D0828620

GREEK ART
AND ARCHAEOLOGY

Western Nebr. Comm. College
Library
1601 East 27th Street, NE
Scottsbluff, NE 69361

GREEK ART
AND ARCHAEOLOGY

John Griffiths Pedley

HARRY N. ABRAMS, INC.
Publishers, New York

MAY 25 1993

In Memoriam
Felix Needham Dowson
George Maxim Anossov Hanfmann

Half-title Terracotta jug, from Thera. Height 17 ins
(43.5 cm) LB I. National Museum, Athens

Frontispiece Parthenon, Athens, east frieze: seated deities
(Poseidon, Apollo, Artemis). Marble. Height 3 ft 6 ins
(1.06 m). 447–438 BC. Acropolis Museum, Athens

Designed by Andrew Shoolbred
Picture research by Sara Waterson
Index by Vicky Robinson

This book was designed and produced by
CALMANN & KING LTD, London

Library of Congress Cataloging-in-Publication Data

Pedley, John Griffiths.
   Greek art and archaeology/by John Griffiths Pedley.
     p. cm.
   Includes bibliographical references and index.
   ISBN 0–8109–3369–1
   1. Greece—Antiquities. 2. Art, Greek. I. Title.
   DF130.P44 1992
   938—dc20   92–9707
                                  CIP

Copyright © 1993 by Prentice Hall, Inc.

Published in 1993 by Harry N. Abrams, Incorporated,
New York
A Times Mirror Company
All rights reserved. No part of the contents of this book
may be reproduced without the written permission of
the publisher

Printed and bound in Hong Kong

Contents

Preface

The main purpose of this book is to introduce beginning students, whether at university or at home, to the major monuments of Greek archaeology. Questions of terminology are important. By definition, archaeology includes art, and yet it is often thought to refer only to excavated materials and objects which may be more artefactual than aesthetic, or to the process of the recovery of information rather than the study of accumulated evidence. By convention, the visual arts are often thought to comprise painting and sculpture, but not always architecture. Since the basic themes of this book are the developments in architecture, architectural sculpture, sculpture, painting, and pottery (some of which is painted, and some not), it seemed best to give the book the title it has.

Another purpose is to make the principal documents of Greek art and archaeology more easily accessible. So there is emphasis on the range of the illustrative material, and the text has been planned in a systematic framework to allow users to find their way about easily. Each chapter begins with a section on the historical background. In chapters 1 to 3 the art and archaeology of Bronze Age Greece is explored by region, focusing in turn on Crete, the Cyclades, mainland Greece and Troy. The remaining chapters 4 to 10 are divided by categories of evidence – architecture, sculpture, pottery, and wall painting. Architecture and architectural sculpture are treated together to give a more cohesive picture of individual buildings.

A glossary at the back of the book provides an explanation of some more unfamiliar or technical terms. At the first occurrence these terms are printed in italics.

The book stems from my teaching an introductory course in Greek archaeology to undergraduates over the past 25 years. It has been helped by my experience of excavation both in Greece and at other Greek and related sites in Italy, Turkey, and Libya. It is proper to focus on the mainland of Greece as the center of artistic creativity – Athens, Corinth, Olympia, and Delphi, for instance, obviously played major roles. But significant advances took place elsewhere too, so that it also seemed proper to include the achievements of other Greeks, not least those who lived in Sicily and south Italy. Similarly, in chronological terms, it seemed useful to begin at the outset of the Bronze Age, so that undergraduates and other interested beginners might, in a single volume, have an account of the whole period from about the years 3000 to 30 BC, however schematically.

Questions of what to include, and what to omit, and questions of emphasis are difficult. Inevitably, given the constraints of time and space, some objects or monuments doubtless considered of great importance by some commentators will have been omitted. For these omissions I apologize. Yet the book is after all an "Introduction," a framework to be filled in by other work or other reading. As to emphasis, there are constant tensions between the different purposes to which archaeological evidence can be put – to the understanding of social history, or economic history, or political history, or art history, and so on. Sometimes these purposes overlap and normally the tensions are creative. Here, the emphasis is, in the main, on the use of the evidence for art history and architectural history, and accordingly in that context, on form and function. There is a particular difficulty with the Bronze Age material where current research tends to focus on the use of archaeological data for the analysis of social systems, demographic patterns, land use, and state formation rather than for the comprehension of architectural and artistic development. Yet, to maintain a coherent focus and coherent themes throughout the book,

I have treated this material also largely in terms of artistic development.

The question of the spelling of Greek names, both of places and of persons, is a constant problem – whether to use the ancient Greek names or their perhaps more familiar Latinized or Anglicized forms. For the most part, I have tended to use Latinized or Anglicized forms where such forms are now part of the English language (e.g. Athens, Rome, Mycenae, Corinth) and where these forms are more familiar to me (e.g. Miletus). Elsewhere, the Greek form of a name is used. However, I doubt whether any author achieves consistency and I suspect there are cases of inconsistency in this book. But those familiar with the difficulty will not, I hope, be irritated, and I doubt whether anyone will be misled.

I have been helped by many friends and colleagues who have saved me from foolish mistakes, replied to many questions of fact and opinion, and offered valuable advice and criticism. I offer warm thanks accordingly to Rebecca Ammerman, Barbara Barletta, and Diane Conlin who read through large portions of the text at different stages; and to Sharon Herbert, Jim Higginbotham, Gail Hoffman, Cathy Keesling, Greg Leftwich, and Laurie Talalay who helped me on specific points with information and advice. I owe a special debt of gratitude to Jerry Rutter who steered me clear of numerous pitfalls in the unfamiliar (to me) territory of the Bronze Age with his unstinting kindness and generosity. I am also grateful to Prentice Hall's anonymous readers for countless suggestions and corrections, and to their editorial staff, and that of Calmann & King in London, for their expert assistance. In Ann Arbor, Michelle Biggs provided indispensable editorial help. Flaws of fact, style, and opinion which remain are entirely my own.

In matters of organization, logistics, and morale, I am enormously indebted to my wife, and for particular matters, about which she knows; the book could not have been written without her. It is dedicated to two teachers. To Felix Dowson, of Kirkby Lonsdale, Westmorland (as it was then), who first opened my eyes at a very tender age to the delights of the Greek language, and by whose kindness I was first able to visit Greece. And to George Hanfmann, a more recent mentor, whose critical judgment and generosity of heart have corrected and supported numerous students, among whom I am privileged to count myself.

Acknowledgements

Many of the line drawings in this book have been drawn by Taurus Graphics, Abingdon. The maps were drawn by Paul Butteridge. Calmann & King Ltd are grateful to all who have allowed their plans and diagrams to be reproduced. Every effort has been made to contact the copyright holders, but should there be any errors or omissions, they would be pleased to insert the appropriate acknowledgement in any subsequent edition of this publication.

Harry N. Abrams, Inc., New York 6.7, 7.6 (from Frederick Hartt, *Art*, 1989), 10.13 (from Marvin Trachtenberg and Isabelle Hyman, *Architecture: from Prehistory to Post-Modernism*, 1986)

Professor Ekrem Akurgal 5.19, 5.21 (from *Alt-Smyrna I: Wohnsichten und Athenatempel*, Turk Turih Kurumu Basimevi, Ankara, 1983)

American Journal of Archaeology (84: 1988) 9.5 (reproduced courtesy of Professor Naomi Norman)

American School of Classical Studies of Athens 4.21, 6.31, 7.17, 9.10, 10.9

Annuano della Regia Scuola Arch di Atena (I: 1914) 5.15

Professor Ernst Berger, Antikenmuseum Basle und Sammlung Ludwig 8.7, 8.10 (Drawings by Miriam Cahn)

British Museum, London 3.39

British Museum Publications, London 3.21 (from John Chadwick, *Reading the Past: Linear B and Related Scripts*, 1987) 6.59 (from D. Williams, *Greek Vases*, 1985)

British School at Athens 4.2 (from J. D. S. Pendlebury *et al.*, "Excavations in the Plan of Lasithi, III. Karphi: A City of Refuge of the early Iron Age in Crete." *Annual of the British School at Athens* 38: 1939)

Chicago University Press, Chicago 1.15 (from E. Vermeule, *Greece in the Bronze Age*, 1964)

Cornell University Press, Ithaca, 6.25, 10.6 (from J. J. Coulton, *Ancient Greek Architects at Work*, 1977)

Deutsches Archäologisches Institut, Athens 5.14, 7.11

Gerald Duckworth & Co., Ltd, London 6.60, 8.1, 10.14 (from Susan Woodford, *An Introduction to Greek Art*, 1986)

Edinburgh University Press, Edinburgh 4.4 (from A. M. Snodgrass, *The Dark Ages of Greece*, 1971, by permission of the British School at Athens)

Hirmer Verlag, Munich 5.18, 7.1, 7.2 (from Gottfried Gruben, *Die Tempel der Griechen,* 1966)

Liverpool University Press, Liverpool 9.5 (from Alison Burford, *The Greek Temple Builders at Epidauros*, 1969)

McGraw-Hill Publishing Co., New York 4.25, 8.29, 9.16 (from R. Brilliant, *Arts of the Ancient Greeks*, 1972); 3.9 (from Sinclair Hood, *The Home of the Heroes: The Aegean before the Greeks*, 1967, by permission of Thames and Hudson)

W. W. Norton & Co Ltd, New York 5.13, 6.13c (from W. B. Dinsmoor, *The Architecture of Ancient Greece*, 1975)

R. Piper Verlag, Munich 4.8, 5.18, 6.12 (from Hans Walter, *Das Heraion von Samos*, 1976

Praeger Publishers, New York 8.24 (from John Travlos, *Pictorial Dictionary of Ancient Athens*, 1971, by permission of John Travlos and Verlag Ernst Wasmuth, Tübingen)

Princeton University Press, Princeton 3.7 (from James Walter Graham, *Palaces of Crete*, 1962); 6.1 (from P. P. Betancourt, *The Aeolic Style in Architecture*, 1977)

Thames and Hudson, London 4.6, 6.14, (from John Boardman, *Greek Art*, 1985); 6.41 (from John Boardman, *Greek Sculpture: The Archaic Period*, 1978); 8.15 (from John Boardman, *Greek Sculpture: The Classical Period*, 1985); 7.17 9.11 (from J. M. Camp, *The Athenian Agora*, 1986); 1.2, 3.30, 3.37 (from Reynold Higgins, *Minoan and Mycenaen Art*, 1981)

University of Cincinnati, Department of Classics 3.42 (courtesy Professor C. W. Blegen)

7.1 (from H. Berve, G. Gruben, M. Hirmer, *Greek Temples, Theatres and Shrines*, London, 1963); 6.18 (from G. Daux, *Fouilles de Delphes, II: Le Deux Tresors*, Paris, 1923); 10.4, 10.5 (from C. Humann, *Magnesia am Maeander*, Berlin, 1904); 2.17, 3.40 (from F. Matz, *The Art of Crete and Early Greece*, New York, 1962); 9.12, 9.13 (from D. M. Robinson, *Excavations at Olynthos*, VIII and XII, Baltimore, 1938, 1946); 9.17 (from M. Schede, *Die Ruinen von Priene*, Berlin 1964)

Photographic Credits

Calmann & King Ltd, the author, and the picture researcher wish to thank the institutions and individuals who have kindly provided photographic materials for use in this book. The majority of photographs were supplied by the museums named in the captions. Other photographs were supplied by the archives listed below.

Aaron M. Levin, Baltimore, © 1985 6.28, 7.37, 7.39
A. F. Kersting, London 9.9
Alison Frantz, Princeton 0.3, 2.3, 2.7, 3.2, 3.5, 3.13, 3.14, 3.18, 3.41, 4.14 (x2), 5.7, 5.16, 5.17, 5.29, 6.6, 6.9, 6.17, 6.19, 6.34, 6.35, 6.36, 6.37, 6.42, 6.43, 6.44, 6.45, 6.49, 6.52, 6.54, 7.3, 7.4 & chapter opener, 7.5, 7.8, 7.9, 7.10, 7.13, 8.3, 8.4, 8.8, 8.14, 8.20 & chapter opener, 8.23, 8.25, 8.27, 8.28, 8.30, 8.31, 8.38, 9.24, 9.33, 10.24
American School of Classical Studies at Athens 1.17, 1.18, 2.16 (by kind permission of Dr. Martha Wiencke); 0.5, 0.6, 4.20, 4.23, & chapter opener, 6.76 (x2), 8.49, 8.50, 8.51, 10.10, 10.11, 10.42 (excavations)
Ancient Art and Architecture Collection, London 2.1, 3.19, 4.6
Antonello Perissinotto, Padua 10.38
Archive Roger-Viollet, Paris 3.35, 8.26
Archivi Alinari, Florence 0.9, 0.14, 0.15, 6.24, 8.37, 9.36, 10.15(x2), 10.33, 10.39, 10.41
Archivio Fotografico Musei Vaticani, cover, 6.68
Barnaby's Picture Library, London 0.8, 1.19, 8.33, 9.21, 10.2, 10.7
Bildarchiv Foto Marburg, Germany 1.4, 7.23, 8.42, 9.7
Bildarchiv Preussischer Kulturbesitz 9.49
British Library, London 3.6 (Restoration after Sir Arthur Evans from the *Knossos Fresco Atlas* © Gregg Press 1967), 9.14, 9.39 (Reproduced from David Robinson's *Mosaics, Vases, and Lamps at Olynthos* Series, Vol. V, © Johns Hopkins University Press)
British School at Athens (Courtesy of the Management Committee) 3.11 (Courtesy of the Department of Classics, University of Columbia USA, photo © L. H. Sackett), 4.9, 4.18 (Courtesy of Professor M. Popham, photos © Dr D. Eveley)
Deutsches Archäologisches Institut, Athens 3.10 (KR 125), 4.7 (NM 5493), 4.11 (OL 1801), 4.13 (OL 2072), 4.17 (KER 14784), 4.22 (75·664), 5.8 (71·1104), 5.11 (MYK 69), 5.23 (OL 4982), 5.30 (SAM 3322), 6.8 (75·885), 6.46 (81·89), 6.47 (1558·14), 6.50 (SAM 2546), 6.51 (5835), 7.11 (OL.175), 8.32 (THES 2514), 9.23 (NM 5357a), 9.29, 10.8 (BAU 115), 10.26 (33·125). 6.46 & 6.47 were reproduced by kind permission of Dr Helmut Kyrieleis, DAI Berlin
Deutsches Archäologisches Institut, Istanbul 9.36
Deutsches Archäologisches Institut, Rome 10.35 (65·101)

Ekdotike Athenon, Athens 2.2, 3.4, 6.38, 9.40, 9.41, 9.42, back cover
French Archaeological School, Athens 6.53, 10.40
Goulandris Foundation: Museum of Cycladic Art, Athens 1.8, 1.10, 1.11
Harvard University, Fogg Art Museum 9.30, 9.31 & chapter opener (Bequest of Mrs K.G.T. Webster)
Hirmer Fotoarchiv, Munich 0.2, 0.12, 2.5, 2.6, 2.8, 3.3, 3.8, 3.12, 3.15, 3.17, 3.20, 3.23, 3.24, 3.31 & chapter opener, 4.3, 6.20, 6.21, 6.29, 6.39, 6.40, 6.61, 6.62, 7.7, 7.14, 7.19 (x2), 7.22, 7.24, 7.25, 7.26, 7.30A, 7.31, 7.32, 8.12, 8.13, 8.17, 8.18, 8.40, 9.2, 9.8, 9.27, 9.37, 10.20, 10.27, 10.28, 10.30, 10.52
Mansell Collection, London 6.16
Metropolitan Museum, New York 1.9 & chapter opener (Rogers Fund), 3.54 (Louisa Eldridge McBurney Gift Fund 1953), 4.10 (Rogers Fund 1921), 6.33 (Fletcher Fund 1932)
Museum of Fine Arts, Boston 0.8 (Francis Bartlett Collection), 6.32 & chapter opener (William Francis Warden Fund), 6.73 (x2) (H.L. Pierce Fund), 7.33 (James Fund and by Special Contribution)
Peter Clayton, Hemel Hempstead 2.22, 3.25, 8.5
Photo Bulloz, Paris 10.23
Professor John G. Pedley, Ann Arbor 0.7, 6.27, 6.30, 7.16, 9.48, 9.50
Professor M. Petsas, Athens 10.37 (Photo courtesy of Thames and Hudson Ltd)
Réunion des Musées Nationaux, Paris 2.12, 5.6, 5.27, 6.48, 6.71, 6.74, 6.78, 7.34, 7.35, 8.21 & chapter opener
Scala Fotografico, Florence 3.22, 3.32, 4.19, 5.3
Sonia Halliday Photos, Buckinghamshire 0.4, 10.2
Soprintendenza Archaeologica di Calabria 8.35 (x2), 8.36; di Napoli e Caserta 7.20; di Ostia 7.21; di Roma 7.30 (bottom right and left), 10.19; di Trepani 0.13 (Photo Studio Capellani)
Staatliche Antikensammlungen und Glyptothek, Munich 1.16, 5.2, 5.10, 6.11 (x2), 6.75
T.A.P. Services (Archaeological Receipts Fund), Athens Half title, 1.12, 1.13, 2.13, 2.14, 3.16, 3.26, 3.27 & chapter opener, 3.31, 3.32, 3.32A, 3.33 (x3), 3.34, 3.46, 3.47, 3.48, 3.51, 4.6, 4.12, 4.15, 4.16, 5.9, 5.22, 5.25, 5.28 & chapter opener, 6.14, 6.55, 6.56, 6.58, 6.68, 7.27, 7.28, 7.40, 8.22, 8.39, 8.41, 8.43, 9.25, 9.34
University of Cincinnati, Department of Classics 3.43, 3.44 (Watercolours by Piet de Jong reproduced from Blegen and Rawson: *The Palace of Nestor at Pylos* Vol I © Princeton University Press, 1966), 3.35 (By kind permission of Dr Elizabeth Schofield)
University of Syracuse, Sicily 9.22

Introduction

What does the phrase "Greek Art and Archaeology" mean to most people? Probably the Acropolis in Athens, the Parthenon, and the Elgin Marbles in the British Museum. These monuments, in fact, mark the culmination of a long period of artistic development and reveal an early civilization of extraordinary achievement. For in Greece lie the foundations of much of our Western civilization. Its great philosophers, historians, poets, dramatists, architects, sculptors, and painters still influence the way we think and act and create today.

As far back as the fifth century BC, Greeks were being entertained by the tragedies of Aeschylus, Euripides, Sophocles, and the comedies of Aristophanes. Thucydides was analyzing historical events, and Socrates was developing his philosophy. The greatest of Greek sculptors, Phidias, the architect, Iktinos, and their colleagues were at work on the Acropolis.

Athens was also the first place to develop a democracy, though it relied heavily on slaves, and women were very much treated as inferior. But this newly democratic state almost singlehandedly drove back the Persian invasion at the battle of Marathon in 490 BC. It played a major role in the Greek victory over the Persians at the naval

0.1 The Greek world

BLACK SEA

Danube

Halys

MACEDONIA

• Troy

PHRYGIA

ASIA MINOR
(ANATOLIA)

Tigris

• Pergamon

LYDIA

*AEGEAN
SEA*

Smyrna

Maeander

MESOPOTAMIA

EUBOEA

Delphi

Ephesos •

CILICIA

Antioch •

Athens •

Samos

Priene •

CARIA

Al Mina •

SYRIA

Corinth

Didyma •

Euphrates

Mycenae •

Delos •

Orontes

Olympia •

LYCIA

PELOPONNESE

Sparta •

Melos •

Thera •

Rhodes •

CYPRUS

PHOENICIA

Knossos •

CRETE

MEDITERRANEAN SEA

PALESTINE

• Cyrene

Alexandria •

Naukratis •

LIBYA

Nile

EGYPT

battle of Salamis in 480 BC, and in 479 BC took part in the victory over the Persian army at Plataea. So, it is not surprising that many will think of the Acropolis at Athens when they hear the words "Greek Art and Archaeology."

But Athens of the fifth century BC is far from the whole story. Evidence of art and archaeology in Greece can be traced back to the beginning of the Bronze Age two and a half thousand years before that and even beyond. Material evidence of human activity in the Bronze Age is considerable, especially of the Minoan and Mycenaean civilizations of Middle and Late Bronze Age Greece. Moreover, people in Greece in the Bronze Age, and perhaps even before, spoke Greek. So, this book begins at the beginning of the Bronze Age, that is about 3000 BC.

The periods during which written records existed which can now be brought to bear on historical problems are called "historical" periods. Where there are no significant written documents (with certain exceptions), the periods are termed "prehistoric." In Greece, the Bronze Age is considered prehistoric. Among the major centers of prehistoric Greece were Mycenae on the mainland and Knossos on Crete.

Although Athens, with its fortified acropolis, had been a political center in the Bronze Age, it did not have anything like the power of Mycenae. The city is important, however, for the period between the end of the Bronze Age and the Greek renaissance of the seventh century BC since remains of pottery in the cemeteries show that people lived there continuously from the eleventh to the eighth century BC. But for different reasons other city-states have more importance up to and including the seventh century BC. Among these are Corinth and Samos, the Greek states of Asia Minor, like Smyrna, and the Greek states of the West, like Syracuse. Thus, the geographical range of this book is wide (fig. **0.1**).

The Western Greeks, those who left Greece and established themselves in Sicily and south Italy from the eighth century BC onwards, are not

0.2 The Propylaia to the Acropolis, Athens, from the southwest. 437–432 BC often mentioned in books on Greek art and archaeology as their contribution to progress in Greek sculpture was minimal, and to vase painting only small, until a great burst of creativity in the fourth century. However, Western Greek experiments in temple architecture are astonishing, and the Western Greeks pioneered some aspects of architectural sculpture. They found solutions in the Doric order of architecture which anticipated by some two generations those arrived at in Greece and finally used in the Parthenon itself.

In the fifth century BC the city of Syracuse in Sicily certainly saw herself as the cultural rival of Athens, both in the arts and in literature. It may have been this, along with Syracuse's great riches and commercial prosperity, that provoked Athens' ill-fated attack in 415 BC, ending in the death or capture of so many Athenians in 413 BC. Thereafter, it is for vase painting that Western Greeks are best known. The major centers of Greek vase painting in the fourth century BC are in south Italy, and it is in the West that Greek

vase painting enjoyed its final flourish in the third century BC. So the Greeks in the West play a considerable role and their achievements are included in this book.

The recovery of antiquity

Some ancient Greek buildings always remained visible, while parts of others were incorporated into newer structures. On the Acropolis at Athens, the Propylaia (fig. **0.2**) was built into a fort, while the Parthenon (fig. **0.4**) and the Erechtheion (fig. **0.3**) became churches. Near the *agora*, the Hephaisteion (fig. **0.5**), too, became a church, and in the agora the *Stoa* of Attalos (fig. **0.6**), or parts of it, were built into the city's defenses. At Agrigento in Sicily, which the Greeks had called Akragas, and in south Italy at Paestum (fig. **0.7**), called Poseidonia by the Greeks, Greek temples stood abandoned or were converted to churches.

0.3 *Left* The Erechtheion, Athens, from the southeast.
430s–406 BC

0.4 *Above* The Parthenon, Athens, the east façade.
447–432 BC

0.5 *Left* The Hephaisteion, Athens, from the east. c. 450–415 BC

0.6 *Below* The Stoa of Attalos in the Agora of Athens, from the northwest. c. 150 BC, reconstructed AD 1956

0.7 The city of Poseidonia, from the east gate.
Engraving by Thomas Major, AD 1768

0.8 Gilt-bronze quadriga, St Mark's, Venice. Possibly
Greek of the 4th century BC, possibly a Roman copy or
adaptation

By the second century BC, the Romans had begun to collect Greek sculptures and other objects, and fourteen hundred years later, in thirteenth-century Italy, there was a great resurgence of interest in Greek works of art. The great quartet of bronze horses which used to stand above the entrance to St Mark's in Venice (fig. **0.8**) was brought from Constantinople in 1204. It had been taken from Chios, perhaps as early as the fifth century AD. These horses may be the work of a late Classical or early Hellenistic sculptor, or of Lysippos himself. Or they may just be Roman copies or adaptations. Italians began to gather ancient coins, Greek and Roman, and mold-made pottery for private enjoyment. By the fifteenth century, important statues had come to light and formed the nucleus of great Italian collections.

One notable statue was the Apollo Belvedere (fig. **0.9**), a Roman marble copy of a Greek bronze original made during the last years of the fourth century BC, possibly by Leochares. The Apollo was acknowledged for many years as the paragon of Classical beauty and the Classical ideal and was thought of in those terms by the great eighteenth-century critic, Winckelmann. It was Winckelmann who first drew distinctions between Greek and Roman art, and who first classified Greek art into the periods still used today. To our eyes, the Apollo appears more unbalanced, more open, and more sensual than the fifth-century BC concept of the ideal would allow. Another sculpture known in the fifteenth century was the Belvedere Torso (fig. **0.10**), much admired by Michelangelo and later by Winckelmann; it is a fine example of Hellenistic art.

By the seventeenth century, English gentlemen were beginning to visit Greece. Among

0.9 *Left* Apollo Belvedere. Roman marble copy of a Greek bronze original of the later 4th century BC. Height 7 ft 4½ ins (2.24 m). Vatican Museums, Rome

0.10 *Below* Belvedere Torso. Marble copy of the 1st century BC after an original of c. 200 BC. Height 5 ft 2 ins (1.59 m). Vatican Museums, Rome

them were the Earl of Arundel, who acquired several Greek antiquities, many of which may be seen today in Oxford, and Sir George Wheler, who, accompanied by a French doctor, Jacob Spon, went to Athens in 1675. In 1678, Wheler and Spon published journals of their tour. But it was not until the eighteenth century that the real recovery of the physical world of antiquity began.

THE EIGHTEENTH CENTURY

The Greek temples discovered at Agrigento (Akragas) in Sicily were explored and published in 1732 by Pancrazi and those of Paestum (Poseidonia) by the French architect, Soufflot, in 1764. Soufflot had visited Paestum in 1750 and the site soon became a place of importance for the intellectual explorers of that time. Winckelmann saw the temples in 1760 and made them the starting point for his influential *Remarks on the Architecture of the Ancients*. Giovanni Battista Piranesi drew the temples and made a set of engravings, finished by his son, which ensured that knowledge of them became widespread. Interest in Paestum (Poseidonia) was doubtless stimulated by the discovery of Herculaneum in 1738 and the beginning of excavation at Pompeii in 1748. All three sites are relatively close to Naples.

At the same time interest in Greece itself increased. In 1750 two Englishmen, James Stuart and Nicholas Revett, were sent to Athens by the London Society of the Dilettanti to measure and to draw the ancient buildings. Their drawings were later published in *Antiquities of Athens* (1762–1816). The French, as usual, were quicker. Le Roy visited Athens in 1754 and published *Les Ruines des plus beaux monuments de la Grèce* in 1758, though this was not as complete or detailed. Elsewhere, too, Greek and Roman buildings were the objects of scrutiny. The English and Irish together explored the temples at Palmyra and Baalbek and published them in the 1750s, while Robert Adam himself investigated (1757) and published (1764) the late Roman palace at Spalato.

Sir William Hamilton, a diplomat at the court in Naples in 1764, developed a strong interest in Greek vases, which were then being recovered in large numbers from tombs of the sixth and fifth centuries. Within a few years he had amassed a remarkable collection, which was sold to the British Museum in 1772, and became the foundation for one of the most significant collections of Greek vases in the world.

Collections of Greek and Roman sculptures became a mark of upper-class distinction among the English gentry. Rome was the source for such collections, where entrepreneurs were busy prying loose old Italian collections from needy nobles and organizing excavations for treasure hunting. Perhaps the most influential of these English gentlemen collectors was Charles Townley, whose agents included one Thomas Jenkins, a man who had close connections with successive popes. Townley's collection was put on display at his town house in London (fig. **0.11**), where it received many visitors. It is all now in the British Museum.

0.11 Charles Townley and friends, human, marble, and canine. Oil painting by Zoffany. Canvas 4 ft 2 ins × 3 ft 3 ins (1.27 × 0.99 m). AD 1781–83. Towneley Hall Art Gallery and Museums, Burnley

THE NINETEENTH CENTURY

The Parthenon marbles were acquired by the British Museum in 1816 and rapidly came to influence both artists and scholars in their views of Greek sculpture. At about the same time, the pedimental sculptures of the Temple of Aphaia on Aegina were sold to the Prince of Bavaria and may now be seen in Munich. Cockerell and Hallerstein discovered, measured, and drew the Temple of Apollo at Bassae, and brought the sculptured frieze blocks to London.

In the second half of the nineteenth century, more systematic excavation than had previously been practiced in the cemeteries of Etruria and south Italy began. Notable discoveries of Greek sculpture were made on the Athenian Acropolis by Greek archaeologists. The newly independent government of Greece encouraged German-sponsored excavations at Olympia which continue to this day. At the same time, archaeologists were unearthing great quantities of other materials at these and other sites, and realized the need to classify their findings of bronzes, *terracottas*, pottery, lamps, and so on into types and periods. Thus, the antiquities of Greece of the historical period – the period illuminated by written sources – came gradually to the attention of the world, slowly in Italy from the thirteenth century on, more rapidly by far after the middle of the eighteenth century.

Though the Lion Gate at Mycenae (fig. **0.12**) had stood visible since antiquity, its age and meaning were unknown, and almost nothing was known of the archaeology of prehistoric Greece until the excavations of Heinrich Schliemann. Schliemann came to archaeology late in life. He had been entranced by the Homeric poems since boyhood. Throughout his career as a businessman in America at the time of the gold rush in the 1840s and in Europe where he worked both in Germany and Russia, he had maintained his enthusiasm for Homer and was convinced that the poems reflected historical events. Once he had acquired a fortune, he devoted it and the rest of his life to excavating and interpreting the sites with which the poems are primarily concerned. Scholars had discussed whether Homer's narrative in the *Iliad* could be

true, but it was Schliemann's work at the site identified by him and many others as Troy which showed that history might be found in Homer. Schliemann excavated at Troy between 1870 and 1879, 1882 and 1884, and in 1890, and on the mainland of Greece from 1874 onward. Schliemann followed hints in a surviving description of Greece written by Pausanias in the second century AD, and in 1876, while he was excavating inside the walls of Mycenae, he found *shaft graves* belonging to the royal family. Subsequently he worked at Tiryns and Orchomenos. He had already made exploratory trenches on Ithaca. His work revealed a whole new civilization, termed "Mycenaean." Its geographical distribution seemed to tally nicely with the account of the states involved in the expedition against Troy, given in Homer's catalogue of ships in Book Two of the *Iliad*. But how old was this civilization?

Archaeologists were now recognizing characteristic pottery from this, Mycenaean, civilization and, most importantly, finding it alongside Egyptian artefacts, which could be dated. They found datable Egyptian objects such as *scarabs*, bearing royal names in houses and cemeteries at Mycenae itself too. A scarab with the name of Queen Ty, wife of Amenophis III, was one example. This meant that these archaeologists could now date the Mycenaean pottery, using the Egyptian chronology. Moreover, they now realized that Egyptian tomb paintings of the eighteenth Dynasty portrayed Mycenaean objects, to which approximate dates could then be given. Thus they concluded that this Mycenaean civilization had flourished between about 1600 and 1300 BC.

Further excavations were made in the 1890s in the islands of the Cyclades in the southern Aegean, and hundreds of tombs were recovered. They yielded stylized idols and new varieties of pottery, and from these scholars were able to identify yet another civilization, the "Cycladic," which once more could be dated alongside the Egyptian chronology. What they now wanted to know was whether this was the direct precursor to the Mycenaean culture. Some eyes were already turned to Crete, where Schliemann had wished to excavate, but had been denied.

0.12 Lion Gate, Mycenae, from the northwest. c. 1250
BC

THE TWENTIETH CENTURY

The English scholar, Arthur Evans (later Sir
Arthur), originally went to Greece to carry out
research on sealstones in the Ashmolean
Museum in Oxford and on early writing. In 1900
he was able to start excavations at Knossos.
Within a few years he had uncovered most of the
palace, and discovered clay tablets with writing
in what he termed a "Linear B script." He continued to excavate until 1932 and published the
monumental four-volume *Palace of Minos at Knossos* between 1921 and 1935. Evans was able to
show that this new prehistoric civilization, which
he called "Minoan," after the legendary king
Minos, was the main precursor to the
Mycenaean culture on mainland Greece. By
examining the sequence of archaeological layers
(stratigraphy) of earth, artefacts, and debris, he
worked out a relative chronology of prehistoric

Crete. Soon after Evans had discovered the
palace at Knossos, work began at other sites on
the island. The Italians started to excavate the
palace at Phaistos, the Greeks at Mallia, shortly
before World War I, and an American archaeologist, Harriet Boyd (later Boyd Hawes), started
work at the town of Gournia.

In the 1920s, another American, Carl Blegen,
began to investigate the predecessors of the
Mycenaeans on mainland Greece, and again by
careful stratigraphic work he was able to unravel
the chronology of Greece right back to the beginning of the Bronze Age. He termed the various
phases of the chronology "Helladic," after the
word *Hellas* which meant "Greece" in antiquity,
as it still does today. In 1939, with a Greek
archaeologist, Kouroniotis, Blegen also discovered the Mycenaean palace at Pylos. Here
they found more Linear B tablets and these were
eventually to lead to the decoding of all the
tablets in 1952 by Michael Ventris. The decipherment of the Linear B script as an early form of
Greek is among the great intellectual feats of the
second half of the twentieth century. Other sites
have now been discovered, including Lerna on
the mainland, Thera (Akrotiri) in the Cyclades,
and another palace, Zakro, on Crete.

Sites of the historical period have been
excavated systematically throughout the twentieth century, uncovering the major sanctuaries
and urban centers. Delos, Delphi, Samos,
Olympia, Athens, Corinth, and Sparta in Greece,
and Pergamon, Priene, Didyma, and Miletus in
Asia Minor are all examples of such sites. Work
had, in fact, begun at most of these sites in the
last quarter of the nineteenth century, and has
since continued. Syracuse, Selinus, Akragas, and
Gela in Sicily, and Metapontum, Poseidonia, and
Taras in south Italy were also quickly discovered
and excavated by archaeologists. Among more
recently explored sites, Lefkandi in Greece and
Ischia in Italy have yielded important new information, while the Macedonian tombs, notably
the complex at Vergina, have been revelatory.
Both these newer excavations and the older
complexes are far from finished. Samos recently
(1980) yielded more over-lifesize marble statues
of the sixth century BC, while a Carthaginian

0.13 Marble Charioteer, Motya. Height 5 ft 11¼ ins (1.81 m). c. 480–450 BC. Motya Museum

sanctuary at Motya in Sicily produced the astonishing marble Charioteer (fig. **0.13**). Chance finds, too, can be informative. The discovery in 1972 of the two big bronzes (figs. **0.14** and **0.15**) in the sea near Riace in south Italy revolutionized thinking about styles of Greek sculpture in the mid-fifth century BC.

At the same time, in both Greece and Italy, extensive surveys and excavation of country areas have produced important information. For example the survey of the territory of Metapontum in south Italy tells us much about the number and distribution of farm sites from the sixth century BC through to the early third century BC.

Literary sources

Little relevant written material has survived from Classical and Hellenistic periods. No treatise written on architecture or sculpture has come down to us, though we know that such treatises were written. Chance references, such as the mention in Euripides' play, *Ion*, of the façade of the Temple of Apollo at Delphi, are scarce. From the first century BC on, however, several sources are useful. The geographer Strabo, who wrote in the late first century BC and early first century AD, is illuminating about the topography and history of the Greek world of his time. Cicero, writing in the first century BC, reveals contemporary attitudes towards art. When he requests friends in Athens to send him Greek statues suitable for his villa, he does not ask for specific statues or sculptors, but statues which suit the various rooms of his villa. The most helpful of the other sources are Vitruvius, Pliny, and Pausanias.

Vitruvius was a Roman architect of the later first century BC whose handbook on architecture has survived till today. It offers a useful description of contemporary techniques, defines architectural terms, and puts forward recommendations about proportions to be used for temples, though no temple has been found which corresponds in every respect to his advice. He went into considerable detail, advising, among other things, that corner columns should

0.14 Riace Warrior A. Bronze with copper lips and nipples, silver teeth, and eyes inlaid. c. 460–450 BC. Height 6 ft 9 ins (2.05 m). National Museum, Reggio Calabria

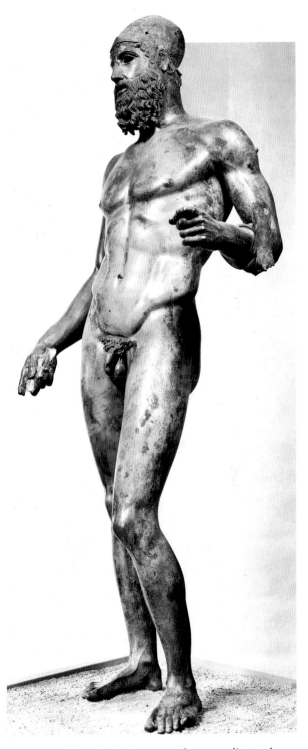

0.15 Riace Warrior B. Bronze with copper lips and nipples, and eyes inlaid (one preserved). Height 6 ft 6 ins (1.96 m). National Museum, Reggio Calabria

be thicker than others. Through Vitruvius we dis-cover that in wall painting perspective first appeared in painted stage scenery of the fifth century BC. Both Vitruvius and other Roman sources drew liberally on Greek or Hellenistic predecessors.

Pliny the Elder wrote a *Natural History* which covered numerous topics and drew on many written sources. He died in the eruption of Vesuvius in AD 79. He is most interesting in the attention he gives to Greek sculpture, devoting separate sections to bronzes, terracottas, and marbles. The section on bronze statues is by far the largest. He lists sculptors and their most famous works, dating them by Olympiads (periods of four years) and gives critical judg-ments of statues which probably reflect the view of his Hellenistic source. Through his descriptions experts have been able to identify Roman copies of Greek originals, though using this method can be controversial. His writing on painters and paintings is similarly of great interest. He admired Polygnotos, describing his many innovations. He lists the titles of important Classical paintings, and says that large-scale mythological groups like ''Perseus freeing Andromeda'' were especially popular in Greek times, and were favored again in his own time.

Pausanias wrote a *Description of Greece* in the second century AD as he traveled around the country. He described the sites he visited and the statues and other objects he saw. His detailed walks through Olympia or the Athenian Agora, for example, are invaluable, but also maddening. Where his information can be verified he often makes errors, leading us to believe that he relied on hearsay. Yet he gives important news: his des-cription of Polygnotos' paintings in the Lesche of the Knidians at Delphi, for example, is critical to our understanding of how Polygnotos suggested depth in space on the flat surface of a wall.

Writing, other than literary, is also an import-ant source. The decipherment of the Bronze Age Linear B script of Knossos as an early form of the Greek language told us that Greeks were in Knossos in the fourteenth century BC and that the tablets themselves were archives (mostly inventory lists). Inscriptions on pots and sherds of the later eighth century BC tell us when the skill of writing was learnt again in Greece after its Dark Ages. Writing was then later used on pots to identify characters in painted scenes and for the signatures of potters and painters. An inscription of the fifth century BC gives details of expenditures on the Erechtheion at Athens, while another of the fourth century BC gives the costs of the construction of the temple of Asklepios at Epidauros. Yet another fourth-cen-tury inscription gives the specifications for the Arsenal at Piraeus. Statue bases give information about the identity of the donor of the statue and of the sculptor. In the sixth century BC such inscriptions even appear on the statue.

The development of Classical archaeology

The monuments and objects of antiquity which attracted the earliest students were temples, statues, coins, and inscriptions. Accordingly, historians of architecture and urbanism, historians of art, *numismatists*, and epigraphers were in the forefront. Style and *iconography*, the study of sculpture, painting, and other visual arts, were of major importance from the start. Once artefacts began to be recovered through excavation, the field expanded to include other aspects of cultural history, especially those involved not with high art but with daily life. Archaeological evidence began to be used to tell us about social and economic history, and people began to realize just how important pottery was, both as art when painted and as artefact when plain.

Pottery breaks easily but is not easily destroyed entirely and survives in the earth. When broken into sherds, a pot has little intrinsic value. Fragments often remain where they were initially discarded. Since making pots from fired clay was the commonest craft in antiquity and since pots had many uses – for cooking, eating, drinking, for storage, and for offerings in sanctu-aries and tombs – pottery provides the largest category of archaeological evidence that has survived. It is not perishable like textiles and woodwork, which have virtually disappeared from the record, though we know they existed. It is not, like bronze or marble statues, likely to be recycled. Artisans could burn marble for lime, or melt down bronze. So it has survived in large quantities and is invaluable evidence for social history. The uses to which it was put are studied, as well as its painted scenes depicting customs, beliefs, and rites. How the wares were distributed, trade connections and patterns, tell us about economic history. Then it can also tell us about its evolution as an art form.

Such are the quantities which have come down to us that scholars have been able to work out the stages of development of various shapes and systems of decoration, and have been able to relate these stages to historically recorded events. Accordingly, pottery has become a critical tool for dating archaeological contexts, and for dating buildings or objects by stylistic analogy. For example, the temple of Apollo at Thermon is dated by similarity between the style of the painted *metopes* and that of firmly dated Corinthian pottery. Coins are another useful dating tool since they exist in large numbers and are often dated themselves by internal evidence; hence, they can help date the context in which they are found. Historical records, pottery, and coins are therefore the more traditional means of establishing a chronology. More scientific methods such as *dendrochronology*, which allows the estimation of dates by examining growth rings on trees or dead wood, *thermoluminescence*, which dates clay objects by measuring radioactively accumulated energy, and radiocarbon dating (see p. 32) are helpful but costly.

A relatively recent new field of activity is underwater archaeology. Many ancient coastal sites are now submerged, or partially so, and exploring such sites and their harbor installations is yielding much valuable new information. Similarly, the careful excavation of shipwrecks is revealing cargoes which greatly expand our knowledge of trade and chronology. The Late Bronze Age wreck off Ulu Burun in Southern Turkey (p. 64) provides a good example. Research in the field is now equally divided between excavation and survey. In any excavation, all artefactual material and bones must be kept and the sites conserved. More recently, in the decade 1950–60, the importance of the collection of soils, seeds, and pollen was also recognized. Excavation is now often preceded by an aerial photographic survey or by a *resistivity survey*, using electrical currents in the ground to detect ancient remains, and by surveys using other scientific methods. A field survey of the zone to be excavated and its immediate surroundings is then carried out. Regional survey aims at covering much larger tracts of ground; it is labor intensive and often addresses different kinds of questions than those traditionally posed by architecture, sculpture, coins, pottery, inscriptions, or other evidence retrieved by excavation.

Such questions are concerned more with settlement patterns, demographic studies, agriculture, animal husbandry, and other land use than they are with the history of architecture, or religion, or art, or political history. They require a very wide range of studies and skills, and demonstrate the broad scope of the categories of evidence and questions covered by archaeology today. It is large enough to encompass many types of information, some to explain the social behavior of a group, others to focus on the skills and aspirations of an individual. How did the Greeks farm their land? How did a master craftsman like Exekias paint an *amphora*?

In the realm of art, students pay increasing attention to the social, political, and religious contexts, and to purpose. Why was a particular image or object or monument chosen? Who chose it? Who commissioned it? What relation do monuments have to political events? Integration of the archaeological evidence into wider contexts reinforces the need for a firm grasp of chronology.

This book concentrates on description and chronological sequence, which are the first steps, and only the first steps, in understanding ancient monuments and objects. Combined with exploration of the broader contexts, this study should lead to a fuller comprehension of the workings of Greek minds and their essential concerns.

1
The Aegean in the Third Millennium
c. 3000–2000 BC

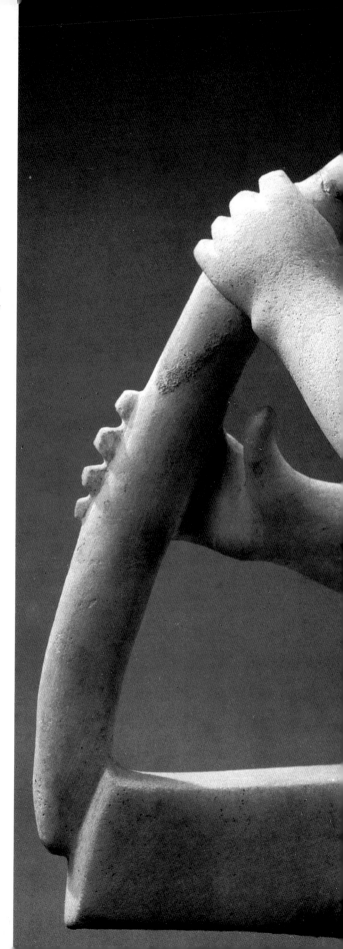

Humans had inhabited Greece for many thousands of years before the Bronze Age. They lived by hunting, fishing, and gathering fruit, nuts, berries, and grains. They were living in Epirus (fig. **1.1**) in northwest Greece perhaps as early as 40,000 BC. One important early site is the Franchthi Cave in the Argolid (near Argos in the Peloponnese), which people were using by 20,000 BC at least. *Obsidian*, volcanic glass used to make cutting and scraping tools, was found on the Franchthi site in contexts dating to around 10,000 BC. It originally came from the island of Melos some 90 miles (145 km) away, which shows that there was communication across the Aegean Sea at that time.

New peoples arrived about 6000 BC, and at the same time a new life style,

Opposite Marble figure of a harpist, detail of fig. **1.9**. EC II. Metropolitan Museum of Art, New York

based on permanent settlements and dependent on agriculture and domesticated animals, was introduced. To judge from similarities between some of their artefacts and contemporary materials in Anatolia, and from the distribution of their sites (in the east of Greece) the newcomers came from Anatolia. People now lived either in caves which offered ready-made shelters and often a supply of water, or in settlements in open countryside suitable for animals and crops.

In some areas those who lived in settlements in the open built the walls of their houses of wattle (interwoven saplings) in a timber frame with wooden posts to support the roof, and in others they used stone and mudbrick. Soon after 6000 BC, they began to use fired pottery instead of wood or basketry vessels. They also made stone or terracotta (baked clay) figurines, many of which, in the traditional view, represented the

Mother Goddess, the miraculous giver of life to humans (and by extension to animals and crops). She had exaggerated breasts, thighs, and buttocks. This was evidently a society whose religious beliefs were rooted in the miracles of birth and growth, and of agriculture. Around 4000 BC fragmentary evidence for metalworking begins.

There seem to have been more population movements around 3000 BC, the date which loosely marks the beginning of the Bronze Age. In Greece the transition from the Final *Neolithic* Age, characterized by primitive farming methods and the use of polished stone and flint tools and weapons, to Early Bronze was smooth, but there were newcomers in the Cyclades, who may have come from mainland Greece, and others in Crete who may have arrived from Anatolia. (We have been able to deduce this by comparing their pottery.) Soon after these movements, people began to cultivate olives and grapes as well as cereals. Their knowledge of metals advanced rapidly in the first part of the third millennium. Artisans

1.1 Minoan Crete and the Bronze Age Aegean

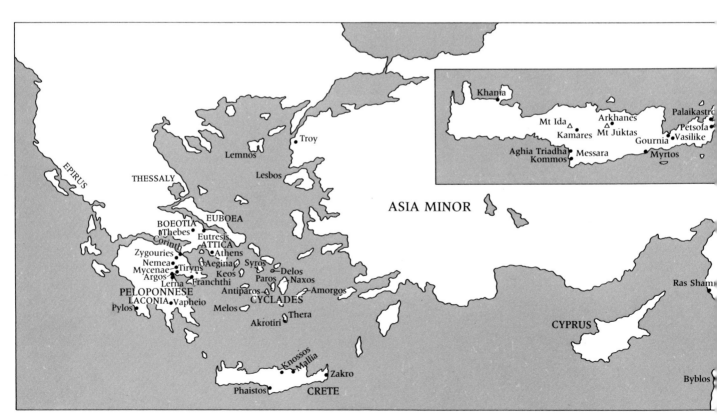

now made implements both from copper, an "element" which can be made into a rather soft tool, and from bronze, an "alloy" (consisting principally of copper, but mixed, usually, with tin) which produces a much harder and more durable tool. These were better than stone tools for woodworking, shipbuilding, construction, and agriculture. Copper and bronze were also a form of wealth, and as such a source of competition. This had a significant impact on the emergence of leaders and the formation of society. About 2900 BC, on the coast of Asia Minor and guarding the approaches to the Black Sea, the first city of Troy was built.

Major Neolithic settlements have so far been found in the Cyclades only on Saliagos and on Keos. Settlers had however arrived in Crete by about 6000 BC, in boats large enough to carry cattle, goats, sheep, and pigs. They established themselves at Knossos. A depth of over 19½ feet (over 6 m) of Neolithic stratification was unearthed beneath the west court of the Bronze Age palace, and beneath the central court excavators found remains of houses. Small, rectangular, cell-like units and small cobbled areas cluster into what may have formed a pair of dwellings. Walls were of stone in the lower part, and mudbrick above. Interiors were furnished with benches and platforms. As on the mainland of Greece, the life of the inhabitants changed little for 3000 years. Then, when the new peoples arrived, around 3000 BC, a new phase began. Metal artefacts appeared in Cretan graves.

Chronology

Through examining the stratification at Knossos and the pottery found in it, early excavators began to associate pottery styles with chronological phases, and thus to establish a relative chronology. An Egyptian chronology had already been made in three parts: the Old, Middle, and New Kingdoms (fig 1.2). By finding what looked like correlations between these periods and the strata at Knossos, the excavators identified three major prehistoric periods of human activity on

Crete after the Neolithic period. These were described as Early, Middle, and Late Minoan, taking their name from Minos, an early legendary ruler of Crete, mentioned in Homer and subsequent Greek writers. These three periods were then subdivided, in accordance with pottery styles, into Early Minoan (EM) I, II, and III; Middle Minoan (MM) I, II, and III; and Late Minoan (LM) I, II, and III. These periods were further subdivided, using the letters of the alphabet, when distinctions became discernible, for example, LM IA and LM IB. Subsequently, similar systems were adopted for the Cyclades (Early, Middle, and Late Cycladic) and the mainland (Early, Middle, and Late Helladic), and similar abbreviations have come into use: EC, MC, LC

1.2 Chronological Table of the Bronze Age in Crete, the Cyclades, mainland Greece, and Egypt. MM II almost only at Knossos and Phaistos. LM II only at Knossos

BC	CRETE	CYCLADES	GREECE	EGYPT	DYNASTY
3000					
2800	E M I	E C I	E H I	ARCHAIC	II
					III
2600					IV
2500				OLD KINGDOM	
2400	E M II	E C II	E H II		V
2300					VI
2200					
2100	E M III	E C III	E H III	1st INTER	VII - X
2000					XI
1900	M M I	M C I		MIDDLE KINGDOM	XII
1800	MM II	M C II	M H		
1700				2nd INTER	XIII - XVII
1600	M M III	M C III			
1500	L M I A		L H I		
	L M I B		L H II		XVIII
1400	L M II			NEW KINGDOM	
	L M III A		L H III A		
1300					
1200	L M III B		L H III B		XIX - XX
	L M III C		L H III C		
1100					
1000	DARK AGES			LATE PERIOD	XXI
900					

and EH, MH, and LH. Crete, the Cyclades, and mainland Greece are the three major geographical zones of inhabitation in the Greek Bronze Age. Close to the Greek World, and of great importance, was the site at Troy in Asia Minor.

The Early Minoan, Early Cycladic, and Early Helladic periods are more or less contemporary, as are Middle Minoan, Middle Cycladic, and Middle Helladic. Likewise, Late Minoan, Late Cycladic, and Late Helladic are, generally speaking, contemporary. EM, EC, and EH represent the Early Bronze (EB) Age in the Aegean; MM, MC, and MH represent the Middle Bronze (MB) Age; and LM, LC, and LH the Late Bronze (LB) Age. Unfortunately pottery styles do not always follow one another neatly, and sometimes they overlap chronologically. The details of the relationship of style to chronology are constantly being refined, so that a system such as this becomes awkward to use. On Crete, an alternative system exists, using the destruction levels of the palaces, but many commentators continue to use the older system, and it will be used here. At Troy the chronology is defined by the seven cities built one atop the other on the site. Troy I–V correspond in general terms to the EB period, Troy VI lasts from the start of MB to well into the LB period, and Troy VII covers the last two centuries of the Bronze Age.

The "relative chronology" achieved by examining the stratification of a site establishes that certain artefacts were made earlier – that is to say, further away from the present day in time – than others. An "absolute chronology" will yield dates in years BC and is much to be preferred, though it is more difficult to arrive at. It depends largely on Egyptian and Mesopotamian "synchronisms" (when firmly dated foreign objects appear in Greek contexts, or Greek objects in firmly dated foreign contexts, the Greek object or context may be dated to the same time as the already dated foreign material). Civilizations in Egypt and Mesopotamia, which enjoyed the practice of writing and kept records, give a generally reliable absolute chronology as far back as the third millennium. Accordingly, dated Egyptian objects found in a Cretan context will help give a date for that context. Such

synchronisms are more reliable in the MM period, but earlier Egyptian seals of the First Intermediate Period appear in tombs in the south of Crete and help to establish the date of these tombs. There are of course pitfalls. Such objects may be heirlooms and give nothing more than a *terminus post quem* (a date after which) for the context in which they appear.

Another means for arriving at absolute dates for organic objects is radiocarbon dating. This measures the amount of carbon 14 left in an object. Since we know the amount of C14 in any organic object, and since, after death, the C14 decays at a fixed rate, it is theoretically possible to measure the amount of C14 in, for example, an animal bone or wooden object, and determine when the animal perished or the tree was cut down. This method has been enhanced by the adjustment of radiocarbon dates, based on the C14 dating of tree rings all the way back to the sixth millennium. Yet there are still considerable differences between dates provided by many C14 samples. The more available other sources of chronological information become – coins, inscriptions, correlations with written records – as they do in the historical period, the less useful the C14 technique becomes. Yet for the third millennium – and earlier – it is crucial.

The chronological framework set out in figure **1.2** is a simplified scheme and there is much uncertainty about many dates. In the third millennium, inaccuracies of up to 200 or 300 years may still be expected.

Crete

EARLY MINOAN I (c. 3000–2500 BC)

Pottery is the most significant feature of the EM I phase. There are many different shapes. Decoration is either in a single color (monochrome), which can be gray or red, or it makes use of two contrasting colors, designs being painted in white on a dark background or in a dark color on a light background. There are two major categories, named after the sites where significant examples have been found. Gray "Pyrgos ware" is sometimes burnished and sometimes has incised

1.3 Onouphrios ware beak-spouted jug from Aghios Onouphrios. EM I. Height 11 ins (28 cm). Iraklion Museum, Crete

decorations, and the chalice is its most characteristic shape. "Aghios Onouphrios ware," on the other hand, often thought to have arrived with newcomers from Asia Minor, introduces new shapes, including round-bottomed jugs decorated with dark red, black, or brown paint on a light background. This decoration sometimes includes crosshatching of diagonal lines to form lozenges repeated around the surface of the vessel (fig. **1.3**).

EARLY MINOAN II (c. 2500–2200 BC)

The second EM phase is a period of great prosperity. On the hilltop at Vasilike in the east of Crete, a settlement took shape which consisted of several buildings, built at different times and arranged for the most part to the east of a paved "west court" (part of one structure was actually built on top of the court). The size of the complex is impressive, but individual spaces are very small, comparable in scale to the cellular units of the Neolithic houses at Knossos. Walls of stone and mudbrick were supported by wooden *tiebeams*, and surfaces were coated with a rough *stucco*, a plaster made from ground limestone and sand, which was painted solid red.

Also in the east of the island, and close to the south coast, a community of farmers and artisans lived in the village of Myrtos. Stone-built dwellings, set on the hilltop as at Vasilike, resemble rooms or cells more than houses. Sharing party walls, they too call to mind the buildings of Neolithic Knossos. The scale of the individual spaces is tiny. Streets, little more than passages – two people cannot walk abreast here – link different parts of the village. Different zones have different functions. There are storage areas with rooms of *pithoi* (large storage vessels), living areas and working areas, and a shrine. There is much evidence of agricultural and industrial activity. The inhabitants grew barley, wheat, olives, and vines and reared all the usual domesticated animals: sheep, goats, pigs, and cattle. They made pots, terracotta and stone figurines, and loom-weights. They wove and decorated textiles and painted pots. The site presents a compelling picture of a proto-urban Minoan society.

Some of the dead in EM I had been buried in *cist* graves, rectangles cut in the earth and lined with stone slabs. This practice continued in EM II, but now tombs varied greatly. Notable are *chamber tombs*, these consisting of two or three stone-built rooms, constructed entirely above ground, and therefore always visible. In the

1.4 Stone jug, from Mochlos. EM II. Height 4¾ ins (12 cm). Iraklion Museum, Crete

south of the island in the plain of the Messara, another type was popular: the circular tomb or *tholos*, which appeared first in EM I and lasted until the end of the millennium. These structures were of monumental size, and like their north Cretan house-tomb counterparts, built entirely above ground. How they were roofed remains uncertain. These massive stone-built chambers appear to have served whole communities for centuries. While there appears to be a formal connection between them and the later Mycenaean *tholoi*, their functions were, however, quite different.

The Early Minoan's familiarity with working stone extended to making vases in brightly colored alabaster, breccia, schist, serpentine and steatite (fig. **1.4**), mostly stones native to Crete. This flourishing technology, which appeared in EM II and continued through EM III, was adapted from Egypt and the Cyclades, where it was widely practiced. The interior of the vase was worked with a tubular copper drill, moved by a bow, and using an abrasive powder, probably emery from the island of Naxos. The exterior was modeled by hammering with stone hammers and polishing with emery or sand. The range of shapes is very broad, perhaps even broader than that in the contemporary Cyclades where working in stone was highly favored. Striking is the sophisticated use of the veining of the stone to create flowing and moving designs and effects.

1.5 Ivory seal, from Platanos. EM II. Length 1⅕ ins (3 cm). Iraklion Museum, Crete

1.6 Vasilike ware cup and jug, from Vasilike. EM II. Height (cup) 2⅜ ins (6 cm); (jug) 5½ ins (14 cm). Iraklion Museum, Crete

Most seem to be miniatures, perhaps purpose-made for use in tombs. Some stone vases are equipped with lids, and some stone lids with handles are in the form of recumbent greyhounds. Here one can see the Minoan interest in naturalistic forms and in the animization of the lifeless. The ivory seal (fig. **1.5**) reveals this same interest. Its handle is in the form of an ox and it was found in a tholos tomb of EM II date.

Metallurgy flourished too, with artisans excelling in the manufacture of jewelry. Their skill can be seen in the rich finds in the tombs of Mochlos: gold diadems, hair ornaments in the shape of petals and leaves, as well as beads and pendants.

The typical pottery style of later EM II is the so-called "Vasilike ware." Typical shapes are the long-spouted jug and cup (fig. **1.6**). The decoration relies on a mottled effect, thus imitating the surface of stone vases. A lustrous reddish-brown wash covers the surface and forms the background for the darker floating forms of the principal decoration. These darker spots, or passages, are sometimes arranged symmetrically, as in figure **1.6**, and here they are balanced by the painted linear ornament on the spout. There are several ways the mottled effect could have been achieved: by holding a hot stick against the surface while the pot was fresh and still hot from the kiln, or by an early form of the three-stage firing process used later (see p. 182.) Typically Minoan is the sense of movement and the freedom of decoration. Pellets of clay attached to the spout on either side have been taken to suggest the eyes of birds, and thus introduce a *zoomorphic*, or animal, element into the ornament.

EARLY MINOAN III (c. 2200–2000 BC)
This period is full of problems, chronological and other. Yet a different kind of pottery decoration seems to have emerged. It continued to use the shapes popular in EM II with a tendency to reduce exaggerated spouts (fig. **1.7**). Mottled decoration has been abandoned, to be replaced by a dark, black background on which diagonal, horizontal, vertical, and sometimes curvilinear designs are drawn in thick white paint with varying degrees of precision.

1.7 Spouted jug, provenance unknown. EM III. Height 3½ ins (9 cm). Ashmolean Museum, Oxford

The Cyclades

The islands of the southern Aegean, called the Cyclades, almost belie their name, since they can only with some generosity be described as forming a circle, a "kuklos," around Delos. They did, however, from earliest times, when the sea was as much a highway as a barrier, provide a chain of anchorages and watering-holes between Asia Minor, Crete, and Greece. It was certainly by this route that Asiatic cultures reached Europe. They also formed part of early patterns of communication, as the obsidian from the island of Melos found on Neolithic sites shows. Late Neolithic sites on the islands of Saliagos (near Antiparos),

which flourished around 4200–3700 BC, and on Keos at Kephala (c. 3500–3000 BC) were succeeded by settlements of newcomers who probably arrived from the west (mainland Greece) at the beginning of the Bronze Age. After a slow start the immigrants discovered metals, marble, emery, and obsidian, and as in EM II Crete, the archaeological records show that EC II is a period of great prosperity. EC I is associated principally with the islands of Naxos and Melos, EC II with Syros, Keros, and Amorgos, and EC III with the first period of the site at Phylakopi on Melos.

EARLY CYCLADIC I (c. 3000–2500 BC)
Little evidence of architecture remains from EC I, but sculptured marble figures have survived. Pottery is limited in shapes and decoration. Shapes include the so-called "frying pan," and lidded cylindrical boxes thought to be containers for cosmetics. Decoration is limited to incised or pressed patterns on a monochrome ground.

EARLY CYCLADIC II (c. 2500–2200 BC)
On Syros a double fortification wall of stone, some 230 feet (70 m) long, can still be seen. It was built at the site of Khalandriani to protect a small town. The inner wall was protected by five horseshoe-shaped towers, with the space between the walls very cramped. Entrance through either wall was narrow or devious, and the planners evidently knew their business. Similar fortifications appeared on Naxos. Such fortification is unknown in Crete, but does appear at this time on the mainland at Lerna, while contemporary Troy boasted a fortification system beside which others pale. Houses in the islands began to be built of local stone, though walls are insubstantial (a thickness of 19½ inches (50 cm) is exceptional), and roofs of branches and clay needed the support of wooden posts. Plans are either rectangular or curvilinear according to the lie of the land and the availability of space.

Cemeteries were often located on slopes of nearby hills. Graves, like houses, were either rectangular or curved in plan, and built of stone, either in slabs (so-called cist graves) or in smaller flat stones like bricks, built up in *corbeled* fashion until a single slab could close the opening at the top. Graves did not vary appreciably in size, and relatively few – except on Syros – were reused. No precise orientation of these Cycladic graves is discernible.

The Cyclades of the third millennium are most famous for their marble sculpture. Important quarries, especially in Naxos and Paros, were now exploited to provide material for the largest of the figures. Most of the smaller figures and figurines could well have been worked from ordinary beach pebbles and larger stones. There are four major themes: female figures, male figures, musician figures, and "violin" figures, the last being the earliest. These are totally abstracted versions of the rotund Neolithic Mother Goddess type, now shown with elongated head, arms reduced to stumps and legs drawn up, uncannily

resembling violins in shape; they appear in late Neolithic times, and are popular in EC I.

It is in EC II, however, that the Cycladic sculptors enjoyed their heyday. They worked from thin rectangular blocks of marble using tools of bone and copper, and the powerful abrasive, emery. They knew that the large grained brilliant marble would split easily, and so concentrated on essential forms, leaving details to paint. Thus, they produced an uncompromisingly abstract style. The vast majority of the figures represent females shown in schematic manner (fig. **1.8**). But most striking for their exploitation of the marble and for their artistic freedom and virtuosity are the musician figures, seated harpists (fig. **1.9**), and standing figures playing the pipes. There are also warrior figures, some wearing helmets, others with baldric and

1.8 *Left* Cycladic marble figures and head. Spedos type. Height (smaller figure) 13 ins (33 cm); (larger figure) 25 ins (63.4 cm); (head) 4⅖ ins (11.2 cm). EC II. Museum of Cycladic Art, Athens

1.9 *Above* Marble figure of a harpist. Height 11½ ins (29.5 cm). EC II. Metropolitan Museum of Art, New York

1.10 *Above* Marble head and neck of a figurine. Plastiras type. Height 4 ins (10.4 cm). EC II. Museum of Cycladic Art, Athens

1.11 *Right* Marble female figure. Khalandriani type. Height 12 ins (30.5 cm). EC II. Museum of Cycladic Art, Athens

dagger, articulating a theme which was to be current throughout Greek sculpture.

Among these Cycladic figures, a number of different types have been distinguished, some more schematic than others. The Plastiras type, so called from a cemetery on the island of Paros, is dated to EC II. The head (fig. **1.10**) is oval, the nose aquiline. The ears are in relief, and the mouth sometimes, too, as in the illustration. Eyes are sometimes rendered with a boring instrument or are painted while the neck is conical and long. The arms of more completely preserved figures are not folded, and the navel is shown. Occasionally, the eyes and navels are inlaid. This is the most naturalistic of the Cycladic types. Rarely do examples of the type exceed 10 inches (25 cm) in height. Often, if broken, they were repaired. They are found in only a handful of islands south of Delos: Naxos, Paros, Antiparos, and Despotiko.

The Spedos type is more schematic (fig. **1.8**). It is datable to EC II. Examples of the type are

among the so-called "folded-arms figurines" characterized by a backward leaning head, an oval face, a pronounced ridge of the nose, a long neck, sloping shoulders, abbreviated arms folded one above the other, slim hips, curving contours, and legs bent at the knee. The eyes, mouth, ears, and hair are often rendered in paint; they may reach a height of about 5 feet (1.53 m).

Another type, the Khalandriani type (fig. **1.11**) also uses the folded-arms formula, but offers angular shapes, with a square torso, the shoulders at right angles to the neck, a triangular head, and short legs.

So much variety of form, especially within the Spedos type, and such artistic freedom were displayed that commentators have identified a number of stylistically definable subgroups of figures, which are regarded as evidence of the existence of different studios and studio traditions, and individual artists have been isolated. It is also now clear that these prehistoric artists used a modular canon of proportions, over one thousand years earlier than sculptors of the Archaic and Classical periods. The canon in use in Archaic Greece, however, was derived from Egypt, rather than inherited by some miraculous means from these island precursors.

The figures range in size from just under 8 inches (20 cm) in height to a few giants almost 5 feet (1.5 m) tall, though some miniatures exist too. They are as popular today for their powerful abstract quality as they were in the Bronze Age Aegean. There was demand in Crete and on mainland Greece where examples have been discovered. They are found mostly in graves, as companions of the dead, and some had even to be broken to fit into the grave. Some have also appeared in domestic contexts. A number of theories have been advanced to explain their function, none wholly convincing. Were they servants of the dead, or respected ancestors, or playthings, or even substitutes for sacrifice? Alternatively, were they heroes, nymphs, or divinities? Most likely the female figures were a new version of the Neolithic Great Mother, the spontaneous naturalism of the plump Stone Age fertility figures giving way to schematic, conceptualized, rigid forms. They exploit a new

material, marble, and a new scale. These are not figures to be carried about, stroked, and handled like their predecessors. They are idols, magically imbued, created to dwell with their owners both in life and death.

The Cycladic marble workers also made vases, whose elegant, simple design echoes their pottery counterparts. Collared jars, beakers with lugged handles, and handleless footed cups are favored shapes. Cycladic artisans also created zoomorphic forms in stone – sheep, for example, and the famous "Dove Tray."

EC II pottery both emulates the shapes of contemporary stone vessels like the collared jar with spreading foot and copious belly, and continues the interest in cosmetic boxes and pans (fig. **1.12**). Potters continued to use incised decoration, often now in spiral designs inlaid with a chalky white; impressed triangles are popular too. The underside of the "frying pan" illustrated shows a high-prowed, oared ship, with a prow-ornament in the form of a fish and interconnected spirals representing waves. Terracotta pans like this have been interpreted as fertility charms in the form of wombs, with the smaller field beneath taken to represent female genitalia, as on some marble figures. Yet the pan, which has a rim several inches high, is evidently intended as a container. Did these pans hold water and act as mirrors? Some pots have a painted design, sometimes in angular patterns against a buff ground, sometimes as a dark monochrome covering their entire surface.

1.12 Terracotta pan, from Syros. Height 2⅜ ins (6 cm). Diameter 11 ins (28 cm). EC II. National Museum, Athens

1.13 Terracotta hedgehog, from Syros. Height 4¼ ins (10.8 cm). EC II. National Museum, Athens

Potters, like their counterparts who worked in stone, were also interested in zoomorphic forms such as the terracotta hedgehogs (fig. **1.13**) from Syros, Corinth, Naxos, and Aghia Eirene on Keos which show both humor and naturalism. Representational art is the special strength of the Cyclades, varying from stonework and zoomorphic forms to decorated terracotta. In this respect Cycladic culture was advanced, Crete came a distant second, while the mainland lagged far behind.

EARLY CYCLADIC III (c. 2200–2000 BC)
At Phylakopi on Melos stone-built houses clustered closely together provide the first

1.14 Terracotta *kernos*, provenance unknown. Height 10 ins (25.7 cm). EC III. Ashmolean Museum, Oxford

1.15 Lerna, ground plan. EH II

evidence for a small town on the site. Marble idols and vases continued to be made during EC III, but production declined. Idols were reduced to schematic forms. But a new matt (non-shiny) paint was developed to decorate pottery ware, and a new shape, the kernos (fig. **1.14**), makes its appearance. This was a multiple vase for making simultaneous offerings, like grain, to a deity.

Greece

Theories vary as to whether new peoples arrived at the beginning of EH I. But this may not have happened until the violent end of the culture of EH II.

Small scattered communities have been revealed by surface survey in Laconia and in the Nemea valley near Corinth. Larger townships have been found at Lithares in Boeotia, and at Manika in Euboea. Here considerable evidence

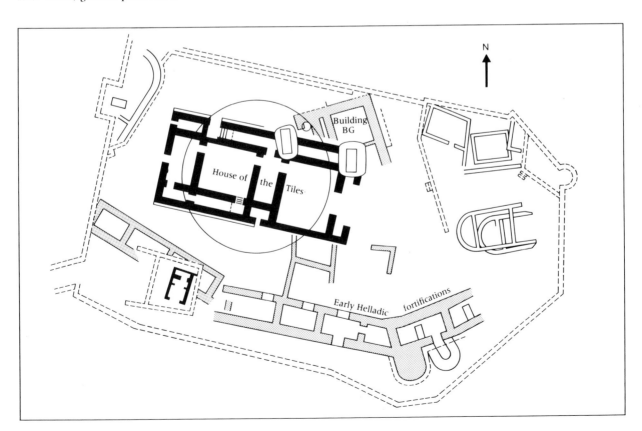

points to the working of obsidian imported from Melos. Some settlements like the village at Tsoungiza near Nemea existed throughout the whole of the EB period. Others like Lerna, with its two large buildings, flourished only in EH II. Sites with imposing big buildings imply a centralized authority in the zones they dominate. Elsewhere, the countryside was dotted with villages of apparently equal size and status, and with more isolated, scattered farms, or groups of rural buildings.

EARLY HELLADIC I (c. 3000–2500 BC)

Lithares was a large township, nearly 48,000 square yards (40,000 square m) in area, with houses opening off a long axial road. This is comparable to the underwater site at Astakos in northwest Greece where a survey has revealed an EH site of some 60,000 square yards (50,000 square m). The fragile, handmade pottery – simple bowls, small jugs, and jars – is decorated with paint or left monochrome and burnished.

EARLY HELLADIC II (c. 2500–2200 BC)

Like EM II in Crete and EC II in the Cyclades, EH II is a period of rapid development. Lerna, near Argos in the Peloponnese, is among the more informative sites. Its two big buildings, possibly palaces, followed one another on the same spot (fig. **1.15**). The excavators called the earlier of the two "Building BG" and its successor the House of the Tiles.

The two buildings show similar techniques of construction, each having a tile roof, similar shapes of rooms and corridors, and similar proportions. But associated with the first building, BG, is a number of closely packed houses with gravel streets between them, all arranged haphazardly, with little sense of planning. The dense little town was protected by a ring of fortifications provided with towers, similar to those on the island of Syros at Khalandriani.

Still within the EH II period, the House of the Tiles was built over the ruins of BG at a time when the fortification circuit too had gone out of use. The new building measured approximately 82 × 39 ft (about 25 × 12 m), and was almost rectangular. Entrances on all four sides gave access to corridors and rooms arranged with some degree of symmetry, while staircases at north and south led to at least one upper storey. Foundations are of stone, floors are of hard tamped clay, walls are of mudbrick and over a yard (1 m) thick. The roof is of both terracotta and schist tiles. The tiles alone imply a gabled roofing system. Most walls were stuccoed, but a few built of fieldstones laid in herringbone fashion left their patterned surfaces visible. This house, built directly above the debris of BG, was itself suddenly destroyed around 2200 BC. The ruined site was left untouched for several generations, though it was eventually built over.

So-called "corridor" houses, like the House of the Tiles, have been found elsewhere in the Aegean world. They represent an important architectural tradition, as significant perhaps as the later traditions of palatial architecture on Crete, and of fortress architecture in LB Greece. The sheer size and planning of the buildings are striking, and the invention of tiles – to be forgotten for over 1500 years – was a precocious innovation.

Large central buildings are not however usual in EH Greece. Other sites of densely packed townships like Eutresis in Boeotia or Zygouries in the Argolid do not have similar buildings. At Tiryns, however, a large circular structure, more than 30 yards across (about 28 m) and with two floors, was built of mudbrick on stone foundations. It seems to have been supported by horseshoe-shaped buttresses. For this staggering building a circumference of no less than 96 yards (88 m) has been proposed. Remains of terracotta and schist tiles have been found here, so the roof was evidently tiled, though how rectangular tiles would have been fitted on to a conical roof remains problematic. Equally puzzling is the function of this building: was it a communal granary? A contemporary example of a building for grain storage is the stone model of a multiple granary, said to be from Melos (fig. **1.16**).

Tiryns had another important building. This was used for working obsidian from Melos, as at Manika. It seems that lead was also used. Doubtless this was imported from Siphnos or from Thorikos in Attica, where silver and perhaps copper were being mined as well at this time. Thus

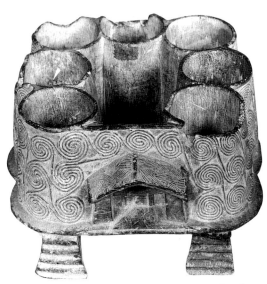

1.16 Stone model of a multiple granary, said to be from Melos. Height 4 ins (10 cm). EC II. Staatliche Antikensammlungen, Munich

1.17 Pottery "sauceboat," from Lerna. Height 7⅘ ins (20 cm). EH II. Argos Museum

the flourishing metallurgical industry was supplied with ores, and the success of skillful EB artisans is evident at many sites across the Aegean such as Mochlos in Crete and at Troy.

How people buried their dead at this time can be seen in the cemetery at Aghios Kosmas (near Athens airport). Here, stone-lined cists, some built in the earth, some above ground like minuscule houses, show a Cycladic influence. Multiple burials were accompanied by pots. A similar phenomenon appears at Marathon in eastern Attica, while at Zygouries in the northern Peloponnese pit graves were used, and burials were accompanied by pots and some jewelry. Rounded underground chamber tombs appear occasionally. Neither here, as grave offerings, nor elsewhere is there much evidence for sculpture beyond clay figurines, and a number of marble figurines imported from the Cyclades.

Pottery began to diversify during this period. New shapes include the "sauceboat" (fig. **1.17**), obviously some kind of pouring vessel (though some claim it could be used for drinking). Beak-spouted jugs and saucers are also in vogue. The surfaces are finished with a dark, shiny, early gloss, often described by the German term, "Urfirnis." "Sauceboats" were ubiquitous, thin-

walled, and fired very hard, the glossy finish perhaps suggesting a metal prototype. Examples of metal "sauceboats" have, in fact, come to light. Metal vessels are, however, rare in this period. Another suggestion has been that the sauceboat shape is derived from an obliquely sliced *gourd*. If so, could the "Urfirnis" have followed the color of the gourd?

EARLY HELLADIC III (c. 2200–2000 BC)

An important development in architecture is found in the Peloponnese. This is the long house, with either an *apsidal* or rectangular plan. The plan had appeared earlier in Thessaly and at Thebes, and is the architectural antecedent of the LB *megarons*, also a type of long house with a porch and a long hall, which dominate the Mycenaean fortresses. Evidence for sculpture is very scrappy.

A typical assemblage of pottery seems mostly to consist of solidly painted or plain dark burnished wares. For the rest, there are pattern-painted pots, decorated in both light-on-dark and dark-on-light in the form of interlocking tri-

1.18 Tankard, from Lerna. Height 4½ ins (11.7 cm). EH III. Argos Museum

angles, lines winding continuously backwards and forwards (*maeanders*), and *chevrons*, ornaments in the shape of an inverted "v". A familiar shape is the two-handled tankard (fig. **1.18**). There are also large jars with trumpet mouths and lug handles, and small cylindrical cups, dubbed by their excavators as "ouzo" cups from their similarity to the glasses which Greek tavernas still use today. But wheelmade pottery has also been found in small quantities at one or two EH III sites in the Peloponnese. This is the ancestor of the so-called gray "Minyan ware," which was to become important in Middle Helladic Greece.

The appearance of the fast-turning potter's wheel made of stone or fired clay or wood called for an apprentice to control it, whether by stick or hand. The wheel was turned by the apprentice, and the potter was thus free to use both hands to lift and form the clay. The wheel probably appeared in the later phases of EB II, but, perhaps surprisingly, was hardly used until the Late Bronze Age on mainland Greece.

Troy

An important site of the Aegean Bronze Age world was found in northwestern Asia Minor (modern-day Turkey). It was excavated and published by Schliemann and later by the University of Cincinnati as Troy. Inspired by episodes in the story of the great war between Greece and Troy recorded in the Homeric poems and in later authors, and guided by geographical clues in Homer, Schliemann excavated a hillock known as Hissarlik and identified it as Troy.

The site stands in a commanding position, at the end of the land route from Asia to Europe traveled by many migrants, and was thus a recognizable channel for cultural ideas. It also was handily situated to control shipping making its way through the Dardanelles from the Aegean to the Black Sea and vice-versa. Here Schliemann discovered the remains of several citadels, one atop the other, to which he gave sequential numbers, Troy I being the lowermost settlement he retrieved. His assertion that Troy II should be equated with the Troy of the Homeric poems has been shown to be misguided, but this should not detract from recognition of the magnitude of his achievement. Almost singlehandedly he began the recovery of the Bronze Age cultures of the Greek world.

Troy was fortified from the beginning. Troy I was furnished with huge, stonebuilt (in their massive lower courses) walls, still visible today. A projecting bastion with sloping walls protected the south gate, little more than a narrow passage through the bastion. Within the walls, inhabitants lived in dwellings of rectangular plan with a porch. Walls are built of mudbrick and timber above a stone socle (plinth).

Troy II is even more massive, and brings to

1.19 Troy II. Paved ramp leading to southwest gate

mind the fortified sites of Greece and the Cyclades built during the same period. It covers an area of some 9500 square yards (8000 square m) (fig. **2.17**, p. 60). A huge fortification wall built of stone and mudbrick was strengthened by numerous towers and bastions; paved ramps (fig. **1.19**) led to the gateways providing entrance to the citadel. Within, several smaller residences were overshadowed by the central unit, a megaron, larger than the House of the Tiles at Lerna. The building had a porch, a hall twice the size of the porch, and in all probability a back chamber too. Walls were almost 5 feet (1.5 m) thick; foundations were of stone, the walls themselves of mudbrick and timber above a stone socle course. A courtyard stood in front of the entrance, the whole complex giving an impression of great space and ease. Dressed stone blocks were used for the broadened end of the flanking walls, the *antae* of the megaron in one of

its phases, and for column bases in the courtyard. Comparably advanced urban planning may be seen nearby in the northeastern Aegean at Thermi on Lesbos and at Poliochni on Lemnos. At the same time, the citadel complex at Troy is a far more impressive statement of the power of the local ruler than anything on the Greek mainland or in the Cyclades.

The inhabitants of Troy II were energetic potters, and produced numerous monochrome shapes which were sometimes embellished with clay human faces below the rim. They also wove textiles. They are probably best known, however, for their metal goods: gold, silver, and bronze cups and bowls, and much jewelry to which the so-called "treasures" stand witness. The Great Treasure alone produced over 8000 gold beads along with numerous silver, bronze, and gold objects. It is an eloquent testimony to the wealth of the city and the skills of its craftsmen.

2
The Middle Bronze Age
c. 2000–1550 BC

Great changes appear towards and at the end of the third millennium. Crete rapidly grew prosperous, while in the Cyclades independent development was checked, and conditions deteriorated. On mainland Greece, the arrival of new peoples coincided with a period of cultural poverty. Across the Aegean at Troy, the sixth city arose on the site.

The construction of palaces in Crete shows that profound political and social changes took place at the end of the third millennium. In the absence of comprehensible written records – a hieroglyphic script, as yet undecoded, was used in the first palaces – this situation is not entirely easy to understand. In Egypt, a single central monarch had already controlled the country for almost 1000 years. The presence of several palaces on Crete, however, suggests that political power was now dispersed. The villages of the EM period, like Myrtos, gave way to

Opposite Terracotta jug, from Melos, detail of fig. **2.14**. MC III. National Museum, Athens

the MM palatial complexes. Power seems to have resided in regional centers, thus implying a much tighter control on agriculture and the economy. Legend records that the great ruler of Crete, Minos, expelled his brothers from the island, a story which may contain a grain of truth, reflecting a moment at which one leader gathered all power to himself and unified the island under the leadership of Knossos.

In the Cyclades, though life seems to have been largely uninterrupted at the end of the EB age, the high level of achievement of the third millennium was not maintained, and the islands were increasingly influenced by Crete. Marble idols were no longer made. Was it because Crete was coming to dominate the Aegean? Or was it that the social function they had performed was no longer required?

In Greece the influx of new peoples toward the end of the third millennium had interrupted life and introduced a period of cultural torpor. These new peoples were evidently unambitious in terms of architecture and the arts, and indeed other aspects of their living conditions. What evidence of their culture survives contrasts sharply with that of Crete and Troy. At Troy the MB period was to see the building of a new fortified citadel, Troy VI.

Crete

ARCHITECTURE

Somewhere around 2000 BC great palaces were built at Knossos and Phaistos. At Mallia and Zakro, we cannot be certain whether the LM palaces copied MM predecessors whose plans significantly resembled the structures of the Late Minoan period. At Zakro, however, there may have been a central court. The first palaces at Knossos and Phaistos, and the buildings at Mallia and Zakro were destroyed by earthquake in around 1700 BC. At Knossos and Phaistos the palaces were repaired and expanded, and at Mallia and Zakro comparable palaces arose on the debris of the ruined structures. The spectacular remains of these second palaces can still be seen today. Good evidence for other palaces has recently been found.

The ruined palaces mask much of the earlier structures beneath them, so that it is difficult to discuss their original design in precise detail. Yet, Knossos and Phaistos do show a large rectangular central court with access on all four sides and a considerable court outside to the west.

At Knossos, a group of separate architectural units seems to have surrounded the central court, and then been linked together into a single complex. A façade was added to face the west court, with storage units behind, and an approach road from the south was built. The palace had a complex drainage system using terracotta pipes throughout.

At Phaistos, the central court was flanked by a *colonnade*. Direct access from the paved exterior west court to the central court was through an entrance corridor, running from the center of the west façade. Many corridors and small cell-like units lay behind this impressive west façade. Some were used for religious purposes, others for storage, and others were evidently living rooms equipped with much splendid pottery.

At Mallia, there was a different and more significant architectural development. A large structure to the west of the later palace has many rooms with stuccoed walls, staircases, and storage units filled with pottery. Clay sealings and hieroglyphic inscriptions on vases suggest an administrative purpose for this building. Rooms with significant deposits of metal objects existed on the west side of the later court, but it is uncertain whether there was a court in this phase. Separate, uncoordinated buildings existed elsewhere, for example, around the so-called Agora. It seems likely that a palatial organization functioned from separate architectural units, and that no integration took place until after the earthquake in c. 1700 BC.

In these first palaces, façades were constructed of dressed stone, walls of rubble and mudbrick, and columns of wood. Here can be found the

2.1 Faience snake goddess or attendant, from Knossos. Height 11½ ins (29.5 cm). MM III. Iraklion Museum, Crete

2.2 Gold pendant, from Mallia. Height 1⅘ ins (4.6 cm). MM III. Iraklion Museum, Crete

earliest use of cut stone in the southern Aegean, especially in the large slabs used to form the lower course of the walls (*orthostates*) of the west façades and in the projecting plinth course on which the orthostates sat. Dowels were used for the first time to attach the wooden beams, used as leveling courses, to the top surfaces of the orthostates. Small rectangular spaces with steps leading down to them (*lustral basins*), and small courtyards (shafts) designed to let in light and air, called *light-wells*, made their first appearance (at Mallia). The first paved causeways and storage silos can be seen in the west courts at Phaistos and Knossos. And these palaces show the first significant use of columns in the southern Aegean (previously in evidence in Troy II).

At Knossos and Phaistos the great central court is the major feature. It emphasizes the Minoan interest in the free flow of air, light, and people within the palace. The absence of restrictive palace fortification walls allowed the gradual expansion of the complex as the need arose, so that the architecture is in a sense organic. The plan – as far as is discernible – suggests connec-

tion with Near Eastern palaces, many of which enjoyed large central courts, corridors, and many rectangular units. One such was that of Zimrilim at Mari on the Euphrates. This palace dates to the eighteenth century BC in the state in which it is best known, but incorporates parts of a complex of the earlier twenty-first century BC. Differences are that oriental complexes were heavily walled, and expansion was therefore restricted. The accent was more on keeping out the sun and heat, than on admitting light and air. Minoan and Mesopotamian palaces were similar then in their function of controlling independent city states, but different in the spirit of their architecture. (Useful comparison may also be made with the contemporary palace at Beycesultan in Anatolia and with Egyptian buildings.)

Increased contacts with Egypt and the Near East doubtless influenced the Minoan planners, who then modified the rigidity of their plans by introducing features that allowed for freedom, movement, air, and light. The Minoan planners may also have blended in local architectural traditions, as exemplified by the EM II houses at Vasilike, whose somewhat elementary architecture used corridors, small rectangular units, and a paved court to the west.

After the palace, the French archaeologists at Mallia went on to excavate the private houses nearby. Here again, though most housing dates to after the earthquake of around 1700 BC, plans of individual rectangular houses with several rooms may be discerned. To get some idea of the external face, the *elevation*, of private houses, the so-called ''Town Mosaic'' from Knossos is helpful. The term is misleading since this is not a mosaic, but a group of small polychrome plaques made from an opaque glaze called *faience*, which may originally have decorated the sides of a wooden chest. Found beneath the flooring of the rebuilt palace at Knossos, these plaques date from the time of the first palace there. They show (fig. **2.3**) the façades of houses of some architectural elegance, having two or three storeys, central doorways, a normally symmetrical arrangement of windows, sometimes shuttered, and flat roofs. They are built of brick and timber, with beamheads often visible. The many windows again speak for Minoan interest in air and light for ventilation. The terracotta model of a house (fig. **2.4**), found at Arkhanes – though of a later phase – gives more good evidence for the upper storeys of houses, and shows staircases opening out on to the flat roofs.

An intriguing structure was built at Aghia Photia on the northern coast of the island. Rec-

2.4 Terracotta house model, from Arkhanes. Height 9¼ ins (23.5 cm). LM I. Iraklion Museum, Crete

tangular in shape, it measured approximately 29½ × 21 yards (27 × 19 m), and consisted of more than thirty rooms arranged around a narrow court laid out on an east–west axis. The plan somewhat resembles that of Minoan palaces, and the early date (around 2000–1900 BC) is significant since it may mean that the palatial plan was an indigenous development. The building's function is unclear. It was not a palace since there was no provision for storage in pithoi, large clay storage vessels. Nor is there differentiation of use between groups of rooms. A freestanding wall protecting the site on the seaward side is unique on Crete, but is somewhat reminiscent of defensive arrangements at EB Khalandriani on Syros.

2.3 Faience plaques in the shape of houses, perhaps inlays from furniture, from Knossos. Height 1⅕–2 ins (3–5 cm). MM II. Iraklion Museum, Crete

SCULPTURE

From the hilltop sanctuary at Petsofa come some of the earliest (MM I) examples of Minoan sculpture, in terracotta (fig. **2.5**). These terracottas represent human figures, animals, and even human limbs, evidently offerings to the divinity. The tallest is no more than 9 inches (23 cm). Male figures stand to attention, arms raised to the chest in an attitude of respect, and wear nothing beyond a belt, a codpiece, and occasionally a dagger. Female figures have arms raised and extended in front of them, they wear bell-shaped skirts, elaborate hats, and have their breasts bared. The treatment of the heads is impressionistic, with facial features, other than nose and

2.5 Terracotta figurines, from Petsofa. Height (female) 5$\frac{1}{2}$ ins (14.3 cm); (male) 6$\frac{4}{5}$ ins (17.5 cm). MM I. Iraklion Museum, Crete

2.6 Ivory bulljumper, from Knossos. Length 11$\frac{4}{5}$ ins (29.9 cm). MM III. Iraklion Museum, Crete

chin, hardly delineated. These naïve figurines nonetheless reveal an attention to proportions – slender waist, broad shoulders – and conventions of posture, gesture (for female figures), and garments which were to continue for many centuries in Crete.

The high point of Minoan sculpture of this period is the group of female faience figurines of Snake Goddesses or attendants found at Knossos in stone-lined pits, the so-called "Temple Repositories." Sealed below debris of an earthquake which took place near the end of the MM period they are accordingly MM III in date. The largest figurine (fig. **2.7**) is 13$\frac{1}{2}$ inches (34.5 cm) tall, and is one of the largest surviving examples of Minoan sculpture in the round. She wears a bell-shaped, flounced skirt, a tight belt, and a short apron; her breasts are bare. Snakes curl down and along her arms and around her waist and shoulders, while another circles her lofty hat. Arms outstretched, bird perched on the hat, her large ears and unwelcoming expression create an imposing impression. The other figures (fig. **2.1**, p. 47) wear similar clothing, all brightly colored with shades of red, blue, and green. All show similar posture and proportions. This figural style, dependent on geometric shapes – cones (skirts), cylinders (arms, waists), triangles (faces) – with large eyes and joined or almost joined eyebrows, shows demonstrable links with earlier Near Eastern and Mesopotamian figures. Formality and naturalism co-exist, with geometry, symmetry, and elaborate decoration countering the evident interest in naturalism.

An acrobat in ivory with hair of gilt bronze (fig. **2.6**) 11¾ inches (29.9 cm) in length, also found in the palace at Knossos and also MM III in date, reveals Minoan mastery of other materials, as well as interest both in naturalism and movement. He seems to be in movement in midair, and may have belonged to a group of figures depicting the bull sports, representations of which have survived in a wall painting of the LM age from Knossos (fig. **3.5**, p. 69) and in a bronze group in the British Museum. He leaps, then, between the horns and over the back of the bull in a daring somersault manoeuver. Details of musculature, fingers, and veins are all minutely shown with realistic modeling. This diminutive vaulting jumper pioneers the notion of the sanctity of athletics which was to permeate the sanctuaries and festivals of the Greeks of the historical period. In Minoan Crete, however, the figure is shown in streamlined movement, in a captured moment, while later victorious athletes (with one or two exceptions) appear as solid timeless reality.

Another acrobat – part sculpture, part weaponry – appears on the eighteenth-century gold covering of the pommel of a great ceremonial sword (fig. **2.8**, p. 52) found in the palace at Mallia. The circular covering of the pommel, worked in raised *repoussé* relief, is entirely filled with the body of the acrobat, so arched that the tips of the toes touch the hair of his head. Realistic in representation from the curls of his hair to his upraised hands and his ribcage, his belted kilt and knobbly knees, the circular motif and willowy shape of the youth are typically Minoan. Another sword from Mallia has a pommel of rock-crystal, and a hilt of gray limestone covered with gold foil, so it appears that these weapons were elaborately decorated. (Crete, incidentally, produced the first swords of

2.7 Faience snake goddess or attendant, from Knossos. Height 13½ ins (34.5 cm). MM III. Iraklion Museum, Crete

2.8 Gold cover of sword pommel, from Mallia. Diameter 2¾ ins (7 cm). MM III. Iraklion Museum, Crete

the Aegean world, fragile bronze rapiers, many of which were used as dedications.)

Also from Mallia, also naturalistic and also hybrid – in this case, sculpture and jewelry – is the gold pendant (fig. **2.2**, p. 48). It shows two hornets confronting each other over a honeycomb, with three suspended granulated discs. New techniques of working gold are employed: *filigree*, that is, decorative metalware made of thin wire, *granulation*, where globules of gold or silver were soldered onto jewelry, and *embossing*, a technique of decoration raising the surface into projecting knobs or studs (bosses), doubtless acquired from new contacts with Syria and the Near East. Not much gold is found in palatial Crete, but vessels of silver existed, as is shown by a deep, two-handled drinking cup (*kantharos*) found at Gournia. The paucity of sculpture in the round or in relief, on any substantial scale, may be explained by the accidents of survival or of discovery. It may also be because the Minoans preferred miniature figural art, an interest which found expression in seal-engraving.

Rings and seals were used to stamp the clay with which knots of rope, which bound boxes and chests of goods, were secured, thus identifying as well as fastening the goods. Seals were also thought to have magical powers. And they were admired for the colors and shapes of the stones, as well as for the designs engraved upon them.

2.9 Chalcedony seal mounted in gold, in the shape of a cylinder, showing two men and a huge dog. Length 10½ ins (26.5 cm). LM I. Iraklion Museum, Crete

In the EM phase – from around 2300 BC – materials used for seals were bone, steatite (a stone soft enough to be carved with a copper knife), and ivory. The variety of shapes is enormous, including animals with engravings on the base (fig. **1.5**, p. 34), as is the range of topics engraved – animals, humans, abstract designs. In the period of the first palaces, the materials used include rock-crystal, jasper, agate, and carnelian. Flat or convex discs and prisms are popular shapes, and topics in favor were animals, geometric designs, and hieroglyphs. From around 1700–1550 BC, the range of shapes continued to expand to include the "amygdaloid" (an almond-shaped stone) and the flattened cylinder. Topics engraved – animals, humans, and religious scenes – reflect the contemporary enthusiasm for naturalism. Signet rings in bronze and gold appear. Production continued unabated in the new palaces after 1550 BC, and the seal in light blue chalcedony mounted in gold provides a fine example of the time (fig. **2.9**).

The engravers of these rings and seals were highly skilled, and their output huge. The materials on which they worked were tiny, and required a delight in figural art on a tiny scale.

POTTERY

The building of the palaces was matched by a new style of pottery and a new technology: the potter's wheel. The palaces seem to have allotted considerable space to the workshops of artisans, not least potters, and the new palaces evidently encouraged, and perhaps even enforced, the centralization of artistic production. High on the side of Mt Ida overlooking the palace at Phaistos was a cave sanctuary called the Kamares cave. This is where the new pottery was first found, and it is from the cave that the pottery has taken its name.

"Kamares ware" (MM I and II) was an almost *baroque* elaboration of the earlier light-on-dark wares of EM III. It was a palatial ware, rarely found outside Knossos and Phaistos. It may be the product of only very few workshops. There are two fabrics: an eggshell-thin table ware and a heavier, coarser ware for storage and pouring vessels. Shapes which are popular are the single-handed cup, the spouted jar, and the beak-spouted jug. Decoration is in white-on-black with much added yellow, red, and orange, in a true polychrome style while designs range from abstract spirals around the vessel to natural forms. Motifs, whether spirals, coils, petals, or leaves, are repeated around the pots, urging the eye to move. Human figures are excluded altogether.

Raised designs of diagonal ridges, or patterns of dots or bosses or prickles – so-called "barbotine decoration" – show that decorators explored texture as well as color. Architecture also reveals an interest in texture as shown in the variation introduced into the west façades of palaces by multiple recesses, and in the use, in a single wall, of cut stone (for orthostates), exposed beams, and mudplastered rubble.

The eggshell ware (fig. **2.11**) is the most famous pottery type of the period, mostly found in the teacup shape, of which there are numerous varieties. Its manufacture requires skillful manipulation of the wheel and firing. A white scale pattern encircles the cup in repeated and linked registers accompanied by motifs drawn from the natural world of abstracted floral buds in orange and white.

2.10 Kamares ware beak-spouted jug, from Phaistos. Height 10⅗ ins (27 cm). MM I. Iraklion Museum, Crete

2.11 Kamares ware cup, from Phaistos. Diameter $4\frac{3}{4}$ ins (12 cm). MM I. Iraklion Museum, Crete

The repetition of design motifs around the pot and the linkage of motifs also occur on a beak-spouted jug (fig. **2.10**) made of the coarser fabric. The decoration is as energetic and vibrant – pairs of spirals are linked by repeated oval motifs, all situated diagonally on the surface. A pellet of clay on the spout is reminiscent of a zoomorphic shape. Sometimes designs on Kamares wares become so complicated it seems that the surface is decorated with a firework-like display. The variety in MM pottery is astonishing.

Interestingly in this period, though artisans used painted plaster, they did not apply figural art to walls. Painted pottery, on the other hand, achieved perhaps the status of high art, and some of the finest artists applied themselves to pottery. Yet, at a more humdrum level, they were also prepared to repeat their designs on different shapes to produce groups of matching vessels.

Kamares ware continued after the reconstruction of the first palaces in the new palaces of MM III. Its design became calmer and more naturalistic, yet with a certain stiffness and formality. Vegetal motifs – lilies, grasses, and palmtrees – were elegantly repeated around the vases' surface. Kamares ware was popular outside Crete. It was shipped to mainland Greece, the Cyclades, Syria, and Egypt, and in Egypt a Kamares ware vase took pride of place in a burial group found at Abydos.

The Cyclades

ARCHITECTURE

The second town at Phylakopi on Melos provides important evidence of the Middle Cycladic phase. Excavation revealed a good portion (some $87\frac{1}{2} \times 54\frac{1}{2}$ yards (80×50 m)) of this settlement, and uncovered winding and narrow streets and houses with many rooms which were built of local stone. Middle Minoan pottery was imported here, as was Minyan ware from mainland Greece. At Aghia Eirene on the island of Keos there is only fragmentary architectural evidence for an EB settlement. After a gap at the end of EB, this was superseded by a settlement surrounded by a gateway and a towered fortification. Here both mainland and Minoan pottery were imported. A second phase of MB Aghia Eirene saw a stronger fortification wall replacing the earlier circuit, all somewhat after the collapse of the first palaces at Knossos and Phaistos.

POTTERY

The pottery at first shows little change from EC III, but in MC II it comes into its own. The favorite shape is the beak-spouted jug, painted with the same matt paint that decorated the wares of the mainland. The decoration is, however, more ambitious, displaying spirals and curls (fig. **2.12**) as well as bands of horizontal lines and groups of dots, often referred to as rosettes. Lines emphasize the neck and belly of the jug in a typically sparse arrangement. Relief breastlike forms appear below the neck and are emphasized by paint; sometimes a pair of eyes painted on the spout intensifies the zoomorphic feel of the pot. Spiral designs echo Kamares ware but the exaggerated beak-spouted shape seems to have its origins in Anatolia.

This dark-on-light style flourished especially on Melos, where in MC III vegetal motifs, birds, and fish were introduced into the decorative vocabulary – one exceptional vase stand (fig. **2.13**) proudly displays four fishermen and their catch. Birds in flight (fig. **2.14**) are especially favored, the dark matt paint often enlivened by patches of red. They float on the surface of the

pots, as if the tight design of earlier periods had been freed under the influence of Minoan style, creating new interest in movement, and the natural world. Cycladic painters made the bird their particular motif, and some of these vessels were admired enough to find their way as exports to the Minoan and Mycenaean centers.

2.13 *Below* Terracotta stand for a vase, from Melos. Height 6¾ ins (17 cm). MC III. National Museum, Athens

2.14 *Left* Terracotta jug, from Melos. Height 10¼ ins (26 cm). MC III. National Museum, Athens

2.12 *Above* Beak-spouted jug, from Thera. Height 10¼ ins (26 cm). MC. Musée du Louvre, Paris

Greece

ARCHITECTURE

Some towns continue on the site of EH settlements while some are new. All are characterized by narrow, three-roomed houses, apsidal or rectangular in plan, built of mudbrick, with roofs of reeds and clay supported by timbers. These tripartite houses with long halls (megarons) were already present in Greece in EH III. The main room of the house has a hearth, and sometimes benches against walls, while the back room has storage bins. Streets are in chaotic order. Characteristic sites are Eutresis in Boeotia, Lefkandi in Euboea, and Lerna. The site at Kolonna on Aegina was already fortified in the EH III phase, and by the beginning of the MH period, these walls were the largest fortifications in the Aegean world, after those at Troy. Later in the period defensive walls were added at Argos but not, curiously, at coastal Lerna.

Burial customs are reasonably standard. "Intramural burial" (burial beneath house floors) was typical for infants and very young children. Older children and adults were usually buried in individual cist graves or pits, sometimes within the settlement, but, increasingly as time passed, in extramural graveyards. Groups of graves often become formalized into "tumuli" (burial mounds), holding dozens of cists, pits, and pithos burials. Such tumuli doubtless formed the burial place of members of the same family or other social group. Grave gifts are poor but became richer towards the end of the period. On the island of Aegina a burial in a shaft grave was accompanied by a sword, a dagger and spear, and pottery (both local and imported). Graves like this announce the social standing of the buried person by the wealth of the accompanying gifts and anticipate the great richness of the shaft graves of Mycenae.

POTTERY

"Minyan ware" – so-called by Schliemann after his discovery of it at Orchomenos, home of the legendary king, Minyas – is the pottery often regarded as characteristic of this period, though it was not found at all sites. Though it had first appeared in EH III at Lerna, it is in the Middle Helladic period that it is best known. The fabric is fired very hard and has few or no coarse, heavy particles of clay in it. The surface is glossy and has a greasy feel. The color is gray at first (Gray Minyan), then yellow (Yellow Minyan), and always monochrome. Shapes are few: thick-stemmed goblets (fig. **2.15**) and two-handled bowls (kantharoi) are popular. They are sharply profiled, reflecting the use of the fast wheel. It is worth repeating here that the wheel was only infrequently used for many centuries. The matt painted pottery made alongside the Minyan is quite different, being handbuilt, decorated with unadventurous geometric designs (fig. **2.16**), and coarse of fabric. Beak-spouted jugs, huge storage jars, and kantharoi are popular shapes.

The limited repertoire of pottery shapes, the poverty of the architecture, and the absence of sculpture do not say much for the artistic aptitudes or aspirations of these Middle Helladic peoples. It is often plausible to associate breaks in the archaeological profile of a country or zone, such as those towards or at the end of the third millennium, with the arrival of new peoples. Since the Greek language was in use in the fourteenth century BC, as shown by the Linear B tablets (see pp. 78–9), and since there is no break

2.15 Minyan ware goblet, from Mycenae. Height 7½ ins (19 cm). MH. British Museum, London

2.16 Matt-painted storage jar, from Lerna. Height 24⅘ ins (63 cm). MH. Argos Museum

in the profile between the beginning of the MH period and the end of the Bronze Age, many take the view that the MH peoples were the first Greek speakers to dwell in Greece. A recent theory has proposed, however, that even in Neolithic times the residents were speaking an early form of Greek. Pottery very similar to Minyan has come to light in Troy in contexts contemporaneous with MH Greece, and this has suggested to some that the Trojans and Greeks of the MB period may be of the same racial stock. What surprises, however, is the sharp difference between the cultural poverty of Greece and the might of Troy.

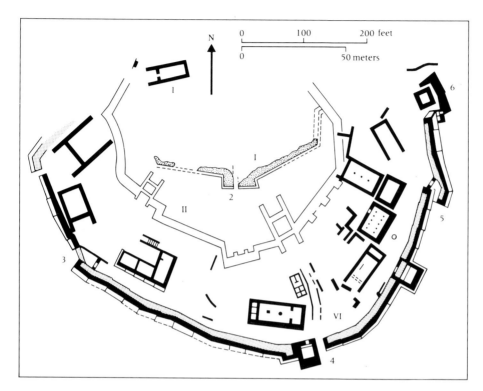

2.17 Troy VI, with Troy I and II, showing comparative sizes

Troy I
1 Megaron
2 South gate, EB I

Troy VI
3 West gate
4 South gate
5 East gate
6 Northeast bastion and water supply,
  c. 1800–1300 BC

2.18 Troy VI, stretch of eastern fortification wall from the south

Troy

In this period the site at Troy expanded to about double the size of the third millennium citadel. It is known now as Troy VI – that is, the sixth city built on the site – though it does not appear to have taken the monumental form in which it is best known today until the very end of the period. The top of the site was shaved down by builders of later (Hellenistic and Roman) times, so that the disentangling of buildings and archaeological levels has been a daunting task. Despite Schliemann's inventive efforts, much of the systematic refinement of the phasing and chronology was made by the University of Cincinnati.

Troy VI lasted from the beginning of the MB age in Asia Minor well into Late Bronze. The excavators give absolute dates of around 1800–1300 BC for this city, detecting eight strata and three chronological phases. The top of the hill was doubtless crowned by large buildings from the beginning of the MB age, all trace of which was lost in later remodeling. A fortification wall (fig. **2.17**) was built at the outset and was constantly under repair so that different stretches of it correspond to the three phases of the city itself. It took its massive form towards the end of Troy VI, enclosing houses which stood individually, at any rate on the lowest terrace close to the wall. The wall itself (fig. **2.18**) was built, in its lower courses, of squared masonry presenting a sloping face and vertical offsets towards the enemy. The plan shows the main gate at the south, flanked by a protective tower, with other gates through the wall to east and west. The gate to the east was formed from overlapping walls, while another exterior defensive tower stood close by to the south. To the north a great masonry bastion protected the water supply. A stretch of the paved road leading from the main gate into the citadel and pointing to the top of the hill suggests a spoke-like plan of streets within the fortress, all emanating from the palace on the top and leading down to the gates.

The sophistication of the military architecture at Troy can be compared with that of the palatial architecture in Crete. It is surely the proximity of these rapidly advancing cultures along with profound social changes on the mainland itself which ensured that Greece could not remain much longer in the doldrums.

3
The Late
Bronze Age
c. 1550–1100 BC

In Crete, the palaces now enjoy their period of maximum prosperity, and they all show similar arrangements and similar elasticity of plan. None was ever fortified, which suggests a civilization full of confidence and ease. They were destroyed around 1450 BC, along with all other major sites on the island. Only Knossos, less seriously damaged, was repaired and continued in less grand circumstances until around 1375 BC. Knossos is the largest palace, though they are all evidently taken from a single design. They have central courts of about the same size, about 51 yards long by 25 yards wide (47 × 23 m), with the exception of Zakro which is smaller. The plan at Knossos is very complicated, and it is this complexity which may have given birth to the legend of the labyrinth at Knossos. The palace, which alone covered about 3 acres (1.2 hectares), was the center of a city, of which a number of

Opposite Gold mask, from Mycenae, detail of fig. **3.31**. LHI. National Museum, Athens

houses and villas have been excavated. But the population figures and the density of the population, in spite of hints from Homer (*Iliad* 2:649), remain unknown.

For one hundred years, the influence of Crete continued to spread. In the Cyclades, islanders maintained some of their own traditions, keeping the typically Cycladic shapes and decorations for their pots. Yet imports increased, and architectural forms and wall paintings derived from Crete appear. The site of Akrotiri on Thera provides good evidence of the mingling of Cretan and Cycladic elements in the years prior to around 1500 BC. After about 1450 BC the Cyclades fell wholly into the orbit of mainland Greece.

The shift in mainland Greece from MH to LH life is signaled by the grave circles at Mycenae, which imply a centralization of power. During the LH I-II period a group of leaders emerged to seize power and establish a feudal (that is, a hierarchical) society. From the evidence of the shaft graves of Circle A, they were warriors. These Late Helladic Greeks, it seems, enjoyed both an indecent appetite for war and a mastery of navigation. They entered into contact with foreigners and, around 1450 BC, appear in Knossos, where they stayed for about 75 years. Elsewhere in the Aegean their presence, as traders, is documented by their increased commerce in painted pottery, and, doubtless, in the contents of some pots (oil and wine, for example). During the fourteenth century BC Late Helladic wares were exported eastward to Cyprus, the Syro-Palestinian coast, and to Egypt. Materials recovered from the fourteenth-century BC Ulu Burun shipwreck off southern Turkey suggest what was expected in return. For the ship's cargo consisted of metal, including about two hundred *ingots* of copper, and about a ton of terebinth (a resin used for perfume) stored in Canaanite amphoras; quantities of figs, grapes, almonds, sumac, coriander, safflower, and pomegranates; bronze tools and weapons, gold and silver jewelry, faience and amber beads; African ebony, hippopotamus and elephant ivory, ostrich egg shells, and other exotica.

The term "Mycenaean" is used both as an adjective applied to the city of Mycenae itself, and, more frequently, as equivalent to "Late Helladic." In the latter instance, it is applicable to all artefacts made by Late Helladic Greeks. Mycenaean Greeks, in this sense, do not necessarily come from Mycenae but might equally well come from Tiryns or Pylos or elsewhere. At home they built great fortress citadels, like Mycenae, which stand as witness to the continuity of their centralized power. The bureaucracies and the society they built appear vividly in the Linear B tablets. Mycenae is not the only highly organized social unit revealed by archaeology, but it is the best known. Others include Tiryns, Pylos, Athens, and Thebes, the relative size and power of which are echoed in Homer's catalogue of ships in Book Two of the *Iliad*.

At Athens a section of the fortification wall can still be seen on the Acropolis, and the line of the wall has been traced. But little has survived the subsequent use of the site, nor has much, beyond sections of the circuit wall, been retrieved at Thebes, hidden for the most part beneath the modern town.

Crete

ARCHITECTURE AND WALL PAINTING
Knossos. The plan (fig. **3.1**) shows the four main entrances at the points of the compass. The names of rooms in the palace are, of course, modern. The west court offers the most pleasing point of arrival. It was furnished with altars (7) for sacrifice, and has analogies in the west courts at Mallia and Phaistos. The visitor arriving here was directed down the Corridor of the Processions (8), the walls of which were painted with processions of people bringing offerings. A circuitous route led to the staircase up to reception rooms on the second floor: the longer, the more meandering the approach, the greater the impact at the moment of arrival.

An alternative route could take the visitor into the central court. Here, the west side is the major façade, comprising three floors and rising to a height of 46 feet (14 m). The main staircase (2) to the upper floor(s) was flanked by the so-

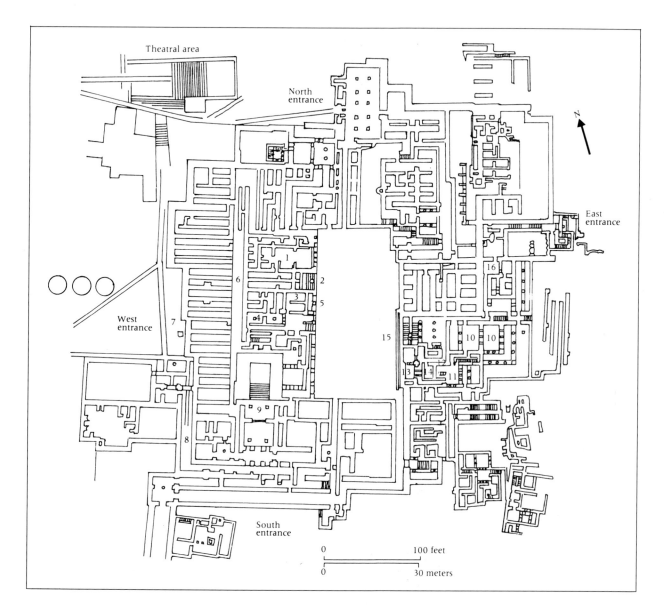

called "throne room" (1) and the main shrine of the palace (5).

The "throne room" is small and intimate, not built to impress. It may have served more as a shrine than as a royal reception room. Immediately to the left, on entering, there is a small rectangular space with steps leading down into it, a so-called lustral basin. The function of this space may have been associated with initiation rites. Against the right hand wall stood an ornate highbacked chair, the "throne," flanked by

3.1 Plan of the palace at Knossos. Late Minoan

1 Throne room
2 Staircase
3 Temple repositories
4 Pillar crypt
5 Main shrine
6 Corridor access to magazines
7 Altars
8 Corridor of the Processions
9 Staircase
10 Hall of the Double Axes
11 Queen's Hall
12 Bathroom
13 Lavatory
14 Storeroom
15 Grand staircase
16 Lapidary's workshop

3.2 Knossos, grand staircase adjacent to the royal living quarters, LM I

frescoes depicting huge *griffins* heraldically arranged on either side. The main shrine, signaled by "horns of consecration," is small. It was from here that the faience figures of the snake goddesses were retrieved from the temple repositories (3), pits lined with stones, at a lower level. Here there was also a pillar crypt (4), that is, a chamber with one or two pillars decorated with incised images of double axes. Scholars conjecture that this chamber was used for ritual purposes. Behind these public rooms, and the state apartments above, a long corridor (6) provided access to numerous magazines, or storage units. Here, in huge pithoi (fig. **3.3**), olive oil and grain (taxed goods?) were stored.

Outside the palace proper, but linked to it by raised paved walkways across the west court and to the north entrance, was a rectangular area with what appear to be steps on two sides. These were in fact seats, so that this is an *al fresco* theatre, or "theatral area." The north entrance of the palace is marked by a pillared hall from which a narrow passageway led up to the central court: monumental forbidding entrance below, pleasant painted porticoes above.

To the east of the central court were workshops, a lapidary's (16) for example, and to the south, the residential apartments of the monarch (10–14). The slope of the hill on which the palace stood was cut into to accommodate these apartments which descended in several storeys from the level of the central court. Access to this domestic quarter from the central court was by means of a grand staircase (15). The staircase descended alongside an open air shaft, ending at ground level in a small court (fig. **3.2**). Such courts, not always accompanied by staircases, were open to the heavens and are termed light-wells. At the foot of the staircase was another light-well, forming the first unit of the Hall of the Double Axes, named after the motif of double axes incised on its walls. Eastward from there was the Hall itself, with its pier-and-door construction. Piers alternating with doors in three separate rows allowed for great variety in the amount of space used, and for the amount of air and light. Doors could be open or shut, and the space curtailed or expanded accordingly. To the south more light-wells ran along the side of another smaller hall (11), called the Queen's Hall by some, next to which were rooms with a lavatory (13) and a bath tub (12). The palace was provided with a sophisticated drainage system.

3.3 Knossos, basement storerooms (magazines) from the east, showing storage vessels, LM I

Walls of the palace were decorated with fresco paintings. Unlike true frescoes, which were painted on the wet plaster, these were painted on already dry surfaces, and a binding agent was used to fix them to the walls. Only the smallest fragments have survived from the painting of the first palaces. Most of the legible fragments surviving come from the reconstructed palaces but even these are fragmentary and many paintings are heavily restored. Colors used were red, yellow, black, white, green, and blue while motifs are derived from the natural world and from the courtly life of the palace. Scenes were bordered by decorative geometric friezes.

At Knossos, fragments of a larger fresco depicting pairs of seated figures saluting one another (the Campstool fresco) yielded a striking profile of a woman instantly called "La Parisienne" (fig. **3.4**). It is very primitive, though bold use of color and the loose lock of hair at the front show a certain control. Another fresco shows a scene from the bull sports (fig. **3.5**). Here one female figure, conventionally shown with white flesh, grasps the bull's horns in preparation, another female, on the right, completes her somersault over the back of the bull, while a third, male, figure is in mid vault. The bull's position, with all four hooves off the ground, is termed the "flying gallop." Vivid naturalism is the hallmark of "La Parisienne" while movement and naturalism are those of the bull jumpers. Other frescoes, known as the Miniature Frescoes, of which the so-called "Grandstand Fresco" provides a good example, are larger and less detailed (fig. **3.6**). Impressionistic, rapid brushstrokes create visions of massed dancers, chattering crowds, landscape elements, and architectural features. Occasionally, fresco painters rendered their figures in plaster in low relief before painting them, thus lending a third dimension to their scenes.

The palace walls were built of stone, either carefully dressed *ashlar* blocks or large rubble. Rubble walls were heavily plastered, and all walls were secured with huge horizontal and vertical wooden tiebeams. Gypsum was used for the orthostate course of some important walls, the exterior of the west wall, for example. Wood was

3.4 Fresco fragment, so-called "La Parisienne," from Knossos. Height 9⅘ ins (25 cm). LM I. Iraklion Museum, Crete

used for the plentiful columns, tapering in shape. There were numerous colonnades and windows and roofs were flat. The architectural vocabulary consisted of courts, stairways, light-wells, porticoes, narrow rooms, corridors, theatral areas, lustral basins, all arranged around a central court, and designated by pre-arranged plans for ceremonial, storage, residential, and workshop use.

Today Knossos is heavily restored, mostly on secure archaeological evidence, but with several questionable points. Evans himself – relying for elevations on the evidence of depictions of buildings on wall paintings as well as on the actual excavations – was responsible for much of the restoration, but students should be aware of what meager conservation techniques were available to him in his day.

3.5 *Top* Restored fresco showing scene from bull sports, from Knossos. LM I. Iraklion Museum, Crete

3.6 *Bottom* Reconstruction of the so-called "Grandstand Fresco," from "Knossos Fresco Atlas." After Sir Arthur Evans. LM I. Original in Iraklion Museum, Crete

Phaistos. Minoan palaces show variations in siting, combinations of spaces, and changing arrangements. At Phaistos (fig. **3.7**) the new palace combined the theatral area with the west court, and replaced the weaving labyrinthine approach of Knossos with a huge staircase. The central court (fig. **3.8**) was aligned north–south on Mt Ida. To the west, as at Knossos, were storage units opening off a corridor. The thickness of their walls implies the existence of upper storeys. To south and east, much of the palace is lost, but to the north lay the residential quarter, located here to catch the prevailing summer breeze.

The central court had colonnaded porticoes on both east and west sides. There were doors protecting all the entrances onto the court, and a puzzling masonry platform in the northwest corner. At Mallia cuttings in the *stylobate* (the course of masonry on which columns stood) of the col-

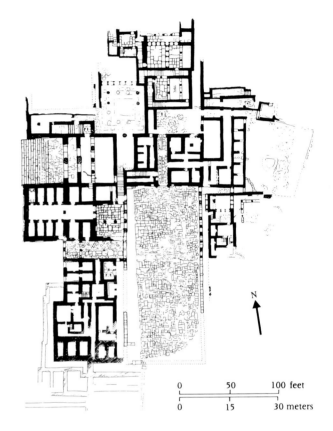

3.7 *Right* Plan of the palace, Phaistos. Late Minoan

3.8 *Below* Central court of the palace at Phaistos, from the south with Mt Ida in the background

onnade on the east side of the court and in the sides of surviving blocks of piers show that there were temporary barriers between piers and columns. It may be that so-called bull sports took place in the central courts. The barriers would keep bulls from swerving into the colonnade, and the masonry platform would enable athletes to execute a particularly tricky leaping manoeuver.

At the north, access to the domestic quarter was gained through an elaborate doorway. Engaged half columns stood on either side, each flanked by a rectangular niche and piers. Beyond the passageway was a *peristyle* courtyard with a surrounding colonnade, pier-and-door construction giving access northward, and a further rectangular unit with an alabaster floor, light-wells, and more pier-and-door arrangements. Basically similar in plan to Knossos, this palace introduced new features: an impressive entrance staircase, porticoes on two sides of the central court, a monumentalized approach to the living quarters, and a peristyle court. As at Knossos, there is no trace of fortification; unlike Knossos, there are few of the riches associated with a functioning palace.

Aghia Triadha. This villa, so called from the nearby church of the Holy Trinity, and some 6 miles (10 km) from Phaistos, has yielded examples of much of the rich paraphernalia of palace life: fresco fragments, stone vases with relief scenes, copper ingots (measures of weight and wealth), and evidence of writing – clay tablets inscribed in the Linear A script.

It is to be expected that a culture sophisticated enough to build mighty and lavishly decorated palaces would have the capacity to write, and it did. The earliest script used in the first palaces (see p. 53) was hieroglyphic, and it has been found on clay tablets, on vases, and on stone seals. It was apparently copied from Egyptian prototypes. The hieroglyphic system was evidently thought too cumbersome so it was simplified and linearized to become the script called Linear A (to distinguish it from Linear B which was to come later). By the time of the new palaces, only Linear A which was a syllabary (a set of syllables) was in use. As well as at Aghia Triadha,

tablets inscribed in Linear A have been found in the palace at Zakro, in townhouses at Khania, in fact at over twenty Minoan sites. But scholars have as yet been unable to decipher it.

The plan of the site is difficult to read, since it was built over in the LM III period. To the west, however, narrow porches and colonnades lead to a residential quarter equipped with stairs, lightwells, pier-and-door construction, lustral basins, and vestiges of a peristyle court. Gypsum and alabaster are used lavishly for paving and veneering of walls and benches while fresco fragments evoke the vitality and energy of the natural world. Was this also a residence of the prince of Phaistos?

From the adjacent cemetery comes a limestone sarcophagus offering important evidence about Minoan painting. One side (fig. **3.22**, p. 80) perhaps shows offerings to the dead in front of a tomb, another (fig. **3.23**, p. 80) preparation for sacrifice.

Foreshortening of figures might explain the smaller figure in front of the tomb, who might be thought of as further away from the spectator than those carrying offerings. The painter's interest in spatial illusionism is obvious. Images (birds and headdresses) explode beyond the controlling frame. There is much overlapping. On one side the woman pours her libation behind the sacred post, the musician's lyre is partly hidden behind the attendant's pail, legs of the model animals of the adjacent frame overlap each other. Are we intended to envision figures advancing abreast, flattened out into single file for us to see? On the other side, one leg of the sacrificial table is drawn in front of the animal victims with the other leg beyond so that the head of the ox may be thought of as in a more distant plane than the rump, while the tree standing behind the façade of the shrine offers similar suggestions of space. Are we intended to imagine a rectangular space enclosing the altar, with the shrine forming one side and the sacrificial table, parallel to the shrine, another? Such considerations suggest the presence in Bronze Age Crete, even after the collapse of the palaces, of painters wrestling with the problems of the representation of figures and objects in three-dimensional space.

Gournia. A complete Minoan town was excavated at Gournia in the east of the island by Harriet Boyd Hawes in the early years of this century and published with exemplary speed. The plan (fig. **3.9**) shows the town at the time of the new palaces, in LM I; it was without fortification. Characteristic of Crete in being built on rocky ground to preserve arable land, the site covers about $6\frac{1}{2}$ acres (2.6 hectares). Circular, winding streets were connected by staircases (streets) (fig. **3.10**) to a central hub, the "palace" or residence of the governor and the public court with its theatral steps to the north. There is a small shrine identified by cult objects. The miniature palace is demarcated by cut ashlar masonry and is thus set apart architecturally, yet there is no separation of the palace from the houses nearby except by a narrow street, implying a close relationship between governor and governed. Houses were built on two levels up the slope of the rocky knoll, with perhaps shops below and living quarters above. The tools of many artisans were found here – of blacksmiths, carpenters, and potters – promoting the notion that this was a city of craftsmen. Gournia has a comfortable and intimate feel about it, in striking contrast to Mesopotamian practice. There, shrines were not embedded in the fabric of towns, but were separate, raised, and massive. It is different too from Egyptian towns for workmen which were built in grim, standardized, grid-controlled blocks.

Mansions. As well as palaces like Knossos or Zakro which were surrounded by large houses, and towns like Gournia with smaller houses, there existed independent mansions or villas of grand dimensions. Examples include the country mansion at Vathypetro where olive pressing and wine making took place, the coastal mansion at Nirou Chani which stored bronze double axes and other ritual objects, perhaps preparatory to shipment, and the mansion at Nerokourou in the west of the island. A terracotta model (fig. **2.4**, p. 49) from Arkhanes of a Minoan villa gives a good idea of the elevation of such mansions with staircase, light-well, columned roof, and balcony.

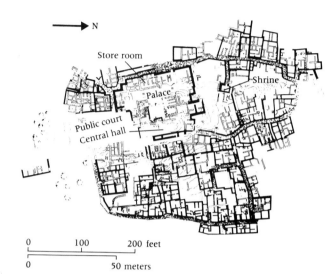

3.9 *Above* Plan of the town of Gournia. LM I

3.10 *Below* Stepped street in Gournia. LM I

SCULPTURE AND POTTERY

Sculpture. The tradition of working ivory exemplified by the MM acrobat (fig. **2.6**, p. 50) continued, as can be seen in the statuette found at Palaikastro (fig. **3.11**). Torso, arms, legs, and feet were made of ivory (hippopotamus teeth). Fragments of gold foil still attached to the ivory and gold sandals were found nearby, showing that this was originally a *chryselephantine* (of gold and ivory) figure. The head was carved from gray

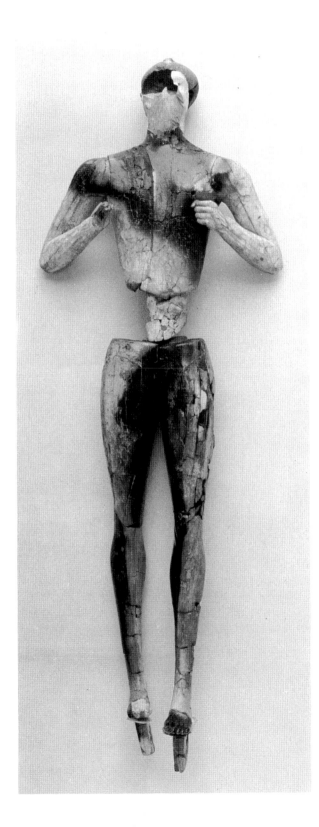

serpentine with eyes of rock-crystal and eye-brows and ears of ivory. This rich panoply of materials, and the unusually large size (the figure stood some 19½ inches (50 cm) high) suggest that this was a cult image. Arms and hands hold the posture first articulated in Petsofa terracottas centuries before, while the left foot, slightly advanced, adopts a walking stance.

The male and female types, first expressed in terracotta in the Petsofa figurines appear in bronze too (fig. **3.12**). Proportions, scale, posture, garments, and even the impressionistic handling of the facial forms follow the Petsofa prototypes. The gesture is changed. The right hand now is raised to or towards the forehead in the worshippers' gesture of salute, while the left arm (of males) is held by the side. This style is different from that of the faience female figurines of MM date from Knossos (figs **2.1**, p. 47 and **2.7**, p. 51) with their oriental overtones, and may represent a more indigenous tradition.

3.11 *Left* Gold and ivory (body and garments), serpentine and rock crystal (head and eyes) statuette, from Palaikastro. Height (with base pegs) 20¾ ins (52.7 cm). LM I. Siteia Museum, east Crete

3.12 *Below* Bronze figure of a worshipper, from Tylissos. Height 6 ins (15 cm). LM I. Iraklion Museum, Crete

The surface of these bronzes is commonly quite rough. This may be due to the low percentage of tin in the metal, which often makes it nearly one hundred per cent copper, or the deliberate absence of retouching of the cast bronze, or the undetailed modeling of the wax of the *cire perdue* (lost wax) method. This method consisted first in modeling the object in wax, covering the wax model with clay, and heating the clay so that the wax melted away through holes left in the now hard clay. Molten bronze was then poured into the hollow clay mold, now empty of wax, and allowed to cool. When cold, the clay was broken away and the bronze figure revealed, cast solid.

A number of stone ritual vases (*rhyta*, sing. *rhyton*) were decorated with relief scenes. Some were found with flakes of gold leaf still attached, so that it is probable that all were gilt. One, depicting a hilltop sanctuary, comes from Zakro and is discussed below (pp. 79–80) while three important examples come from Aghia Triadha: the Chieftain Cup, the Boxer Vase, and the Harvester Vase (fig. **3.13**).

The Chieftain Cup shows a Minoan prince issuing instructions to a military figure, or, as a more recent theory has it, young Minoans engaged in a ceremony marking the transition to manhood. The Boxer Vase shows a series of sporting events in four registers. The Harvester Vase is a rhyton made of serpentine and in the shape of an ostrich egg but only the upper part is preserved. The sculpted scene shows an elderly man with long hair, ceremonial dress, and staff, leading a procession of workmen. They carry winnowing fans for the harvest. At the back of the vase (fig. **3.14**) a figure shakes a "sistrum" (a musical instrument) with his right hand, keeping time with his left, while behind him a trio join him in song, mouths wide open. Twenty-seven figures appear in all. Aside from the main figures they are grouped in pairs, one figure slightly in advance of another, as if distanced from the viewer in spatial recession. The hilarity and movement disguise the fact that figures in the further plane are no smaller in size.

Rhyta were sometimes entirely zoomorphic, as is the case with the bullshead rhyton from

3.13 *Above*, **3.14** *Below* Upper part of a steatite rhyton, so-called "Harvester Vase," from Aghia Triadha. Diameter 4½ ins (11.5 cm). LM I. Iraklion Museum, Crete

Knossos (fig. **3.15**), where a hole in the mouth acts as the spout with another in the neck for filling. The stone is serpentine, the eyes of rock-crystal set in a pinkish stone to give a bloodshot appearance. A white band of shell surrounded the nostrils and the horns were of gilt wood. Curls are engraved between the bull's horns as are the long straggling hairs of his coat down the face and neck. This rhyton is full of naturalism and energy.

Bulls, and their capture, are the subject of the famous gold cups found on mainland Greece at Vapheio, in a context dating them to around 1500–1450 BC. There are two cups, each (fig. **3.16**) consisting of two sheets of gold, the outer decorated and the inner plain, with a gold handle riveted on. One cup shows a bull caught in a net, in a perspective close to a bird's eye view and known in Minoan wall painting. The third dimension is absent, and objects or landscape elements in the vertical plane appear to float in space, unconnected realistically to the scene of which they are a part. Two bulls escape, one on either side, one kicking up his rear hooves and making off at the Minoan flying gallop, the other tossing one lithe Minoan, as another man falls to the ground, arms outstretched. The second cup shows a quieter capture in a landscape setting, where again the third dimension is missing. Recent opinion suggests that one of these cups is of mainland Mycenaean manufacture. Yet many still believe that both represent the high point of Minoan metalwork, and indeed of relief sculpture. They are full of movement and naturalism, showing conscious use of light and shade to create the effect of shape and mass, a technique known today as *chiaroscuro*.

In the period after the destruction of the palaces, a series of terracotta female figures preserved the tradition of female deities or adorants. These figures, so-called household goddesses, are characterized by wheelmade lower bodies, hands held aloft, and complicated headdresses, sometimes as here (fig. **3.17**) embellished with poppies. Some stand as tall as 2 feet $6\frac{1}{4}$ inches (77 cm). Their popularity lasted some three hundred years, and they were followed by a similar Dark Age type (fig. **4.3**, p. 106).

3.15 *Above* Rhyton in the shape of a bull's head, serpentine, limestone, and rock crystal, from Knossos. Height $10\frac{1}{4}$ ins (26 cm). LM I. Iraklion Museum, Crete

3.16 *Below* Gold cup embossed with scenes of capture of a bull, from Vapheio. Diameter $4\frac{1}{4}$ ins (10.8 cm). LM I. National Museum, Athens

3.17 Terracotta statuette, a so-called "household goddess," from Gazi. Height 2 ft 6¼ ins (77 cm). LM III. Iraklion Museum, Crete

3.18 *Opposite* Floral Style vase, from Palaikastro. Height 9⅗ ins (24.5 cm). LM IA. Iraklion Museum, Crete

Pottery. Before the destruction of the palaces around 1450 BC, the pottery of Late Bronze Age Crete is characterized by dark-on-light decoration rather than the light-on-dark favored in the first palaces. The Pattern Style and the Floral Style, both designated LM IA, are popular to begin with. The Pattern Style used abstract motifs such as linked spirals, derived from the borders of wall paintings, while the Floral Style concentrated on naturalistic motifs such as grasses and flowers. A fine example of this Floral Style (fig. **3.18**) has papyrus plants coiled in spirals repeated around the pot. This echoes a design which first appeared in Crete in EM I (fig. **1.3**, p. 33). Common shapes for either style are jugs with horizontal spouts, large egg-shaped storage jars, and the teacup.

To the Pattern Style and Floral Style of LM IA is added around 1500 BC the Marine Style, designated LM IB. Cuttlefish, dolphins, nautili, starfish, and octopuses sprawl across the surface of pots, interspersed with seaweed, shells, and rocks, in lively, free floating arrangements. Favored shapes include the pilgrim flask, the ewer (a horizontally spouted jug with one handle) and the rhyton. The pilgrim flask from Palaikastro in the east of the island (fig. **3.19**) may be the most famous example of the Marine Style: the head and body of the octopus are placed on a diagonal axis of the pot, while tentacles writhe freely, giving a sense of continuous movement.

After the widespread destructions in the middle of the century the Palace Style appears, known only in Crete at Knossos. It is taken as evidence of the presence of Greeks in the damaged palace. Really a mainland Greek style, called in Crete LM II, it adapts Minoan motifs, both floral and marine, to its own stylistic preferences. The decorations of the pot are now often in panels, which confine the naturalistic motifs, so that they present stylized, anchored octopuses, or stiffened motionless plants (fig. **3.20**). While LM II was popular at Knossos, it is possible that LM IB was still being made elsewhere on the island. Great chronological difficulties and uncertainties still surround the pottery styles of Crete in the fifteenth and fourteenth centuries BC.

Greeks in Knossos and the Linear B Tablets.
The question of the Greeks in Knossos is complicated. Palace Style pottery is only part of the evidence for establishing their presence there from around 1450–1375 BC. There were also new kinds of tombs, the appearance of weapons in tombs, a new style of fresco painting, characterized by motionless, rigid figures, and a new writing system. This system, known as Linear B, was deciphered as an early form of Greek by Michael Ventris in 1952, and is the clearest evidence for the Greeks in Knossos. The decipherment revolutionized our thinking about the history of Bronze Age Greece. Previously, since the vast majority of tablets in Linear B had come to light in Crete, and far fewer had appeared in mainland Greece, historians had advanced the theory that the language of the

Linear B tablets must be Minoan, and that Minoans might have controlled the mainland. The decipherment changed all that.

The Linear B tablets are made of clay fashioned into page-shaped leaves or thin labels. They are flat, gray-brown, and baked hard by the fires which ruined the palaces. Upwards of 4000 of these Linear B tablets were found at Knossos, but it was only after the discovery of quantities of them at Pylos on mainland Greece that the decipherment was made. It seems that the Greeks adapted the Linear A system they found to their own use. About 20 Linear A signs ceased to be used, and their place was taken by 10 new ones. There are 87 signs in all in Linear B, too many for an alphabet, and too few for a pictographic script. The system therefore is a "syllabary," each sign representing a syllable. Alongside

3.19 *Below* Marine Style pilgrim flask, from Palaikastro. Height 11 ins (28 cm). LM IB. Iraklion Museum, Crete

3.20 *Right* Palace Style three-handled amphora, from Knossos. Height 2 ft 6¾ ins (78 cm). LM II. Iraklion Museum, Crete

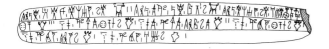

3.21 Linear B tablet, terracotta, so-called "tripod tablet," from Pylos. LH IIIB

the syllabic system were ideograms (fig. **3.21**), of great and obvious help in the decipherment. The tablets are mostly inventories, lists of flocks and herds, of olive trees and saffron, of chariots and weapons. Thus, they are the recording system of a bureaucracy, detailing amounts of taxed goods and movements of men and commodities. They also shed some light on the religion of these Late Bronze Age Greeks. Though it displays some similarities with Minoan religion, it is unlikely to have been identical. Of the later Greek Olympians, Hera, Zeus, and Poseidon appear, but there are more mysterious figures, too: Pipituna and Potnia Dapuritojo, for example. The gifts they received, barley, fennel, coriander, oil, honey, and wool, were not sacrificial. In contrast with the evidence of the Aghia Triadha sarcophagus, they were without blood.

The Linear B tablets from Knossos are associated with the final destruction of the palace, though the actual date of this is debatable. A few scholars claim it to be around 1200 BC, while most believe that it took place in the early years of the fourteenth century BC. The causes remain puzzling: did the Greeks themselves destroy the palace, perhaps in an episode of civil war?

MINOAN RELIGION
The Aghia Triadha Sarcophagus. There is much conjecture about the complicated and difficult topic of Minoan religion, since much of the evidence is inconclusive. The Aghia Triadha sarcophagus may be a suitable starting point. This painted limestone coffin is dated to around 1400 BC and is important evidence both for Minoan painting and for religion. One longer side (fig. **3.22**) shows two scenes, though the background is divided into three sections. To the left a woman pours a libation (a drink offering) into a large vessel. This is positioned between posts crowned with double axes, on which birds perch. Behind

her come an attendant carrying more vessels slung across her shoulder, and a man playing a lyre. The other scene moves in the opposite direction: three men, carrying models of animals and a boat, approach a stepped altar, a tree, and a cloaked figure in front of a tomb. Is this the dead man rising as a phantom from the grave? Or is he gazing at rituals expediting his passage to the next world? Is this evidence for a funerary cult, or for a cult of the dead?

The other longer side (fig. **3.23**) shows a procession of women, led by a man playing the double flute, a trussed ox on a sacrificial table beneath which are two terrified animals, and a woman who stands in front of an altar rolling her eyes heavenwards. The altar stands in front of a bird perched on double axes supported by a post, behind which is a shrine in front of a tree. In the background a basket of fruit and a Kamares ware jug complete the scene. Sacrifices and offerings to the dead seem to be the subjects depicted on both sides of this sarcophagus.

Cults. The evidence of the Aghia Triadha sarcophagus along with objects of daily use found in tombs has suggested a Minoan belief in life after death. Some scholars have also maintained that the dead were deified and received divine rites, that is, that there was a cult of the dead.

Votive offerings (objects dedicated or vowed to a deity) especially of human and animal figurines, and of pottery, show that divinities were worshiped in hilltop sanctuaries and caves, and in small shrines in villas, palaces, and towns. A household shrine in EM Myrtos was furnished with a terracotta female cult figurine set on a stone stand. By the end of the millennium sanctuaries were being built on mountain tops. Caves such as the Kamares cave and the Diktaion cave received worshipers from the beginning of the MM period. Hilltop sanctuaries proliferated all over the island, good examples being those at Petsofa and on Mt Juktas. A hilltop sanctuary is depicted in low relief on a fifteenth-century BC rhyton of serpentine found in the palace at Zakro (fig. **3.24**). The door of the shrine is decorated with spirals, altars stand in front, and the walls are decked with numerous "sacred horns,"

3.22 *Top,* **3.23** *Bottom* Painted limestone sarcophagus, from Aghia Triadha. Height (of figured scene) 6 ins (15 cm). c. 1400 BC. Iraklion Museum, Crete

3.24 Rhyton of serpentine, showing hilltop sanctuary, from Zakro. Height 9½ ins (24 cm). LM I. Iraklion Museum, Crete

symbols of power. Two pairs of mountain goats recline on the roof, flanking a sacred image, while others skip down the mountainside. Hawks fly overhead, no human is to be seen, the divinity is within, and birds and animals rule the mountain.

Some shrines in palaces and villas were supported by pillars, incised with the double axe sign. These pillars doubtless were the manmade versions of the extraordinary natural rock formations which attracted worship in caves. Pictures of religious activity often show altars, shrines, and trees together, and often the tree or trees become the focus of attention. So, trees and rock formations, mountains, and pillars were apparently objects of worship. As such, they seem to have represented the world of Nature.

The evidence of rings and gems points in another, but overlapping direction. A female figure, accompanied by women attendants, often takes pride of place and appears in control of wild animals or trees. Is this the old Mother Goddess – the goddess of fertility – descended from Neolithic times? She is sometimes shown with her son or consort, a boy-god. On rings and seal-stones she can appear in motion and bare-headed, her hair floating in the wind. The faience statuettes from Knossos (figs **2.1**, p. 47 and **2.7**, p. 51) present a more refined version. As a divinity or divinities of nature, earth, trees, and wild animals, she or they may have been thought of as being present in rocks, caves, and mountain tops, and when pillar crypts were built she may have been thought of as the establisher of houses. Whether she was a single divinity who took many aspects (as Mistress of Animals, Household Goddess, Goddess of Fertility) or many different goddesses is a matter of debate. She was certainly closely identified with a vegetation cult, the fertility of the earth and of those who lived off it.

Practices. Shrines in palaces and villas often had benches around the walls and offering tables of stone or terracotta, some perforated with holes to take the liquid offerings poured presumably for a spirit beneath the earth. Other equipment included stone and terracotta storage vessels, lamps, shells, and painted pottery. A mainstay of religious practice was evidently the giving of gifts, whether terracotta figurines, pottery, fruit and grains, liquids, or animals.

There is ample evidence of animal sacrifice. The Aghia Triadha sarcophagus shows a sacrificial scene, and the mountain sanctuary of Kato Syme, for example, has revealed the residue of numerous sacrifices of animals, as well as the terracotta vessels used for pouring liquids. Human skeletons were found in the ruins of a shrine on Mt Juktas, one of which, on a table, seems to provide evidence for human sacrifice at the moment of the building's collapse around 1600 BC. Further evidence comes from Knossos, where human remains suggest the sacrifice of children around 1450 BC. Many bones were cut by knives suggesting the preparation of flesh for cooking and eating.

Wall paintings which decorate a lustral basin and an adjacent chamber at Akrotiri on Thera have suggested the use of these basins for initiations. The paintings show women engaged in ceremonial activities; the painting above the dado of the basin itself shows a seated woman holding her bleeding foot, while another beside her gazes at an altar with blood dripping from it. On the wall of a room above the basin, women gather crocus stamens and offer them to a seated deity. These scenes have been interpreted as religious initiations.

While the purpose of altars, offering tables, and rhyta to pour libations is clear, what are we to make of "the horns of consecration"? What of the double axes, incised in pillars or frequently found as votive offerings in caves?

THE LM III PERIOD

The period around 1375–1100 BC (LM III) remains hazy. Did Crete become a dependency of the great Mycenaean (mainland Greek) warlords? It was a quiet period with a certain degree of good fortune, for the island seems to have avoided the far-reaching destructions which began to strike the mainland around 1200 BC.

The site of Kommos in the south of the island reveals a large public building of the LM I–II period, identified as a stoa by the excavators,

with a pebble courtyard and flanked by paved roadways leading to the Libyan Sea. This stood intact though derelict in LM III, while at the same time the largest LM III building so far recovered in Crete was built. This was made of coursed ashlar masonry, or of ashlars and rubble in a timber framework. It had long galleries with windows and flat roofs. Cypriot and Canaanite materials found in LM III Kommos point to the existence of a trade network, and this building has been identified as a warehouse for commodities. Alternatively, it could have been used as shipsheds.

The Cyclades

KEOS

At Aghia Eirene on Keos, additions were made to the fortification system in a period approximately equivalent to that of the grave circles at Mycenae (see p. 87). In the period of prosperity which followed, chronologically parallel to LM IB in Crete, much building took place. This included part of a sanctuary where a large number of terracotta figures (fig. **3.45**, p. 96) were found. This sanctuary which first saw life in the MB period continued in use, intermittently perhaps, for some eight centuries.

MELOS: PHYLAKOPI III

Massive fortifications of polygonal masonry were built to protect the third town on the site at Phylakopi, similar now to the fortified site at Aghia Eirene on Keos. Streets, as at Gournia on Crete, were almost 5 feet (1.5 m) wide, but little more than footpaths with flights of steps. Construction techniques vary, but most walls were of rubble and about 2 feet 3 inches (0.7 m) thick. Blocks of limestone and basalt occur occasionally, and there is ample evidence that timber was used to stabilize walls. Houses have two or three rooms, and some suggest Minoan influence. A pillared room for example looks very much like a pillar crypt.

One major building, larger by far than other houses, doubtless had a special function. The discovery close by of an inscribed clay tablet, apparently listing commodities, suggests the existence of an archival system, and that this large structure served an administrative purpose. All the fragmentary frescoes from Phylakopi may be considered of this phase. They include the flying fish fresco (fig. **3.25**) depicting blue and yellow fish in circular motion among stylized rocks and the spray of the sea. In style and subject matter, this fresco is wholly Minoan. There is ample evidence of Minoan influence on local vase painters too, again in terms of style and subjects.

The Minoan Thalassocracy. So distinctly Minoan are some of these features that Minoans probably lived at Phylakopi, some as traders, some perhaps as administrators, some certainly as builders and artists. A similar situation occurs at Miletus on the coast of Asia Minor, on Rhodes, and on the island of Kythera. So there may be some truth in the report by the fifth-century BC historians, Herodotos and Thucydides, of a thalassocracy (control of the sea) by Minos, the legendary ruler of Knossos. It is worth recalling how widespread the popularity of Kamares ware pottery was. Late Minoan I pottery also enjoyed a wide vogue, being traded to Cyprus and Egypt, and to Aegina, Thera, Naxos, Keos, and Melos.

Pottery. Cycladic potters continued producing vases until around 1450 BC, becoming more and more influenced by Crete. The beak-spouted backward leaning jug, equipped with "breasts," hallmark of MC, continued, though now more globular in shape. The "askos," a baggy-shaped, low pouring vessel, stayed in production and

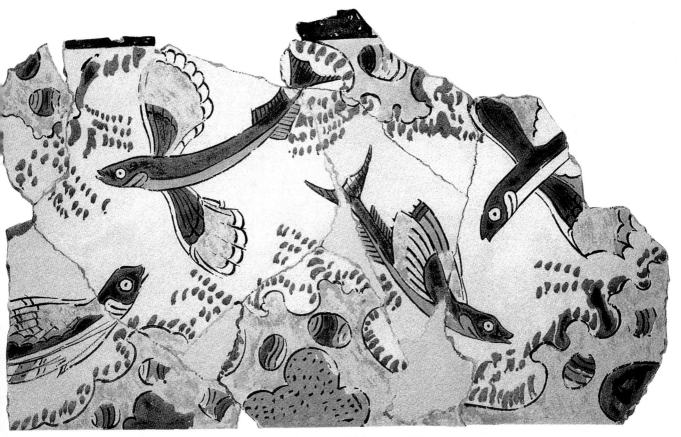

3.25 Restored fresco of flying fish, from Melos. LB I. National Museum, Athens

3.26 Terracotta cup, from Thera. Height 4¼ ins (11 cm). LB I. National Museum, Athens

3.27 *Right* Terracotta jug, from Thera. Height 17 ins (43.5 cm). LB I. National Museum, Athens

spouted jars and singlehandled jugs continue. The rhyton and some varieties of cup shapes are introduced from Crete. Birds continue their popularity as decorative emblems, joined by Minoan-inspired marine and vegetal motifs (fig. **3.26**). The plump-bodied jug (fig. **3.27**) from Thera introduces from Crete a marine motif, the dolphin, uncharacteristically bold-eyed and bad-tempered, however, and sharp of snout.

Thera. New evidence for the Cyclades has come from excavations at the site of Akrotiri on Thera. Much of a LC town, enshrouded in the debris discharged by a volcanic eruption which changed the shape of the island, has been excavated. It has justly been termed an Aegean Pompeii. As to architecture, houses have adjoining walls, and are two, three, and four-roomed with plenty of windows for light and air. Some are several storeys high. Streets show little organization. No "palace" or more imposing building has yet come to light. There is clear

evidence of Minoan presence with pier-and-door construction, light-wells, and a lustral basin.

Lower levels at the site, surprisingly, show no contact with Crete and Greece in the third millennium. MC Akrotiri, however, has yielded Kamares pottery from Crete and matt-painted pottery from the mainland. The site was destroyed by earthquake in MC III at about the same time as the MM III destruction of Knossos.

As to wall paintings, the scrupulous excavation of the LC town has allowed the reconstruction of entire rooms. The techniques, colors, and conventions of the paintings are similar to those on Crete. Some themes are new — children boxing, antelopes — while some emulate Crete — blue monkeys, for example. One astonishing painting almost 23 feet long (7 m), and in the style of the miniature frescoes of Crete, depicts a landscape with houses, scenes of warfare, and worship, and a great flotilla of ships. Interpretations of this scene vary from a navigational festival to a naval regatta, or acts of piracy. Another shows a young

priestess (fig. **3.28**) wearing a long heavy garment, earrings, bracelets, a necklace, an elaborate coiffure, and carrying a clay incense burner. In another, more Minoan in tone, people are absent and all three preserved walls celebrate nature – polychrome rocks, vigorous bichrome lilies, and mating swallows (fig. **3.29**). Pottery, both local and imported at Akrotiri, is a poor match for this blaze of wall painting. As, however, with the pottery, the origins of the wall painters remain enigmatic. How strong the local Cycladic elements are, and how strong the influence of Crete was in the culture of Akrotiri, is debatable, but there is little doubt that the site reflects Minoan culture at its height.

Did the volcanic eruption of Thera destroy the palaces and other sites on Crete? The chronology does not support this. According to the excavator of Akrotiri, the eruption took place around 1500 BC. Even earlier dates going back to c. 1600 BC have been proposed whereas the destructions on Crete are thought to have occurred around 1450 BC. The eruption, with its accompanying aerial blasts and tidal waves, certainly did damage to Crete, but it seems that something yet more dreadful (the Greeks?) was responsible for the calamitous events of around 1450 BC. Recent research on the island of Mochlos off the coast of Crete has recovered remains of a number of houses, contemporaneous with the palaces in their LM phase. One of these houses is of LM IB date. Beneath the floor, a stratum of volcanic debris from Thera was found, and beneath the ash, pottery of LM IA. Accordingly, LM IA and LM IB appear to be wholly distinct chronologically, at any rate in certain zones of the island. It seems the volcano blew up during LM IA and that Crete continued to flourish during LM IB.

Melos: Phylakopi IV. From the middle of the fifteenth century BC, the Cyclades fell under the influence of mainland Greece. Cycladic pottery styles lost their identity and became submerged in a uniform Mycenaean (Late Helladic) style which spread right across the Mediterranean. At a

3.28 Fresco of a priestess, from Thera. LB I. National Museum, Athens

3.29 Fresco of a landscape with swallows, from Thera. LB I. National Museum, Athens

number of sites there is evidence of the arrival of Mycenaeans. The fourth town at Phylakopi on Melos, built atop the ruins of Phylakopi III, boasted some houses which stood individually, and a dominant central building displaying Mycenaean characteristics: a megaron with flanking corridor and a court in front. This megaron, built in the early years of the fourteenth century, was positioned directly on top of, but was even larger than, the big building of Phylakopi III. Some distance away, a small shrine was built, the finds from which are largely Mycenaean in character and include typical terracotta figurines. A new stretch of fortification wall reinforced the existing system. This is the period (around 1400–1200 BC) when Mycenaean (Late Helladic) culture spread right across the Aegean and beyond. Among the first to fall into the mainlanders' sphere of influence were the communities in the Cyclades.

Greece

THE GRAVE CIRCLES AT MYCENAE

The transition from MH Greece to LH and from cultural torpor to energetic engagement with other communities outside Greece is marked by the grave circles at Mycenae. There are two: circle A was discovered by Schliemann in the nineteenth century, and circle B in 1952. Both were originally outside the citadel's wall, but circle A (fig. **3.30**) was incorporated inside when the wall was extended in the thirteenth century BC. A few graves in circle B are earlier than the royal shaft graves of circle A, though most are contemporary. In general terms, they cover the period from around 1550–1450 BC.

Almost all the graves in these circles are cist or shaft graves. A cist grave is a shallow rectangular grave lined with four stone slabs with a fifth slab used for the lid. A shaft grave is also rectangular but much deeper, with a floor of pebbles, walls of rubble masonry, and a plank roof some distance from the surface of the earth.

The graves in circle A are surrounded by a double ring of limestone blocks with rubble between them, capped by flat slabs. The wall surrounding circle B is of rough stones only. Graves in both circles were marked by upright rectangular limestone blocks called *stelai* (singular *stele*), grave markers, some of which were sculpted. Grave Circle B, some 142 yards (130 m) west of the Lion Gate, the main entrance to the citadel in the thirteenth century BC, had 24 graves of which 14 were shaft graves, similar to those of circle A, one a late vaulted tomb, and the others simple MH inhumations in cist graves. Funerary gifts in circle B were poorer than those in circle A. The extent to which the materials from these graves were imported or influenced by imports or imported craftsmen, and especially the extent of their relations to Crete and Cretan workmanship remains a lively topic.

Grave Circle A enclosed 6 shaft graves, of which grave IV, the largest, measured about $21\frac{1}{4}$ feet (6.5 m) in length and about $13\frac{1}{2}$ feet (4.1 m) in width. Nineteen people in all were buried in these graves, from two to five in each shaft, men, women, and children. It is the funerary gifts which take the breath away in a great blaze of gold and weaponry. There are gold masks laid over the face of the dead (fig. **3.31**) (their individuality suggests attempts at portraiture),

3.30 Reconstruction of Grave Circle A, Mycenae, c. 1250 BC

3.31 Gold mask, from shaft grave V at Mycenae. Height 10¼ ins (26 cm). LH I. National Museum, Athens

3.32 *Below* Gold signet-rings, from shaft grave IV at Mycenae. Diameters 1⅛, 2 ins (3, 5 cm). LH I. National Museum, Athens

gold signet rings (fig. **3.32**) with scenes of human combat and the hunt, a gold lionhead rhyton, gold panels for attachment to a wooden surface, gold cups, and gold jewelry. Other dazzling gifts include ornate ceremonial weapons (fig. **3.33**) decorated with scenes of the hunt of lions, or with *Nilotic* (river-life) scenes made in a technique derived from Egypt, and a bullshead rhyton made of silver with nostrils, horns, and ornamental rosette of gold.

The sudden accretion of this wealth to Mycenae remains without explanation. The weaponry implies warlike tendencies, so the wealth may come from direct pillage or mercenary activities. It does not seem to imply new peoples in Greece, since there are no archaeological interruptions on sites. There may have been commerce with the north. What is certain is that Minoans played a part in creating the artefacts with which Mycenaeans enriched their lives. The

3.33 *Right* Bronze dagger blades with gold, silver, and *niello* inlay, from shaft graves IV and V at Mycenae. Length 6⅖, 9⅖, 8⅖ ins (16.3, 23.8, 21.4 cm). LH I. National Museum, Athens

3.34 *Below* Three-handled amphora, with panelized marine ornament, from Kakovatos. Height 30¾ ins (78 cm). LH II. National Museum, Athens

bullshead rhyton was obviously inspired by Crete. The Minoan motif of the "flying gallop" is found both on a ceremonial dagger and on gold panels. The figures hunting lions on a ceremonial dagger are cleanshaven and narrow-waisted in the Minoan tradition. Yet there is much that is nonMinoan, too: masks for the dead, scenes of combat and hunt, and mainland vase shapes. Minoan craftsmen probably exported Minoan objects for the new market at Mycenae, executed commissions for Mycenaeans, who required their own kinds of objects and decorated scenes, and also trained Mycenaean apprentices.

The oldest pottery in the grave circles is Minyan and matt-painted ware of the MH tradition. During LH I/II Cretan shapes and Cretan ornaments flooded into Greece, though the exuberant naturalistic motifs of LM IA and B seem to lose vitality in the transfer (fig. **3.34**). Vessels painted with such decoration appear in the shaft graves, and it seems inescapable that Minoan potpainters were at work in Greece.

ARCHITECTURE AND WALL PAINTING

Although little evidence of settlement architecture exists for the period around 1550–1400 BC, pottery proves that settlement was widespread and dense. The Mycenaeans' ability to capture Knossos in about 1450 BC is also an indication of the size of the population and their power.

Mycenae   Mycenae (fig. **3.35**) commands the plain of Argos. It is not just a palace, for houses too are protected by the massive fortification; yet most of the town lay outside the wall. The wall (fig. **3.36**) did not originally include the Lion Gate or the northeast extension. About 1250 BC, however, the wall was extended to include Grave Circle A and the Lion Gate was built. Fifty years later the wall was further extended in a loop at the northeast to guard the water supply. The walls are built partly of roughly dressed but carefully fitted *Cyclopean* masonry (blocks so large that it was believed that only the giant Cyclopes could move them!), partly of coursed ashlars. They follow the lie of the land and are almost 20 feet (6 m) thick. The Lion Gate defended the citadel's entrance by projecting a bastion forward for some 15 yards (14 m) on one side, parallel to the line of the wall itself on the other, so that an enemy would be vulnerable on one side or the other. The gate itself consists of four massive blocks: threshold, *lintel* and jambs, of which the lintel is said to weigh around 20 tons. Atop the lintel sat the thin triangular block, only $27\frac{1}{2}$ inches (70 cm) thick, depicting the lions. The empty space behind the triangular block (fig. **0.12**, p. 23) is termed a *relieving triangle*, since it

3.35 The citadel, Mycenae, from the south

3.36 The citadel, Mycenae. 13th century BC
  1 Lion Gate
  2 Postern gate
  3 Steps to cistern
  4 Northeast extension
  5 Grave Circle A
  6 Ramp up to palace
  7 Houses
  8 Palace
  9 Later Geometric period Greek temple

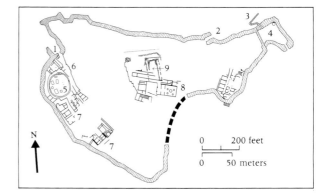

relieves the lintel of unnecessary weight. There is large ashlar masonry either side. A small *postern* gate to the north echoed the plan of the Lion Gate, while the northeast extension safeguarded the underground passage, which ran beneath the wall, before zigzagging down in sawn limestone steps to the subterranean cistern far below.

The palace was sited on top of the hill. It is a good example of a mainland megaron, being rectangular with the entrance in the centre of the short side, having a porch with two columns *in antis* (i.e., between the *antae*, the broadened ends of walls), a vestibule and a hall equipped with a throne, a hearth, and columns. A corridor flanking to the north gave access to that direction, while a court in front of the megaron was approached either directly, or by a staircase to the southwest. There are similarities between Homer's description of the palaces of his heroes and this. His *aithousa, prodomos,* and *domos* find correspondences in the Mycenaean porch, vestibule, and hall. The differences between Minoan and Mycenaean megara, however, could not be more pronounced: Minoan are infinitely expandable, using pier-and-door construction to this end, and welcoming light and air. Mycenaean, on the other hand, are immutable and static and evidently prefer warmth to ventilation.

Outside the palace, on the slope of the hill within the fortification, was a shrine area. Here a cult room was embellished with a staircase, columns, and platforms on one of which stood a female terracotta figurine, almost 2 feet (61 cm) high. Some sixteen other female idols, of the same size or smaller, were in an adjacent chamber, with a pair of coiled terracotta snakes. A connecting chamber was decorated with frescoes. These included a painting of an elegant lady, about half life size, holding what have been interpreted as wheatsheaves. There were three panels of human figures only partially preserved. Other motifs included a frieze of solid discs beneath "horns of consecration." A third room was L-shaped. One arm of this contained vases of LH IIIB and partly worked ivories. In the other was a shrine with figures painted on a platform in one corner. As in the Cretan palaces, places of religious worship were accorded no immediately visible size or shape.

The princes who lived in the palace at Mycenae required that their tombs also reflect the glory of their lives, for a new kind of tomb appears there. This was a specially built, domed chamber, sometimes termed a beehive tomb or a *tholos*. It appears first in Greece, in the western Peloponnese, in the mid-sixteenth century BC, and arrives at Mycenae around 1500 BC. Its origins are obscure. Some say it may have developed from the circular tombs of the third millennium in Crete. Others maintain that tholoi are translations of the native chamber tombs into more lasting form. Yet another view argues that the dome of the tholos represents the vault of the heavens over the open precincts of the graves, as at the grave circles at Mycenae.

There is a sequence of nine tholoi at Mycenae, of which the mistakenly named "Treasury of Atreus" provides the best preserved example (fig. **3.37**). It was built around 1250 BC on a hillside and is approached by a long passage about 38 yards (35 m) long and 6½ yards (6 m) wide, cut out of the rock and lined with ashlar walls (fig. **3.38**). The door, almost 16½ feet (5 m) high,

3.37 Isometric drawing of the Treasury of Atreus, Mycenae. c. 1250 BC

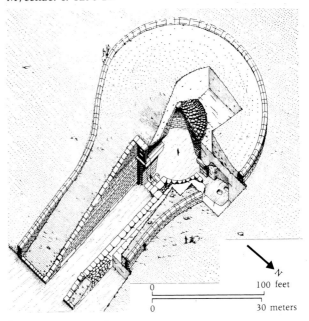

0   100 feet

0   30 meters

3.38 Treasury of Atreus, Mycenae. Approach passage, door, and relieving triangle, from the east. LH IIIB

tapering inwards towards the top, gives access to a corridor beneath two massive lintel blocks, which leads to the vaulted interior. A relieving triangle above spared the lintels the gigantic weight of the superstructure. The interior measures nearly 16 yards (14.5 m) across and is 43 feet (13.2 m) high. It has a corbeled dome, built of cut masonry within the contour of the hill at the lower courses, and then continually buttressed on the outside by earth, when the dome emerged above the ancient surface of the landscape.

Against the façade stood *engaged* columns in red and green marble, the half columns appearing to project from the wall – a pair in red above a larger pair in green (fig. **3.39**). Those below were carved with Minoan chevron and spiral motifs, and supported capitals, also of Minoan type with similar decoration. This façade brings to mind the façade of the north end of the central court at

Phaistos (fig. **3.8**, p. 70). The functional, heavy Mycenaean stone architecture contrasts strikingly with the ornamentalism of the Minoan decorated columns, designed originally for spacious courts and halls, and here slapped unceremoniously onto the exterior of the Mycenaean tomb as a decorative counterweight. This shows another striking contrast between Mycenaean and Minoan attitudes to architecture. Mycenaeans favored *megalithic* possession of space, using massive, irregularly shaped blocks in

3.39 Façade of the Treasury of Atreus, Mycenae. c. 1250 BC

the construction of their fortresses, and megalo-maniac enclosure of it in their tombs. Minoans treated it flexibly in unfortified palaces, which were almost whimsically expandable in their exteriors, and labyrinthine in their interiors.

Tiryns. At the other end of the plain of Argos from Mycenae stood the fortress of Tiryns (fig. **3.40**). Located close to the sea in a position of no geographical prominence, Tiryns enclosed an area of some 23,920 square yards (20,000 sq m) in a circuit of walls about 765 yards (700 m) long.

3.40 The citadel of Tiryns. 13th/12th century BC

1 Gates	4 Courtyard
2 Propyla	5 Megaron
3 Vaulted galleries	6 Lower citadel

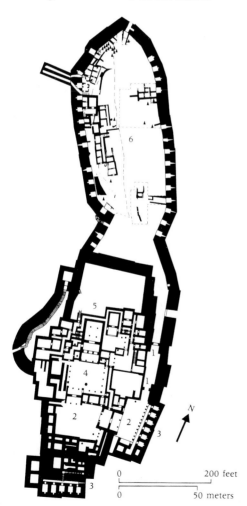

3.41 Tiryns, vaulted gallery in southeast bastion of citadel wall. LH IIIB

What remains of these walls dates from the thirteenth century BC. They are built of Cyclopean or ashlar masonry, as at Mycenae. Within the fortress, in the lower citadel to the north, excavation has revealed considerable construction of LH IIIB/C date, including a number of shrines and provision for access to two underground cisterns. As at Mycenae the water supply was the vulnerable point. To the south a well-preserved megaron of the thirteenth century BC is approached by a winding route. The tripartite megaron is flanked by a smaller one, so the planners evidently enjoyed doublets: there are also two gates with narrowed approaches, and two further *propyla* (monumental columned gate-houses) linking three courts. Massive vaulted galleries (fig. **3.41**) supported bastions in the walls. A large porticoed courtyard stood in front of the megaron, and frescoes decorated the walls. Tiryns emerges as the finest extant example of Mycenaean military architecture. It is a large megaron with dependencies, suitably decorated, spacious columned courts, and monumental gatehouses. And it is all systematically arranged within a tough outer shell of Cyclopean galleries, bastions, and walls.

Pylos. The palace at Pylos in the southern Peloponnese seems rural by comparison. Built, lived in, and destroyed within about a century, perhaps around 1300–1200 BC, it was unfortified. There was a megaron, preceded by a court and a single-columned entrance (fig. **3.42**). By the entranceway is the archive room where the Linear B tablets were found. The domestic unit to the west was probably the earliest to be built and

3.42 The palace at Pylos. 13th century BC
1 Propylon
2 Court
3 Porch
4 Vestibule
5 Hall

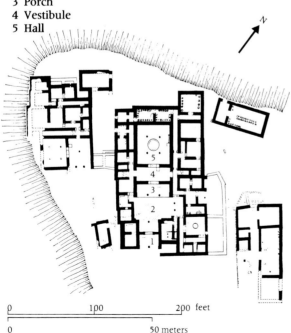

lived in, while the separate unit to the east consisted of a shrine and a repair depot for chariots, armor, and weapons. Walls are built mostly of rubble, with much timber framework and tiebeams. Timber was also used liberally for ceilings and columns. Ashlar limestone blocks were used in wall exteriors, and reinforced corners. Floors were of plaster, often decorated with abstract patterns. Interior walls too were heavily plastered and richly painted, and it is Pylos which has yielded the most information we have about Mycenaean frescoes.

The fresco painters evidently drew on Minoan sources for some of their motifs. These included figured cycles of processions, architectural façades, court figures chattering, mythological beasts (fig. **3.43**), musicians, and even bulljumping. Figures, on the other hand, seem less free, and stiffer, just as Minoan motifs on pots had become more rigid. Some scenes, moreover, are wholly Mycenaean in flavor. Scenes of the hunt and of humans in combat (fig. **3.44**), bizarrely falling about against multicolored backgrounds, find no parallels in Crete, and are characteristically Mycenaean.

Destruction c. 1200 BC. The prince at Pylos will have regretted the absence of fortifications for the site was destroyed by fire and the sword shortly after 1200 BC. Mycenae and Tiryns were luckier; they were badly damaged by earthquake, according to the current excavators, but continued to function. Both were extensively rebuilt and reoccupied, though it seems that the palaces and their bureaucracies were gone, and the townships organized otherwise politically in the twelfth century BC. Many other sites, like Dendra and Thebes, were destroyed, while others, such as Eutresis, were abandoned.

SCULPTURE AND POTTERY
Sculpture. In Grave Circles A and B at Mycenae, the whereabouts of shaft graves was signaled by stelai (fig. **3.30**, p. 87). Some of these, though not all, were decorated with relief sculpture. Topics represented were typically Mycenaean (the hunt, warfare), and may suggest the favored pastime of the deceased.

3.43 *Above* The palace at Pylos. Reconstructon of the hall of the megaron showing the columns, hearth, and throne. 13th century BC

3.44 *Left* Reconstructed fresco with warriors, from Pylos. LH IIIB

The most impressive instance of the Mycenaean sculptor's skill is the famous relief, after which the Lion Gate is named (fig. **0.12**, p. 23). Created around 1250 BC, the relief is almost 10 feet (3 m) high, and shows a pair of lions or lionesses, in profile view, arranged heraldically either side of an architectural column which supports the abbreviated *entablature* (i.e. the horizontal members of the superstructure) of a building. The column stands, as do the front feet of the animals, on a pair of Minoan altars, similar to one found at

Arkhanes on Crete. The lions' heads, worked separately of a precious material and fixed on by means of tenons, are now lost. There are similar scenes on Minoan gems and seals, but the lion is characteristically a mainland motif, and this enlargement from a miniature scale is surely the work of a Mycenaean. Nothing has survived in Crete to challenge the successful marriage of architecture and sculpture exemplified by the Lion Gate, the earliest example of monumental Greek sculpture to have come down to us. It is surprising that no trace has yet emerged of commemorative sculpture or historical reliefs, given these autocrats' enthusiasm for mighty architectural statements in their citadels and tombs.

A sanctuary on the island of Keos, just off the coast of Attica, has yielded fragments of numerous (perhaps as many as 50) terracotta female figures, which range in height from about $27\frac{1}{2}$ inches (70 cm) to almost life size (fig. **3.45**). Traces of color on the surface show that they were brightly painted in white, red, and yellow. Some may date from as early as the MB age, others from the fifteenth century BC. Most wear a flattened skirt and a heavy belt, baring their breasts. Proportions, shapes, and garments call to mind their Minoan counterparts. Yet similarly attired and proportioned figures appear in mainland frescoes, as for example at Pylos in the thirteenth century BC. Though the sanctuary was destroyed around 1400 BC, the head of one of the figures was used again in a shrine of Dionysos on the same spot in the eighth century BC. Thus, the religious function of this site continued into the Dark Ages, and the sanctity of the Bronze Age image was preserved for centuries.

From Mycenae came the painted plaster head of a female, perhaps a sphinx (fig. **3.46**), dated to the thirteenth century BC. It is almost lifesize. It was painted white, and then enlivened by bright reds and blues. The hair is bound by a red fillet and eyes are dark blue like the Homeric gods'. Her hat is pale blue. Cosmetic beauty spots decorate her cheeks and chin with dot-rosettes; her mouth is scarlet. The coloring is dramatic, while hypnotic eyes and sardonic mouth create a distinctive, if not fearsome, impression. The terracottas from Keos and the head from Mycenae are

3.45 Terracotta female figure, from Keos. Height 3 ft 2 ins (98.8 cm). LH II. Keos Museum. Courtesy of the University of Cincinnati

the only examples of large-scale sculpture in the round to have survived.

On a smaller scale, ivory was a popular medium. From Mycenae comes the fourteenth or thirteenth century BC ivory group (fig. **3.47**) of two identically dressed women sharing a cloak and an embrace. They crouch on the ground, while watching a child playing in front of them.

The full rounded forms of arms, legs, breasts, and face are characteristic of ivory work of the Levant. The ivory itself came perhaps from Syrian elephants (though much ivory is rhinoceros tusk), and the style of working the ivory may also depend on Syrian origins. Most carved ivories are in relief and were used for cosmetic boxes, mirror handles, furniture inlays and other *objets de luxe*. Topics chosen for decoration include sphinxes, griffins, combats, a warrior wearing a boar's tusk helmet such as that described by Homer (*Iliad* 10:261–5).

Also on a small scale is the lead figure of a youth from Laconia (fig. **3.48**) normally dated to the fourteenth century BC. Dress and proportions are Minoan, but the gesture with the hands held horizontally, the detailed treatment of the facial features, and the quizzical smile suggesting individuality are not. Moreover, though the Mycenaean figure adopts the posture of the Minoan types (fig. **3.12**, p. 73), he seems quite different from his Minoan counterparts. For the Minoans, the contour was like a restless arabesque, to be valued for itself and for its motion. For the Mycenaeans it defined the volume of the figure. The Minoan figure moves in space, while the Mycenaean figure seizes it.

By far the commonest examples of Mycenaean sculpture are the terracotta female figurines (fig. **3.49**) of the fourteenth and thirteenth centuries BC. They have been found far and wide at Mycenaean sites – both in houses and tombs – all the way from south Italy to Syria. They range in height between about 2 inches (5 cm) and 5 inches (13 cm). There are two principal types, named "psi" and "phi" figurines after the letters of the Greek alphabet which they resemble. Psi figurines hold their arms aloft, phi hold theirs lowered in front of them. A triangular head sits atop a circular or "lunate" torso, supported by a cylindrical stem. Details such as clothing, hair, the nose, and eyes are added in paint; pellets of clay represent breasts. Occasionally a figurine was portrayed cradling a child. These highly stylized, diminutive, doll-like figurines are a far cry from contemporary figures in ivory or bronze, and can barely be called works of art. There is nothing Minoan about them, and

3.46 *Above* Painted plaster head, from Mycenae. Height 6⅗ ins (16.8 cm). LH IIIB. National Museum, Athens

3.47 *Below* Ivory group of two females and a child, from Mycenae. Height 2¾ ins (7 cm). LH IIIA/B. National Museum, Athens

3.48 Lead figure of a youth, from Laconia. Height 4¾ ins (12 cm). LH IIIA. National Museum, Athens

3.49 Terracotta "phi" (*left*) and "psi" (*right*) figurines, perhaps from Melos. Height 3 ins (8 cm). LH IIIA. British Museum, London

their popularity marks them as distinctively Mycenaean. They were made by the same artisans who made the pottery of this period.

Pottery. The pottery of the period, LMH IIIA and B, from around 1400–1200 BC, is known for its sparse decoration and for its fine fabric. Technically it is sophisticated, if aesthetically humdrum. It was exported all over the Mediterranean, and enjoyed a wide vogue. Shapes became uniform and endlessly repeated: tall-stemmed drinking cups (*kylikes*) (fig. **3.50**), tankards, *stirrup jars* (fig. **3.52**), so-called from the stirruplike handle next to the spout, *kraters* (mixing bowls), and *alabastra* (ointment containers) were popular. Decoration became repetitive: the naturalistic motifs of LH II, which were already constrained, became more and more rigid, until they were reduced to severe abstractions. Horizontal bands of paint began to dominate the surfaces. This style is sometimes referred to as the Pattern Style but should not be confused with the Pattern Style of the preceding century on Crete. By contrast, some potters plucked up courage enough to decorate kraters with schematic scenes of chariots, horses, and charioteers, often seriously impeded by linear ornaments crowding the space around them. Others painted dappled bulls, angry geese, and mythological beasts on deep open bowls. This style is called the Pictorial Style.

The transition from LH IIIB to LH IIIC (1200–1100 BC) is marked by the Warrior Vase (fig. **3.51**), a pictorial style krater, from Mycenae. It is a unique example from this era of narrative decoration of a vase. It shows a line of armed warriors marching in single file and in sombre mood to the right while a woman at the left bids them farewell. The standardization of shapes and decoration of the two preceding centuries now breaks down, and though shapes remain largely unchanged in LH IIIC, the period is characterized by variety of decoration of which there are two major styles, the Granary Style and the Close Style.

The Granary Style, named after the building at Mycenae where it was first found, hardly catches the eye. It is a style of restricted imagina-

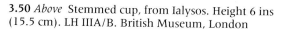

3.50 *Above* Stemmed cup, from Ialysos. Height 6 ins (15.5 cm). LH IIIA/B. British Museum, London

3.51 *Above right* The Warrior Vase, from Mycenae. Height 16 ins (41 cm). LH IIIB/C. National Museum, Athens

3.52 *Below* Stirrup jar, from Aegina. Height $7\frac{4}{5}$ ins (20 cm). LH IIIA/B. Ashmolean Museum, Oxford

3.53 *Below right* Three-footed tankard, from Miletus. Height $8\frac{1}{4}$ ins (21 cm). LH IIIC. Izmir Museum, Turkey

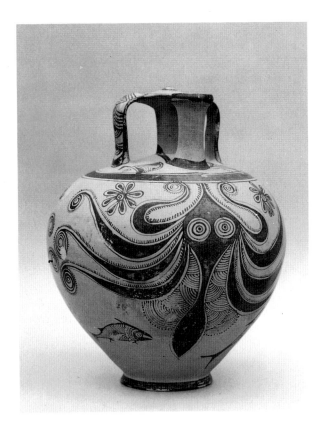

3.54 Stirrup jar. Height 10¼ ins (26 cm). LH IIIC. Metropolitan Museum of Art, New York, Louisa Eldridge McBurney Gift Fund

Troy and the end of the Bronze Age in Greece

The palace at Pylos was violently destroyed around 1200 BC. At about the same time, it seems that Athens was attacked (houses at the foot of the Acropolis were destroyed), and Mycenae and Tiryns were felled by earthquake. Many other sites perished or were abandoned, though some, including Athens, Lefkandi, and Nichoria in Messenia, survived. Greece entered a period of uncertainty, in which populations moved from vulnerable areas, either inland (for example, to Achaia in the Peloponnese), or to the coast, or to the islands, or to Cyprus. All this destruction and upheaval was in the context of a wider disturbance in other Mediterranean lands. Towards the end of the thirteenth century BC, Egypt came under attack from the Sea Peoples (about whose identity there is no agreement). Attacks were repeated in the twelfth century BC. The Egyptians and Hittites were at one another's throats and warfare continued intermittently between them, until the Hittite empire collapsed in the twelfth century BC. The Hittite records speak of the Ahhijawa, taken by many to be Greeks, making a nuisance of themselves in Asia Minor. The great city of Troy VI was destroyed around 1300 BC.

It is after a few Greek pots of the LH IIIB style had reached Troy that the city was destroyed. The fortification wall was damaged, and houses collapsed. But the city was not looted, nor was it burnt, so that Schliemann's eager view that this was the city described in the *Iliad* is unlikely to be correct. Troy VI was evidently destroyed by earthquake. It was succeeded by Troy VIIa, a city exactly the same size as its precursor. The disturbed walls of Troy VI were repaired; houses were now squeezed together, sharing party walls, and butted up against the interior of the city walls. These were new departures in terms of the planning of the citadel, without precedent in any city of Troy. They suggest that space was in short supply, and that people were crowding together. Moreover, uniquely in this phase of the city, pithoi for the storage of oil and grain were sunk in the floors of houses, thus saving space. Condi-

tion, consisting almost exclusively of horizontal dark bands and the occasional wavy line. The Close Style, on the other hand, covered the surface with closely packed crosshatched net patterns or files of swans and other water-happy birds. Sometimes this style, especially in the islands or on the coast, became so adventurous that it has been termed the Wild Style (fig. **3.53**). Birds dance underwater with fish, crabs, and other marine beasts. The octopus came to the fore again, sometimes a melancholy reflection of his vigorous LM IB predecessor, and sometimes more flamboyant and accompanied by other ocean denizens (fig. **3.54**). There is a weird exuberance about this style, the last gasp of the Mycenaean world before the end of the Bronze Age.

tions in Troy VIIa were consistent with a city under siege. This city was destroyed by fire. Accordingly, though we are uncertain about the true facts of the Trojan War, it is possible that the city of Troy VIIa was the city destroyed by the Greeks, an episode firmly embedded in the Greek mind. Only a handful of pots were imported into Troy VIIa, which makes the date of the destruction a matter for controversy. Proposed dates range from around 1260 BC to the end of LH IIIB, but before the destruction of Pylos in Greece.

The pottery styles of LH IIIC were thus produced in a period of international political and social uncertainty. The disasters in Greece at the end of LH IIIB were not terminal for Mycenaean civilization, but they were a harbinger. Between about 1200 and 1100 BC, the period during which LH IIIC pottery was produced, the Mycenaean world went into slow decline. There were more destructions and dispersals of people throughout the century, and by the end, Lefkandi and Argos, among others, were abandoned. At Koukounaries on the Cycladic island of Paros, a twelfth-century settlement was built, and lived in, and burnt, and destroyed by human agency. Yet Mycenae and Tiryns continued to be occupied into the eleventh century BC. So the twelfth century BC witnessed both

widespread movement of peoples, and continued substantial occupation of the old centers of Tiryns and Mycenae. The Mycenaean world was not yielding easily.

The identity of those who wrought havoc intermittently in Greece during this century is a vexed question, to which there may be several answers. The mysterious Sea Peoples may have played a part, especially at sites vulnerable from the sea like Pylos. The myth of the Seven Against Thebes preserves a tradition of war in early times between Greek municipalities, so that civil war may have been one element. The most insistent tradition is, however, of the arrival of a new wave of Greeks, who spoke a Doric dialect. The language of the Linear B tablets contains no Doric elements, yet in later Greece the Doric dialect is securely established. So it is logical to think of its arrival at the time of the great upheaval, and of Dorian Greeks taking advantage of the weakness of the Mycenaean world. The withdrawal of survivors to villages in the hills, which had begun during LH IIIC, now accelerated. It is here and in Athens, alone of the great Mycenaean feudal centers, and in the diaspora across the sea, that are found what shreds of cultural continuity survived into the Dark Ages.

4
The Dark Ages and Geometric Greece
c. 1100–700 BC

During the Bronze Age, three principal cultures were discernible in the Greek world: those of Crete, the Cyclades, and mainland Greece. The third millennium BC was the period of greatest difference between the three. This was followed by an era when Cretan culture was paramount, and began to influence the others, and then by the period of mainland Greek supremacy. Accordingly, the archaeological and artistic evidence fell conveniently into major geographical regions.

Such divisions are no longer pertinent after the beginning of the Iron Age, when the evidence of major cultural developments begins to come not only from Greece, Crete, and the Cyclades, but also from further afield, from Asia Minor at first, and later from Sicily and south

Opposite Detail of a Geometric oinochoe from Dipylon cemetery, Athens, fig. **4.22**. c. 750 BC. National Museum, Athens

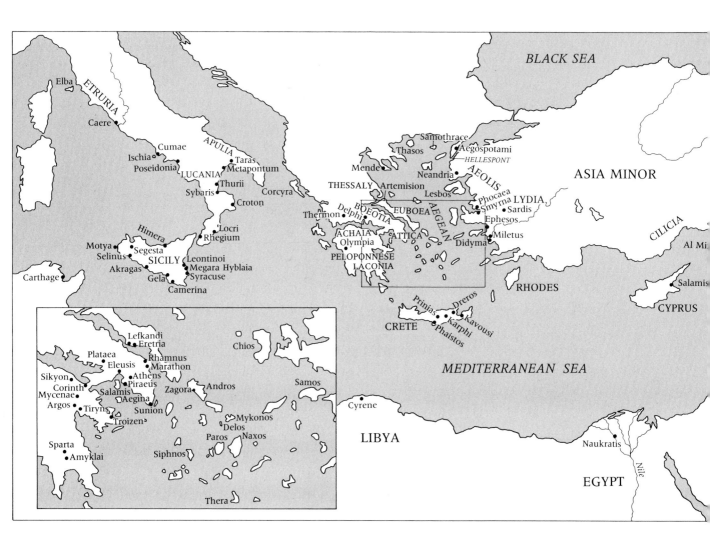

4.1 The Greek world to c. 400 BC

Italy (fig. **4.1**). So it seems best to present the evidence as a coherent chronological narrative in familiar categories – architecture, pottery, and sculpture – but taking in important examples of regional development where it is significant. At first in isolation, and later under influences from the East and Egypt, Greek communities developed separate answers to common problems. One example is the bewildering complexity of the earliest Greek epichoric (regional) alphabets, developed in the eighth century BC. Another is that of the differing approaches taken by pot-painters to decorating their pots.

Innovation. Sometime during the eleventh century BC cremation of the dead was introduced at Athens, and sometime during the same century ironworking skills also appeared in Greece. We do not know whether these important innovations occurred at the beginning of the Dark Ages, but some commentators have suggested that the new practice of cremation burial was connected to the catastrophe at the end of LH IIIC and with the appearance of new peoples in Greece. Did the destructions at the end of LH IIIC mark the arrival of Dorian-speaking Greeks, who brought with them the practice of cremation? Were they also versatile enough to work iron, or were these developments entirely unrelated? We cannot say for sure. But we do know that Greece now passed from the Bronze Age to the Iron, and, in spite of this watershed event, lapsed into almost total decrepitude.

Transition. With the destruction of the Mycenaean palaces went the social system of which they were the centers. Kings, subordinates, scribes, and the knowledge of writing all disappeared. With them went also the knowledge of masonry and construction using cut blocks, of wall painting, the working of ivory, precious metals, and sculpture in stone. In a word, all the sophisticated achievements of the Greek Bronze Age vanished. Society was decapitated and then dispersed. Mycenaean survivors made their way inland, to the islands, to Crete, to Asia Minor, and to Cyprus. The Dark Ages in Greece, characterized by depopulation, impoverishment, and solitude, closed in. The period was to last some two hundred years. The revival began slowly in the ninth century BC and gathered pace during the eighth. This span of two centuries (c. 900–700 BC) is termed the Geometric period, from the mathematically precise way in which potpainters decorated their vases.

Continuity. Little or no archaeological evidence has been found to reveal links between the Mycenaean world and the Dark Ages. The Lion Gate at Mycenae was always visible, and the shattered remains of fortresses and palaces should have provided some stimulus to architecture. Echoes of Mycenaean architecture can be detected in the later architecture of classical temples, but for the immediate aftermath there is little in view. Pottery shows some continuity, of a bedraggled sort, between the Granary Style of LH IIIC and a style suitably called subMycenaean, which used LH III shapes, but they were badly thrown and shakily decorated. After this came a new style, the Protogeometric, in around 1050 BC. Later writers claimed that Athens survived the destructions at the end of the Bronze Age, and a continuous series of graves at Athens from

subMycenaean through Protogeometric lends some support to this. Sculpture in terracotta continued to be made, not of the widespread phi and psi types of female figurines so much as of a LM III "goddess" type on Crete. Blood, language, and some aspects of religion too survived – to judge by the historical Olympians, some of whom we saw had appeared in the Linear B tablets – so tenuous strands of continuity may be perceived. The poems of Homer, originally recited from memory by professional bards, and written down perhaps in the later eighth century BC, reflect a mixture of conditions in the Bronze Age, the Dark Ages, and the Geometric period, and to that extent they may be said to connect the periods.

Conditions. Conditions in the Dark Ages were of immense poverty. People lived in ramshackle hovels, built of mudbrick and thatch or fieldstones, in small rural communities which were not conducive either to art or architecture. They depended on a subsistence economy, and were controlled by landowning aristocracies. No one could read or write. Warfare was endemic, and hostilities between neighbors frequent. Contact with the outside world was spasmodic, though, exceptionally, the site of Lefkandi has provided evidence both of an ambitious building project and of imports from abroad (p. 107). But after three gloomy centuries, Greece emerged in the eighth century BC with new political regions. These were the "poleis," independent states which were at first controlled by landowning and horse-rearing aristocrats. They included countryside and mountains as well as townships, and were defined by natural frontiers, that is, mountains, rivers, and oceans. The polis of Athens, for example, included all the territory of the peninsula of Attica as far south as Sunion and east as Marathon. Populations now grew rapidly. Agriculture and economic conditions improved. Trading centers were set up in the east (Syria) and in the west, where the lure of metals was a powerful magnet. These changes were not, however, equal to the needs of the increasing populations. As the century advanced, more and more Greeks came to seek their fortunes overseas.

Architecture

Around 1100 BC, refugees scrambled up to a hill-top in the east of Crete and built themselves a new town on the site of Karphi. The small and congested dwellings were primitive, and the plan (fig. **4.2**) shows the random nature of the building. Houses huddle cheek by jowl, apparently uncoordinated in plan. Yet streets or pathways are cobbled and there is both a Great House (the excavators' terminology) with associated court-yard and storage units, and a shrine equipped with altar and terracotta statuettes (fig. **4.3**). Crudely constructed tholos tombs provided for the needs of the dead, which some connect with Mycenaean burial practice, while the settlement shows similarities with LM Gournia. So there were some distant echoes of Bronze Age archi-tecture. The site was abandoned around 1000 BC.

Recent excavations near Kavousi promise more information. In one zone, a settlement of LM IIIC, furnished with pottery kiln and a shrine with more statuettes like those from Karphi, pro-vided buildings used in the eighth century BC as a burial plot: no continuity then is visible yet here.

4.3 *Above* Terracotta female figure, from Karphi. Height 26⅔ ins (67 cm). c. 1000 BC. Iraklion Museum, Crete

4.2 Plan of the hilltown, Karphi. 11th century BC
 1 Shrine   2–3 Great House

4.4 *Below* Plan and reconstruction of an oval house, Smyrna. 10th century BC

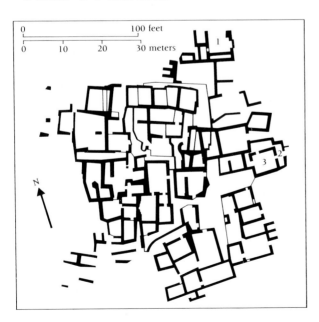

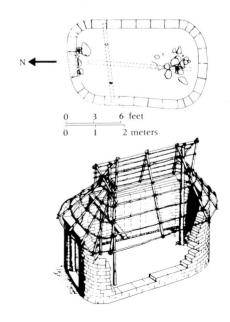

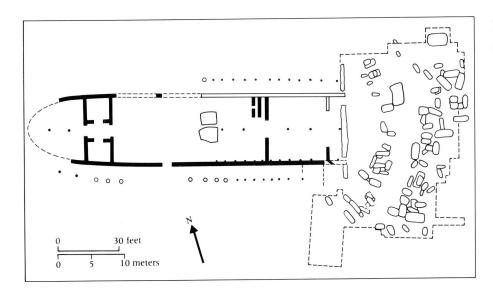

4.5 Heroon and cemetery, Lefkandi. Heroon 10th century BC. Cemetery 9th century BC

0   30 feet

0   5   10 meters

In another zone, however, excavation of buildings has shown stratification from LM IIIC through Geometric times, and suggests the site was continually occupied from the Bronze Age through the Dark Ages.

In Crete, they made for the hills. From Greece, they made their way across the Aegean to Asia Minor, as well as to the islands and to Cyprus. In Asia Minor, they established coastal settlements which can be recognized from finds of Protogeometric pottery, imported (or brought with them) from Athens, and locally made. One such site is at Smyrna, near modern Izmir. The refugees arrived here about 1000 BC. Excavations have revealed the relics of a small late tenth-century BC house (fig. **4.4**). This single room structure was oval – or double apsidal – built of mudbrick on a stone socle, and probably thatched. It is one of the earliest post Mycenaean houses yet found, and may hark back to Bronze Age predecessors. The house was built over in the ninth and eighth centuries BC by other houses, all rectangular in plan, which were encircled by a fortification wall, unparalleled in mainland Greece at this time, but again echoing Bronze Age structures.

The stone foundations of a large building at Lefkandi in Euboea, and its adjacent cemetery, recently discovered, have given us a glimpse of a richer world. Apsidal in plan (fig. **4.5**) the structure was almost 55 yards (50 m) long and 11 yards (10 m) wide. Buried within this huge building were a warrior (cremated), a woman, and a number of horses. The size of this tenth-century building and the burials within suggested that it had functioned as a *heroon*, a site for the worship of a hero, a semidivine person such as a prince or leader heroized after death. Clustered in an arc around the east end of the heroon was a cemetery with 69 tombs and 23 pyres. (Both cremation and inhumation were practiced.) The graves are mostly shaft graves. There is another horse burial, and graves of children are confined to one corner. The whole cemetery is thought to date to the ninth century BC. Bronze and faience bowls imported from the Near East and Egypt were found, revealing contact with these more flourishing cultures. Objects of gold and jewelry also suggest the occupants of these graves were wealthy and important. This looks like the burial place of a local dynastic family, part warlike, part mercantile, already in touch with the East.

Worship of the gods took place in the open air, in sanctuaries defined only by an enclosure wall and a hallowed spot, sometimes recognized by an altar. Placation of the gods by gifts of votive offerings – sometimes tiny terracotta figurines, sometimes more prestigious goods – was routine. During the Geometric period the Greeks began to house the images of their gods. A temple of the

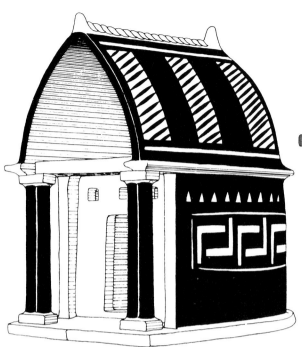

4.6 Restored terracotta model of a shrine (or house?), from Perachora. Height (as restored) 13 ins (33 cm). Later 8th century BC. National Museum, Athens

4.7 Terracotta model of a shrine, from Argos. Length 14 ins (36 cm). Later 8th century BC. National Museum, Athens

tenth century BC at Kommos in Crete still has its rectangular plan. A fragmentary wall in the Sanctuary of Hera, at Perachora near Corinth, with votive offerings nearby, may belong to an early temple, apsidal in plan. This plan is echoed in terracotta fragments of a small eighth-century model of a building found as a votive offering at the site (fig. **4.6**). This miniature of what is probably a religious building has just a single chamber with a central doorway behind two pairs of wooden posts forming a porch, mudbrick walls, and a high thatched roof with wide eaves.

A similar eighth-century model (fig. **4.7**), found in the Sanctuary of Hera at Argos, may represent the first temple there. It is rectangular in plan, with a pair of single posts forming the porch, and separate roofing systems for porch and chamber. At Eretria, in Euboea, a diminutive structure, built around 800–750 BC and found beneath a later Temple of Apollo, was probably a temple. Horseshoe in plan, the elevation was almost entirely of wood and other perishable materials. A more imposing building, a hundred-footer (i.e., a *hekatompedon*, one hundred feet long) was built nearby in the middle years of the century. Both apsidal and rectangular plans echo Bronze Age predecessors.

Remains of the eighth-century temple at Dreros in Crete preserve the rectangular plan of a stone-built structure, with a central hearth flanked by two stone bases for wooden posts and a bench against the back wall. A similar arrangement is at Temple B in the sanctuary at Kommos, also in Crete, while the Temple of Artemis Orthia in Sparta also has a back wall bench (about 700 BC). Was this bench, on which, at Dreros, three bronze statuettes were found, the prototype for cult statue bases? Was it in later temples, pulled away from the wall to become the free-standing cult statue base? The interior arrangement of hearth and posts, as at Dreros, reminds one of Mycenaean megara with their hearths, chimneys and columns. At Mycenae and Tiryns themselves, early temples are built directly over the sites of Mycenaean megara. Thus temporal power was superseded by divine.

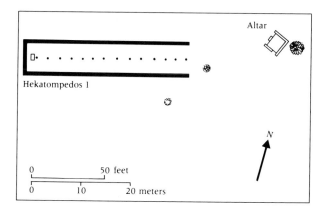

Altar

Hekatompedos I

N

0   50 feet

0   10   20 meters

4.8 Conjectured plan of the first Temple of Hera, Samos. Probably 8th century BC. Altar 8th century BC

We cannot be certain of the early history of the important Sanctuary of Hera on the island of Samos. The first temple may have been built in the eighth century BC, and it may have been a long skinny building of mudbrick, with a central row of wooden posts (fig. **4.8**) as roof supports. But these posts would have hidden the cult statue, if the stone base for the image had not been nudged into the north aisle. On the other hand those remains may simply be the foundations of what is called the second temple. In any event, a temple of advanced plan existed by around 650 BC with a peristyle around it and a double row of wooden posts at the front. Such a temple implies the existence of an eighth-century predecessor, whether on the same spot (which is likely) or not.

The site at Zagora on Andros is a good example of domestic architecture of the Geometric period. Here a settlement of the eighth century BC used local island stone to build houses close packed to one another. They have two basic plans: one is the megaron arrangement with columned porch in front of a main room with hearth and posts, while the other is a square house equipped with benches or sleeping platforms. It seems that cult activities took place around an altar in an open courtyard in front of an imposing house, perhaps that of the ruler. There is no temple here until the sixth century BC. Towns similar to Zagora existed on other islands, notably on Chios and on Siphnos.

Sculpture

Though the skills necessary to produce work like the Lion Gate (fig. **0.12**, p. 23) had been lost, sculpture in terracotta continued, especially in Crete. The female figures from Karphi in Crete (fig. **4.3**, p. 106) – perhaps divinities, perhaps worshipers – followed a Late Minoan fourteenth- and thirteenth-century predecessor (fig. **3.17**, p. 76). The similarities are obvious. The frontal type with cylindrical body and upraised arms is the same. Yet the headgear is different, and with the Dark Age example, the legs and feet of the figure are included. Note that the "horns of consecration" on the headgear of the example from Karphi show another mark of continuity from the Bronze Age. The head and arms were added, handmade, to the wheelmade cylinder of the body, while legs, also made separately, were slung beneath. The whole sculpture was then fired like a vase, so that figures like these were as much the work of potters as of sculptors.

The repertoire of these potter-sculptors also included animals and hybrid creatures, of which the late-tenth-century (about 900 BC) centaur from Lefkandi (fig. **4.9**) is a famous example. Human torso, head, and legs are solid and made by hand, while the cylindrical horsy horizontal part of the body is wheelmade. Ears have centrally pierced holes (one wonders why), and the circular hollows of the eyes were inlaid with bone or shell. Was this Dark Age image from the world of Greek myth a specific centaur? There is no doubt he was highly prized. Head and body were found in separate graves, both serving as needed companions after death.

As the population grew and living conditions improved, the Greeks converted some local shrines into Panhellenic sanctuaries, and to these – at Olympia, Delphi, Delos – were brought multitudes of votive offerings of terracotta and bronze. Olympia has been a particularly rich source of these, and many date from the eighth century. Animal figures were at first cut out from bronze or copper sheets. There are mares and foals, deer and fawn, birds, and bulls. Later, they were hammered flat, until the technique of solid casting was introduced, though the figures were

4.9 *Left* Terracotta centaur, from Lefkandi. Height 14 ins (36 cm). 10th century BC. Eretria Museum

4.10 *Below* Bronze horse. Height 7 ins (17.6 cm). c. 750–700 BC. Metropolitan Museum of Art, New York

4.11 *Left* Bronze tripod cauldron, from Olympia. Height 2 ft 1½ ins (65 cm). 8th century BC. Olympia Museum

still formal in appearance, for instance, the horse in figure **4.10**. Figures like this sometimes stand on openwork plaques, and sometimes may have been suspended from trees. Others served as attachments to the handles of big bronze tripod-cauldrons (fig. **4.11**).

Such tripods, enlargements of valued household objects, were used both as offerings and as prizes in the games (and probably as both; first a prize, and then an offering). Some were huge, even man-size. While the cauldron itself was hammered, legs and ring handles, sometimes decorated with geometric designs (concentric circles and zigzags, for example), were cast. Molds for making tripod legs, found at Lefkandi, show that cauldrons were being made in Greece as early as around 900 BC.

Among human figures, the warrior was a common type. The example shown here was cast solid (fig. **4.12**). But arms were subsequently hammered to take a spear on the right, and a shield on the left. Legs were elongated, torso triangular, and facial features stylized. Like the animal figures, some were suspended in sanctuaries, some attached to cauldrons, and others were freestanding. Occasionally votive offerings celebrated a victory like the belted and helmeted charioteer from Olympia (fig. **4.13**). This is a theme to be made famous by Polyzalos' dedication at Delphi some 250 years later (fig. **7.24**, p. 220). Others may have been cult statues (fig. **4.14**). Two female figures and one male figure, from Dreros in Crete, provide evidence of another technique, sometimes known as *sphyrelaton*, of hammered bronze plates fixed to a wooden core. These figures may thus have echoed the earliest cult statues of which we know. Called *xoana* by later writers, they were made of wood.

Similar in proportions to the Dreros figures is the ivory figurine of a young woman (fig. **4.15**), found with four similar companions in a grave in Athens, dated by its pottery to around 730 BC. The reappearance of ivory in Greece suggests oriental sources, as does the nudity of the figure emulating the Near Eastern Astarte. Her long legs, triangular torso, sharp features, and her maeander decorated *polos* (hat), however,

4.12 *Above* Bronze figurine of a warrior, from the Acropolis of Athens. Height 8¼ ins (21 cm). c. 750–700 BC. National Museum, Athens

4.13 *Right* Bronze charioteer, from Olympia. Height 5¾ ins (14.5 cm). c. 750–700 BC. Olympia Museum

4.14 Bronze statuettes, from Dreros. Height (female) 15¾ ins (40 cm); (male) 2 ft 7½ ins (80 cm). c. 700 BC. Iraklion Museum, Crete

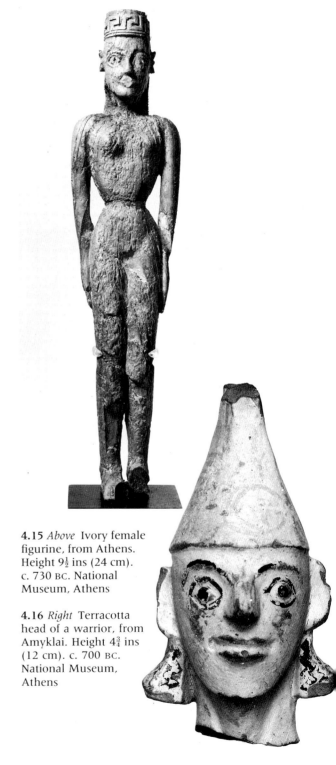

indicate a Geometric Greek sculptor at work, borrowing from abroad and emending to local taste. Terracotta remained a popular medium and the head of a warrior from Amyklai (fig. **4.16**) near Sparta provides a good example. The conical helmet was decorated, like the hat of the ivory from Athens, with maeander design, while the clay was covered in painted details.

These representations of divinities or devotees, of animals such as horses and bulls (either commemorating successes in the games or standing as substitutes for sacrifices) offer the first glimmerings of Greek sculptural invention after the devastation at the end of the Bronze Age.

4.15 *Above* Ivory female figurine, from Athens. Height 9½ ins (24 cm). c. 730 BC. National Museum, Athens

4.16 *Right* Terracotta head of a warrior, from Amyklai. Height 4¾ ins (12 cm). c. 700 BC. National Museum, Athens

Pottery

The Mycenaean fortress on the Acropolis at Athens seems to have avoided the worst depredations at the end of the Bronze Age, and numbers of refugees from the destructions elsewhere evidently made their way to Attica, and thence across the sea to Asia Minor. It is in Athens that developments in pottery first took place. Numerous examples of pottery of this period have come to light in the Kerameikos (potters' quarters) cemetery (fig. **4.17**). The style called Protogeometric appeared in Athens around 1050 BC and lasted till about 900 BC. It was followed elsewhere – in Argos and Boeotia, for example – and there are sufficient variations in products of different centers for us to identify the quirks and tastes of different workshops. Athens, however, was the mainspring.

Shapes of Protogeometric mostly derive from Mycenaean, the commonest being the amphora (for storage), the krater (for mixing wine and water), the *oinochoe* (for pouring), and various shapes of cups. These pots were now being made on a faster wheel. Their contours are crisper and more precise. However, their decoration was still limited. Groups of concentric circles or semi-circles precisely drawn with multiple brushes or

4.18 Protogeometric amphora, from Lefkandi. 9th century BC. Eretria Museum

4.17 Protogeometric pots from the Kerameikos cemetery, Athens. Height (of *skyphos*) 6 ins (15.5 cm). Late 11/10th century BC. Kerameikos Museum, Athens

4.19 *Opposite* Geometric amphora, from Dipylon cemetery, Athens. Height 5 ft 1 in (1.55 m). c. 750 BC. National Museum, Athens

4.20 *Left* Geometric vases from the burial shown in fig. **4.21**. 9th century BC. Agora Museum, Athens

4.21 *Below* Agora, Athens. Cremation burial with geometric vases. 9th century BC

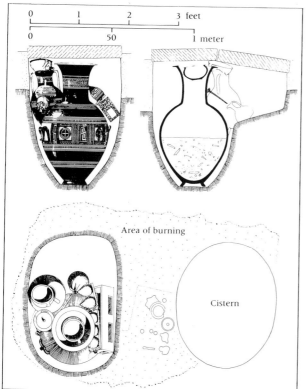

compasses replace the freehand error-prone wavering lines of subMycenaean decoration. There are also crosshatched triangles, panels, and zigzags symmetrically arranged. Decoration is there to emphasize form. The plump amphora found at Lefkandi (fig. **4.18**) but manufactured in Athens shows the rich black gloss which Protogeometric painters of pots used. Ornamental designs – concentric semicircles with checkerboard centers on either side of a crosshatched triangle – emphasize and are confined to the shoulder of the amphora.

The full Geometric style developed from Protogeometric, in the years after 900 BC. Again Athens took the lead, once more followed by regional workshops. Sharply defined amphora, krater, oinochoe, and cup, with their taut, clean lines, remained the most important shapes. In decoration the maeander became the dominant decorative device. Of various shapes (key maeander, battlement maeander) and sizes, it was accompanied by the familiar battery of crosshatched or wavylined lozenges, squares, and triangles. Painting the whole surface with some zones completely dark, setting off the geometric friezes, or with geometric friezes one after the other, became a requirement. A ninth-century burial from the Agora of Athens has yielded a remarkable group of pots (figs. **4.20**, **4.21**). A large amphora, in which the bones and ashes of the deceased were found, has the foot, body, neck, and lip firmly distinguished. The main decoration with motifs arranged in vertical panels was placed between the handles. An unusual *pyxis*, lavishly decorated with maeanders, has five beehive-shaped objects (representations of granaries?) atop, similarly decorated. More than 50 other pots found in this burial provide a rare gallery of geometric shapes and decoration of the ninth century BC.

In the eighth century BC, painted human and animal forms were introduced. Animals appeared first in stylized repeated forms: grazing deer, feeding birds, recumbent goats looking backwards encircle the vase like the abstract friezes that accompany them. They are not visualized as living organisms, but are repeated as patterns. At long last, after almost four centuries of geometric patterns, humans appear; they are sticklike silhouette figures, with elongated legs, triangular torsos and dabs of paint for heads (though later the eye is shown). Mourners tear their hair by funeral biers, showing their lamentation through their gestures. Charioteers' bodies are hidden behind the shields they carry, while they ride in airborne chariots, both wheels shown in curious perspective. Similarly, horses whose stylized forms copy their sculpted bronze counterparts, with cylindrical bodies and trumpet shaped heads, show all their legs (fig. **4.22**).

A number of large vessels decorated in this way were used as gravemarkers and were found in part of the Kerameikos cemetery called the Dipylon, after the city gate nearby. The mid-eighth-century Dipylon amphora (fig. **4.19**) is monumental in scale (5 ft 1 in (1.55 m) high). There are bands of dark paint around the foot, the lip, and the joint of neck and body. Decorative friezes of geometric designs and files of grazing deer and seated goats – each image an abbreviated symbol – run continuously around the pot and cover the rest of the surface. The

4.22 Geometric krater, from Dipylon cemetery, Athens. Height 4 ft (1.22 m). c. 750 BC. National Museum, Athens

panels between the handles show the most important scene, that of *prothesis*, the laying out of the dead body on the funeral bier. The shroud is raised to reveal the corpse: arms, fingers, and all. The painter paints not what is visible but what he thinks is there. The mourners, carefully separated from one another and enveloped in filling ornaments (no space was to be left undecorated) tear their hair. They are shown with profile head and legs and frontal torso. This topic was a common one: other popular subjects were chariot processions and scenes of warfare.

Some of these scenes introduce the concept of narrative; some carry specific allusion. The oinochoe from a grave in the Athenian Agora (fig. **4.23**) shows two joined warriors (even their helmets are linked) mounting a chariot in flight.

4.23 *Right* Geometric oinochoe with narrative scene, from a grave in the Athenian Agora. Height 9 ins (22.8 cm). c. 730 BC. Agora Museum, Athens. *Below* detail

4.24 Late Geometric krater, from Thebes. Height (of figured panel) 3½ ins (9 cm). c. 730 BC. British Museum, London

Siamese twins were rare enough in antiquity and it is difficult not to see here reference to the Moliones twins of whom both Homer (*Iliad*, 11: 709–10) and Hesiod speak. Other images have suggested more familiar mythological themes. A Late Geometric krater (fig. **4.24**) made in Athens depicts a huge oared ship, fully manned. A male figure still on dry land holds the wrist of a female companion with his right hand and climbs on board. Is this Theseus and Ariadne, as some have proposed? Or Paris and Helen? Or a generic scene of abduction? Or even a farewell scene? Identification is still uncertain.

Settlement overseas

If the Moliones oinochoe seems to allude to the world of the *Iliad*, others perhaps evoke that of the *Odyssey*. A krater found at the site of Pithekoussai on the island of Ischia (fig. **4.25**) off the coast of Italy near Naples presents a complex scene of shipwreck: capsized boat, sailors floating or swimming in a dangerous sea crowded with fish, one wretched fellow with his head in the jaws of a shark. Such shipwrecks occur in Homer's narrative of the *Odyssey* (e.g. 7: 249–52), and such incidents would not have been unknown to the oceangoing Greek adventurers of the eighth century BC, who were already busily exploring the Mediterranean.

Greeks were at Pithekoussai on Ischia as early as the second quarter of the eighth century BC, and the settlement there seems to have been the earliest long-lasting Greek establishment in Italy. They were not alone. Egyptian faience objects and scarabs, Syrian flasks, and pottery made locally but inscribed in Aramaic and Phoenician tell of Near Easterners on the island, too. What was the great attraction? Excavation has produced evidence of early iron working – including slag, bellows, and *blooms* – and this provides the explanation. The search for metals had been resumed. Iron was mined on Etruscan Elba to the north, and Ischia may have been the closest that Greeks and others could get.

4.25 Detail of a Geometric krater with shipwreck scene, from Ischia, Italy. c. 725–700 BC. Ischia Museum

The settlement at Pithekoussai was followed rapidly by others. Opposite Ischia, on the mainland of Italy, Cumae was settled in about 740 BC. In Sicily, Naxos was founded about 735 BC, and Syracuse, soon to become the greatest of Greek cities in the west and in the fifth century a rival to Athens herself, was founded around 733 BC from Corinth. Sybaris was settled in about 720 BC from Achaea and Troizen in the Peloponnese, and Taras from Sparta in the last decade of the century. So many were the Greek establishments in Sicily and south Italy, and so powerful did many become, that the area came to be called *Magna Graecia*, Great Greece.

The search for metals was not the only reason for establishing these settlements. Population growth and shortage of land, combined with drought, famine, and oligarchical systems of land tenure, were also powerful motivators. The new settlers did not come from parts of Greece blessed with ample tracts of land like Thessaly, but from areas pinched between the mountains and the seas: from Corinth, Achaea, and the Argolid, and from the islands. Trade, too, and the search for new commodities and ideas played their part.

The Greeks who settled at Pithekoussai came from the island of Euboea, and it is the Euboeans who had taken the lead in exploring the opening world. They had gone east as well as west. In their search for commerce they had already, by the ninth century BC, established a presence at the mouth of the river Orontes in Syria at a site called Al Mina. Here they lived and traded alongside Cypriots and others, and it is through Al Mina and similar small sites nearby, and in Cilicia, that eastern objects and ideas had begun to be channeled into Greece. In the course of the eighth century BC objects decorated in new styles wholly different from those of Greek geometric art made their way into Greece, and were to have a profound impact. Eastern artisans, too, it seems, came to Crete and Greece bringing with them materials, motifs, and techniques, which were new to the Greek world. Parallel with these developments in the spheres of metal working, ivory carving, pottery, and jewelry, an alphabetic script was introduced to Greece for the first time. This alphabet may have arrived in Greece through an area where populations were mixed, such as at Pithekoussai in the west. Whether this was the point of contact and transmission or not, the signs of the new Greek alphabet are unmistakably Semitic in origin. The arrival of an alphabet resulted both in the appearance of chaotic local scripts and in the epics of Homer being written down from their oral predecessors. Under this energetic oriental stimulus, the Greek world re-awakened.

5
The Orientalizing Period
c. 700–600 BC

The pace of life quickened in the seventh century BC. Greek prose and poetry came to life; new techniques of working raw materials produced a new kind of sculpture, a new architecture, and a new metallurgy, and new oriental designs changed the face of Greek pottery. Eastern ideas had their greatest impact on the Greeks during the seventh century BC which is therefore often referred to as the Orientalizing period. Egyptian ideas too had an impact, particularly on the creation of buildings and statues in stone. However, the Greeks always seem to have modified their borrowings according to their own sense of proportion, form, or pattern.

Some Greeks had been driven to find their livelihoods abroad in a series of population movements known as

Opposite "Woman at the Wndow," limestone relief, from Mycenae, detail of fig. **5.28**. c. 640 BC. National Museum, Athens

colonizations, and they were already well ensconced in Sicily and south Italy. These migrations continued in the seventh century BC. New Greek cities were founded at Gela in Sicily, Poseidonia (Paestum) in south Italy, Cyrene in Libya, and Naukratis in Egypt. Some Greeks also headed northward to the Black Sea coast, where they settled at sites like Istros and Olbia. Those who stayed behind found themselves clustered together in discrete geographical zones, in which towns and their dependent countrysides functioned institutionally as poleis, or city-states. During the course of the seventh century BC many poleis fell into the hands of individual masters, called "tyrants," a term which for Greeks at that time carried no negative overtones. A tyrant was a powerful individual who had seized and held all constitutional and military power. Under tyrants many states, notably Corinth, flourished. Trade, industry, and public works were all encouraged. At the same time Greek states vied with one another for land and business, notably neighbor with neighbor, so that complex alliances sprang up between distant cities. Thus, the spirit of competition, fear, and envy, which was to culminate in the long rivalry between Athens and Sparta in the fifth century BC, was nurtured.

Since oriental ideas appear most copiously as designs on pottery, and since the chronology of Protocorinthian (c. 725–625 BC) and Corinthian (c. 625–550 BC) pottery is the key dating tool for the Orientalizing and early Archaic periods, this chapter will deal with the pottery first.

Pottery

Broken pottery is by far the most common material recovered in excavations. Since pottery broke easily, and, once broken, had no intrinsic value it was discarded. As well as using pots, Greeks admired them. Prized pieces were placed in tombs as gifts for the dead alongside other specially made brand new but coarser pots, and whole pots have thus come to us from the excavation of ancient cemeteries. Through

5.1 Protocorinthian aryballos. Height 2¾ ins (6.8 cm). c. 720 BC. British Museum, London

studying the sheer volume of sherds and intact pots retrieved, their shape and decoration arranged according to developments in style and technique, and through the study of the strata in which they were found, we are able to give approximate dates for their manufacture, and hence for the context in which they were found. For 700–500 BC, the margin of error in dating pots narrows from about 25 years to as little as a decade. For archaeologists, pottery is of prime importance for this ability to date contexts. But it is also valued for what its uses – storage, mixing, pouring, drinking, etc. – reveal about social and economic activity. It can also tell us about vase painters, their places of work, the range of their trade, the development of local styles and taste, and the popularity of the various themes they painted.

Orientalizing influences on vase painting can be seen in Corinth as early as the eighth century BC. Many of these pots were exported to the Greek West (that is, Sicily and south Italy), or were carried by settlers. The discovery of sherds of Protocorinthian and Corinthian pottery found in the lowest levels of the colonial sites has helped provide the dates for the pottery types. The starting point for the chronology of these colonies is the narrative found in Book VI of the fifth-century historian, Thucydides. The chronology hinges on Syracuse. Thucydides gives a number of relative dates for its foundation, from which an absolute date of around 733 BC may be derived by the confirmation of other sources. Pottery from the lowest levels at Syracuse is of the first phase of the Protocorinthian style. This phase of Protocorinthian may then be dated around 725–700 BC.

CORINTH

A Geometric style of pottery was being produced in Corinth in the eighth century BC. But this lacked both the figural decoration and the longevity of Athenian Geometric. Vase painters in Corinth were therefore more open to innovation than Athenians. Their city, which had harbors opening both east and west from the isthmus linking the Peloponnese to the rest of Greece, was well placed for communications and commerce. Orientalizing motifs appear in Corinth around 725 BC. The style which they exemplify was applied first to the decoration of pots called Protocorinthian (as precursor of the Corinthian style), the vogue for which lasted about one hundred years.

Popular shapes of Protocorinthian are the *aryballos* (a perfume or oil flask), the *olpe* (a broadlipped jug), the oinochoe (another pouring vessel), and the *kotyle* (a cup). Orientalizing motifs include floral and vegetal designs, and animals of all shapes and descriptions. There are "panthers" (lion-like or other felines shown with frontal face), lions, boars, bulls, birds, dogs, geese, hares, and hybrids (for example, the siren, a bird with the head of a woman). The filler most conventionally used was the dotted rosette. At first, the figures were drawn either in the old-fashioned geometric silhouette manner or in outline; an aryballos (fig. **5.1**), made in the last quarter of the eighth century BC, shows a central stylized oriental Tree of Life drawn in curved lines, flanked by a horse drawn in silhouette

5.2 Protocorinthian olpe. Height 12⅗ ins (32 cm). c. 650–625 BC. Staatliche Antikensammlungen, Munich

(with an outline human behind), and an outline bird. There are other echoes of the Geometric style here in the bands of paint encircling the foot and in the crosshatched triangles rising from the baselines of body and shoulder decoration.

Later, however, figures are drawn in silhouette, but with anatomical details picked out by incision. This allowed the color of the clay to appear in thin sharp lines and thus to suggest forms. Patches of red and white were also used as a means of depicting forms. This technique – using silhouette with incision and added color – is termed *black-figure*. It was introduced in Corinth almost a century earlier than in Athens. It relied heavily on clear, crisp draftsmanship, on precise contour, and the effects of color. An olpe (fig. **5.2**), made around 650 BC, displays the

5.3 *Above* Protocorinthian aryballos, the "Macmillan" aryballos. Height 2¾ ins (7 cm). c. 650 BC. British Museum, London

5.4 Protocorinthian olpe, the "Chigi" vase. Height 10¼ ins (26 cm). c. 650 BC. Villa Giulia Museum, Rome

characteristic registers of black-figure animals, the dotted rosette fillers, and the upward pointing triangles at the base, last vestige of the Geometric tradition.

Human figures appear much less frequently than animals, but two pots from the middle years of the seventh century BC display warriors in action. These represent, perhaps, the high point of the Protocorinthian style. The so-called "Macmillan" aryballos (fig. **5.3**) is a very small vase, only about 2¾ inches (7 cm) high. The upper part is rendered as a lion's head, and there are no fewer than five registers of decoration beneath. There is a luxuriant floral design, drawn in curved lines, on the shoulder, striding and collapsing warriors in combat on the body, a cavalcade, hare and hounds, and upward-pointing triangles (or rays) at the foot. The figures are all drawn in a single plane, with no thought of perspective. The Chigi olpe (fig. **5.4**), now in the Villa Giulia Museum in Rome, is rather larger, about 10¼ inches (c. 26 cm) high. In a dashing display of polychrome painting, the artist depicted three registers of figures. The lowest shows a scene of humans, hounds, and hares. Above it, a procession of chariot and horsemen and a lion hunt are separated on one side (the front) by a double-bodied sphinx, and, on the other (the back), by a mythological scene, the Judgment of Paris, much of which is unfortunately lost. But it is the main frieze on the shoulder which catches the eye. Greeks fight Greeks: lines of heavily armed foot soldiers (hoplites), wearing crested cheek-pieced helmets, bronze cuirasses and greaves, and carrying spears and emblazoned shields are on the point of engagement, egged on by a smaller (a boy?) musician playing the pipes strapped to his mouth. More lines of hoplites follow. Yellows, reds, and whites are the colors used. The wealth of incised detail adds to the intensity. The frieze of animals, so popular in Protocorinthian, is omitted in this masterpiece. This vase gives us important information about military history, showing as it does the beginning of the ascendancy of drilled foot soldiers over cavalry. But, most importantly, it exemplifies, both in terms of technique and style, the very best of Protocorinthian vase painting.

Around 625 BC the Protocorinthian style gave way to full or "Ripe" Corinthian. Orientalizing animals and mythological beasts were still used as decoration, though beasts were now enlarged and less carefully drawn. Splinter rosettes replaced dot rosettes as fillers, and began to clutter the background (fig. **5.5**). The first phase of Corinthian (from around 625–600 BC) was very popular, not least in the West, and it was widely copied.

5.5 Early Corinthian animal style amphora. Height 13¾ ins (35 cm). c. 625–600 BC. British Museum, London

ATHENS

In Athens the pottery of the Orientalizing period is called "Protoattic". It does not use the black-figure technique of Corinth until the end of the century, nor does it enjoy the popularity of Protocorinthian. It is rarely found abroad. The amphora and krater are important shapes, though the oinochoe and skyphos (a two-handled drinking cup) too are popular. Smaller, and closed, shapes were evidently imported from Corinth – a preference which hampered local production. Painted scenes are much larger than in Protocorinthian, and continue the monumental scale of the Attic Geometric tradition. There are fewer eastern animals and hybrids than at Corinth. Vase painters seem to have focused more on human figures, with all the inherent opportunities they offer for storytelling and genre scenes.

An amphora by the Analatos Painter (fig. **5.6**), made around 700–675 BC and so called from the spot where a vessel painted by him was found, is an early Protoattic pot. A register of clumsily drawn (note the back legs!) sphinxes encircles the zone beneath the lip. They are painted partly in silhouette and partly in outline, and surrounded by a blizzard of fillers, the density of which is reminiscent of Geometric pots. A second figural scene on the elongated neck of the pot shows male and female dancers with a piper, again part silhouette part outline, again cluttered with fillers. A third register shows a chariot procession, a motif used during the Geometric period but here modernized by incising details of the horses' manes. Some other elements here derive from the Geometric style too – long legs and angular bodies, the clouds of fillers – while others such as the mythological beasts, the outline drawing, and the rosettes and spirals are more attuned to the seventh century BC.

There was an increasing interest in mythology as the century advanced. A huge amphora of about 650 BC, found at Eleusis (fig. **5.7**) and so sometimes referred to as the Eleusis amphora, depicts on the main frieze, on the body, the Gorgons in pursuit of Perseus. The hero has just decapitated their sister Medusa, and is making off with her head. The figure of Perseus is

5.6 Protoattic amphora, the "Analatos" amphora. Height 31½ ins (80 cm). c. 700–675 BC. Musée du Louvre, Paris

fragmentary, as is that of Athena, who is hindering the Gorgons. But the Gorgons themselves are majestic. Drawn in outline, with some added white paint, they offer frontal toothy and snaky heads and torsos, with profile legs, as they advance, firm-footed on the groundline, their

5.7 Protoattic amphora, the "Eleusis" amphora. Height 4 ft 9 ins (1.44 m). c. 650 BC. Archaeological Museum, Eleusis

faces of his comrades, on the other hand, are painted white, and Polyphemos' face is left the color of the clay. Incision is used for fingers, toes, and Polyphemos' beard, while fillers have only a minor role. The story has combined two episodes into one: Polyphemos howls as the stake penetrates his eye, yet has the winecup in his hand with which the Greeks had stupefied him before blinding him while he slept. Thus, different incidents are squeezed together, and time is compressed. This amphora then shows two approaches to narrative, one on the neck and one on the body, with the single episode (Perseus and the Gorgons) standing for the entire fable, and the synchronized image (Odysseus, Polyphemos, and Greeks) incorporating two different episodes. So well planned a composition with large figures, however awkwardly drawn, suggests an already existing tradition of narrative wall or panel painting. This amphora, like many of its predecessors in the eighth century BC, served a funerary purpose.

The story of Odysseus is shown in a painting of a fragmentary mid-seventh-century oinochoe found on the island of Aegina, where it may have been made. It is Protoattic in style. Slung beneath rams (fig. **5.8**), Odysseus and two of his comrades

5.8 Protoattic oinochoe. Diameter 8⅘ ins (22.5 cm). c. 650 BC. Archaeological Museum, Aegina

steps in unison. Here is a scene from a well-known myth, recognizable by any self-respecting seventh-century Greek. Its message is the triumph of the Greek hero over the world of malignant monsters. An animal combat, with silhouette boar and outline lion, decorates the shoulder. On the neck, Odysseus and his companions blind Polyphemos, the Cyclops who had imprisoned them in his cave (Homer, *Odyssey* 9:370ff.). The literary inspiration is clear, while Geometric influence can still be seen in the silhouette figures. The body of Odysseus and the

escape from Polyphemos' cave as the rams go off to pasture. The blinded Cyclops passes his hands over the backs of the rams without detecting the wily Greeks. The figures are drawn in black outline with added white paint, and some forms are wholly black (Odysseus' hair for instance, and the ram's tail and hooves). A few fillers such as the radial dot rosette and the dotted triangle linger in the field as does the typically Protoattic hook spiral, but the Geometric compulsion to fill all the space with ornament is long gone. This vase is the name piece of the "Ram Jug Painter," details of whose style are distinctive enough for numerous pots to be attributed to him.

In the last quarter of the century (around 625–600 BC) the black-figure technique was introduced to Athens and was used in large-scale scenes of figural narrative. The Nessos amphora (fig. **5.9**) is similar to the Eleusis amphora (fig. **5.7**) in function, and similar in having non-functional handles, the space between handles and neck filled in to provide a decorative or perforated surface. The arrangement of narrative

5.9 Late Protoattic/early black-figure amphora, the "Nessos" amphora. Height 4 ft (1.22 m). c. 625–600 BC. National Museum, Athens

5.10 Wild Goat Style oinochoe, from Rhodes. Height 12⅗ ins (32 cm). c. 625 BC. Staatliche Antikensammlungen, Munich

scenes is also similar, but the pot itself has a less swollen body and firmer foot. The now winged Gorgons, tongues protruding and fangs flashing, kneel or run one after the other to the right. This posture of kneeling or almost kneeling on one knee (so-called "knielauf") is the usual manner in early Greek art of expressing a figure in rapid motion. Though Perseus himself is not shown, a frieze of dolphins below, moving in the opposite direction to the Gorgons, emphasizes the speed of the chase across the ocean. The shoulder of the vase has an Orientalizing, convoluted floral design rather than animals as on the Eleusis amphora. A file of geese plod round the rim, and other birds occupy the filled-in zones between handles and neck, notably the Athenian owl. On the neck the struggle between Herakles and the centaur Nessos is identified by inscriptions, a combination of figures and inscriptions seen here for the first time but which will become common in vase painting. The centaur – part man, part horse – thus midway between the human and the bestial world – had tried to violate Herakles' wife, Deianira. The Greek hero invokes full punishment and is again victorious in his entanglement with a dangerous monster. Herakles grabs Nessos by the scalp, thrusts his left leg into the small of the centaur's back, and prepares to kill him with his sword held in his right hand. Nessos implores Herakles, his arms outstretched to touch Herakles' beard, the conventional gesture of supplication and submission.

This is the black-figure technique beginning to be established in Athens. Fillers are now negligible, though the Protoattic hook spiral is still present, as well as the dotted rosette filler imported from Corinth. The Nessos amphora can be dated to the end of the Protoattic tradition, or the beginning of Attic black-figure, or perhaps, most accurately, as transitional between the two.

ELSEWHERE

Corinth and Athens were two sites which developed dramatically in the seventh century BC, but there were interesting developments in the islands, too. At Rhodes and on the coast of Asia Minor, a style of decorating pots using animal outlines grew up about midcentury. The favorite

beast was the goat (fig. **5.10**). Hence the style is called "Wild Goat," and numerous pots are decorated unimpressively with files of often cheerful, bright-eyed goats, and other animals. More impressive are the calligraphic friezes of lotus and bud which appear beneath. A jug found on Aegina (fig. **5.11**) demonstrates several influences at work. From the Geometric tradition come the panels on the shoulder, the grazing horse, the maeander frieze, and the crosshatched lozenges and triangles. However the motif of lion and prey and the spirals embellishing the triangles towards the base are Eastern. Making part of the pot as an animal or human head was popular in Crete and the Cyclades, so this jug was perhaps the work of a Cycladic painter, around 675–650 BC.

5.11 Griffin jug, from Aegina. Height 15⅜ ins (39 cm). c. 675–650 BC. British Museum, London

5.12 Terracotta relief amphora, from Mykonos. Height 4 ft 5 ins (1.35 m). c. 650 BC. Archaeological Museum, Mykonos

Potters in the islands were also making large pots, decorated not with paint, but with panels of figured scenes in relief. An example found on the island of Mykonos in 1961 (fig. **5.12**), about 4½ feet (1.35 m) high, is datable to about 650 BC, and had been used as a coffin. On its body it shows a series of incidents from the capture of Troy arranged almost in the manner of a strip cartoon. Greek heroes menace Trojan women, and infants are slaughtered. On the neck, the wheeled Trojan horse is shown with the heads of Greeks still inside, as if seen through windows – as one commentator observed, like passengers in a train. Some of the Greeks inside are handing

down huge swords, another hands down a shield, and another a helmet. Those outside are already fully armed, some walking on top of the horse, another still clambering down. In this way, the potter emulated the sculptor, and the two skills overlapped. Familiar tales were told through brand new images, which challenged the narrative diction of the epic poets.

Architecture and architectural sculpture

The Greeks who, sometime before 630 BC, founded the colony of Naukratis in Egypt, and also their predecessors, who paved the way, could not fail to have been impressed by the scale and grandeur of buildings built of stone. This encouraged architects to use more stable materials than mudbrick and wood, and was the starting point for Greek architecture in stone.

The need to shelter sacred places and house the images of gods more permanently was paramount. As with the adoption of Eastern motifs in vase painting, the earliest evidence comes from Corinth and from the Sanctuary of Poseidon at Isthmia, close to Corinth. From a temple at Corinth dating from the first half of the century come masonry blocks and terracotta rooftiles, the weight of which provided another reason for using stone for walls. At Isthmia, too, there are the remains of a temple of the same period. Wooden columns (later replaced by stone) surrounded a deep porch and *cella*, the main room for the cult statue, with more columns standing on individual stone bases in a single row in the interior. Walls are of stone, with terracotta for the rooftiles, and wood for some elements of the superstructure. It is, then, in the early to middle years of the century, that the flimsy mudbrick, wood, and thatch structures began to yield to masonry.

The most complete example of this transition on the mainland may be the Temple of Apollo at Thermon. Here (fig. **5.13**), a peristyle of columns, five on the façades by fifteen on the flanks, sur-

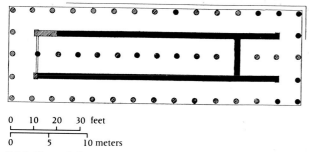

5.13 Plan of the Temple of Apollo, Thermon. c. 640 BC

thodomos. The importance of the building is shown by its exterior columns and its length. Long, narrow proportions were popular in the seventh century BC, and remained so until builders found methods of supporting heavy roofs. After that, more pleasing and balanced proportions became possible. In the seventh century BC, however, the length of *peripteral* temples gave rise to narrow drafty spaces while badly positioned interior columns supporting the roof blocked the view of the cult statue of the deity.

Lower courses of the walls were built of stone, upper courses of mudbrick. The wooden columns of the peristyle were later replaced with stone. Evidence of what the superstructure looked like (fig. **5.14**) has survived. Painted

rounded a cella without a porch, but with a chamber at the back, the so-called *opisthodomos*, to which there was direct access from the exterior. An interior row of columns to support the roof bisected both the cella and the opis-

5.14 Reconstruction of the superstructure of the Temple of Apollo, Thermon. c. 640 BC

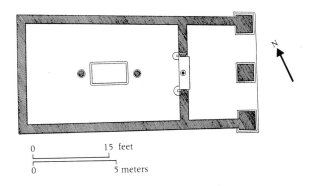

0   15 feet

0   5 meters

5.15 Plan of temple, Prinias. 625–600 BC

terracotta rectangular slabs (metopes) formed part of a decorative frieze, while terracotta heads (antefixes) decorated the edge of the roof. The architectural course (the *architrave*) between the column capitals and the frieze is thought to have been of wood, since no suitable blocks of masonry for such a course have been found.

The metopes show mythological scenes including a scene showing Perseus with the head of the Medusa in a bag under his arm, painted in the Corinthian style. From these we can date the temple's construction to around 640 BC. Accord-

ingly, this building marks a transitional period between structures using primitive materials, such as mudbrick, wood, and thatch, and those built of stone.

Not all temples, however, used exterior columns to signal the presence of the temple or to provide a covered walkway for pilgrims sheltering from rain or sun. At Prinias (fig. **5.15**) in Crete, an irregularly planned rectangular cella boasted a porch with three enormous piers, one exactly on the axis of the building. In the interior of the cella was a hearth or sacrificial pit flanked by two columns, reminiscent of the arrangement of Bronze Age Mycenaean halls. Stone bases on the inner side of the door perhaps supported half columns in an arrangement again recalling Bronze Age practice, for example, at the Minoan palace at Phaistos.

Walls were built of stone, and the temple was decorated by sculpted stone figures, whose style dates the building to 625–600 BC. Limestone seated women (fig. **5.16**) face one another atop a

5.16 Limestone architectural sculpture, Prinias. Height (seated women) 32¼ ins (82 cm), (frieze) 33 ins (84 cm). c. 625–600 BC. Iraklion Museum, Crete

5.17 Limestone architectural sculpture, Prinias, frieze of horsemen. Height 33 ins (84 cm). c. 625–600 BC. Iraklion Museum, Crete

5.18 Plan of the Sanctuary of Hera on Samos. c. 650 BC

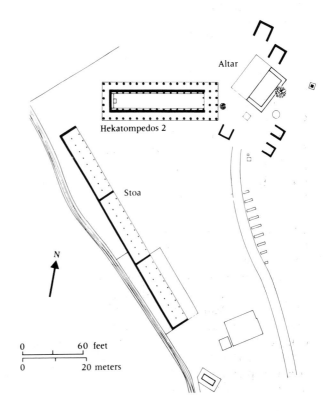

lintel block, the sides of which are carved with Orientalizing animals. Beneath, on the underside of the lintel block, two more standing women look down upon the visitor. A frieze, in relief, of horsemen, showing long-legged, long-tailed horses with diminutive spear-brandishing riders (fig. **5.17**), probably decorated a *dado* (the decorated lower part of a wall) around the porch in Eastern fashion, or may have been situated in the entablature. We do not know for certain whether the lintel with the seated women was above the exterior façade, or over the door to the cella. The frieze itself is the precursor to the great friezes which were to decorate buildings in Delphi and Athens in the sixth and fifth centuries BC. The roofing system is unknown. Advanced in materials and decoration, this temple preferred a non-peripteral plan.

On Samos, architects used columns and colonnades to some purpose. The new Temple of Hera, built around 650 BC (fig. **5.18**), consisted of a single elongated space, having no porch or back room, with a double row of six columns on the façade, which emphasized the entrance. There were also six columns on the back, and 18 on either flank. On the interior, roofing supports were butted up against the walls, so that the cult statue was instantly visible to the visitor. Walls were of limestone, the columns of wood. The roofing arrangement remains unknown. Opposite the temple stood the altar on which

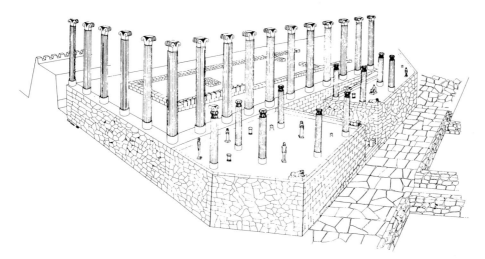

5.19 Hypothetical reconstruction of the Temple of Athena, Smyrna, c. 600 BC, showing terracing with votive columns and statues, the approach road, and the wall beyond

sacrifices were made, and nearby was the stoa. This long, rectangular building, consisting of mudbrick walls at the back and sides and rows of wooden columns – which were little more than posts and brackets – supporting the roof at the front, served to protect pilgrims from the elements. The stoa was to become one of the most frequently used architectural types for the Greeks, equally adaptable to religious and secular use, and a commonplace therefore in Greek sanctuaries and market places.

Megara Hyblaia in Sicily and Smyrna, on the coast of Asia Minor, are good examples of domestic architecture and town planning. Megara Hyblaia was a new colonial foundation of the later eighth century BC, and, as such, was probably planned more systematically than older towns, which were allowed to grow randomly. Excavation here has recovered the plan of a 650–600 BC town laid out in regular blocks around an open agora or market place. Smyrna had been occupied by refugees from Greece during the tenth century BC; and around 640–600 BC it enjoyed a period of considerable prosperity. The town had long been fortified, and this Orientalizing settlement was protected first by an earlier system, and then by a new fortification. This, actually the third wall around the town, was completed near 600 BC and was almost 60 feet (18.3 m) thick.

Within the fortification, streets were laid out in an approximately rectangular grid plan, which followed a north–south, east–west orientation. But these conformed more to the lie of the land than strictly to the points of the compass. One prominent north–south street was paved with precisely fitted polygonal flags. Within the grid, houses were built facing south to catch the sun in winter, and separated from one another by narrow alleys some $23\frac{1}{2}$–$27\frac{1}{2}$ inches (60–70 cm) in width. The dwellings are mostly stone-built from smoothly finished polygonal masonry, with upper courses of mudbrick.

The inhabitants of Smyrna were right to protect themselves with heavy ramparts, though, when the blow came, they were of little avail. Alyattes, King of Lydia – famous for its capital city of Sardis, for its gold, and for its next ruler, Alyattes' son Croesus – built an enormous siege mound and took the city in around 600 BC. Both the domestic quarter and the Sanctuary of Athena suffered badly. Yet the excavations have shown that there was no serious interruption in temple activities, and that the work on expanding the temple, already under way at the time of the attack, was continued. Thus the temple stands as a good example of Greek construction during the period of around 620–590 BC, marking the transition from the Orientalizing to the Archaic period.

5.20 Temple of Athena, Smyrna, limestone "mushroom" capital. c. 600 BC. Izmir Museum, Turkey

The excavator's hypothetical reconstruction (fig. **5.19**) shows the terraced sanctuary, with its retaining wall of polygonal masonry, approach road of polygonal paving stones, the temple itself, and votive dedications. A bewildering variety of stone capitals was used. Some capitals have *volutes* (spirals) springing from the base with floral *palmettes*, consisting of leaves arranged like a palm shoot, in between. Other floral and leaf motifs decorate other parts of each capital, so that this group of capitals presents a veritable galaxy of ornament. These capitals are called "Aeolic," and, though of various sizes and profiles, are thought by the excavator to have belonged to the temple itself. Fragments of 24 such capitals were found. The ornamental forms are all of oriental derivation, with volutes and vegetal motifs enlarged much beyond the scale of their original use in the Near East. Capitals of another shape, the so-called "mushroom" capital (fig. **5.20**), either alone or in combination with Aeolic capitals (fig. **5.21**), may have formed the tops of votive columns. This is a type of dedication often later found in Greek sanctuaries alongside statues, tripods, and the like. The mushroom capital, named obviously from its shape, was carved in low relief, with a leaf pattern on one register, and an alternation of leaf and floral on the

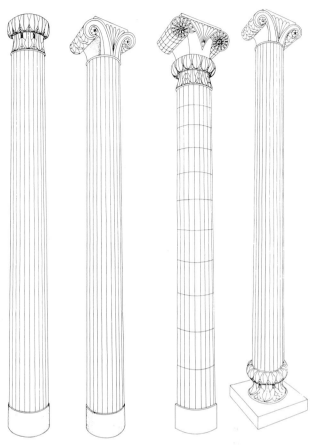

5.21 Reconstruction of the columns, capitals, and bases of the Temple of Athena, Smyrna. c. 600 BC

other. Fragments of some seventeen such capitals were retrieved in the excavation.

By the end of the seventh century BC, architects had turned from mudbrick and wood to stone as the preferred material. They had seen columns with carved capitals and bases elsewhere, and had shown both a liking for them and the way they were placed around temples. In the East, at any rate, they were enjoying the rich variety of oriental motifs, as they strove to decorate their religious buildings with due ceremony. They favored forms which showed variety rather than uniformity. The Temple of Athena at Smyrna shows how elastic was the thinking of Greek planners at the turn of the century.

5.22 *Opposite* Bronze youth, from Delphi. Height 7½ ins (19 cm). c. 625 BC. Delphi Museum

5.23 *Above* Bronze attachment to a cauldron. Height (head and neck) 3½ ins (9 cm). c. 700–675 BC. Olympia Museum

Sculpture

The fratricidal conflicts of the Greek city-states, as depicted for example on the Chigi vase (fig. **5.4**, p. 124), assured that the male warrior type would continue to be a favorite subject of dedications in sanctuaries. Similarly, the cessation of hostilities in order to allow the Panhellenic games to take place assured that the athletic male form would be a focus of attention.

Bronze continued to be a prized material. The tripod-cauldron of the Geometric period was replaced by the (separate) tripod and cauldron decorated with animal or mythological *protomes*. Such protomes (the independent upper part – head, or head and neck – of an animal or mytho-logical creature) were perched on the necks or

5.24 Bronze male figurine, the "Mantiklos" bronze, from Thebes. Height 7⅘ ins (20 cm). c. 700–675 BC. Museum of Fine Arts, Boston

rims of cauldron bowls, and normally faced outwards, though not always. Protomes of griffins and siren head attachments were especially popular. The siren head attachment (fig. **5.23**) with its full, rounded form suggests this was of Eastern manufacture, and possibly an import.

Interpreting anatomy as geometric forms at first continued. The Mantiklos bronze (fig. **5.24**) is a statuette from Boeotia dedicated to Apollo. It shows cylindrical thighs, triangular torso, pyramidal neck, triangular face and hemispherical crown. But forms from 700 BC are less two-dimensional and more rounded than those of predecessors. Greek enthusiasm for using the newly found skill of writing knew no bounds, and here the dedicator, Mantiklos, proudly defaces the thighs of his gift with two hexameter verses: "Mantiklos dedicated me to the Far-shooter with the Silver Bow from his tithe; grant, Apollo, something good in return." It is worth noting the familiarity between mortal and immortal, the metrical know-how, and the pronoun used to suggest the living or lifelike quality of the bronze.

More anonymous is the bronze from the first quarter of the seventh century BC (fig. **5.25**) found at Olympia beneath the foundations of the Temple of Hera (see pp. 148–9). A young warrior stands facing the front, wearing only a crested helmet and a wide belt. His right arm, held aloft, originally held a spear. The hair, carefully coiffed in horizontal loops or waves, adopts a style which was to become, in a more elaborate form, a hallmark of the seventh century BC.

A later bronze, made around 625 BC, comes from Delphi (fig. **5.22**, p. 136). Here the long legs have given way to more naturalistic, though still stretched, proportions. The left leg edges forward. The arms are held by the side, fists clenched, following an Egyptian convention. He wears a belt, of a type familiar on Crete. The face is a narrow triangle. The forehead is low, the nose and eyes big, the skull flat. He has no ears! The hair, horizontally hooped and falling in dense masses, appears like a beehive from the

5.25 Bronze warrior, from Olympia. Height 9⅔ ins (23.7 cm). c. 700–675 BC. National Museum, Athens

5.26 Terracotta torso of a female "Daedalic" figurine. Height 7 ins (17.5 cm). c. 650–625 BC. Iraklion Museum, Crete

used as votive offerings, whether representing donor or divinity, in many sanctuaries.

The hairstyle, already seen on the bronze from Delphi, and variants of it (forehead curls, divided vertical locks, knoblike endings) is common among many terracotta female figurines produced about 680–625 BC. These figures share the following traits: frontality (they face forwards), rigidity, and flatness (the profile view is so compressed that sometimes the ear is not shown), they have triangular faces, low brows, big noses and eyes, and flat skulls. We can be reasonably sure of their chronology, since a number of Protocorinthian vases, firmly dated, terminate in similar terracotta heads. Thus, a stylistic development within the series can be identified. The more detailed the hairstyle, as here (fig. **5.26**) and the more apparent the anatomy, the later in the series is the figurine. Though they were widely distributed across the Greek world, the major centers of production seem to have been at Corinth, Crete, Sparta, and Rhodes. The style they exemplify is called "Daedalic," after the legendary early sculptor Daedalus. Female figurines are by far the most numerous examples of the style, though beardless youths also appear. Terracotta is the most usual material, but the style found expression also in figures in bronze, as we have seen (fig. **5.22**), in ivory, gold, and, most significantly, in stone.

The "Lady of Auxerre" (fig. **5.27**), a limestone statuette 25½ inches (65 cm) tall and named after the city in France where she was first exhibited (she is now in the Louvre), is an enlargement from the mold-made terracottas and a translation into stone. She typifies the Daedalic style, and probably came originally from Crete. Standing frontally, she wears a long dress, elaborately decorated on the skirt with incised concentric squares which were originally painted. A similar design decorates the upper border of the garment at the neck. A broad belt pinches in the high narrow waist. Actual bronze belts like this have been found dedicated in sanctuaries. A cloak covers both shoulders. Her face is triangular, and her brow is low. Her hair is arranged in vertical strands and horizontal waves, also taking on an

back and sides and like triangles on either side of the face from the front. This may be an attempt to copy an Egyptian wig, but became a convention for thick hair, combed and brushed.

The Greek world was also flooded with small mold-made (hence, mass-produced) terracotta female figurines. Some early ones resemble oriental representations of the nude Eastern goddess Astarte. But they are soon dressed and addressed as Aphrodite. Others certainly represented other female deities, and all were

5.27 *Left* Limestone statuette, so-called "Lady of Auxerre." Height 25½ ins (65 cm). c. 640 BC. Musée du Louvre, Paris

5.28 *Above* Limestone relief, from Mycenae, the so-called "Woman at the Window." Height 15¾ ins (40 cm). c. 640 BC. National Museum, Athens

approximately triangular shape on either side of the face. Large feet emerge from beneath the shapeless skirt. She holds her large left hand flat against her leg and her large right hand across her body between her breasts, in a gesture often thought to mean adoration.

Her counterparts in architectural sculpture come from Prinias, as we have seen, and from Mycenae. The Mycenae relief figure (fig. **5.28**), only 15¾ inches (40 cm) tall, has hair which, as preserved, is more obviously triangular and wig-like than that of the Lady of Auxerre. Yet, like the Lady of Auxerre, the forehead is low and the hair above the brow ends in fancy curls. The Mycenae figure pulls her cloak either over or away from her head in a modest gesture often associated with brides. Some scholars have thought that the relief was a metope, part of a frieze decorating the superstructure of a Doric building. Fragments of other limestone reliefs also come from Mycenae, and may have belonged to the same frieze. But such a frieze is more likely to have adorned the dado course of a building, as seems to have been the case with the frieze of cavaliers from Prinias (fig. **5.17**, p. 133), in the Eastern manner. Both the Lady of Auxerre and the Mycenae "Woman at the Window," as she is sometimes called, are thought to have been made around 640 BC.

At about the same time, Greek sculptors turned to a new material, marble, and a new scale. As with architecture, the impetus for change came from Egypt. From the early years of the century, visiting Greeks had seen not only gigantic buildings made of stone, but also lifesize and colossal statues of standing and seated figures. Egyptian sculptors frequently used very hard stones, granite, and porphyry, which they worked laboriously with abrasives and stone pounders in an age-old technique.

5.29 Marble female statue, "Nikandre", from Delos. Height 5 ft 9 ins (1.75 m). c. 625? BC. National Museum, Athens

Up to this point Greek sculptors, working soft limestone, had needed little more than carpentry skills to create statuettes like the Lady of Auxerre. Now, Greeks began to use the crystalline white marble with which the islands of the Cyclades, notably Naxos and Paros, were so liberally endowed. Marble quarries on Samos too were open by the end of the century. Though the influence on Greeks of Egyptian buildings and statues is inescapable, the earliest Greek marble-quarrying techniques are most closely paralleled in Anatolia, and not in Egypt.

The blocks themselves were worked with an iron point, a flat chisel, and an abrasive, probably emery, from Naxos. From an early date, a drill, worked with a bow, was used for details and to free arms from bodies. The new large figures were first roughed out at the quarry site, to judge from the unfinished blocks midway between quarry and harbor on the island of Naxos. This preparatory step would have reduced the cost of shipment from quarry to the site of dedication, though occasionally work was damaged in transit from quarry to port.

The style at first is Daedalic, though, almost at once, the diminutive scale associated with Daedalic was left behind. A Naxian aristocrat named Nikandre made a dedication on Delos which, though battered, has survived (fig. **5.29**). This is the first lifesize marble Greek statue which we have. The anonymous sculptor worked edgily on the thin planklike rectangular block, nowhere thicker than 8 inches (20 cm), and presented the normal Daedalic forms, a triangular face, wiglike hair, and a frontal and rigid pose. An inscription boldly placed on the side of her skirt reads: "Nikandre dedicated me to the Far Darter, the Arrow Shooter, outstanding of women, daughter of Deinodikes of Naxos, sister of Deinomenes, wife of Phraxos." The statue shows the Naxian aristocracy's pride in their lineage as well as the originality of the sculptor. The figure has been variously dated. Though some have said it dates pre-650 BC, as a marble figure she would be oddly isolated. A date of about 625 BC is more likely, since a fragment of a larger marble female of about that date comes from Samos. Nikandre did not choose to name the sculptor of her statue,

but the début of the artistic personality was not long delayed. The base of a statue for a male figure, dated about 600 BC, reads: "Euthykartides dedicated me, the Naxian, and he made me."

The first male figures in marble are lifesize or bigger from their first appearance. Enough fragments of these huge figures have been retrieved to make a reconstruction of the type. They follow Daedalic conventions for the hair and head. They are naked, except for a belt, and stand with one leg slightly advanced, like their Daedalic precur-

5.30 Kneeling ivory youth, from Samos. Height 5¾ ins (14.5 cm). C. 625 BC. National Museum, Athens

sors, for example the bronze from Delphi (fig. **5.22**, p. 136). They appear in sanctuaries as dedications (on Delos, for example), and in cemeteries as gravemarkers (as on Thera).

The Egyptian influence on their appearance is striking. Egyptian standing male figures are strictly frontal. Many were wrested from their rectangular blocks by a system of proportions, which was sketched in a grid on all four surfaces of the block. The Greek method of working marble was similar, working inward from the surface all the way round the block at the same time, removing mantle after mantle of stone. Similar "quadrifrontal" figures (figures worked on all four sides) emerge, though there are differences. Egyptian figures stand one leg advanced, as do the Greek. Yet the Egyptian figure stands more stiffly, back leg locked, while the weight of the Greek figure is more evenly distributed, and the pose is not so forced. Egyptian figures are clothed, while the Greeks are naked. Though there are obvious similarities of form, it is the method of working stone (the approach from all four sides, working from linear diagrams on each surface) and system of proportions that show to a greater extent the influence of Egypt. The sheer size of the Egyptian statues also had an obvious impact.

On a less imposing scale, sculptors refined their skills, turning to smaller figures, which are of conspicuous beauty. Such is the kneeling youth from Samos (fig. **5.30**), who originally formed one arm of a lyre, and was made around 625 BC. An ivory figure, he has eyes, brows, earlobes, earrings, and pubic hair inlaid in another material, now lost. His triangular torso, long thighs, and ornate belt depend on Daedalic prototypes, yet the head is quite different. Gone is the flatness of feature, the wiglike hairdo, the shape of the face and low-browed skull. Gone too are the fuller rounded forms, which might have pointed to an Eastern origin, and which are commonly found among some ivories in Greek sanctuaries of the same period. Simply carved major forms of arm, leg, torso, and cheek are matched by the detailed precision of hair, mouth, belt, and hand. Side by side with the marble giants, this small figure exemplifies the close of the Orientalizing period. From now on, all things – vase painting, art, and architecture, included – whatever their sources of inspiration may have been, were to be Greek.

6
Archaic Greece
c. 600–480 BC

The prosperity of the seventh century BC continued into the sixth; so did the rivalries between states, the intensified interest in commerce, and the energetic expansion of colonies already founded abroad. Commercial enterprise and competition brought the Greek states face to face with other expanding Mediterranean powers: the Etruscans and Carthaginians in the West, and the Persians in the East. Many states continued to be in the hands of tyrants, but by the end of the sixth century BC democratic constitutions had been set up in some, for example Athens. The Archaic period opens around 600 BC with architects and sculptors striving for monumentality in stone in competing city-states thriving on commercial prowess. It ends around 480 BC with the great battles between East and West: Greece against Persia, and Greeks in the West against Carthage. These military and

Opposite Detail of an Attic black-figure hydria: fountain-house scene, fig. **6.32**. c. 510 BC. Museum of Fine Arts, Boston

naval conflicts mark the culmination of dramatic changes in the arts, as shown in sculpture in the round, in vase painting, and in architectural sculpture.

ATHENS

Athens, which had shown the way ahead in the Geometric period, now came to the fore again. She had not participated in the colonizing ventures of the late eighth and seventh centuries BC. This was probably due to a decline in population which is revealed in the fact that in the Attic cemeteries there are many fewer graves of the early seventh century BC than of the later eighth century BC and that there were only half the number of wells in use in what was later the Agora of Athens in the seventh century.

The relative obscurity of seventh-century Athens was replaced by a period of political, commercial and artistic activity. In the early sixth century BC the struggle for power between the aristocrats and the rest resulted in the appointment of a citizen called Solon, both politician and poet, as chief magistrate with powers to settle the differences. Aristotle, writing over two hundred years later, says that Solon used the old property classifications to divide the citizens into four groups: five hundred bushel men (those with the land providing five hundred bushels of grain), horsemen, teamsters, and workers. But some commentators believe that Solon himself was the one who introduced these divisions to emphasize the importance of wealth as well as birth, and so initiated constitutional progress towards democracy. All agree that he set up an elected council chosen from the old tribes to prepare business for the assembly, and allowed access to the lawcourts for all. His reforms aimed to reconcile the populace with the aristocracy. Predictably, perhaps, he pleased no one.

In the second quarter of the century a tyrant, Peisistratos, appeared on the scene. He and his sons Hipparchos and Hippias controlled the city, more or less continually, until 510 BC. Disagreements between the classes were suppressed, while commerce prospered and the arts were encouraged. Sculpture and vase painting flourished, and large-scale building programs were begun. Peisistratos died in 527 BC, Hipparchos was assassinated in 514 BC, and Hippias was driven into exile in 510 BC. Political argument and civic strife then resumed, until the reins of power passed to Kleisthenes whose wideranging reforms, instituted in 508/507 BC, ushered in the democracy. Kleisthenes broke the stranglehold of the four old tribes by setting up ten entirely new ones, each consisting of citizens from the three geographical zones of Attica (the city, the coast, the inland). Members of one of the new tribes, who lived on the coast, might live far from fellow tribesmen, who lived inland, or in the city, and so on. There were other reforms, notably a new council of five hundred, 50 from each tribe, but new membership rolls for the ten new tribes were the constitutional ingredient which forged the new democracy. In this way Kleisthenes strove for the integration of Attica.

New challenges faced the fledgling democracy at once. Summoned to support the Greek cities of Ionia in their revolt against the all-conquering Persians in 499 BC, Athens shared in the surprise attack on Sardis, the capital city of a Persian satrapy, and burnt it down. This became the ostensible reason, the *casus belli*, for the Persian invasions of Greece which followed. The landing at Marathon, at which the geriatric exiled tyrant Hippias was present on the Persian side, took place in 490 BC. The Athenian hoplites won, almost singlehandedly, over the Persians. Only a small contingent from Plataea arrived at Marathon in time to help the Athenians in their assault. This astonishing victory, long to be remembered, provided a huge boost to the confidence of the young democracy. Moreover, it forced other cities to recognize the power and energy of Athens. Ten years later, in 480 BC, when the Persians returned with another armada, the Athenian general Themistokles and the Athenian fleet played an important role in the victory at Salamis, and, though the city itself was laid waste by the Persians, Athens' prestige among the Greeks soared. The land victory over the Persians at Plataea in 479 BC was managed by the traditional land power of Greece, Sparta. From then on, Athens and Sparta became rivals for the leadership of Greece. As the Archaic period ended, most cities of the Greek world found themselves within the political orbit of one of these two states; the only exceptions were to be found in the West, where cities like Selinus prospered independently and where, following their success against Carthage at the Battle of Himera, Syracuse and Akragas nursed their own ideas of grandeur.

The period is everywhere one of excitement, expansion, exploration, and revolutionary change. As sculptors came to grips with the problems of representing the ideal in the observed, so rational advances in philosophy and the natural sciences struggled with a world in which the gods were close at hand and to be feared. The notion that the gods resented and punished acts of human aggrandizement was keenly felt. So, too, was the sense that human success, whether on the battle-field or in athletics, was only acquired in godgiven moments of exceptional talent.

Architecture and architectural sculpture

The building of temples for the gods continued to command priority. They were now regularly sur-rounded by colonnades. These colonnades formed part of the exterior of the temples, for which the so-called architectural "orders" were designed. The two principal orders in stone, the "Doric" and the "Ionic," dimly discernible at seventh-century Thermon and Samos, now find full expression.

THE ORDERS

The "Doric" order (fig. **6.2**) presents columns without bases, but with flutes joining in a sharp ridge (the *arris*) and capitals in two parts, an oblong or square flat slab, the *abacus*, above the cushion-like *echinus*. There are echoes here of Mycenaean columns (compare the Lion Gate) and of Egyptian. Above the capital came the entabla-ture in three parts: the architrave, the frieze, and the *cornice*. The architrave regularly consisted of undecorated ashlar blocks, undecorated except

for a narrow projecting band (a taenia) at the top to which were attached small rectangular shelves (regulae) with pegs (guttae) fixed to their under-sides. The frieze comprised an alternating series of *triglyphs* (upright members, each with three bars conventionally thought to represent the transla-tion into stone of carpentry prototypes) and metopes (frequently decorated). The cornice pro-vided an horizontal capping member on the flanks of the building, and both horizontal and angled members framing the gables at the ends. The end gables (the *pediments*) were often decorated with sculpture, at first in relief, but by the end of the period entirely in the round, standing on the floor of the pedimental triangle.

The "Ionic" order (fig. **6.2**) separated the shafts of the columns from the stylobate (the course of masonry which supported the colonnade) by horizontally fluted bases. It had more vertical flutes on its columns than did the Doric. It also, later, separated flute from flute with a flat fillet.

The capitals of the order are related to, but distinct from, some of those richly varied capitals (mushroom and "Aeolic" capitals) used in the Temple of Athena at Smyrna at the turn of the century. Used elsewhere with a distinctive regional flavor, for example at Phocaea, Larisa, and Neandria, "Aeolic" capitals (fig. **6.1**) often have volutes springing upward and outward from separate stems, with a palmette between the two, and collar(s) of leaves below. All the decorative elements (florals and volutes) are drawn from the Eastern vocabulary. In the Near East, these motifs had never been anything grander than small-scale elements in wood and bronze elaborating, for example, furniture. Where they had appeared on a large scale, in Phoenician volute capitals, they had not belonged to any coherent order.

6.1 Aeolic capital, Neandria. c. 600 BC

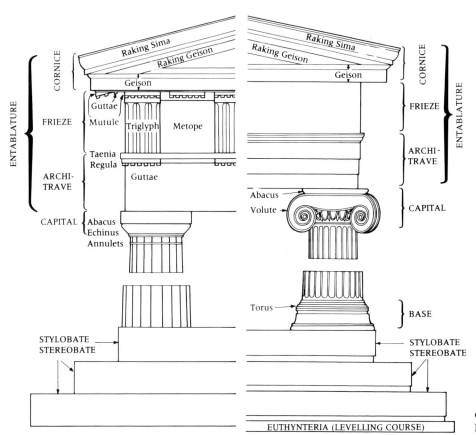

6.2 The Doric (*left*) and Ionic (*right*) orders

In Ionic, the two volutes are joined, seemingly pressed down with carved decorative *molding* beneath, and palmettes (conventionalized palm-leaf ornaments) relegated to corners beneath the volutes. Sometimes a narrow abacus above supports the entablature. In the entablature, the architrave is often broken into three horizontal planes (*fasciae*). The most important feature is the frieze, which is continuous, sometimes carved with figures, sometimes denticulated (looking like precisely gapped rectangular teeth). Cornices provide the crowning members.

In general terms, the Ionic order is more restless visually, with much ornament and much variety. The Doric seems more integrated and more sturdy. Doric is popular on the mainland of Greece, and among the Greeks in the West, and Ionic among Greeks in the East (Asia Minor) and in the islands. These orders appeared on the exterior of temples whose plans (fig. **6.3**)

remained straightforward. A box for the cult statue, the cella, was preceded by a porch (*pronaos*). In the Doric order the temple also had a back chamber (an opisthodomos or *adyton*).

DORIC TEMPLES

Two examples of Doric temples of the sixth century BC can be seen in the Peloponnese. The Temple of Hera at Olympia, built around 590 BC, marks the end of the transition from elementary materials to stone. The plan (fig. **6.4**) shows six columns on the front, by sixteen on the flank, porch, and opisthodomos, each with two columns *in antis*. Porch columns, front and back, are aligned with columns of the façades, thus tying peristyle and central block together. The cella has interior columns and spur walls which no longer obstruct the view of the cult statue. The upper elements of the temple were of mudbrick and timber and are lost, but stylobate, platform, and

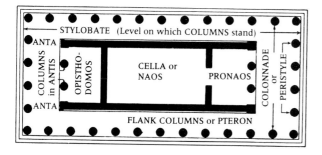

6.3 Typical ground plan of a Doric temple

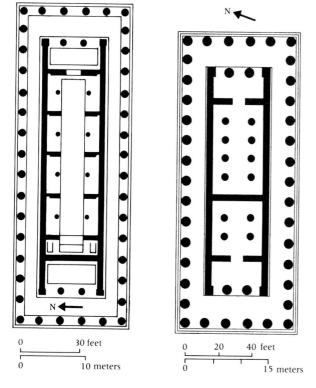

6.6 Temple of Apollo, Corinth, surviving columns from the northwest. Limestone (with white stucco surface). c. 560 BC

6.4 *Above left* Plan of the Temple of Hera, Olympia. c. 590 BC

6.5 *Above right* Plan of the Temple of Apollo, Corinth. c. 560 BC

lower courses of the walls were of cut masonry. The columns were originally wooden, gradually replaced by stone. Many years later, Pausanias writes that he saw an oak column still standing in the opisthodomos. This confirms that the building was transitional in terms of building materials. This temple is double the area of the seventh-century temple at Thermon.

Better preserved, in terms of the elevation, is the Temple of Apollo at Corinth built in the second quarter of the century. The plan (fig. **6.5**) shows six columns on the façade, by 15 on the flank (showing that architects were reducing the more elongated proportions of earlier structures). There is a columned porch and opisthodomos. Porch columns align with those on the façade. It also has the unusual feature of two inner columned chambers. Of these, the eastern one would have accommodated the cult statue. Would the other have sheltered Apollo's treasures, or have been a place for oracular activity? Seven of the columns of this temple still stand with an architrave block or two still in place (fig. **6.6**). The squatness or slenderness of Greek columns is often described in terms of proportions, with the height stated as a multiple of

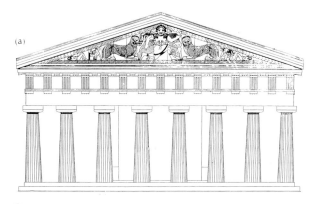

(a)

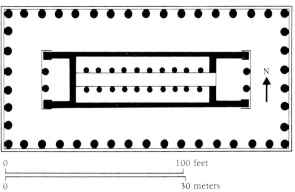

(b)

N

| 0 | 100 feet |
| 0 | 30 meters |

6.7 (a) Restored elevation and (b) plan of the Temple of Artemis, Corcyra. c. 580 BC

dependency of Corinth (fig. **6.7a** and **b**). Built around 580 BC, this temple, of which the blocks of the platform, walls, and columns are almost completely lost, showed in plan eight columns on the façades, by 17 on the flanks. It had a columned porch, cella, and back chamber. New is the broader space between the colonnade and the walls leaving enough room for a second row of columns, a so-called ''pseudo-dipteral'' arrangement. A few fragments of carved limestone metopes have survived, and, miraculously, so has the relief sculpture of the limestone pediment from the west end of the building. Most of the triangular space is taken up by a huge central Gorgon figure, almost 10 feet (3 m) tall, flanked by Pegasus and Chrysaor (fig. **6.8**), the children born at the moment of her death. This trio is flanked in turn by two enormous felines. On a much smaller scale, Zeus, on one side, thunderbolt poised, attacks a giant. On the other, a seated figure, backed by what might be a city wall,

the lower diameter. At Corinth, the height of these sturdy columns is 4.15 times the lower diameter at the front of the building, 4.40 times on the flank. The columns are monolithic (i.e. carved from a single quarry block) made of limestone, and have an outward swelling, cigarlike, contour. This is termed *entasis*, a refinement aimed at correcting the optical illusion that straight lines, whether vertical or horizontal, appear to sink in towards the midpoint. Another Doric refinement, practiced here for the first time, is the upward curvature of the stylobate. The echinus of the capital bulges visibly, giving a baggy profile. The profile of Doric capitals provides a valuable, if relative, chronological marker. The baggier the profile, the earlier the capital.

The superstructure lost from the temples at Olympia and Corinth is partly preserved among the fragmentary remains of the Temple of Artemis on the island of Corcyra (modern Corfu), which, for a long while, was a

6.8 Temple of Artemis, Corcyra, limestone pediment: central figure of the Gorgon, Medusa, with her son Chrysaor to her left. Height (of Gorgon) c. 9 ft 4 ins (2.85 m). c. 580 BC. Corfu Museum

stretches out an imploring hand to the lost figure whose spear threatens his throat. Is this Priam, King of Troy? Prostrate dead or dying figures fill in the corners. The composition is symmetrical. Heraldic felines speak of the power of the goddess within (and of the Gorgon), under whose control they are. This power is available to well wishers and is ready to chastise non-Greek malefactors. Narrative groups stand as metaphors for the conquest of barbarism by the civilized world of Greek deities and heroes.

The limestone groups which decorate the pediments of the Temple of Athena built on the Acropolis at Athens in the early years of the tyranny solved in a new way the problem of what to do with the corners of a triangular shape. They were filled with snaky-tailed monsters (fig. **6.9**), or with struggles between heroes like Herakles and mariners like Triton, whose fishtail could writhe away conveniently into acute angles. These limestone figures were richly painted with blue, white, red, and green to present a brilliant, if not garish, appearance. This Temple of Athena may be associated with the foundations visible between the Erechtheion and the Parthenon (dotted plan on fig. **8.1**, p. 237).

Developments in Doric building throughout the century culminate in the Doric Temple of Aphaia on the island of Aegina. The plan (fig. **6.10**) has six columns on the façade, and 12 on the flank, columned porches front and back and a

6.9 *Above* Athens Acropolis, limestone pedimental group: three-bodied, snaky-tailed monster. Height c. 3 ft (90 cm). c. 550 BC. Acropolis Museum, Athens

6.10 *Below* Plan of the Temple of Aphaia, Aegina. c. 500 BC

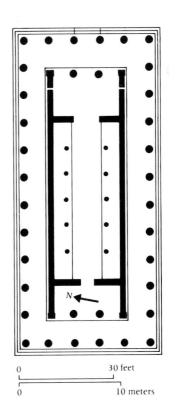

0	30 feet
0	10 meters

columned cella. The temple is accordingly less elongated, and there are Doric refinements. Columns lean inwards slightly, and corner columns are thicker than others. Strictly applied numerical ratios governed the heights of members of the elevation. The height of the columns is now 5.33 times the lower diameter, yielding much more slender proportions than in the columns of the Temple of Apollo at Corinth. Angle contraction – already used as early as the Temple of Hera at Olympia – was used at the corners. Spacing between columns adjacent to corner columns was narrowed. This became necessary when builders wished to align triglyphs of the frieze with the centers of the columns, to push end triglyphs to the corners of the building, and to avoid having elongated metopes at the corners. The only solution was to contract the whole of the corner of the building.

The temple has left fragments of three pediments, two from the east end, and one from the west, which clearly present problems. The

somewhat ungainly stiff angular style of the figures of the west pediment (fig. **6.11**) suggests a date of around 500 BC. Those of the replacement east pediment (fig. **6.11**) show more natural movement and realistic expressions and may date from 480 BC. The composition was accorded a push-and-pull treatment, a contrast of centripetal and centrifugal movement in the two pediments. In the west, the action is centrifugal with the battle flying outwards; in the east, it moves inwards from collapsed figures in the corners (one even beginning to roll out) to striding figures near the center. In either instance the tableau is of the Aeginetan heroes at war, perhaps at Troy, presided over by Athena, the only figure drawn to a scale larger than others, as befits a divine being. The choice of topic allows

6.11 *Top and bottom* Temple of Aphaia, Aegina, pediments: top, west pediment; below, east pediment. Marble. Height (of Athena in west pediment) c. 5½ ft (1.68 m). Width c. 49 ft (15 m). c. 500–480 BC. Staatliche Antikensammlungen, Munich

for unity of scale with figures striding, kneeling, lunging, and collapsing, filling the space all the way into the corners. These pediments mark the transition from the Archaic period to the Classical.

IONIC TEMPLES

The earliest indisputably Ionic temples were erected in Asia Minor, at Ephesos and Didyma, and in the Sanctuary of Hera at Samos. On Samos, a new temple of gigantic size, 54½ yards (50 m) wide by almost 110 yards (100 m) long, was built by the architects Rhoikos and Theodoros. Begun after 575 BC, it was completed by about 560 BC. There were eight columns on the front, by 21 on the flanks, with ten at the

back (fig. **6.12**). A double colonnade encircled the deep porch and columned cella. No capital from this building has survived. This temple was the centerpiece of an elaboration of the sanctuary, with a new monumental gateway, altar, and other outbuildings. When it collapsed around 530 BC, an even bigger and more ambitious replacement was begun (fig. **6.13a**), now to be surrounded by a triple colonnade at front and back, and with a double colonnade on the flanks.

Not to be outdone, the Samians' neighbors to the north at Ephesos began a gigantic temple for their divinity, Artemis, at about the same time. Of the same width, it was nearly 126 yards (115

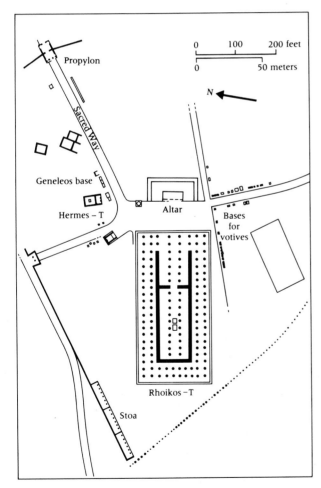

6.12 Plan of the Sanctuary of Hera on Samos. c. 560 BC

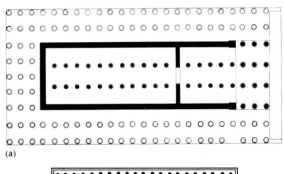

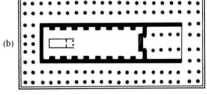

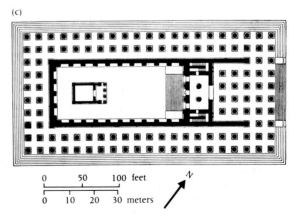

6.13 Plans of Ionic temples showing relative sizes
(a) Temple of Hera, Samos. c. 530 BC and later
(b) Temple of Apollo, Didyma. c. 550 BC
(c) Temple of Apollo, Didyma. c. 330 BC and later

6.14 Restored elevation of the Temple of Artemis, Ephesos. c. 560 BC

m) long with a triple row of columns on the façade. Unlike most Greek temples which were oriented towards the east, this one faced west. Horizontally fluted bases supported tall columns (fig. **6.14**), some endowed with sculptured drums above the base, and surmounted by volute capitals, some of which survived and are to be found in the British Museum. Precious fragments of an inscription, confirmed by the fifth-century Greek historian Herodotos, tell us that the king of Lydia, Croesus, contributed to the cost. This provides an important chronological marker, for Croesus lost his kingdom in 547 BC. It is probable therefore that the columns to which the inscription refers were in place before that date.

A third example of Ionic gigantism, similarly built in the mid-sixth century BC, appeared at the Sanctuary of Apollo at Didyma near Miletus on the coast of Asia Minor, close to Samos. This temple (fig. **6.13b**) has an open-air interior sheltering a small shrine – a temple within a temple. It also has relief sculpture, which decorated not only the lowest drums of exterior columns (as at Ephesos), but also the corners of the architrave above (gorgons and lions). When the temple was rebuilt in the fourth century BC and later a similar plan (fig. **6.13c**) was followed, though on an even more monstrous scale.

The functions of these temples were varied, and they should not be thought of in the same way as we think of churches, synagogues, or mosques. They do not seem to have been built only for purposes of worship. Some were indeed built to shelter hallowed places, or ancient venerable images with special powers, or an altar, or a tree. These held appropriate religious ceremonies: worship and sacrifice, the reception of initiates, the consultation of an oracle. Attachment to a particular holy or magical place explains perhaps why temples are often built repeatedly on the same spot, as for example the two sixth-century temples on Samos. Other temples seem to have been purpose-built as houses for images of anthropomorphic gods (gods having the attributes of humans), or for sheltering new cult images. These were elaborate and costly offerings from the city to the divinity concerned.

In the same vein, temples were also used to guard the offerings of other states or individuals, and other possessions of the god. This function was evidently more in the realm of banking and finance than of religious ceremony. Since gifts and goods were inventoried, temples became record offices as well. This function was sometimes expanded to include caring for administrative or business archives and citizen lists. Many liturgies were enacted outside the temple near open-air altars, but some acts of worship and sacrifice (with an indoor altar) took place inside.

TREASURIES: DORIC AND IONIC

Altar and temple were the focus of sanctuary life. But, in the more famous sanctuaries, architects also constructed smaller buildings, called treasuries, to safeguard the offerings of individual cities and to stand themselves as offerings, and marks of gratitude and devotion. At Delphi, for example, numerous states including Athens, Sikyon, and Siphnos built treasuries in the Archaic period. Normally simple in plan, a rectangular box to hold the offerings preceded by a two-columned porch, these treasuries were embellished with the architectural orders on their exteriors. Between 575 and 550 BC, the tyrant of Sikyon, a Peloponnesian state which faced Delphi across the Corinthian gulf, built a Doric treasury in the sanctuary. For this he commissioned sculptured stone metopes to decorate the frieze. There were 14 metopes in all, of which four are almost entirely preserved. One of these (fig. **6.15**) shows the Greek heroes, Castor and Pollux (the Dioskouroi), and two friends, on a cattle raid. Another shows the departure of the ship *Argo* in search of the golden fleece, while another shows the Calydonian boar. Occasionally the action spills over, across the triglyph from one metope to the next as is the case with the *Argo* episode, but

6.16 Treasury of the Athenians, Delphi, from the east. Marble. c. 490–480 BC

6.15 Metope from the Sikyonian Treasury, Delphi: the cattle raid of the Dioskouroi. Limestone. Height 2 ft (63 cm). c. 560 BC. Delphi Museum

otherwise the subject matter seems unconnected. The absence of Herakles in such a series of metopes at this period is notable. There is much paint, and painted inscriptions identify the figures. Relief is high; long hair and garments are shown in detail. Heads of oxen appear engagingly in frontal and profile view. There is ample sense of recessive planes, as spears held in the right hands precede the receding heads of the captured cattle, with other spears or goads held in the left hands in the background. Here is the literal petrification of the painted terracotta metopes of the preceding century (cf. Thermon, p. 131).

Sometime after the battle of Marathon, in the decade 490–480 BC, the Athenians dedicated a treasury at Delphi, now wholly rebuilt (fig. **6.16**) on its site in the sanctuary. The Doric order was used with sculptured metopes. These depicted the exploits of Herakles at the back and on the northern side, and those of Theseus, hero of the new democracy, on the more visible southern

6.17 *Above* Metope from the Treasury of the Athenians, Delphi: Herakles and the hind. Marble. Height c. 2 ft 2 ins (67 cm). c. 490–480 BC. Delphi Museum

6.18 *Below* Perspective reconstruction of the Treasury of the Siphnians, Delphi. c. 530 BC

flank. The front of the building, facing the Sacred Way, showed an Amazonomachy (battle between Greeks and Amazons), but metopes here are so damaged that neither Theseus (the more likely candidate) nor Herakles is discernible. The metopes now show cycles of events rather than isolated incidents. Here (fig. **6.17**) Herakles leaps on the back of the hind, his cloak and quiver parked behind him. Sharply cut details of patternized beard, ribcage, and abdomen contrast with the natural energy of the pose.

The most dazzling treasury in the sanctuary is the Treasury of the Siphnians (fig. **6.18**). Traditional understanding of literary evidence holds that this Ionic building was constructed out of the wealth which came to Siphnos from its gold and silver mines, before the island was overcome by Samians in 525 BC, and before its mines were flooded by the sea. This treasury is highly important, not only for its rich and varied ornament but also because it is securely dated, and can therefore act as a valuable chronological marker for the development of Greek sculpture. The two columns of the porch were replaced by female figures carved in the round, known to Vitruvius as *Caryatids*, but probably called "Korai" at the time. The Greeks came to think of religious build-

6.19 Treasury of the Siphnians, Delphi, east pediment. Marble. Height (at middle) 2 ft 5 ins (74 cm). c. 530 BC. Delphi Museum

ings often in terms of the human body, but such literal humanization is unusual. Another city-state, Knidos, had already built a treasury at Delphi with Caryatids in the porch, but the most famous example of this phenomenon, the Erechtheion on the Acropolis of Athens, was yet to come. Each gable end of the Siphnian treasury was decorated with *pedimental sculpture*, apexes of the building were enhanced with carved figures (*akroteria*) standing against the sky, and a continuous frieze ran all the way around the structure (fig. **6.18**). The building faced west, so that, paradoxically, the sides of the building most visible to the pilgrim climbing the zigzag Sacred Way were the back and the north flank.

The pedimental sculpture from the back is preserved. The central figure of Zeus arbitrates between Herakles and Apollo who struggle for the Delphic tripod (fig. **6.19**). Chariots and horses flank the central scene with smaller scale, standing, striding, and recumbent figures adapting their poses to the triangular space. The composition is unevenly balanced, asymmetrical, and figures seem motionless and stilted.

The frieze beneath this pediment showed two conflicts, the space equally divided between them. There is the verbal argument between divinities, seated on Olympus, over the fate of the heroes at Troy, and an actual encounter at Troy between heroes (fig. **6.20**), dismounted from their chariots, over the body of a fallen warrior. The relief is high, the composition symmetrical and unified. New are the three-quarter view of the chariot horses, the further parts shown in paint on the background, the pathos of

the dead warrior in his awkward foreshortened pose, and the dramatic gesture of the end figure closing the composition at the north.

The matching short frieze at the front of the building was divided into three scenes (fig. **6.18**). A winged Athena mounting a chariot, and Aphrodite descending from a chariot are the two scenes preserved. The third was probably Hera with her chariot and Paris, the whole representing the famous Judgment of Paris.

The long continuous north frieze showed the battle between gods and giants (fig. **6.21**). It is thick with overlapping figures, diagonal movement, foreshortening, and continuous variation of posture, attitude, and shape. One incident shows Themis in her chariot and Dionysos attacking giants. In another, Apollo and Artemis are firing in unison at giants who advance like hoplite infantry, shields abreast. Themis, Dionysos, Apollo, and Artemis are all identified by painted inscriptions. One of Themis' lions munches vigorously on the midriff of an unfortunate giant. The sculptor magisterially combines descriptive detail of the lion's mane with three-dimensional roundness of body in plastic, somewhat flattened forms. The signature of this sculptor is inscribed around the circular edge of a giant's shield. Though the name itself is lost, the inscription claims that he worked the friezes at north and east, and stylistic similarity between the friezes supports this claim. The style of the south and front friezes is quite different. This sculptor worked almost fussily in the very front planes, cutting back drastically around his figures to the back of the relief.

With every suitable surface decorated with sculpture, enlivened with paint, and even metal additions for things like weapons, this was a dazzling building. Complex sculpture in relief gave

6.20 *Above* Treasury of the Siphnians, Delphi, east frieze: combat of heroes at Troy. Marble. Height 2ft ⅘ in (63 cm). c. 530 BC. Delphi Museum

6.21 *Below* Treasury of the Siphnians, Delphi, north frieze: gigantomachy. Marble. Height 2ft ⅘ in (63 cm). c. 530 BC. Delphi Museum

visual form to narrative themes of permanent power. The topic of the triumph of the Greek gods (Good) over superhuman barbaric giants (Evil), for instance, became a perennial favorite, and had already been used in the pediment at Corcyra. Such themes set in such brilliance make this Ionic treasury, jewellike in scale, the most compelling document of architectural sculpture of Archaic Greece.

SICILY AND SOUTH ITALY

Greek architects in the West preferred from the first the elevation of the Doric order for their temples and treasuries, as a rapid glance at any site will show, whether Syracuse or Selinus in Sicily or Metapontum or Poseidonia (Paestum) on the Italian mainland. This apparent emulation of Doric temples in mainland Greece, sometimes disparagingly referred to as provincialism, did not however extend to the layout of temples. Especially with reference to the plans, but also with reference to the introduction of Ionic elements into the elevations, exterior, and interior, Greek architects in the West, in fact, showed consider-

able flexibility and brilliance. Their buildings demonstrate new thinking, great vitality bordering on exuberance, and a true regional style. At Syracuse, Locri, and Metapontum, moreover, there is evidence of temples built entirely in the Ionic order, once more with great novelties of plan and detail. The Ionic temple at Syracuse was begun in the Archaic period, while the other two were built in the subsequent, Transitional period, around 480–450 BC.

Syracuse became in the fifth century BC a commercial and cultural rival of Athens and then a bitter enemy. A Doric temple to Apollo, built there between 570 and 560 BC, displays both the ingenuity and limitations of Western builders. Proportions of the plan, *hexastyle* by 17, are long (fig. **6.22**) and of the elevation cumbersome, and lack of experience in building in stone is shown by the close spacing of the columns. Yet there were innovations. There was a double row of columns at the front, and secondary stairs to allow access, giving the front of the temple special emphasis. There was a closed chamber, an adyton rather than the opisthodomos at the back.

Moreover, the broad *ambulatory* (the side and end passages all the way round) is almost pseudo-dipteral, echoing either the plan at Corcyra or developments in the Ionic order (e.g., Samos, Ephesos, Miletus), or both. This is the only Greek temple to carry an inscription identifying the architect-builder, Kleomenes.

Selinus, the westernmost Greek colony in Sicily, witnessed the construction on the Acropolis of two sixth-century temples and a further pair on a ridge to the east of the city. One of these, however, the great Temple G, though begun around 530 BC remained unfinished at the end of the Archaic period, and even at the time of the Carthaginian sack of the city in 409 BC.

On the Acropolis, Temple C (perhaps a Temple of Apollo) built around 560 BC is the oldest and the grandest. It displayed both a Doric exterior and a plan (fig. **6.23**) similar to that of the Temple of Apollo at Syracuse. However, columns are more broadly spaced and more slender, so that proportions are much less squat. A flight of eight

steps signaled the front of the building, further emphasized by a second row of columns, as at Syracuse. However, there were no columns on the interior of either the porch or the cella. Thus alignment of columns of the porch with those of the peristyle was not an issue, and the heart of the temple could accordingly be positioned freely. Sculptured stone metopes decorated the frieze at front and back. Of these, three survive, and show Athena, Perseus, and Medusa on one, Herakles and the Kerkopes on another (fig. **6.24**), while a third shows a chariot group with Apollo and Artemis. Heads face outward frontally to magnetize the visitor, drawing attention to the deeds of Greek heroes and gods, and what fates await malefactors. These are not the earliest metopes to appear at Selinus but, together with another series associated with Temple Y and dated to 570–560 BC, point to a vigorous group of sculptors at work in Selinus at that time. Above the frieze course of Temple C terracotta revetments bright with painted geometric and floral

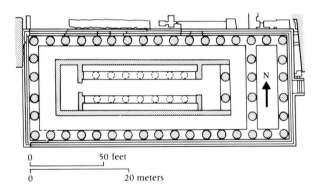

6.22 Plan of the Temple of Apollo, Syracuse. c. 560 BC

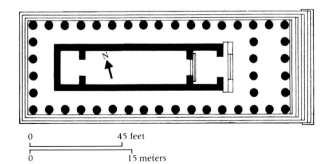

6.23 Plan of Temple C, Selinus. c. 560 BC

6.24 Metope from Temple C, Selinus: Herakles and the Kerkopes. Limestone. Height 4 ft 9½ ins (1.47 m). c. 560 BC. National Museum, Palermo

polychrome designs enhanced the cornices, while a huge terracotta Gorgon head, 9 feet (2.7 m) tall, stood at the center of the pediment.

Much about the building seems rough and ready. Spacing between columns varies, they have different numbers of flutes, while some columns are monoliths with others comprising several drums. There is no entasis of the columns and metopes vary in size. Yet there is no gainsaying the novelty of the plan, the impact of the metopes and the brilliance of the architectural terracottas. The discovery inside the temple of numerous sealings (clay impressions of seals), used to seal official documents, shows that the building functioned partly as an archive, perhaps even of the city itself, and sheds intriguing light on the various functions of Greek temples.

6.25 Plans of Temple G, Selinus, and the Temple of Zeus, Akragas, showing relative sizes
   (a) Selinus, Temple G. c. 530–409 BC
   (b) Akragas, Temple of Zeus. c. 480–406 BC

On the eastern ridge, Temple G was of colossal dimensions (fig. **6.25a**), some 60 yards (55 m) wide by $125\frac{1}{2}$ yards (115 m) long, with columns over 52 feet (16 m) tall. It was evidently intended by its size alone to challenge the gigantic temples of Asia Minor built in the Ionic order. The plan again illustrates the versatility of Greek architects in the West. Pseudo-dipteral, it has a porch with four columns *prostyle* (forward of the antae) and six columns in all, quite unprecedented. It also had a triple entranceway to the celia. The cella had a double colonnade leading to an inner shrine echoing the arrangement at Didyma (fig. **6.13b**, p. 153), and an opisthodomos. Partially fluted columns show that the building was never finished, while some Doric capitals are Archaic and others early Classical. An inscription found here records thanks for a victory (unidentified) to Zeus, Phobos, Herakles, Apollo, Poseidon, Castor and Pollux, Athena, Demeter, Pasikrateia, and the other gods, but especially to Zeus. This gives a good sense of the contemporary hierarchy of

6.26 Poseidonia. 6th-century Doric temples showing plans and sizes
   (a) Temple of Hera I. c. 550 BC
   (b) Temple of Athena. c. 500 BC

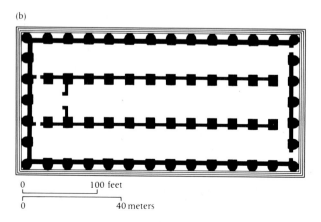

(a)

(b)

0   100 feet

0   40 meters

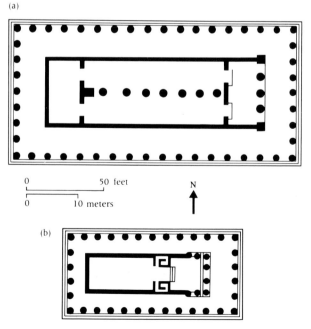

(a)

0   50 feet

0   10 meters

N

(b)

locally influential gods and heroes. The inscription continues to record that "a golden tablet with the names of the gods be placed in the Temple of Apollo, and that 60 talents of gold should be spent to this end." The temple is variously identified as a Temple of Apollo or of Zeus.

On the Italian mainland at Poseidonia (Paestum) stand two important temples of the sixth century BC. The earliest, often erroneously termed the Basilica, and now generally known as the Temple of Hera I, was constructed in the middle years of the century to a novel plan (fig. **6.26a**). It has nine columns by eighteen, a broad ambulatory, a porch with three columns *in antis*, an axial colonnade in the cella terminating in a spur wall, and an adyton at the back. This was a new kind of Doric architecture. Unlike Sicily, the peristyle and cella are closely linked; columns of the porch and cella are the same size as the columns of the peristyle and align with them. The whole building was bisected by the line of the axial colonnade of the cella. This division into two equal parts seems to have served religious purposes, providing similar space and visibility for two statues. Inscriptions and terracotta

figurines found in the sanctuary identify the principal divinity here as Hera. Accordingly, this temple is for her, and probably also for her consort, Zeus, for whose presence in this sanctuary there is also epigraphic evidence.

The columns (fig. **6.27**) display the usual Doric entasis, but introduce *anthemion* (leaf) decoration onto the necks of the shafts of the columns. At the back of the building, even the actual echinus of the capital is decorated with similar encircling tendrils, rosettes, palmettes, and petals. Such floral ornamentation, more in keeping with the Ionic order, would have been picked out in paint. Nothing is preserved above the frieze course, and there is no trace of architectural sculpture. Many fragments of painted architectural terracottas which decorated the eaves of the building have, however, come to light. Registers of palmettes, tongue patterns, swastikas, and quatrefoils are accompanied by painted gutter spouts in the form of lions' heads.

This temple provides a new rapport between cella and peristyle, the unparalleled bisection of the whole building to serve two gods, and rich and varied decoration. It suggests an imaginative

6.27 Temple of Hera I, Poseidonia, from the southwest. Limestone (travertine) and sandstone. c. 550 BC

architectural flair, open to various impulses. In this, it contrasts both with the increasing conformity of Doric in Greece and with the often unbalanced and irregularly aligned plans and plainer elevations of Sicilian.

The other standing sixth-century temple at Poseidonia is the Temple of Athena. Smaller in size than the Temple of Hera I, it displays even more astonishing innovations (fig. **6.26b**, p. 160). The exterior colonnade of six by 13 columns anticipates the ideal proportions of canonical Doric of the Classical period, and contrasts with the unbalanced proportions of the interior, which provide a very deep porch in front of the cella and no back porch at all.

The columns (fig. **6.28**) show distinct entasis. A floral collar decorates the neck of the capital, and the echinus has the baggy Archaic profile. The frieze course above is bracketed by string courses of sandstone (otherwise the stone is the local travertine), decorated with architectural moldings. The frieze itself has no sculptural decoration, nor does either end of the building, since the horizontal cornices are absent. Rather, the architect chose to draw attention to the roof, by projecting the raking cornices forward and decorating them with elaborate *soffits* (the underside of lintels, arches, or cornices).

The exterior displays plenty of imagination, the interior even more. Here columns of the Ionic order with Ionic volute capitals were introduced for the porch. This is the first building in the whole history of architecture to use both Doric and Ionic columns. As such, it is the clear predecessor of developments in Attica some 50 years later. The innovations in the building are numerous: the mix of textures and colors of stone in the frieze and the arrangement of

6.28 Temple of Athena, Poseidonia, from the northwest. Limestone (travertine) and sandstone. c. 500 BC

triglyphs and metopes, the triglyphs becoming the decorative elements, the absence of horizontal cornices on the ends, the extended raking cornices with ornamental soffits, the use of the Ionic order in the interior. The profile of the capitals and other architectural details suggest it was built around 500 BC.

The northern boundary of the territory of Poseidonia was marked by the river Sele, and here at Foce del Sele, the mouth of the river, a sanctuary to Hera was built, some 5 miles (8.5 km) from the city. Within the sanctuary a temple, altar, and stoa have been found, together with another building variously identified either as a treasury or as the first temple on the site. It is for the quality and quantity of sculptured stone metopes that this sanctuary is to be remarked, especially those which decorated the oldest sacred building, built around 570–560 BC. Over 30 sculptured sandstone metopes were found in the excavations. Most depict the exploits of Herakles or aspects of the Trojan War, and the decoration was evidently thought of in terms of cycles of events. Although the use of cycles on Doric friezes was to become commonplace in the Classical period, this is the earliest known example that we have. Most of the metopes show topics familiar to the Greek world of the sixth century BC (Herakles wrestling with the giant Antaios; Herakles bringing the famous boar to Eurystheus), but some are less well known. One (fig. **6.29**) showing Herakles carrying the Kerkopes bound hand and foot on a pole slung over his shoulder was popular in the West, but was not widespread.

Some metopes are in high relief, some in low, while others present figures as two-dimensional contours only (fig. **6.30**). The presence of the cutout type has led to the theory that these metopes were unfinished. It is perhaps easier to imagine, in this age of experimentation, artists ready to fill in details in paint, evoking the pictorial origins of decorated metopes in *trabeated* architecture (i.e. buildings depending on horizontal wooden beams and vertical posts). The series as a whole documents various artistic approaches, of which high relief ultimately became the most popular as the metopes of the

6.29 *Above* Metope from the Heraion at Foce del Sele, Poseidonia: Herakles and the Kerkopes. Sandstone. Height 2 ft 8 ins (81 cm). C. 570–560 BC. Paestum Museum

6.30 *Below* Metope from the Heraion at Foce del Sele, Poseidonia: suicide of Ajax. Sandstone. Height 2 ft 8 ins (81 cm). C. 570–560 BC. Paestum Museum

Parthenon, with some figures almost entirely in the round, demonstrate. If this is seen as the victory in the fifth century BC of mass over flat design, paint continued to be lavishly used, even when high relief was called for.

Selinus and Foce del Sele produced far more sculptured metopes in the early sixth century BC than the rest of the Greek world combined. Their production is contemporaneous with those of the treasury of the Sikyonians at Delphi. But if quality and quantity count for anything, it seems that the origins of sculptured stone metopes are to be sought in the Greek West. Moreover, Selinus and Foce del Sele, which produced the vast majority of metopes in the West, were frontier sites. Selinus faced the Carthaginians to the west, Foce del Sele faced the Etruscans across the river Sele to the north. So perhaps these metopes in frontier sanctuaries served not only as pleasing ornament sending encouraging and admonitory messages to Greek pilgrims, but also as baleful signals to menacing foreigners: "See what happens to those who tangle with Greeks." As with other architectural sculpture of the period the narratives are outside time. Order is produced from disorder, the Greek gods win out, Greek heroes suffer and survive.

Problems of architecture and architectural sculpture were under close scrutiny in the West. Experimental solutions were advanced, some of which were to become critical components of developed forms (the juxtaposition of Doric and Ionic, sculptured metopes), and some not (an uneven number of columns on façades, abandonment of the horizontal cornice). Though geographically peripheral and representing regional thinking, some of these developments were to be influential in the Greek heartland.

ATHENS

Access to the Acropolis was improved by building a great ramp, and the sanctuary was graced by two temples, one built in the second quarter of the century with which the limestone snaky-tailed monsters are associated (fig. **6.9**, p. 151), and a second in the last quarter adorned with marble statuary groups. Almost nothing of these temples can be seen today. The sanctuary also

had a number of small treasuries, numerous dedicatory statues and a small temple to Athena Nike, immediately outside the entrance. Much of the glorification of the cult of Athena Polias, tutelary deity of the city, may have been due to the tyrant Peisistratos, who seems even to have lived up on the Acropolis (with the gods!) for part of his tyranny. Another temple was begun, it seems, after the battle of Marathon, on the spot where the Parthenon was later to be built. This building, unfinished and surrounded by its scaffolding, was destroyed by the Persians, along with everything else on the Acropolis, when they captured the city in 480 BC.

During the Archaic period, an area northwest of the Acropolis, bounded on the north by the Eridanos river, on the west by a slope known as the Kolonos Agoraios, and on the south by the Areopagos hill, was transformed from a zone reserved for housing and cemeteries into the civic center of the city, the Agora (fig. **6.31**). This transformation was not instantaneous but gradual, and may be linked to the activities of the leading political figures of the age, Solon, Peisistratos and his sons, and Kleisthenes. Administrative and religious buildings were to stand along the western edge at the foot of the Kolonos Agoraios. The earliest of these, beneath the later Bouleuterion, may have been built to accommodate the new council of the four hundred installed by Solon.

The period of the tyranny saw the construction of several new buildings, as houses were pulled down and wells filled in to allow expansion south and east. A large building at the south end of the buildings along the foot of the Kolonos Agoraios may have been another palace for Peisistratos, while close by rose one of the principal lawcourts built around mid-century. To the north, the Altar of the Twelve Gods, surrounded by a low perimeter wall, was put in place around 520 BC. Famous as a place of refuge, this Altar was also the spot from which distances were measured in Attica, as a preserved milestone tells us. Greek tyrants seem to have favored large public construction programs, among which temples and hydraulic systems were prominent. The Athenian tyrants were no excep-

6.31 Plan of the Agora, Athens. c. 500 BC

tion. They may have been responsible for at least one of the temples on the Acropolis, and they certainly began the work on the gigantic Temple of Olympian Zeus to the southeast of the Acropolis. In the Agora they built the southeast fountain house, and the aqueduct which fed it. These installations were popular with the people, as their frequent representation on vases (fig. **6.32**) of the later sixth century BC suggests. They offered a rare opportunity for social intercourse for women and for slaves, and it was simpler by far to take water from a spout directly into a *hydria* (water jar) than draw it up from a well.

In the last decade of the century, the new democracy of Kleisthenes needed new administrative buildings. Accordingly, a new bouleuterion was built atop that of Solon. This was a rectangular chamber with provision for seating the five hundred members of the "boule." A stoa called the Royal Stoa was also built, so called since this was the office of the "archon basileus" (the king archon), the second most powerful official in the state. Other topographical matters may be noted. The principal route across the Agora, the Panathenaic Way, ran northwest–southeast, and had existed as a thoroughfare before the sixth century BC when this was a residential area. This road was used for the procession, which made its way from the lower city up onto the Acropolis, at the time of the great festival for Athena, the Panathenaia. Inscribed boundary stones "horoi" were in position by the end of the century, proclaiming boldly, "I am the boundary of the Agora," and written either left to right or right to left. Their purpose was to define the area of the Agora and to prevent infringement by unauthorized buildings or people.

6.32 Attic black-figure hydria: fountainhouse scene. Height 22⅔ ins (57.5 cm). c. 510 BC. Museum of Fine Arts, Boston

Sculpture

Greek sculptors were at work in marble on the islands of Naxos, Paros, and Samos before the end of the seventh century BC, and, before long, evidence of their work appears on the mainland, too. The two major types of sculpture in the round prevalent in the sixth century BC were the standing nude male, the *kouros* (plural, *kouroi*) and the standing clothed female, the *kore* (plural, *korai*). Throughout the period, the kouros develops on one level from over-lifesize abstraction to more naturalistic human proportions and scale. On another level sculptors were attacking the issue of how best to represent divine beauty in human form, the ideal in the real. The kore explores the relationship between garment and body, moving from complete obscuring of anatomy through hints of the body beneath, to daring revelations of limbs, in some late archaic korai. Paradoxically, the more opportunities for rendering drapery folds ornamentally in varied textures, patterns, and colors, the more visible the body became.

The huge kouroi now appear naked. The belt worn in the seventh century BC is discarded, though one or two old-fashioned figures cling to it, and there are other oddities. A kouros in the Metropolitan Museum in New York (fig. **6.33**) made around 600 BC, wears only a neckband, while the twins at Delphi (fig. **6.35**) wear boots and nothing else. Male nudity need not cause surprise, since it had occurred in the Geometric period in sculpture (bronzes), though belted, and since in life men appeared naked in the gymnasia. But there is probably more to it than that. No other nation with which the Greeks came into contact allowed male nudity, so this may have served to distinguish the Greeks from the rest. At the same time, it allowed the body, shared attribute of gods and men, to be fully revealed.

The kouroi stood in sanctuaries or cemeteries, occasionally as representations of divinities (at one time they were all thought to be images of Apollo), but most often as votive offerings to the gods, or as commemorative markers over graves. Towering, vibrant statues, they stood four square with one leg advanced and arms by their sides, held straight or slightly bent with fists clenched. The broken fragments of one such kouros were found buried in a pit in the sanctuary of Poseidon at Cape Sunion (fig. **6.34**). His massive head is larger than natural proportions would allow. Huge eyes stare determinedly ahead, again larger in proportion to the rest of the face than nature would dictate. The anatomical landscape is treated as pure pattern: ears, ribs, and knees are fixed in the surface of original marble block or figure, the sculptor preferring to define the human form by line rather than by mass. This Sunion kouros was made around 580 BC.

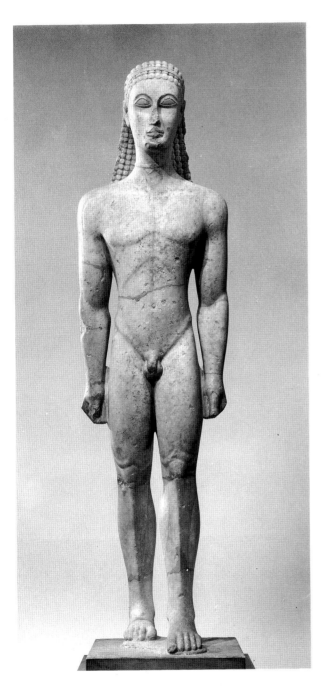

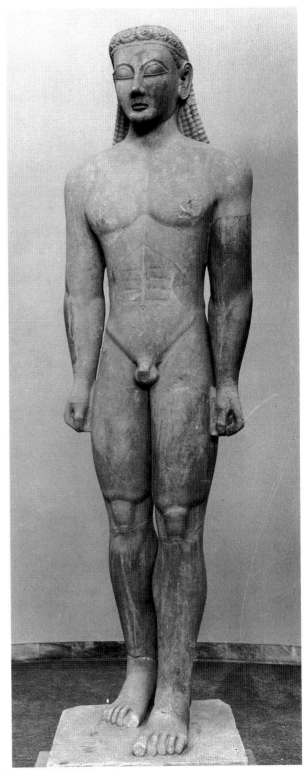

6.33 *Above* Marble kouros, the ''New York kouros,'' said to be from Attica. Height 6 ft (1.84 m). C. 600 BC. Metropolitan Museum of Art, New York

6.34 *Right* Marble kouros (left arm, left leg, and part of face restored), the ''Sunion kouros,'' from Sunion. Height 9 ft 10 ins (3 m). C. 580 BC. National Museum, Athens

The twins at Delphi (fig. **6.35**), most probably identifiable as the Dioskouroi, are shown stepping forward together. Hairstyle is reminiscent of the Daedalic Style of the preceding century. Anatomy is all pattern and line. Their short, square torsos and stocky proportions are different from those of the New York kouros or the Sunion kouros, and are associated with a regional Argive workshop. An inscription gives, infuriatingly, only half the sculptor's signature,

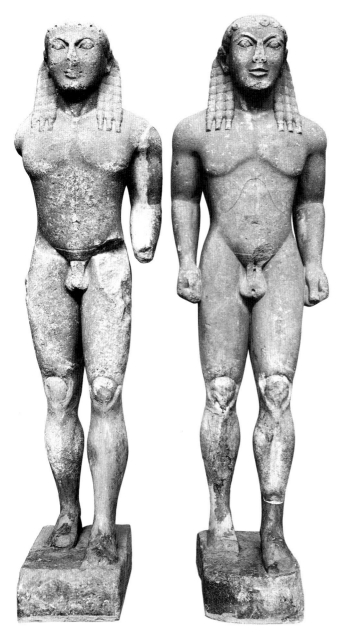

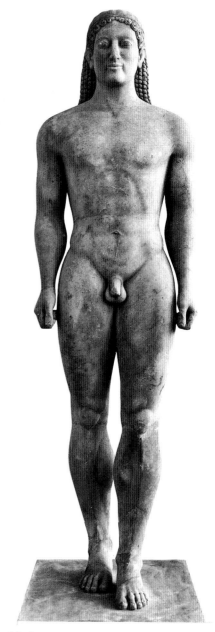

6.35 Marble kouroi, twins (possibly the Dioskouroi), from Delphi. Height 6 ft 6 ins (1.97 m). c. 580 BC. Delphi Museum

6.36 Marble kouros, the "Anavysos kouros," from Anavysos, Attica. Height 6 ft 4½ ins (1.94 m). c. 530 BC. National Museum, Athens

"... medes," but says he came from Argos. He made these handsome dedications, surely a state offering, about 580 BC.

The changing appearance of kouroi through the sixth century BC is often thought of as a progression from abstraction to naturalism. And this is part of the story. The Anavysos kouros, named after the village in Attica where he was found (fig. **6.36**) and dating to about 530 BC, shows advances towards more naturalistic proportions and more supple contours. The sculptor has penetrated the block to a greater depth, and thus achieved greater three-dimensionality. The so-called Archaic smile, not a reflection of an emotional state but an index of vitality, has appeared. Yet posture and gesture, bilateral symmetry, patternized anatomy, and hair have not relented. Some thirty years on, around 500 BC, the Aristodikos kouros (fig. **6.37**), so called since it was the gravemarker of Aristodikos, is yet more naturalistic, with shorter, though still patterned hair, the arms moving away from the flanks, and sinew and bone and knee and shin more realistic. Yet, sculptors were evidently not emulating the bodies they observed around them, though their strivings to find more compelling and worthy images to represent both gods and men were leading them away from superhuman scale and abstract linear form. The tortured struggle to emerge from the conceptual to the representational, or indeed to hold the two ideas in the same figure, continued in this chronological context until the appearance of the Kritios Boy (fig. **7.19**, p. 216). In this statue, the capacity for movement inherent in the kouroi, the sense of a functioning anatomy, at last broke loose. But there is still no attempt to differentiate in terms of age, and the kouroi are emotionless.

By the middle of the sixth century BC, other male statues in the round were being produced. In about 560 BC, the Moschophoros (Calfbearer) (fig. **6.39**) was dedicated on the Acropolis at Athens. The bearded figure, whose beaded hairdo finds parallels among early kouroi, wears a thin cloak and carries the calf, his offering, on his shoulders. Human head and animal head present patterned contrasts. Similarly found on the Acropolis at Athens was the Rampin Horse-

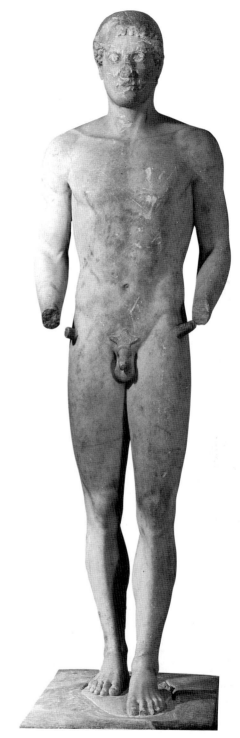

6.37 Marble kouros, the "Aristodikos kouros," from Attica. Height 6 ft 5 ins (1.95 m). c. 500 BC. National Museum, Athens

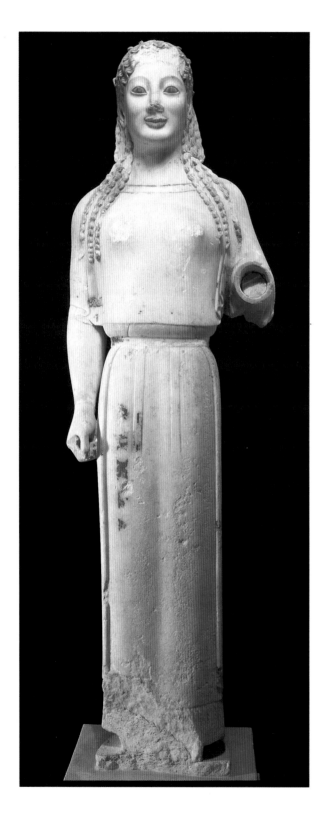

6.38 *Left* Marble kore, the ''Peplos kore,'' from Athens. Height 4 ft (1.21 m). c. 530 BC. Acropolis Museum, Athens

6.39 *Above* Marble calfbearer, ''Moschophoros,'' from Athens. Height (restored) 5 ft 5 ins (1.65 m). c. 560 BC. Acropolis Museum, Athens

man dated to around 560 BC (fig. **6.40**). The sculptor here wrestles with a complex group of a man and a horse, contrasting broad flat planes of torso and face with the extravagant heavy patterned detail of hair and head. The Acropolis at Athens is one of the major sources of Archaic statuary, since the Persians had overturned everything in their onslaught in 480 BC, and the Athenians had gathered up the shattered

6.40 Marble equestrian statue, the "Rampin Horseman," from Athens. Height (torso) 2 ft 8 ins (81 cm); (head) 11⅜ ins (29 cm). c. 560 BC. (Torso) Acropolis Museum, Athens; (head) Musée du Louvre, Paris

dress apparently depended on three major garments, the *peplos*, the *chiton*, and the *himation* or mantle, all of which amounted to little more than rectangles of cloth, buttoned or pinned, and arranged in different ways (fig. **6.41**). The peplos, often of wool, was folded down from the neck, and worn with a belt. Secured at the shoulder with pins, it was sleeveless and sometimes worn over a chiton. The chiton, often of linen, was like the peplos, a rectangle of cloth. It was buttoned along the upper edge in two sections to allow holes for head and arms and was sleeved and belted. The himation, or mantle, was a smaller oblong of cloth, buttoned along one long side, in such a way that it could be worn over the right

6.41 Diagram of garments

Chiton

Peplos

Mantle

remains and buried them tidily for archaeologists to discover at the end of the last century.

The female counterpart of the kouros is the kore, the draped standing female figure. As with the kouroi the functions of the korai were both votive and commemorative. The kore does not appear until a generation or so after the appearance of the kouroi, which is baffling. Examples continue to the end of the Archaic period, with a specially striking late Archaic series coming from the Athenian Acropolis. It seems that rich dedications to Athena were popular at the court of Peisistratos and his sons.

With korai the changes throughout the period are measured more in terms of the rendering of the drapery than of the anatomy. Female

shoulder and under the left arm. This was most often worn on top of the chiton. Sculptors throve on the multiplicity of patterns offered by the drapery, and on the ornamental qualities provided by creases, folds, and tucks of different textures of cloth. Sometimes they were so carried away by the richness of the patterns that the logic and reality of actual garments is lost.

In Attica, an early survivor is the so-called Berlin Kore (fig. **6.42**), from the decade 570–560 BC. She is notable for her frontal stance, the large features of her face, her big feet and hands, the pomegranate she holds, the simple lines of her garments, and her elaborate jewelry – a bracelet, a necklace, and earrings. She wears a tasseled mantle slung symmetrically over her shoulders, the chiton, and a painted headdress (a polos). Similarly attired, though without a mantle, and bejeweled is Phrasikleia, whose name we know from the epigram written on the base which supported her. The inscribed base which gives her name also bears the signature of the sculptor, Aristion of Paros. A gravemarker of about 550–540 BC from the countryside of Attica, she too stands with her sandaled feet together, wearing the chiton. She is richly decorated with paint. The features of her face are smaller and her proportions slimmer than those of the Berlin Kore, however, so that she may represent a combination of Attic and Island traits.

The Peplos Kore, a dedication on the Athenian Acropolis (fig. **6.38**) provides, as her name implies, an example of a kore wearing the peplos, in this instance over a chiton, the close set folds of which appear at the bottom of the figure. Dated around 530 BC, she is among the last korai to wear the peplos. Smaller than lifesize and richly decorated with paint, of which much is still visible on hair and eyes and clothing, her formal simplicity is modified through subtle asymmetries of slightly turned head, barely advanced foot and shoulder. The left forearm carrying the gift was worked separately.

With the last quarter of the century, the fashion in clothing changed, and the cross-slung himation worn over the crinkly chiton finds favor. Together with extravagantly complex hairdos, these garments offered all kind of variety in

6.42 Marble kore, the "Berlin Kore," from Keratea, Attica. Height 6 ft 3 ins (1.90 m). c. 570–560 BC. Staatliche Museen, Berlin

terms of surface decoration. Moreover, at the same time as the brilliance of the drapery is stressed, anatomical forms beneath appear more forcefully. For example, korai of this period often use one hand to pull the drapery against the limbs, thus revealing the shapes of the body beneath, as in Kore No. 682 (fig. **6.43**) from the

6.43 Marble kore, no. 682, from Athens. Height 5 ft 11½ ins (1.82 m). c. 520 BC. Acropolis Museum, Athens

Athenian Acropolis. With Kore No. 674, made around 500 BC, a new mood is discernible (fig. **6.44**). Complex patterns of coiffure, grouped folds of the chiton, and weightier textured himation folds contrast with the somber expression of the face. At the end of the series the Euthydikos Kore (fig. **6.45**) suggests that the freshness of Archaic Greece is almost at an end, and sobriety is at hand. In spite of increased three-dimensionality, with undercutting of the locks of hair at the temples, and pronounced plasticity of eyes, nose, and mouth, drapery folds are rendered almost mechanically, and the figure's expression carries more interest for the observer than delight in pattern. She, too, was found on the Athenian Acropolis, where developments are most easily followed.

In the earlier part of the century, down to around 540–530 BC, sculptors in different parts of the Greek world took different approaches to the same problems, and it has been possible to suppose a number of regional schools, though they are based only on stylistic gathering and a small body of evidence. Workshops with distinguishable traits have been identified for Naxos and Paros in the islands, and for Argos in the Peloponnese. In spite of the ample evidence of architectural sculpture from Foce del Sele and Selinus and the presence therefore of workshops in the West, Sicily and south Italy are poorly represented in kouroi and korai. There was no local marble, which may have been an inhibiting factor, and local sculptors seem to have worked more readily in terracotta. Yet at Megara Hyblaia a physician called Sombrotidas was responsible for a marble funerary kouros, dated around 550 BC. This is the earliest of the few we have from Sicily. An unfinished late-Archaic marble kore survives from Taras. Both may have been imports.

The great Sanctuary of Hera on Samos, however, has yielded much statuary, and indeed is a source of evidence second only to the Athenian Acropolis. Moreover, Samos seems to have been the location of an active workshop of sculptors, who took sharply different approaches from those pursued in Attica. The major types, kouros and kore, are the same.

6.44 *Left* Marble kore, no. 674, from Athens. Height 3 ft (92 cm). c. 500 BC. Acropolis Museum, Athens

6.45 *Above* Marble kore, the "Euthydikos kore," from Athens. Height 22⅘ ins (58 cm). c. 490 BC. Acropolis Museum, Athens

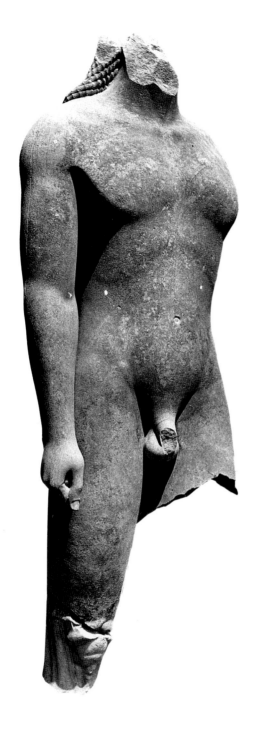

An enormous kouros (fig. **6.46**), taller even than the Sunion kouros, was dedicated here as early as the decade 580–570 BC. Though the hair is patterned into a vertebra-design, the Samian artist eschews other patterning. Posture, gesture, and theme are as in Attica, but the anatomy is treated in a more fluid, almost boneless manner. It is flesh that is sculpted rather than bone, sinew, and muscle. The face too (fig **6.47**) has a quite different shape from Attic faces, and different shapes for the eyes, mouth, and nose. Later Samian kouroi display spherically shaped heads. Hair is brushed back from the forehead and bunched up into closepacked locks over the ears in conventions unknown in Attica.

6.46 Marble kouros, from Samos. Conjectured height of whole figure, including the head 15 ft 5 ins (4.75 m). c. 580–570 BC. Samos Museum

6.47 Head (face) of marble kouros seen in fig. **6.46**, from Samos. c. 580–570 BC. Samos Museum.

An early headless kore from Samos is the so-called Hera of Samos (fig. **6.48**), a contemporary of the Berlin Kore in Attica, with whom she may be compared. Feet together, her right arm by the side, and her left brought across in front of the chest, she stands motionless and frontal. She is conspicuous for the three garments she wears. There is the chiton whose parallel vertical folds decorate the cylindrical lower body. Then there is the mantle, slung crosswise over her right shoulder and under her left arm, introducing a diagonal line into the composition. Finally, the *epiblema* (cloak) covers the back and right flank of the figure, and tucks into the belt at the front. This and similar East Greek figures are the source for the diagonal compositional elements of later Archaic korai in Athens. The sculptor enjoyed the contrasts in texture between the smooth flat epiblema, the chiton with its pleats, and the heavier folds of the mantle. The lower part of the body is lost within the tree-trunklike cylinder; in the upper, however, the contour line takes note of breasts, shoulders, and buttocks, thus initiating the interest in the relationship between anatomy and drapery. The dedicator had his name, Cheramyes, incised along the hem of the epiblema at the front where it was most visible. He must have been a man of substance since he dedicated two other korai in the sanctuary, and a kouros too. Some idea of the head type of these korai is shown in a head from Miletus, a rival state to Samos but quite close by, whose sculptors followed conventions similar to those on Samos. This head (fig. **6.49**), though veiled by the epiblema over the crown, is spherical in shape, and is characterized by narrow eyes, prominent cheekbones, full lips, and broad-winged nose. The sphere and cylinder shapes of these korai find parallels in the neo-Babylonian empire, so there may be an Eastern influence at work. While the origin of the kouros is to be sought in Egypt, that of the kore may derive from Mesopotamia.

6.48 Marble kore, the "Hera of Samos," dedicated by Cheramyes, from Samos. Height 6 ft 3½ ins (1.92 m). c. 570–560 BC. Musée du Louvre, Paris

About mid-century, a sculptor called Geneleos signed a group of figures which all stood together on the same base in the sanctuary at Samos (fig. **6.50**). They present a gallery of types: a seated figure, a clothed youth (a so-called draped kouros), korai, and a reclining figure. The seated figure, named Phileia, and the reclining male whose name is partly lost (. . . arches) may be parents of the quartet arranged between them. The draped kouros is an uncommon type which occurs mostly in the Greek East. The korai, two of whom are named, Ornithe and Philippe, wear long patternized hair and chitons. The folds of the chitons are pulled up to fall over the belt in slack pouches. One hand tugs the dress to reveal the rounded contours of the leg the other side.

6.49 *Left* Marble head of a kore wearing the epiblema over her hair, from Miletus. Height 8¼ ins (21 cm). c. 550 BC. Staatliche Museen, Berlin

6.50 *Below* Marble family group (limestone base) by Geneleos, from Samos, with names inscribed: Phileia (seated); boy, lost; girl, lost; Philippe; Ornithe, in Staatliche Museen, Berlin; . . . arches, the dedicator (reclining). Height (Ornithe) 5 ft 6 ins (1.68 m). c. 560–550 BC. Samos Museum (except Ornithe)

This motif would be much used in Athens later. A major characteristic of these sixth-century Samian korai is the hesitant revelation of the body underneath abstract linear drapery. Korai appear in other materials: a bronze (fig. **6.51**) from Samos on a smaller scale emulates lifesize marble figures, and a terracotta perfume vase (fig. **6.52**) reveals its East Greek origin through its garments, gestures, hairstyle, and the shape of its eyes and nose.

Female figures other than korai were appearing by mid-century. One is the Sphinx dedication by the Naxians at Delphi around 560 BC (fig. **6.53**). The dedication consisted of tall column, Ionic capital with widely separate volutes, and the sphinx crouching menacingly some 33 feet (10 m) in the air atop the column. Another is the personification of Nike (Victory) (fig. **6.54**), dedicated in Apollo's sanctuary on Delos, shown in the Archaic kneeling-running posture. Many see her as the earliest example of a winged Nike that has survived, the most beautiful later example of which is the Hellenistic Nike of Samothrace (fig. **10.23**, see p. 333). This early Nike wears a peplos over a chiton, the peplos lavishly painted. Dowel holes in earlobes and headdress show that metal attachments also adorned the figure.

Sculptors worked figures in relief as well, not just as decorative friezes and pediments on buildings, but also, like kouroi and korai, as votive offerings to the gods and as grave monuments. The grave stelai in Attica consist of rectangular slabs surmounted at first by capitals, then by back-to-back volute scrolls, with sphinxes atop. Later the sphinxes were replaced by palmettes. The face of the slab is most often carved in relief with a male figure or, rarely, a group of figures. Sometimes incised and painted panels appear above and below the main scene. The fragment

6.51 Bronze statuette of a woman, from Samos. Height 10⅜ ins (27 cm). c. 560–550 BC. Samos Museum

6.52 *Far left* Terracotta alabastron in the form of a woman holding a bird, from Thebes. Height 10¼ ins (26 cm). c. 560–550 BC. National Museum, Athens

6.53 *Left* Marble sphinx, dedication of the Naxians, from Delphi. Height (of sphinx) 7 ft 4⅞ ins (2.25 m). c. 560 BC. Delphi Museum

6.54 *Right* Marble statue of a Nike figure (or possibly Artemis), from Delos. Height (without base) 2 ft 11½ ins (90 cm). c. 550 BC. National Museum, Athens

6.55 Fragment of a marble grave stele, from Athens. Height 13¾ ins (35 cm). c. 560 BC. National Museum, Athens

6.56 *Left* Grave stele of Aristion, by Aristokles. Height 7 ft 10½ ins (2.40 m). c. 510 BC. National Museum, Athens

6.57 *Right* Bronze krater, from Vix. Height 5 ft 4½ ins (1.64 m). c. 510 BC. Châtillon-sur-Seine Museum

of around 560 BC from Athens (fig. **6.55**) shows the head of the dead youth framed by the discus carried on the shoulder – an athlete, then. A frontal eye in a face shown in profile is a common convention, while the hair bound with a thin cord is reminiscent of the Berlin Kore. Another frequent type is the warrior, of which the relief of Aristion by Aristokles (fig. **6.56**), identified by inscription, provides a good example. The bearded Aristion wears a helmet, a *cuirass*, *greaves*, and carries a spear in his left hand. The background was painted red, as was the hair, while blue was used on cuirass and helmet. The overall impression is of a free-standing kouros, now armed. The hairstyle points to a date around 510 BC.

Reliefs appeared in bronze too; they include the figures decorating the frieze and handles of the enormous bronze krater (fig. **6.57**) of around 510 BC found in the grave of a Celtic princess at Vix near Châtillon-sur-Seine in France. This gives evidence for a trade network reaching up and down the rivers of France, and for the interest of non-Greek chieftains in Greek goods. The handles of this huge krater are decorated with gorgons' heads and lions, and there is a continuous scene, in relief, immediately below the

6.58 Bronze Apollo, from Piraeus. Height 6 ft 3½ ins (1.92 m). c. 520 BC. National Museum, Athens

left hand, we can say he represented Apollo and served as a cult statue. Lifesize, he edges the right foot forward with both arms stretched out away from the body, his head inclining downward. Though these gestures are not echoed among sixth-century marble kouroi, most commentators date the Piraeus kouros to around 520 BC, though some date it later.

Bronzesmiths now cast their bronzes hollow, and larger bronzes were made in sections, then soldered or riveted together. Rather than use a core of wax, wax was only used to the anticipated thickness of the metal, and was placed upon a core of other material. This was a refined *cire perdue* method. As used in the Piraeus kouros, the core was built to almost the needed size of the figure and covered with wax which was then modeled. A clay covering was put on top of the wax and attached to the core with rods. The entire apparatus was then fired so that the clay hardened and the wax melted and ran out. Molten bronze was then poured through apertures, to enter between clay and core, and form the figure or limb. After cooling, the clay shell was broken off and the figure or part of the body appeared.

rim, like an Ionic frieze on a building. Four-horse chariots ("quadrigas") with charioteers alternate with dismounted warriors, in repeated groups. The way the heads of the nearest horses turn downward and outward towards the viewer is reminiscent of the varied views of horses' heads in the east frieze of the treasury of the Siphnians at Delphi. It also foreshadows the quadrigas of the Parthenon frieze.

Bronze was even more precious than marble, and easier to reuse, for it could be readily melted down and recast. Thus very little has survived. However, one intriguing lifesize kouros of bronze (fig. **6.58**) has come to light in excavations in Piraeus, the harbor town of Athens, where it was found with a group of later statues. All were apparently ready for export, perhaps sometime during the second century BC, or later when the Romans were making off with captured Greek goods. Since he originally carried a bow in the

Pottery

By the beginning of the sixth century BC Athenian craftsmen were masters of potting and painting. They were using large-scale narrative themes, orientalizing motifs, and the black-figure technique (as on the Nessos amphora, fig. **5.9**, p. 128). Much of this had been learnt from Corinth, and, having learnt the business, Athens was now poised to move in on the markets where Corinthian pottery enjoyed a virtual monopoly. Athens was helped not least by the high quality of her clay, which was malleable and a warm deep orange color when fired.

There are plenty of clay beds in Attica, so supply presented no problem. After the clay was dug from its bed, it needed to be cleaned of natural impurities. This was done by mixing the clay with water and letting the impurities sink to the bottom, a process called "levigation." It was repeated until the clay was clean enough for the potter's requirements. A certain amount of clay was then kneaded with the hands, like dough, to the desired consistency (a process known as "wedging"), then placed on the wheel. As the wheel turned at speed, the clay was pulled up by the fingers into the required shape. The pot was made in several pieces: the body, the spout, and the foot, with handles being made by a different method. Sometimes the body of a larger pot was also made in sections. The separate pieces were then allowed to dry until they had the consistency of leather. The pieces were then joined together with *slip*, which is clay in a more liquid form.

Then the pot was decorated. The terms "paint" and "glaze" are still used, since they are entrenched and convenient, but in fact Greek vase painters used neither; they used special slips, some of which contained pigments from metal. Black is the critical color, contrasted with the orange-red of the fired clay. The "black glaze" (or, more accurately, "gloss") came from highly purified normal clay which turned black in the kiln, thanks to a particular firing process. Other colors which continued to be used in the sixth century BC were a purple-red and white. The white was a fine pure clay, with no iron oxide impurity which would have colored it when fired. The purple-red was made from slip, which was a mixture of the black-producing clay and red iron oxide pigment. These color-producing slips were applied with different kinds of brushes, and then fired in the kiln. Obviously, the firing was all-important.

A number of kilns have been excavated in various parts of the Greek world, so we have a good idea of what they looked like and how they worked. The main point is that in the course of firing, the body of the pot turned red and the "painted" parts black. The firing process had three stages. The pots were first placed in the upper part of the kiln, the firing chamber (fig. **6.59**); the fire was lit and the temperature was raised to about 800 degrees centigrade with air allowed free access. These were oxidizing conditions, and the pots became red all over. The second stage called for placing green wood on the fire and closing off access for air, producing reducing conditions. The temperature first had to go up to about 950 degrees and was then allowed to fall back to about 900 degrees. In the course of this, the pots became black all over. At about 950 degrees the surface of areas covered with black-producing purified clay became partially vitrified. This seal prevented the re-entry of oxygen and the consequent return to red which would occur on the other parts of the pot in the next stage. In this third stage, air was allowed in again, an oxidizing condition, and the kiln allowed to cool entirely. Areas of the pot painted with black gloss remained black, but others turned red once more. By the end of the century, the major shapes of pottery produced by this process were already being made (fig. **6.60**).

6.59 Diagram of a Greek kiln
 1 Stoking tunnel
 2 Firing chamber
 3 Central post
 4 Pierced floor
 5 Stacking chamber
 6 Spyhole and hatch
 7 Removable section of the wall to enable loading
 8 Vent hole
 9 Cover for stoking tunnel

6.60 *Opposite* Shapes of Greek vases

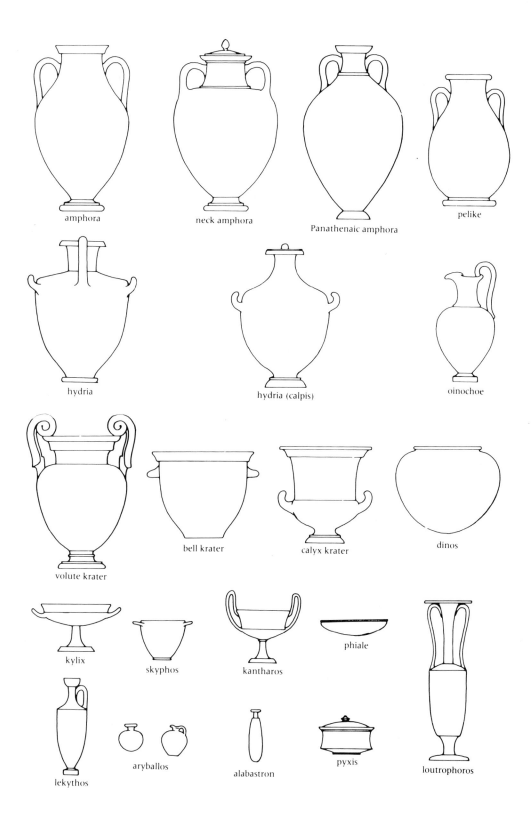

amphora

neck amphora

Panathenaic amphora

pelike

hydria

hydria (calpis)

oinochoe

volute krater

bell krater

calyx krater

dinos

kylix

skyphos

kantharos

phiale

lekythos

aryballos

alabastron

pyxis

loutrophoros

ATHENS

In the first quarter of the century, painters were decorating vessels with animal friezes drawn from the Corinthian vocabulary, rampant floral and palmette passages of Orientalizing origin, and mythological stories. Often the scale is small and the black-figure technique is favored. Sophilos, the first vase painter whose name we know (from the signature proudly displayed, "Sophilos megraphsen") decorated a cauldron (*dinos* or *lebes*) and its stand in this manner (fig. **6.66**, p.188). Friezes of tightly drawn animals and florals appear below the main narrative strip. There is much added purple and white, the white always used for women's faces and exposed limbs. Inscriptions are painted on to identify individual characters. The scene depicts the arrival of guests for the marriage feast at the house of Peleus. Guests include the centaur Chiron and Hebe, conspicuous for her gaily painted peplos decorated with animal friezes which echo the ornament on the vase itself. Peleus welcomes them, offering the refreshing kantharos, while Thetis bides her time within the house whose façade we see: white Doric columns and metopes, purple door, black antae.

The next quarter century sees the high point of the Athenian black-figure miniature style. A volute krater, known as the François Vase (figs **6.61**, **6.62**) after the excavator who found it, came to light in the earlier part of the nineteenth century in Etruria. The Etruscans were always fond of Greek vases, and by now the Athenians were displacing the Corinthians as providers of table wares. The krater is decorated with six figured friezes on either side, of which only one shows the old-fashioned animals and florals. From now on, their appearance is relegated to subsidiary, unimportant zones. The other five friezes show over two hundred figures in closely drawn compositions, many of which are identified by inscriptions. Inscriptions also identify the potter (Ergotimos) and the painter (Kleitias).

Kleitias drew his black-filled figures against

6.61 Attic black-figure volute krater, "the François Vase," by Kleitias and Ergotimos. From the top: Kalydonian boar hunt; funeral games for Patroklos; marriage of Peleus and Thetis; ambush of Troilos. Height 2 ft 2 ins (66 cm). c. 570 BC. Archaeological Museum, Florence

the orange-red ground, starting with contours, then filling in with black and using precise incision to shape interior details. His figures throw their arms in the air expressing delight as their boat comes in (fig. **6.62**, the top register); they leap ashore; they dance. Below, centaurs and Lapiths fight. On the major frieze between the handles, guests in chariots and others walking approach in another version of the procession preceding the wedding feast of Peleus and Thetis. In the frieze below, Zeus and Hera, seated on Olympus, await another arrival, that of the drunken Hephaistos on his excited donkey. The wedding procession is the only scene which travels the whole way around the krater. On the other side, Peleus greets his guests (fig. **6.61**).

Kleitias used architecture – the house of Peleus, the fountain house, the walls of Troy – to suggest locale, and to punctuate compositions. Profile, three-quarter, and even frontal views of figures are shown, as the painter tried to show the human body in varied movement and in space. Figures are massed as many as four deep in the wedding procession, yet only overlapping suggests depth. Kleitias created a masterpiece of draftsmanship and composition, crisp and detailed, and a veritable encyclopaedia of mythological events.

6.62 *Above* Attic black-figure volute krater, "the François Vase," by Kleitias and Ergotimos. From the top: arrival of Athenians; centauromachy; marriage of Peleus and Thetis continued; return of Hephaistos to Olympos. See fig. **6.61**

6.63 Attic black-figure cup, attributed to the Taras Painter. Height 5½ ins (13.9 cm). c. 560 BC. National Museum, Athens

Kraters were used to mix the wine, and cups of various shapes to drink it. The drinking cup (kylix) shown in figure **6.63** was made in Athens around 560 BC and is attributed to the Taras Painter, so named because many cups made by him were exported to Taras (modern Taranto) in south Italy. Sophilos painted and signed the dinos, already mentioned (p. 184), and Kleitias the François Vase, but many vessels like this cup were unsigned.

Pieces made by the same artist can, however, be recognized, in the same way that art historians can attribute unsigned works of Renaissance painting, for example, to different artists, but it is a highly prized skill. It is easier if there is a signed work from which to begin, diagnose characteristic traits, and then attribute unsigned works to the same hand on stylistic grounds. But stylistic grouping can take place even without a signature. An anonymous artist receives his names for various reasons: for the popularity of his work in a particular place, or where his work is now found; or, like the ''Amasis Painter'', because only the potter, Amasis, signed his name.

The exterior of this black-figure cup shows a cavalcade of young, privileged Athenians in regular procession. Detailed incision is limited, confined to salient contours. There is added purple on horses flanking the central horse which was painted white. This was a suitable scene of aristocratic activity on a cup likely to be used in another aristocratic milieu, the symposium.

Two painters dominated production in Athens in the third quarter of the century: the Amasis Painter and Exekias. The Amasis Painter decorated both small and large vessels. He used the precision and delicacy which were characteristic of Kleitias but on an enlarged scale. An amphora, now in Paris, aptly represents his work (fig. **6.65**). The principal surface of the pot is opened up, not cramped by registers, and the major scene is flanked by calligraphic volutes and palmettes. A stately Dionysos (identified by the inscription over his head, the kantharos, the ivy wreath) greets a pair of dancing *maenads*, female members of his retinue. There is precision of draftsmanship here, in the beard and long flow-

ing hair of Dionysos, in the garments and captive animals of the maenads, and delicacy of brushwork in the contours of faces, fingers, arms, and garments. There is also strength in the successfully enlarged and balanced figures, and an engaging lightness and elegance of tone. Painter and potter may have been the same man. If so, it is strange to us that he does not say so. Amasis, the potter, is a Greek form of the Egyptian name, Ahmosis, and it is possible he may have been an Egyptian, or partly Egyptian. But there was a vogue for using foreign names or sobriquets in certain classes in Athens in the middle years of the century.

The representation of emotional states, seen in lighter vein in the Amasis Painter's amphora, and glimpsed too in Kleitias' arriving mariners, is taken up more seriously by Exekias. The sadness and resignation of Ajax as he prepares his suicide (fig. **6.64**), and the emotional intensity of

6.64 *Above* Attic black-figure amphora by Exekias: suicide of Ajax. Height (of field) 9½ ins (24 cm). c. 540 BC. Musée des Beaux Arts, Boulogne

6.65 *Opposite* Attic black-figure amphora by the Amasis Painter: Dionysos and Maenads. Height 13 ins (33 cm). c. 540–530 BC. Bibliothèque Nationale, Paris

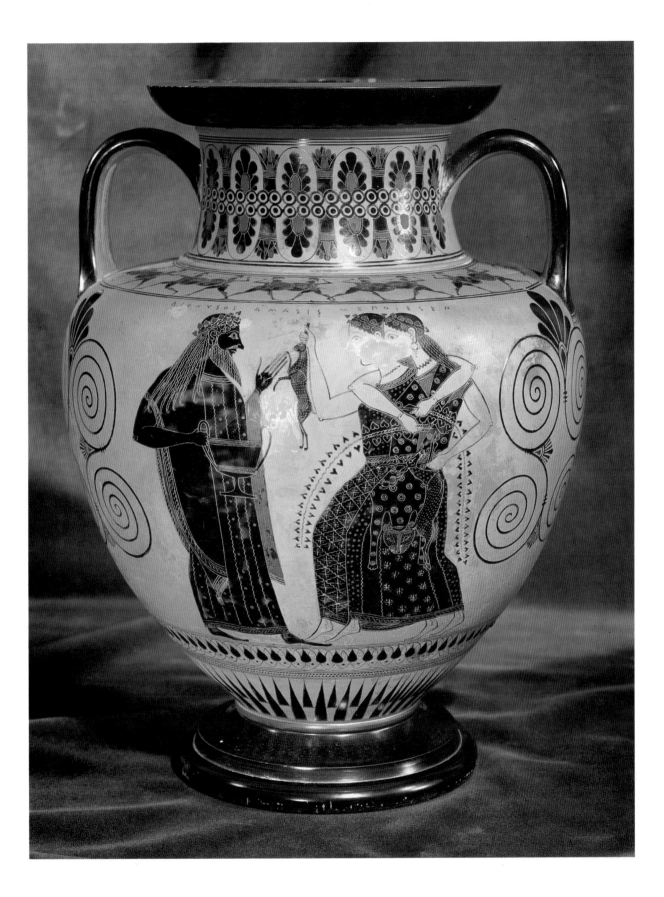

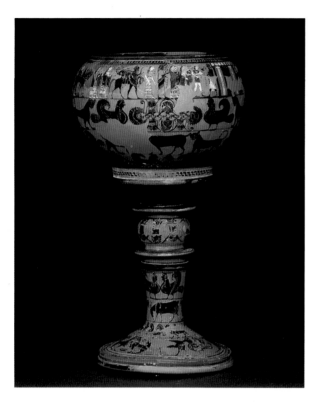

6.66 *Left* Attic black-figure dinos and stand by Sophilos: (dinos) Peleus welcoming gods to the wedding feast; (stand) Animal style registers. Height (of figures) 35 ins (8 cm). c. 580 BC. British Museum, London

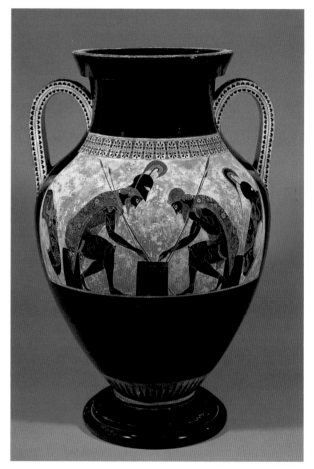

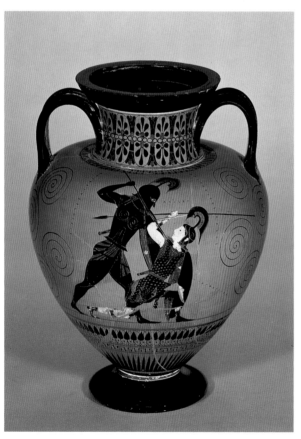

6.67 *Left* Attic black-figure amphora by Exekias: Achilles killing Penthesilea. Height 16⅔ ins (41.6 cm). c. 540–530 BC. British Museum, London

6.68 *Above* Attic black-figure amphora by Exekias: Ajax and Achilles playing a game. Height 2 ft (61 cm). c. 540–530 BC. Vatican Museums, Rome

Achilles and Penthesilea as their eyes lock on each other at the moment of her death (fig. **6.67**) are just two themes successfully rendered. Perhaps Exekias' best known vase is the amphora showing on one side the Dioskouroi at home after the hunt, and on the other Achilles and Ajax playing a game (dice?) (fig. **6.68**). Draftsmanship and brushwork, crispness and control of detail, balance and power of composition may all be taken for granted by this master in this masterpiece. What is so striking is the implied narrative and the implied emotion. The warriors play their homely game, armed, spears and shields at the ready. They are at Troy. Achilles' anger has taken him out of the combat, but the viewer knew he would return, and knew of the dire events which were to follow. Seemingly peaceful, this scene is full of foreboding, ominous with pent-up rage shortly to be released.

Most of the themes used in the earlier part of the century to decorate pots at Athens involved gods and heroes, scenes of myth and aristocratic conduct. During the second half of the century the exploits of Herakles became so popular that it has been proposed that Herakles was used as a propaganda image for the Peisistratid tyranny. Slowly, new motifs of everyday life and social commentary were introduced, alongside more genre scenes of symposia and athletics. By the last quarter of the century, women appear chatting on hydriai (water-jars) at fountain houses (fig. **6.32**, p. 166), conceivably reflecting the newfound enthusiasm for public works (aqueducts and fountains rather than private wells), or even an actual fountain house in Athens. Cobblers are shown at work in their shops.

CORINTH

The Animal Style continued to dominate production but was becoming coarser and less disciplined. Blizzards of fillers packed the background, so that the deterioration of the drawing of the animals was less palpable, but by 575 BC the style was in steep decline and by 550 BC it was obsolete.

As to the figure style, Corinth was soon under great pressure. The Exekias amphora showing

6.69 Corinthian krater by the Three Maidens Painter: a marriage procession. Height 16¾ ins (42.5 cm). c. 560 BC. Vatican Museums, Rome

Ajax and Achilles at their game was found in Etruria, as were many other Athenian vases of high quality of the middle years of the century. Athenians were busy trading with Etruscans and with Western Greeks, and were rapidly depriving Corinthians of their markets. Corinthian artisans reacted sharply. Potters even covered their pots sometimes with an orange-red slip to emulate the more appealing color of Athenian clay. Corinthian painters baulked, however, at the freer compositions of the Athenians, and at the plethora of incision, preferring, it seems, richness and variety of color. A krater (fig. **6.69**) from around 560 BC shows a chariot scene, dense with figures, single, in pairs, and in groups. The married couple in the chariot are surrounded by friends. There is a great deal of added red and white paint. While incision is used for detail on black ground, on white, details are painted. Such vessels found their way to the West, but Etruscan preference for Athenian wares put paid to their production, and by the third quarter of the century, output for export at Corinth was moribund.

ELSEWHERE

In Laconia, the district in the southern Peloponnese whose chief city was Sparta, vase painters who had used the outline technique in the seventh century from around 600 BC began to produce black-figure vases. Most were for local consumption, but some found favor abroad. They were especially popular at Taras in south Italy, a colony of Sparta, and have been found at Cyrene and Tocra in North Africa. The high-stemmed, deep-bowled cup is a familiar Laconian shape. Interiors were decorated with scenes of combat, mythology, or daily life. One interior (fig. **6.70**) offers a rare glimpse of history in Greek art: the king of Cyrene, Arkesilas – hence the painter is called the Arkesilas Painter – is shown seated, supervising the weighing and loading of cargo in a scene full of incident and local color. The Hunt Painter introduced a novel idea, that of showing part of a scene as if through a porthole, simply ignoring the compositional problem posed by the tondo of the cup. So (fig. **6.71**) the circular shape (the porthole) is divided into a lower part which provided the ground line for the main scene and an upper part. Here, in the lower part, or "exergue," a trio of bulky tunny fish are shown. Fishes, dolphins, and other

6.70 Laconian black-figure cup (interior) by the Arkesilas Painter: King Arkesilas of Cyrene supervising the loading of cargo. Diameter 11⅔ ins (29 cm). c. 560 BC. Cabinet des Médailles, Paris

6.71 Laconian black-figure cup (interior) by the Hunt Painter: a boarhunt. Diameter 7⅔ ins (19.5 cm). c. 550 BC. Musée du Louvre, Paris

6.72 Chalkidian black-figure column krater: cocks and snakes. Height 14½ ins (37 cm). c. 530 BC. Martin von Wagner Museum, Würzburg

marine motifs were popular among Laconian painters. Above, hunters pursue a boar of which only the wounded posterior and curly tail are visible. Birds, another common ornamental motif in Sparta, dart about vigorously. The style is mannered, with flat figures, but flourished in mid-century and lasted until about 525 BC.

In the East, the Wild Goat Style of the seventh century BC entered into a period of quiet decline, and though black-figure is introduced alongside the outline, the drawing of animals became coarser and coarser until it petered out around 560 BC. In the West, communities evidently preferred to import painted pottery rather than make it. At first, Corinthian, then Athenian imports dominate. Two groups of pottery, however, deserve attention. Somewhere unknown, though perhaps at Rhegium (modern Reggio) in Italy, a number of vase painters who wrote their inscriptions in Greek and are known as the Chalkidian school produced elegant designs and energetic figures (fig. **6.72**). Their decorative power and precision of drawing are comparable to Athenian black-figure painting. Their production lasted from around 550 to 500 BC, almost all of it retrieved in the West. Another group of pots, hydriai, was produced at Caere in Etruria by an artist (or artists) who wrote in Greek and was familiar with Greek mythology (fig. **6.79**, p. 197). These hydriai are notable for the amount and variety of color used (purple-red, white, and brown) in the black-figure technique, and for their humorous tone.

ATHENIAN RED-FIGURE

Around 530 BC, the conventions of black-figure were becoming stale. Black silhouette, incised detail, added red for hair, beards, and on garments, added white for women's faces and limbs and garments, frontal chests and profile contours, frontal eyes in profile faces, emotion shown by gesture, all began to seem inadequate, at least for expressing the body in realistic motion and emotional states. A number of new techniques, including experiments with a white ground, were tried, of which the *red-figure* technique was the most successful. The method was the reverse of black-figure. The figure now

(a)

(b)

6.73 (a & b) Attic bilingual (black-figure and red-figure) amphora from Andokides' workshop: Herakles driving a bull. c. 520 BC. Museum of Fine Arts, Boston

6.74 Attic red-figure kalyx krater by Euphronios: Herakles struggling with Antaios. Height 19 ins (48 cm). c. 510 BC. Musée du Louvre, Paris

remains the red color of the clay, and it is the background which becomes black. Outlines of figures were drawn with a brush on the surface of the pot, inner details were also drawn, and the background then "painted" black. Contours (outlines) and salient inner lines were drawn with a strong line, which sometimes stands off the surface and is termed a *relief line* (acquired by using a thicker slip), while details of anatomy and drapery were often drawn with a thinner line known as a "dilute glaze line" that fires to brown rather than black. The brush allows more fluidity to line than any *burin*, the instrument used for incising, and obviously made realistic representation of the anatomy in motion, of three-quarter views, foreshortening, garments in motion, and human emotion and moods much easier to portray. Added color almost disappears; dress and anatomy now distinguish males from females.

It is the anonymous painter who painted pots made by Andokides, and hence known as the Andokides Painter, who is most often thought of as the inventor of red-figure. To begin with, he and others demonstrate their versatility by decorating pots on one side in the old-fashioned technique and on the other in the new. Such pots are called "bilinguals." Herakles and a sacrificial bull (fig. **6.73**) appear on one side in red-figure and on the other in black-figure. Frequently, however, the front and the back of the pot show different scenes. Sometimes different painters paint different sides of the same pot.

By the late sixth century BC a group of experimentally minded painters was following the Andokides Painter. They are known as the "Pioneers" because of their daring attempts at new poses and views. One of them was called Euphronios. A panel on one of his kraters (fig. **6.74**) shows an apparently serene Herakles wres-

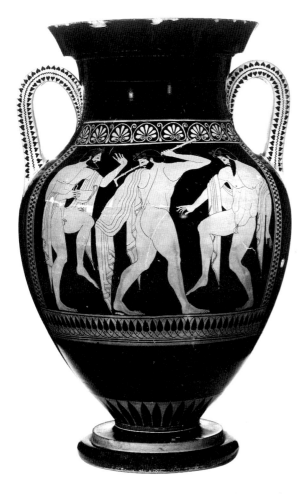

6.75 Attic red-figure amphora by Euthymides: revelers. Height 23⅝ ins (60 cm). c. 510 BC. Staatliche Antikensammlungen, Munich

tling with the giant Antaios in an uncomfortable pose. One of Antaios' arms hangs limp, and he grits his teeth in pain. Euphronios shows awkward postures and emotional states in precisely painted detail and is known for his liking for anatomical detail of bone and muscle, wrinkle of flesh, and vein. Another of the Pioneers was called Euthymides. An amphora by him (fig. **6.75**) shows bearded and older men at their revels. Gestures and poses are varied; relief lines and dilute glaze lines explore the body in motion. The three-quarter view is successfully negotiated, even if the twisting back view fails. The Pioneers knew one another's work well enough. They

used their rivals' names for characters in their scenes. They even issued challenges: on this amphora Euthymides wrote, ''Euphronios never managed anything like this.''

The way Euphronios and Euthymides explored various states of motion has suggested that vase painters led the way in interest in the body in motion. Contemporary work by sculptors working in the round was still obedient to a static code, as the Aristodikos kouros (fig. **6.37**, p. 169) shows. Even figures in relief sculpture on grave monuments remained stiff and automatic like Ariston (fig. **6.56**, p. 180). Yet, in architectural sculpture, in figures from the west pediment at Aegina (fig. **6.11**, p. 152) and in reliefs on statue bases the body is shown in new and varied poses and in motion. So developments in vase painting, in some categories of relief sculpture, and, in architectural sculpture appear to have been happening at the same time. It is plainly the case, however, that enthusiasm for the body in motion was only to come later to sculptors in the round. They preferred the abstract form, and their objectives seem to have gone beyond accurate representation of the anatomy, in motion or not.

A kylix found in the Athenian agora (fig. **6.76**) exemplifies the state of development at about 500 BC. The exterior shows on one side Achilles and Memnon in combat, flanked by two gesticulating women, and on the other Dionysos and his entourage, maenad and satyrs making merry. The interior shows a youth half kneeling, balancing himself with a stick in his left hand and holding a hare by the ears in his right. He wears only a cloak, which frames the torso, and a wreath. Profile and three-quarter views are confidently drawn with relief and dilute glaze lines. His feet are foreshortened and the eye is no longer frontal. Incision is still used for the outline of the hair on top of the head. The potter Gorgos signed on the interior. He may have been the painter, too. The topics he chose to illustrate were those in vogue: an episode from the world of heroes on one exterior side, and on the other a generalized Dionysiac scene of merriment. The scene of everyday life on the interior has erotic overtones (the hare is the lover's gift). The name of

6.76 *Right and below* Attic red-figure kylix by Gorgos: (exterior) Achilles fights Memnon; (interior) half-kneeling youth with staff and hare. Height $2\frac{7}{8}$ ins (7.4 cm). c. 500 BC. Agora Museum, Athens

"Krates" is written on one side, and "kalos" on the other. It means "Krates is handsome." Such "kalos" inscriptions, used to praise a person's good looks (more often male than female), begin in the middle years of the century and last to the end of the fifth. The names change over the years with some rapidity, but serve to identify a favored youth (or courtesan) of the moment.

In the last twenty years of the Archaic period, around 500–480 BC, pupils of the Pioneers came to to the fore. Of these, two, the Berlin Painter and the Kleophrades Painter, concentrated on larger vessels. The Berlin Painter liked elegant single figures or small groups (fig. **6.77**) on groundlines, against a background so dark that the effect is of spotlighting. The Kleophrades Painter liked busier, more energetic scenes with sturdier figures. Both continued to explore space, expressions of mood, and the anatomy of movement. Three-quarter views of faces and of feet attempt to increase the sense of depth in two-dimensional images. Their specialization in larger vessels is paralleled by that of others in smaller ones, especially in cups. Of the cup painters, Douris was especially productive, working from about 500–470 BC, and painting – it has been thought – as many as ten thousand pots in the course of his career. Another, the Brygos Painter (fig. **6.78**), enjoyed decorating some of his cups with mythological scenes, and others with Dionysiac scenes

of revelry and drinking – a suitable ornament, obviously, for a cup. One Dionysiac scene shows satyrs so aroused that they attack the gods; another displays in sombre mood the unfortunate effects of a night on the town. His work is easily recognizable by the dots he sprinkles on the cloaks his characters wear. He paints in crisp waving lines and is a master of mood, sometimes sympathetic, sometimes violent.

By the end of the period, all the skills were acquired to render public buildings in stone, dense with sculptural decoration if required, to sculpt realistic human figures which moved naturalistically, either in the round or in relief, and to paint pots with equally convincing figures moving in suggestive space. The period of experimentation was passed. That of maturity was at hand.

6.77 *Left* Attic red-figure amphora attributed to the Berlin Painter: a reveler. Height 19½ ins (49 cm). c. 490 BC. British Museum, London

6.78 *Above* Attic red-figure cup (detail) by the Brygos Painter: a reveller and companion. c. 490 BC. Musée du Louvre, Paris

6.79 *Opposite* Caeretan black-figure hydria: Herakles running riot among white-shirted Egyptians at the court of King Busiris. Height 17½ ins (44.5 cm). c. 530–520 BC. Kunsthistorisches Museum, Vienna

7
The Period of Transition
c. 480–450 BC

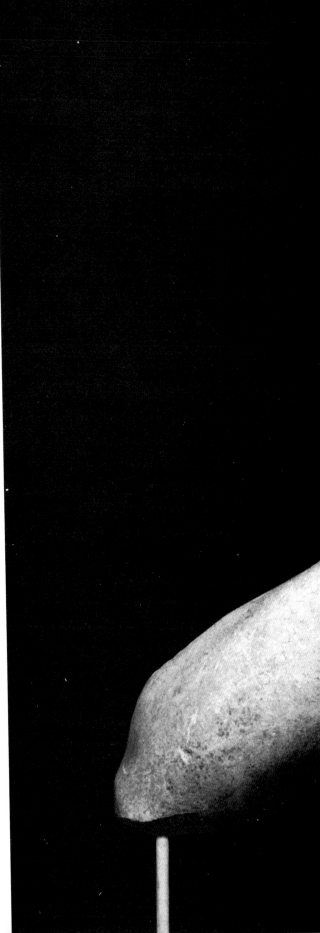

The Archaic era ends conventionally around 480 BC. This is partly because that year marks a critical moment in Greek history, when the Persian invasion was halted. In addition, excavations on the Acropolis at Athens have recovered well-dated deposits of materials shattered by the Persians, and tidily buried by the Athenians in the aftermath. However, some important changes from Archaic to Classical style had begun to take place before 480 BC: in vase painting even before 500 BC, and in sculpture in the period between 500 and 480 BC.

The years from the end of the Archaic era to around 450 BC are known as the Transitional or Early Classical period. The term Transitional is most aptly applied to the sculpture, where human figures were transformed from the stiff Archaic symbols of life into realistic moving images. The style of sculpture is often known as the Severe Style from the

Opposite Detail from the east pediment, Temple of Zeus, Olympia: the seer, Iamos, fig. **7.4**. Marble. c. 460 BC. Olympia Museum

uncompromisingly stern expressions of many figures and from the plain, heavy style of the drapery. However, continued interest in Archaic pattern and measurement restrained the new enthusiasm for representing real life. The balance between anatomical accuracy and expression of the ideal in human form was not achieved until the second half of the century. Similarly, in architecture, experiments continued in terms of proportion and measurement, but it was not until the second half of the century that the need to mix the Doric order with the Ionic was fully realized. In vase painting innovations in studies of perspective anticipated the more elaborate and sensual renderings of the last quarter of the century. And so the term "Transitional period" is a convenient label for the years between the Archaic and High Classical eras.

ATHENS AND THE WESTERN GREEKS

When the Persians withdrew from Greece, no peace treaty was signed and the war continued. The Spartans had little inclination to follow up the victory at Plataea, now that the interlopers were out of Greece, and the field was clear for Athens. By 477 BC the city had set up the Delian League, a consortium of Greek poleis allied against Persia. Its headquarters, ostensibly, and its treasury were on the holy island of Delos in the central Aegean. Member states were to contribute either ships or money for the activities of the League. Some offered ships, but many chose to give money, used to build a huge fleet under the supervision of Athens.

The political direction of the League soon became evident. Athens, the first among equals, *primus inter pares*, encouraged cities to give money rather than ships, since the money converted into ships built and manned by Athenians suited her purpose. Cities were badgered into joining the League, while others who wished to leave the League were not allowed to do so. So, democracy at home practiced empire abroad. All this happened under the leadership of a man called Kimon, son of the great Athenian hero at Marathon, Miltiades.

Operations against the Persians were successful, crowned by a great naval victory at the mouth of the river Eurymedon in the 460s BC, but this was followed by a serious reverse in Egypt in 454 BC. The Athenians used this setback, and the implied insecurity of Delos now exposed to Persian interference, as an excuse to transfer the treasury of the League from Delos to Athens. Henceforth Athena herself was allocated one sixtieth of all monies contributed to the League, while Athens took the rest. The transition from confederacy to empire was complete. The Spartans viewed these developments with distaste, and though they waged land campaigns with their allies against Athens in the 450s BC, this did not succeed in breaking Athens' hold on her empire. Around the middle of the century a peace, the date of which is uncertain (perhaps 449 BC), was made at last between Greece and Persia. The period ends with Athens' star in the ascendancy, major building programs about to begin in the city and in Attica, and with Sparta keeping a jealous eye on Athenian ambition.

In the west, Syracuse emerged as the leading power. The first tyrant, Gelon, brought half the population of Gela with him as well as supporters from Megara Hyblaia and Camarina and ten thousand newly enfranchised mercenaries when he took up the invitation to become tyrant in 486 BC. This new Syracuse was ratified by the victory that he and his fellow tyrant, Theron of Akragas, won over the Carthaginians at Himera in 480 BC. The Carthaginian ships were burnt, their troops enslaved, their leader Hamilcar killed. They were obliged to pay a huge war indemnity. With this, Gelon built a new temple for Athena in Syracuse, much of it still visible today, encased in the cathedral. He also renovated the Temple of Apollo (see pp. 158–9) and built a new agora.

Many West Greek cities had built treasuries at Olympia, and now Syracuse built hers. A gold tripod was dedicated at Delphi. Gelon died in 478 BC and was succeeded by his brother Hieron, who favored the literary arts as much as Gelon had his building programs. Hieron's reign too was strengthened by military success over enemies, this time over the Etruscans at the battle of Cumae in 474 BC. Hieron patronized the great lyric poets – Pindar, Simonides, and Baccylides – welcoming them to his court and giving them commissions.

7.1 Restored elevation of the Temple of Zeus, Olympia. c. 460 BC

7.2 Plan of the Temple of Zeus, Olympia. c. 460 BC

Aeschylus, too, was brought to Syracuse to stage the *Persae*, so that, like Athens, Syracuse became a leading center of both politics and the arts. A third brother, Thrasybulus, succeeded Hieron in 467 BC (a fourth, Polyzalos, remained behind in Gela as tyrant there), only to be supplanted by a democracy in the following year. Rich in land, in natural resources, and in commerce, blessed with two harbors and commanding access to Sicily from Greece, by 450 BC Syracuse, as well as Sparta, was on a collision course with Athens.

The Greeks were so angered by the Persians' destruction of their sanctuaries that, after the battle of Plataea, they took an oath (the oath of Plataea) not to rebuild them; their desolation was to be a perpetual reminder of Persian barbarism. This sentiment was very strongly held in Athens, where the Persians had burnt all the buildings on the Acropolis as well as smaller temples in the agora. There is, therefore, little evidence in Athens of building in sanctuaries between 480 BC and 450 BC.

Architecture and architectural sculpture

OLYMPIA

At Olympia, in the great sanctuary of Zeus, the Greeks decided to build a temple for Zeus himself, alongside the earlier sixth-century BC temple of Hera. The Temple of Zeus (fig. **7.1**) was built by a local architect, Libon of Elis, in the years between about 470 and 450 BC. The Spartans gave a gold shield to be suspended in one of the gables as a thanks offering for a victory in 457 BC, so much of the exterior must have been completed by then. The temple stood for centuries and was seen and described in detail by Pausanias in the second century AD. It eventually collapsed, and a thick deposit of silt and sand caused by floods from nearby rivers washed over the site. The site was lost for many years and little robbed. Thanks to the energetic and careful activity of German scholars it has now produced almost all the sculptural decoration of the temple and enough architectural blocks for the building to be convincingly restored, at least on paper.

The temple was of the Doric order. It followed the Classical fifth-century rule that the number of columns in the flanks should be one more than double that on the façades. Accordingly, the plan (fig. **7.2**) shows six columns on the façade by 13 on the flank, a porch, cella, and opisthodomos. Porch columns and antae align with columns of the façade. Proportions of the elevation have evolved from massive Archaic to more slender Classical, with taller columns and thinner shafts. In height columns measure 4.64 times the lower diameters on the front, 4.72 times on the flank, sturdier than at Aegina, but slimmer than at Corinth. As befitted Zeus, the temple was the biggest finished in Greece before the Parthenon. At a length of nearly 70 yards (almost 64 m), however, it was dwarfed by other temples to Zeus in the West (Akragas, and probably Selinus). The materials used were local limestone, covered with stucco to hide blemishes, for building blocks, and marble for rooftiles and sculptures. Both pediments were decorated with

groups of figures, according to Pausanias, but exterior metopes were blank. However, sculptured metopes did decorate the friezes over the entrance to the porches, six at the front and six at the back. Pausanias' description of the pedimental figures is helpful but also poses problems. For example, he says that Pelops stood on the left of Zeus, but neglected to say whether he means the left of the statue, or the viewer's left. Thus his account presents an intriguing example of the utility and difficulty of primary sources.

East Pediment. The scene in the east pediment shows the preparations for the chariot race between Pelops and Oinomaos, who stand either side the central figure of Zeus (fig. **7.3**), flanked by their womenfolk, grooms, and chariots (fig. **7.1**). The story was superficially suitable for Olympia, since Pelops was long worshipped there, a chariot race was at home at the site of the

7.3 Temple of Zeus, Olympia, east pediment, marble: central figures. Height (of Zeus) as preserved, c. 10 ft 2½ ins (3.10 m). c. 460 BC. Olympia Museum

Olympic games, and Zeus was to be the judge. But for those who knew the outcome of the race, the scene is full of foreboding and deep meanings. The central group standing separately and still ironically impart a sense of tranquility. The action is all in the future, direly anticipated. These five figures leave the automatic Archaic pose far behind. They are full of movement, expressed partly through weight being thrown into one leg, leaving the other free. Gestures vary. Males use garments to contrast cloth and flesh and show off the body. Females now wear the peplos (showing a change of fashion) and reveal the presence of the body by position. (Their Archaic predecessors had used the contour to suggest anatomical form.)

Zeus is larger than the other figures, reasonably enough, and though Pausanias thought this was a statue of a statue, it is more likely he is an apparition who, unseen, sees all. Folds and creases of his garment flow this way and that, for the most part realistically, though Archaic patterns can still be seen in the folds bunched at the

7.4 Temple of Zeus, Olympia, east pediment, marble: the seer, Iamos. c. 460 BC. Olympia Museum

ankle. Beyond the chariots, either side, are seated and reclining figures. One (fig. **7.4**) may be identified as Iamos, resident prophet in Oinomaos' house. The composition is marred by the loss of the right knee on which the elbow rested, and the staff held in the left hand. But age is expressed in the full heavy flesh of the torso and the balding head, and anxiety in the furrowed brow and gesture of hand to chin. This is new in Greek sculpture. Some surfaces are left unworked (moustache, upper part of the beard) to receive paint and to leave major accents of lips and

nostrils unhampered by sculptural detail nearby. In the corner (fig. **7.5**) a reclining figure, a personification of one of the local rivers, the Kladeos, lifts himself to witness events. Drapery contrasts with anatomy, muscle with bone and flesh. The body is lean and young, the hair left undifferentiated, to be painted.

West Pediment. In the west pediment, Lapiths and centaurs fight at the wedding of Peirithoos (fig. **7.6**). There are references to Athens, perhaps in political sympathy. Theseus is here, and Peirithoos' stance echoes that of one of the Tyrannicides (fig **7.20**, p. 217). All is hot activity, presided over by the central figure of Apollo, again invisible to the fighters. The battle is joined, and the issue apparently equally poised. But human Lapiths would defeat bestial centaurs, another image of the victory of the civilized over the barbaric, as those who knew their myths were aware. Apollo (fig. **7.7**) stands with an impassive expression. His arm is outstretched, symbolically, perhaps to signify the range of his control. His torso is framed by drapery. His heavy face with its big chin, flat cheeks, and his eyes bulging between pronounced lids contribute to

the stern expression, which is characteristic of this period. Combatants fight in twos and threes, lunging, parrying, grasping, collapsing, biting, and pulling. A centaur grips a Lapith woman (fig. **7.8**) with his hands and a hoof. She resists calmly, her left elbow banged against his temple. The corners are closed as at the front by reclining figures.

The gods are almost 11 feet (3.35 m) tall, and other figures about $1\frac{1}{2}$ times lifesize. All are fastened to the back of the pediment with rods. The floor of the pediment is about 1 yard (1 m) deep. Most figures are unfinished at the back. Some are sliced flat, and others hollowed out to save weight. They demonstrate many aspects of the contemporary interest in movement, emotion, narrative, and realism. Faces show character as well as mood. Differences in the body, due to age and gender, are explored. Limbs, flesh, and muscle react to movement, and drapery reacts to the motion of the body, swinging, twisting, and bunching. The substance and texture of drapery are contrasted with the human body, human bodies contrast with that of the horse, wrinkly veins and joints contrast with hooves and hocks.

In terms of composition, the two pediments

7.5 Temple of Zeus, Olympia, east pediment, marble: reclining corner figure (personification of the river Kladeos). c. 460 BC. Olympia Museum

7.6 *Above* Temple of Zeus, Olympia. West pediment. c. 460 BC

7.7 *Below* Temple of Zeus, Olympia, west pediment, marble: Apollo. Height (of entire central figure) c. 11 ft (3.35 m). c. 460 BC. Olympia Museum

7.8 Temple of Zeus, Olympia, west pediment, marble: centaur grappling with Lapith woman. c. 460 BC. Olympia Museum

7.9 *Opposite* Temple of Zeus, Olympia, metope, marble: Herakles, Athena, and the Stymphalian Birds. Height 5 ft 3 ins (1.60 m). c. 460 BC. Olympia Museum

7.10 *Above* Temple of Zeus, Olympia, metope, marble: Herakles and the Cretan Bull. Height 5 ft 3 ins (1.60 m). c. 460 BC. Olympia Museum

complement one another. The front is symmetrical and the action focuses inward on the central group. In the back, action is contained by movement and counter-movement presenting the restless struggle in a timeless moment. In the front, Zeus ordains the chariot race and its aftermath. At the back, Apollo arbitrates the battle.

Metopes. The sculptured marble metopes did not decorate the outside of the building, where the pediments were to catch the eye, but were positioned over the front and back porches. They illustrate, as Pausanias painstakingly observed, the labors of Herakles, beginning at the back of the building with the young beardless hero overcoming the Nemean Lion and ending at the front with an older, bearded Herakles cleaning out the

Augean stables. He is assisted by Athena who appears four times, twice at the start and twice at the end, and by Hermes. In one episode (fig. **7.9**) a seated Athena, perching barefoot on a rock, perhaps her acropolis, turns to receive the Stymphalian Birds from Herakles. Her posture, the turning figure, offers a new design, while his presents a profile view of the head and right leg and varying views of the torso turning between the frontal and three-quarter view. His mood is calm, hers gentle. The killing of the armor-piercing birds is over, their mission accomplished and anxiety allayed. In another episode (fig. **7.10**) the action is in full swing, as Herakles struggles with the Cretan Bull. The sculptor needed to suggest the gigantic size of the animal, but could not do so by reducing the size of Herakles in comparison with his size in adjacent metopes. An inspired solution was to portray the bull as bigger than the metope by projecting its head from the background and pulling it back towards Herakles in a turning motion. Motion one way is countered by motion the other in a crossing composition. The combatants' heads face in confrontation, their bodies balance each other, the heroic torso contrasts with the bovine flank. The bull's head is in the round, the neck foreshortened, and the rump in high relief, the whole metope carved from a block only some 15 inches (38 cm) thick.

The sculptural program was completed by Phidias' gold and ivory (*chryselephantine*) statue of Zeus, not installed, however, for some twenty years. It was not designed till after the temple had been built and was positioned on a specially prepared base (fig. **7.11**) at the end of the central passageway formed by the two interior colonnades. These colonnades, with further columns atop forming a second storey, effectively divided the cella into three spaces, the antecedents of the later nave and two aisles of church architecture. We know little of this statue except what can be gathered from written descriptions, and later reduced adaptations or representations on coins. The seated statue reached to the roof and held a statue of Nike (Victory) on an outstretched right hand. Although it cramped the interior of the building, it was said by Quintilian, a Roman critic of the first century AD, to have "added something

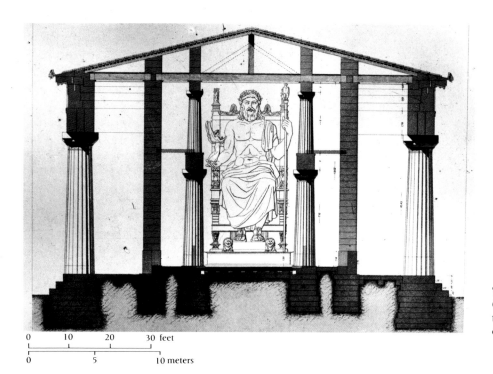

7.11 Temple of Zeus, Olympia. Section showing the cult statue. Later 5th century BC

to religion.'' It was removed, prior to the earthquake in which the temple collapsed, to Constantinople, and perished in a fire in the later fifth century AD. The workshop in which Phidias prepared his great cult statue has been found just outside the sanctuary wall and close by the temple. In it remained sculptor's tools, fragments of ivory, used for exposed flesh, and a number of molds for making the gold drapery.

SICILY AND SOUTH ITALY

The exterior appearance of the Doric order continued to please in the West, and though a pair of Ionic temples were built in their entirety at Locri and Metapontum in Italy, perhaps by Greek refugee architects from Asia Minor, the practice of incorporating Ionic elements into otherwise Doric buildings became less and less popular. In Sicily, temples came to abandon the reduplication of columns at the front, to reduce the pseudodipteral plan, to replace the adyton with the opisthodomos, and to align porch columns with the columns of the façade. Athena at Syracuse, Hera at Akragas, and Temple E to Hera at Selinus show these trends. Sixth-century archi-

tects' innovative thinking seems to have been bred out, as planners came more and more to conform to architectural practice on mainland Greece. The same may be said of their counterparts in south Italy. Yet there were some daring and surprising developments.

The Temple of Zeus Olympios at Akragas (fig. **6.25b**, p. 160), built to emulate the huge Ionic temples of Asia Minor and the nearby vast Temple G at Selinus, measured about 124 × 62 yards (113 × 57 m) at the stylobate. It was doubtless paid for by the indemnity which came to Akragas' tyrant, Theron, after the victory over the Carthaginians at Himera in 480 BC. The open peristyle was abandoned and replaced by a wall varied with half columns on the exterior and pilasters on the interior. Half way up the exterior of the wall, on a ledge, stood sculpted male figures, arms raised aloft to support the architrave (fig. **7.12**). They are nearly 25 feet (7.5 m) high and are known as Atlases or telamones. The order is Doric, but the columns have Ionic bases. Entrance was from the east, where the altar was, but by two doorways, one at either end of the façade, not by a single axial entrance. A local

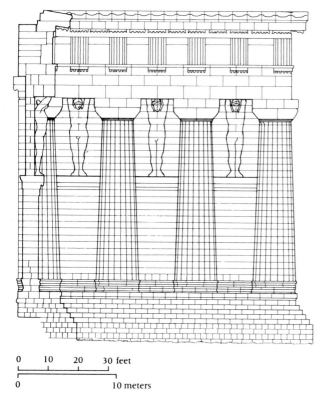

0 10 20 30 feet

0   10 meters

7.12 Restored elevation of the Temple of Zeus, Akragas. c. 410 BC

historian, Diodoros, remarks that a battle of gods and giants decorated one pediment and a capture of Troy the other, both suitable metaphors for the victory of the Sicilian Greeks over oriental Carthaginians. But there is no firm archaeological evidence for this. The puzzling character of the temple continues in the interior. The cella is formed by two rows of 12 massive rectangular piers, each row linked by a screen wall, while spur walls separate the cella from the opisthodomos. It is unclear where the statue might have stood or whether the building was roofed. The architectural origins of this building also remain obscure. Perhaps they are to be sought in gigantic pillared halls as much as in peristyle temples. It is thought that the temple was almost complete at the time when the Carthaginians got their own back, reducing Akragas to rubble in 406 BC.

Temple E (Hera) at Selinus was built around 460–450 BC in the large extramural sanctuary on the ridge to the east of the city, on the site of two earlier temples. The building measures 74 × 27 yards (68 × 25 m), with more elongated propor-

tions than those of the Temple of Zeus at Olympia, though almost the same area is covered.

Sculpted stone metopes decorated the frieze over the porches. There were originally 12, six over each porch, and the figures are almost lifesize. The material used is the local soft limestone, though for exposed female faces and limbs marble was used. So the technique resembles that of *akrolithic* statues (a freestanding akrolithic statue had head, feet, and hands of stone while the body of the figure was of wood.) Here, in the metope depicting Zeus and Hera (fig. **7.13**), Hera's face, arms, and feet are of marble pieced into the limestone. Hera stands in the new post-Archaic posture with a weight leg and a free leg. She wears old-fashioned garments suitable for a divinity: a chiton, a mantle, and an epiblema (cloak) with which she has veiled herself and which she now draws aside to reveal her face to Zeus. She contrasts Archaic clothing rendered in Archaic patterns (zigzags, swallowtails) with a face which is pure Transitional (Severe Style),

7.13 Temple E, Selinus, metope, limestone with marble for Hera's head, feet, and arms: Zeus and Hera. Height 5 ft 4 ins (1.62 m). c. 460–450 BC. National Museum, Palermo

having a big chin, flat cheeks, swelling eyes, thick eyelids, and a serious expression. The rock on which Zeus is seated introduces a landscape element into the relief. Zeus' hair, shown in fine strands radiating from the crown, is typically Severe. His clothing shelters his lower body and exposes the upper, rather like the Zeus from the east pediment at Olympia, though folds and creases here are more decorative. The sculptor still preferred the profile and frontal formula for showing the body even when turned (profile head and legs, frontal upper torso), and the twisting of the torso towards three-quarter views has little of the complexity and fluidity shown by the Olympia Master (cf. Herakles of the Stymphalian Birds metope). Zeus grasps Hera by the wrist, an act often interpreted as a ritual marriage gesture.

Another metope (fig. **7.14**) shows a more active scene. Artemis, with a marble face, arms and feet again, sets Aktaion's own dogs on him, since he has been unintelligent enough to claim he was a better hunter than the goddess and was then unfortunate enough to see her naked when bathing. Artemis has the new Severe stance and features of the face. She adopts the new fashion of the peplos, albeit rendered in agitated patterns. Aktaion offers both frontal and profile views of limbs, his striding posture and gestures full of pathos and motion, and a typically Severe coiffure. Above his head appear the antlers of the deer skin thrown over him to deceive his dogs. The act of arrogance is reaping its reward.

These and other metopes show that this workshop of sculptors continued to work in Selinus through the middle years of the fifth century BC, and that it had absorbed stylistic features popular in mainland Greece. What is peculiar to Selinus is the interest in excessively mannered folds and creases of drapery, the texture of which is thin to the point of transparency, as for example in the Hera and the Artemis. More obviously, the technique of using marble pieces slotted in to otherwise limestone metopes seems especially at home in Selinus.

7.14 *Opposite* Temple E, Selinus, metope, limestone with marble for exposed female flesh: death of Aktaion. Height 5 ft 4 ins (1.62 m). c. 460–450 BC. National Museum, Palermo

On the Italian mainland, both Locri and Metapontum witnessed the perhaps unexpected construction of large temples in the Ionic order. At Locri one was built around 480–470 BC. The building displayed long proportions (six columns by 17), matching front and back porches each with two columns between the *antae*, but no columns in the cella. Columns have volute capitals with lotus and palmette collars beneath. The high quality of stone used cannot be found in south Italy and came, in fact, from Syracuse. This has promoted the suggestion that Hieron participated in the project. Hieron assisted the Locrians when they were attacked by Rhegion in 477 BC. Moreover, Pindar records Locrian maidens singing songs of thanks to the Syracusan tyrant in front of the Temple of Aphrodite at Locri. Could this have been the temple which he mentions?

The other Ionic temple in the Sanctuary of Apollo at Metapontum, constructed around 470 BC, had a large peristyle of eight columns by 20, of which bases and capitals survive. The interior arrangement was old-fashioned, echoing Ionic precursors in Asia Minor, with a deep porch and a cella, but no back chamber at all.

Among the best preserved temples from antiquity is the second Temple of Hera in the great sanctuary at Poseidonia (Paestum) built around 470–460 BC. It is the largest of the three Greek temples at Poseidonia, measuring $65\frac{1}{2} \times 27$ yards (60 × 25 m), and thus approximating the size of the Temple of Zeus at Olympia. The plan (fig. **7.15**) shows a peristyle with six columns by 14,

7.15 Plan of the Temple of Hera II, Poseidonia. c. 470–460 BC

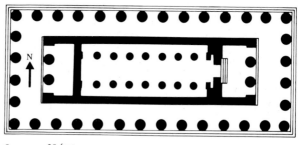

0	30 feet
0	10 meters

7.16 Temple of Hera II, Poseidonia, west façade from southwest. c. 470–460 BC

columned porches at front and back, and a cella with double colonnade. Steps from porch to cella point to the difference in floor levels. The elevation was conventional Doric, yet without any trace of sculptured decoration either of metopes or pediments. The stocky columns (fig. **7.16**) show entasis and are carved with 24 flutes when 20 was the rule in canonical Doric. Proportions of columns are notably old fashioned, the height at the front of the building measuring only 4.20 times the lower diameter, on the flank 4.36 times. They were coated with stucco to cover blemishes in the travertine, a common Greek ruse. The echinus of the capital retains a slightly baggy profile. It has not yet become the straight-sided abbreviated cone of the High Classical period.

Angle contraction is practiced at the corners of the building. Other refinements of the Doric order, which were already in play in mainland Greece, were used in the temple. These include the upward curvature of the stylobate. The horizontal cornices beneath the pediments are similarly curved. Column shafts incline slightly inwards. The rarity of these refinements in the West suggests that the architects were knowledgeable about developments in mainland Greece, and maybe that the temple was the brainchild of a Westerner trained in mainland Greece.

The structure is notably conservative in several respects. A plan of six columns by 14 is distinctly backward looking; conventional Doric required six columns by 13. Similarly retrospective are the rather squat proportions of columns and entablature, which emphasize the weight and bulk of the superstructure, 24 flutes on the columns rather than 20, and the slightly convex profile of the echinus. All these features point to the Archaic style. Yet the Doric refinements and similarities to the Temple of Zeus at Olympia, in spite of the absence of sculptural decoration, date it to the decade around 470–460 BC.

7.17 Perspective reconstruction of the Painted Stoa (Stoa Poikile) in the Agora, Athens. c. 450 BC

ATHENS

The oath of Plataea prevented the Athenians from reconstructing the temples and treasuries on the Acropolis. So they tidied up the debris of the Persian destruction and turned their attention to the Agora. They repaired the Old Bouleuterion and the Royal Stoa, doubtless, and put up two important new buildings. On the north side, close to the northwest corner the Painted Stoa (Stoa Poikile) (fig. **7.17**) was built sometime in the second quarter of the century. The prestigious location of this building provided splendid views along the Panathenaic Way towards the Acropolis. The Doric order was used for the exterior, while the internal colonnade was Ionic, one of the earliest appearances of order-mixing in Athens. Most of the building is limestone, though the Ionic capitals were marble. The stoa is named after the painted wooden panels with which it was decorated. Of these, none survive, but they were described by

Pausanias in the second century AD. They depicted episodes of warfare in which Athenians took part, the most renowned painting being that of the Battle of Marathon in which Miltiades himself was shown. The best known of the painters represented here was Polygnotos of Thasos. Later in the fifth century BC, other buildings were also decorated with paintings: the Propylaia and the Erechtheion on the Acropolis, and the New Bouleuterion and the Stoa of Zeus in the Agora. We are not certain whether paintings were on panels or directly on the walls, but, most likely, they were on wooden panels attached to walls. Many stoas in Athens had specific uses, but the Painted Stoa's functions varied. Beyond being a picture gallery and a museum where war trophies were deposited, it was used as a meeting hall or a lawcourt on occasion, and was often

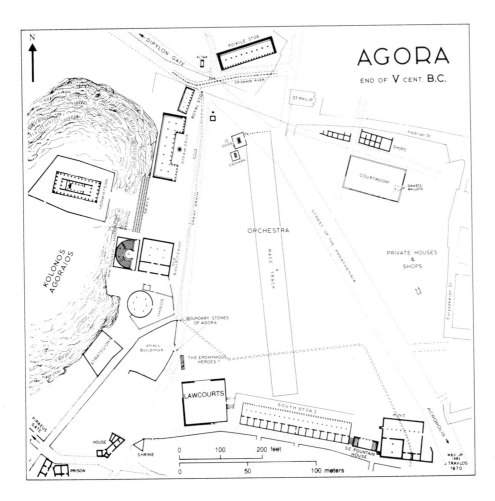

7.18 Plan of the Agora, Athens. c. 400 BC

open to the public. We are told of great throngs of people of all kinds here: entertainers and beggars, fishmongers and philosophers. It is from this stoa that the Stoics, followers of the philosopher Zeno from around 300 BC onward, took their name.

Built at the same time as the Painted Stoa, a circular building, the tholos, was put up at the southwest corner of the Agora (fig. **7.18**). This unusually shaped structure is the lynchpin for our understanding of the topography of the west side of the Agora. Thanks to Pausanias, who wrote of his walk along the west side, we can confidently identify the public buildings at the foot of the Kolonos Agoraios between the Royal Stoa and the tholos. The plan of the tholos is a plain circle, the roof supported by six columns.

This was the place where the fifty members of the "boule" or senate, who formed the executive committee, met to conduct the routine and diplomatic business of the city. This was also the place where they received meals for which the democracy paid. These were modest enough by standards: olives, leeks, barley cakes, cheese, and wine were staples, though fish and meat were occasionally included. Diners probably enjoyed their free meals seated, since there is no room for 50 couches in the tholos to allow them to recline, as was the usual domestic custom. Yet one third of their number who had to spend the night there, so that the city should be always vigilant, were doubtless furnished with couches. Furniture, like crockery and tableware, was easily moved about.

Sculpture

The development of Greek sculpture throughout the Archaic period can be followed readily enough from original statues of kouroi and korai, original groups, original reliefs, bronzes, and terracottas and their counterparts in architectural sculpture.

With the fifth century BC, however, our sources of information become complicated by the wealth of news transmitted by ancient writers, on the one hand, and by the Roman enthusiasm for removing, copying, and adapting famous Greek originals on the other. Ancient writers, among whom Pausanias and Pliny are the most informative, tell us about fifth- and fourth-century Greek sculptors and their products, and the work of later sculptors, too. Pausanias traveled around the sanctuaries and cities of Greece in the second century AD, describing the monuments and statues he saw. He used written sources and information offered by guides whose accuracy may be doubted. He makes mistakes and what he says must be treated with caution. Pliny's *Natural History* contains a long section on bronze statues and a shorter one on marble. He mentions the principal sculptors and their pupils and describes statues individually. These descriptions are sometimes useful in trying to identify from copies what Greek originals would have looked like. They are also useful in telling us what Greek originals were to be seen in Rome in the first century AD.

From the third century BC on, Romans plundered the Greek cities of south Italy and Sicily of their art, and from the second century BC the whole of Greece lay open to their avarice and theft. They removed Greek statues *en masse*, and they copied *en masse*. They were and continued to be unrepentant emulators of Greek art. Some of the statues described by the authors may be spotted among Roman copies or adaptations, especially if a Greek statue was so popular that many copies were made, and several have survived. But questions bedevil these studies: how true to the original is the copy we have, especially if the original Greek statue was bronze and the Roman copy/adaptation is in marble, and how true to the original is the literary description we have? It is sometimes unsound to attribute work to a particular sculptor simply because it bears a stylistic similarity to his. It is best to deal with original statues, if possible, and view the progress of Greek sculpture more in terms of type and style than in terms of shadowy personalities, however intrusive these inevitably may become.

Yet reliance on originals would not yield the whole picture, and copies and adaptations help to fill in gaps. Knowledge of how to reconstruct originals from several Roman copies is therefore critical.

As to originals which have survived, the architectural sculpture from Olympia is paramount in giving a whole gallery of types and activity, physical and otherwise. Yet the preferred material for freestanding statues was bronze, as the unoccupied bases from dedications in the sanctuaries on the Athenian Acropolis, at Delphi, and at Olympia eloquently testify. The statues to which these bases belong have either been melted down and reused, or stolen. A few, however, have survived. Generally they echo developments in architectural sculpture and show the way sculpture in the round progressed. Yet their quality is so startling, and their presence so compelling, that we can only wonder at the impact that dozens of these figures would have created in the sanctuaries and other public places where they stood.

The Kritios Boy (fig. **7.19**), found on the Acropolis in Athens, is both the last of the Archaic kouroi, and the first of the new figures in which the movement of the body is organically explored. Sculpted in marble, and considerably less than lifesize, he displays the new posture with the right leg advanced and free while the weight is on the left. Movement of the horizontal axes follows the pose. The right hip is lowered, the shoulders tilt slightly, the head turns and the body curves a little. The face is characterized by a big chin, flat cheeks, thick eyelids, and a composed expression. The head has hair which radiates in shallow strands from the crown and is rolled up over a fillet. Rolled hair like this is a particular trait of the Severe Style, as is longer hair tied in plaits and wound around the head.

7.19 *Left and below* Marble kouros, attributed to the sculptor Kritios, hence the "Kritios Boy." Height 2 ft 9⅘ ins (86 cm). c. 480 BC. Acropolis Museum, Athens

7.20 *Opposite* The "Tyrannicides." Roman marble copies of original Greek bronzes by Kritios and Nesiotes. Height 6 ft 5 ins (1.95 m). 477–476 BC (original). National Museum, Naples

He is still a frontal figure, but now of realistic bone and muscle, no longer a stiff automaton. He was probably dedicated on the Acropolis shortly before 480 BC, though there is some argument about his precise date.

The Kritios Boy is so called from the similarity of the head to a head in a group made by the sculptors Kritios and Nesiotes and set up in the Agora at Athens in 477 BC. What the precise roles of each artist were remain unclear, but that their collaboration was successful is shown by signed bases for other sculptures found on the Acropolis. The group in question was a bronze group called The Tyrannicides. It depicts Harmodios and Aristogeiton, who had assassinated the tyrant Hipparchus. The use of sculptures for such blatant political propaganda by the new democracy was a new development.

Kritios' and Nesiotes' bronze originals are recognizable without dispute in Roman marble copies (fig. **7.20**). The arrangement of the two figures is, however, controversial. The older man of the pair, Aristogeiton, lunges forward, one arm outstretched with hanging cloak, the other arm holding the weapon held back. Harmodios, the younger man, moves forward with a raised weapon. The striding poses are a common formula and the figures might have stepped out of a pedimental composition. The figures at Aegina (fig. **6.11**, p. 152) are obvious precursors. The anatomy is treated confidently, in the copies anyway. The head of Harmodios, taken to be similar to that of the Kritios Boy, has an Archaic hairstyle (closely packed, patterned curls) juxtaposed to a Severe Style face, while that of Aristogeiton enjoys more consistently Severe Style hair and face.

The more realistic representation of anatomy and mood, shown in the Severe Style, is emphasized by the appearance of portraiture. The arrival of true portraiture at this moment is debatable. Yet a copy of a portrait of Themistokles (fig. **7.21**) seems to provide a good example. Individualized traits of the features are unmistakable as are Severe Style characteristics. Yet the idealizing trend in Classical sculpture was too strong, and the next generation of sculptors rejected realism.

7.21 Themistokles. Roman marble copy, from Ostia, of a Greek original. Height (of head) c. 10¼ ins (26 cm). c. 450 BC (original). Archaeological Museum, Ostia

Ancient writers saw Myron as a sculptor whose work was transitional between the Early and High Classical periods, who followed the path towards realism of the anatomy, while avoiding expression of emotion. A description offered by Lucian of his Diskobolos (discus thrower) has enabled the statue to be identified among Roman marble copies (fig. **7.22**). His hairstyle with its mannered, closecropped curls

seems old-fashioned, reminiscent of some Olympia heads, but his pose is wholly new and unexpected. The original bronze dates perhaps to about 450 BC. Seemingly free and full of movement, the figure is, however, firmly held in two or three receding planes, with only one convincing viewpoint.

Developments from the Archaic marble kouros and kore types in this period can be studied in their counterparts in the pediments at Olympia, where male figures stand in the new relaxed pose, their anatomy realistically portrayed, and standing draped female figures wear the new clothing, the peplos, and hence are called ''peplophoroi'' (fig. **7.3**, p. 202). Though fragmentary, they provide more reliable evidence, being originals, than the numerous Roman copies with all their problems of attribution and identification. The Kritios Boy may be said to introduce the Transitional type of standing male nude figure, and, for the standing draped female figure type, the statue known as Angelitos' Athena, another original, marks the change from Archaic to Transitional. She stands (fig. **7.23**) with a free right leg in the new pose, drapery over the leg revealing the contours clearly. She also wears the new style peplos beneath the aegis, a magic cape or shawllike garment decorated with the Gorgon's head and fringed with snakes. This cape identifies the statue as Athena, as she was often portrayed wearing it. The right hand held a spear, while the left, freed from the Archaic convention of tugging at the skirt, rests flat on the hip. The dedication by Angelitos on the Acropolis at Athens probably took place around 480 BC. Somewhat generalized gravemarkers or gifts to the gods in the Archaic period, these types now become more specific representations, commemorating the prowess of a particular athlete in a dedication in a sanctuary, or representing a specific divinity (most often Apollo or Athena).

A number of bronze originals survive. The Charioteer of Delphi (fig. **7.24**) was a gift of a Sicilian Greek, Polyzalos, tyrant of Gela, to the sanctuary for a victory in the chariot race in 478 or 474 BC. The statue is nearly 6 feet tall (1.82 m) and was originally part of a large group consisting

7.22 Diskobolos by Myron. Roman marble copy of a bronze Greek original. Height 5 ft 1 in (1.55 m). c. 450 BC (original). Museo Nazionale delle Terme, Rome

7.23 Marble Athena, dedicated by Angelitos, hence ''Angelitos' Athena.'' Height 2 ft 6 ins (77 cm). c. 480 BC. Acropolis Museum, Athens

of horses, chariot, charioteer, and groom. With such stupendous dedications did the city-states of the West remind other Greeks of their wealth. The Charioteer was cast in eight pieces: the head in two parts, the body in two, and the limbs. The eyes are inlaid in glass and stone, copper was added on the lips, silver on the headband. The figure's weight is evenly distributed, the lower body, except for the ankles and feet, lost behind the folds of the long racing chiton. There is no trace of the new free/weight leg posture in a composition which is basically static and columnar. Yet slight movement of upper body and head, tension of outstretched arm holding the reins and neck, and the open mouth all breathe life into the figure. Drapery too is enlivened by varied bunching of folds and creases caused by belt, shoulder straps and seams. Heavy features of the face are characteristic of the time, the expression calm and collected. The moment chosen is after the race, since it is aftermath or anticipation, as in the east pediment at Olympia, which sculptors during this period often chose to portray.

Another survivor is the Zeus (fig. **7.25**) removed from the sea off Cape Artemision in Greece. A striding, over-lifesize figure, arms outstretched to aim and hurl his weapon, weight on the front foot and heel of the back foot raised, he is a commanding presence. Yet there are problems. The frontal view of the torso yields no forward movement of the upper body to correspond with the weight on the front foot – though this improves when the figure is viewed obliquely – and the limbs are very long, especially the front arm. The hair on the crown of his head has a strandlike flowing arrangement similar to that of the Kritios Boy but, in contrast to the roll treatment of the latter, the long hair is bound in two plaits carried over the front of the head and tied together. Loose bangs of hair across the forehead explore the fluid possibilities of casting and introduce more plastic movement. Eyebrows and eyes themselves were inlaid in another material. The expression is resolute and

7.24 Charioteer of Delphi. Bronze with copper (lips, eyelashes), silver (headband), and onyx (eyes). Height 5 ft 11 ins (1.80 cm). c. 478 or 474 BC. Delphi Museum

7.25 Bronze Zeus, from the sea near Cape Artemision, hence "Artemision Zeus." Height 6 ft 10½ ins (2.09 m); finger tip to finger tip, 6 ft 10¾ ins (2.10 m). c. 460–450 BC. National Museum, Athens

calm. The comparison with the head of the seated Zeus on the Selinus metope (fig. **7.13**, p. 209) is often made, and marks the broad distribution of the type.

The repertoire of original Greek bronze statues of this period was dramatically increased in 1972 when two more large bronze statues were fished out of the sea near Riace in south Italy. They perhaps come from a shipwreck, doubtless a merchantman carrying spoils to Italy

for Roman patrons. The Riace bronzes (A, the younger man and B, the elder) adopt the Severe Style lateral stance offering a weight leg and a free leg, but the representation of the body shows advances in the understanding of the anatomy in action which go beyond anything at Olympia or in any Roman copy that has survived. These figures, then, may only just be categorized as Severe and stand on the threshold of the High Classical period. They were probably made

around 460–450 BC. The formidable comprehension of the workings of the anatomy together with the expressions of mood portrayed in face and posture underscore what losses antiquity has suffered, and suggest that the Olympia figures may only be rather watered down versions of contemporary freestanding statues.

Riace A (fig. **0.14**, p. 25) originally carried a shield and spear and may have worn a wreath. His eyes are of ivory and coloured stones, his lips and nipples are of copper, and his teeth of silver. His hips tilt one way, his shoulders the other, the head turns challengingly to the right. Riace B (fig. **0.15**, p. 25) also carried a spear and a shield and wore a helmet pushed back (now lost). His eyes were inlaid, his teeth of silver, and his lips and nipples of copper. The figure sways to the right and the left knee advances the front plane. He seems stylistically more advanced, more adventurously engaged in space than his counterpart, and this has suggested to some that the statues were not made at the same time.

These statues show a sophisticated knowledge of muscle, sinew, flesh, bone, cartilage, and of the body in motion. Sculptors now understood that the parts of the body are connected, and that movement in one promoted movement in others. The body was to be seen as constructed and motivated from the inside, and not as a group of separate views seen from the exterior and assembled to suggest symbolic motion. The mainsprings of this change in viewpoint were twofold. Greek physicians were investigating the relationship of bones and muscles to one another, how the contraction of one set of muscles produced relaxation in another, and how muscular activity resulted in movement of bones and sinews. Athletes and warriors were sources of information, and surgery was helping establish the principal systems of movements in the body. Greek philosophers too had long been preoccupied with movement. Parmenides had attempted to break down motion into individual arrested moments. Pythagoras saw the world as moving

geometrical patterns. Abstract and practical alike were concerned with movement.

Not least striking about the Riace bronzes is their exploration of mood. A, the younger man, appears energetic and challenging, almost arrogant, while B is relaxed and calm, almost resigned. These effects were arrived at not just through the different representations of face and hairstyle, but also through the set of the body and the angle of the head (up, down, right, left, oblique). There has been much searching through Pliny and Pausanias to identify groups to which they might have belonged and the sculptors or workshops which might have made them. Stimulating theories have been advanced and the pair have even been attributed to Phidias himself, but there is no consensus and much speculation. Probably they represent Greek heroes and were originally dedications either at Delphi or Olympia.

As well as marble and bronze, sculptors also worked in clay. While not so prestigious an offering, a terracotta figure or group could be impressive. Zeus and Ganymede (fig. **7.26**) from the sanctuary at Olympia stand on a curiously shaped base and are about half lifesize. Zeus strides along, clasping Ganymede with his right arm and holding his traveling stick in the other hand. Ganymede holds a rooster, a love-gift for a lad. Hairstyles are still Archaic, though faces are Severe, so a date of around 470 BC is likely. The group was embellished with much paint: black, brown, red, and yellow. A group like this gives a good idea of what the clay models for bronze statues would have looked like.

Sculptors continued to produce reliefs both for funerary and votive purposes. Sumptuary laws, however, seem to have restricted the production of funerary monuments in Athens, and examples have to be sought in the islands and in Asia Minor. The challenge now for artists was to depict more realistic figures foreshortened in a shallow field. With patterned forms left behind, carved drawing would not suffice. But sculptors were equal to the task, gradually detaching the figures more and more from the background, a skill already exercised in architectural sculpture with some success.

7.26 *Opposite* Terracotta group of Zeus and Ganymede, from Olympia. Height 3 ft 7¼ ins (1.10 m). c. 470 BC. Olympia Museum

7.27 Marble relief of a young athlete, from Sunion. Height 23¼ ins (59 cm). C. 470 BC. National Museum, Athens

A votive relief from the Temple of Athena at Sunion shows a youth (fig. **7.27**) crowning himself. His profile head, oblique torso, his left arm and shoulder pulled back in the front plane are successfully shown in a relief only about 1½ inches (3 cm) in depth. Another relief from the Acropolis in Athens, called the Mourning Athena, shows several hallmarks of the Severe Style. The goddess displays a weight leg and a free leg; she wears a peplos; and her face has a serious expression (fig. **7.28**). She leans on a spear, gazing at what was probably a list of Athenian dead in battle. Undercutting of the long folds of the peplos contributes to the effect of depth. Her attitude – her head inclined downward, her hand to her brow – produces a sorrowful impression. Both reliefs date to around 470 BC.

7.28 Marble relief of Athena, gazing at a pillar, from Athens. Height 19 ins (48 cm). C. 470 BC. Acropolis Museum, Athens

7.29 Marble Enthroned Goddess, from Taras. Height 5 ft (1.53 m). c. 480–470 BC. Staatliche Museen, Berlin

Sculptors and their patrons in the West had to import marble from Greece, and this accounts for their sparing use of it in the metopes of Temple E at Selinus. Yet Pliny tells of renowned sculptors of this period and their work in the West, and a few examples of marble sculpture from Sicily and south Italy show that costs of shipping marble from quarries in the Aegean islands did not deter ambitious commissions.

From Taras in south Italy comes the marble Enthroned Goddess (fig. **7.29**) now in Berlin. The seated figure is an early type already seen in the pediment of the Temple of Artemis at Corcyra (fig. **6.7**, p. 150) and in the Geneleos group from Samos (fig. **6.50**, p. 177). It is especially popular in the East. Here the goddess retains the frontality of the Archaic period, and like Hera in the Selinus metope (fig. **7.13**, p. 209) wears Archaic garments, the chiton and a transverse mantle. Forms are symmetrically arranged, though missing forearms and hands may have introduced variety of gesture. The emphasis is on the decorative qualities of her hairdo, the close-set crinkles of the chiton and the zigzag designs of the mantle. Yet the face is unmistakably Severe with characteristic bulging eyes, thick lids, and flat cheeks. An unknown sculptor made this figure around 480–470 BC.

For a contemporary male figure in marble in the West we turn to the islet of Motya off the west coast of Sicily. Here a Carthaginian sanctuary yielded a big marble draped figure (fig. **0.13**, p. 24). He is a magnificent puzzle. The posture is jaunty, with a weight and a free leg, his right arm raised and his left akimbo, his hand on his hip. He gazes off to the left, self-satisfied. His hairstyle is late Archaic but the face is distinctly Severe (eyes, lids, cheeks, chin). It is the treatment of the drapery, however, which has sparked most interest. The fabric clings to the body, revealing the contours of muscled thigh, hip, and buttock. Folds are bunched together, regularly arranged ridges and channels in some passages, unevenly spaced in others. At the ankles, folds overlap in Archaic patterns. Such transparency of garments, not seen in Greece until the end of the century, should not, however, necessarily surprise in the West. It has already appeared in the metopes at

7.30 Marble reliefs, so-called "Ludovisi throne." Maximum height (of main relief) c. 3 ft 6 ins (1.07 m); (of side reliefs) c. 2 ft 9 ins (84 cm). c. 480–470 BC. Museo Nazionale delle Terme, Rome

Selinus. It seems possible, then, that this statue was the creation of the workshop of Greek sculptors active in Selinus around 470 BC. Many take the garment he wears to be the racing chiton and identify him then as a Charioteer, a worthy marble counterpart to the bronze at Delphi, another West Greek dedication.

Transparent treatment of the drapery, as a West Greek trait, occurs also on the so-called Ludovisi throne (fig. **7.30**). This monument consists of three marble slabs decorated with relief sculpture, which either stood around an open sacrificial pit or adorned an altar. It was not a throne. The front panel (opposite, top) seems to show the birth of Aphrodite from the waves (though there are alternative interpretations). Aphrodite is assisted by women who, arms outstretched, prepare to dry her with the cloth they hold between them. One side panel (opposite, right) shows a heavily draped female taking incense from a box to place on the burner before her. On the other (opposite, left), a girl, naked except for the snood which binds her hair, sits comfortably, playing the pipes. The sculptor's interest in transparent drapery and the body beneath is obvious. Aphrodite's garment clings tightly to the torso, the wet drapery dampened by the ocean, revealing her breasts, nipples, and thorax clearly. The attendant to her left wears the sleeved chiton showing the knees and lines of the lower leg, while the other woman wears the peplos through which, though heavier, the thigh and back leg vividly appear. The musician is the first Greek female nude in sculpture since the Geometric ivories from Athens (fig. **4.15**, p. 112).

Although the figures show errors in their anatomy, the composition is well planned. The nude of one panel matches the draped figure (a priestess?) of the other. Aphrodite reaches up towards balancing figures who lean toward her, their bare feet gingerly touching the pebbles.

These reliefs were found in Rome in the gardens of Sallust, where much Greek sculpture has been retrieved. Aspects of their themes are found among terracotta reliefs from Locri in south Italy. It may be that the Ludovisi throne decorated the altar in front of the temple of Aphrodite built there in the decade 480–470 BC.

This date chimes well with the style of the Ludovisi reliefs.

In the absence of marble in the West, many sculptors turned to clay as a cheap and plentiful medium. This was used to fashion great figures to decorate the superstructure of religious buildings, as had been the case already in the Archaic period, and to make cult statues, of which only fragments have survived. Clay was also the medium for the production of thousands of figurines made from molds, which were therefore mass produced. They were offered as gifts in sanctuaries and represented either worshipers or the gods. These figurines were often reduced versions of larger statues, and can therefore give a good idea of what the large-scale terracotta (or marble or bronze) statues may have looked like.

A good series of such figurines has come from Locri (fig. **7.31**) as have, more remarkably, a

7.31 Terracotta figure of a dancing maenad, from Locri, South Italy. Height 7½ ins (19 cm). c. 400 BC. National Museum, Reggio Calabria

7.32 Terracotta plaque, from Locri, South Italy: Aphrodite and Hermes in a chariot drawn by Eros and Psyche. Height 9 ins (23 cm). c. 460 BC. Taranto Archaeological Museum

series of terracotta relief plaques (fig. **7.32**) also votives. Many of these plaques show scenes of divine activity, of Hades and Persephone, and of Aphrodite. Here Aphrodite is seen in a chariot drawn by Eros and Psyche and accompanied by Hermes. Others show ritual scenes associated with marriage rites, so that divine couplings seem to mirror mortal rites of passage, and lend authority to these important changes of status. The hole in the top of the plaque was to attach it to a tree in the sanctuary.

Pottery and wall painting

The great success of Athenian black-figure, and then red-figure, in the Greek world of the Archaic period drove other workshops to the wall. At Corinth a red-figure technique enjoyed a certain local popularity, but did not last long. It is in Athens that the story continues. One group of

painters, among whom the Pan Painter was prominent, preferred old-fashioned conventions and looked backward admiringly to the sixth century BC. A bell krater (fig. **7.33**) by the Pan Painter shows Artemis drawing her bow to deliver the *coup de grâce* to Aktaion, whose dogs attack him (cf. fig. **7.14**, p. 210). The design is on the surface, without exploration of space; movement and gesture count in a theatrical moment. Quirks include the pouty lips, the small ear, and the eye rendered as a dot. This vase was painted around 470–460 BC.

Another vase, datable to the same period, exemplifies the work of an innovative potter called Sotades. He favored vases with modeled parts such as the sphinx vase in the British Museum in London (fig. **7.38**, p. 233), decorated by his painter, the Sotades Painter. This has a running centaur at the foot, and the legendary king of Athens, the snake-tailed Kekrops, and his daughters on the red-figure frieze below the lip. This was a pouring vessel, as the hole at the front between the legs of the sphinx shows. Closed by a stopper, it would have contained wine to be poured out through the hole when the stopper was removed. Sotades made numerous "plastic" vases like this, following a practice which had flourished in the Orientalizing period. Just as then, contact with the East was now providing stimulation. The Sotades Painter used difficult techniques such as gilding and the use of coral red and much white often as a ground. The work of these two artists was exported far and wide. The British Museum vase was found in Italy, while other examples have come to light in Egypt, Cyprus, and the Greek colonies on the coasts of the Black Sea.

In the same decade, the Niobid Painter attempted to convey space and depth in a new way. A krater (fig. **7.34**) now in the Louvre in Paris shows Apollo and Artemis slaughtering the children of Niobe. Niobe had boasted of the number of her children to the goddess Leto, who had only two children (but what a pair: Apollo and Artemis!). Niobe's act of "hubris," or pride, required divine retribution, and here we see its enactment. The painter has distributed his figures over the surface of the vase in various postures,

7.33 Attic red-figure bell krater by the Pan Painter: death of Aktaion. Height 16½ ins (42 cm). c. 470–460 BC. Museum of Fine Arts, Boston

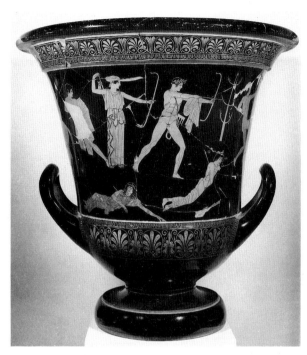

7.34 Attic red-figure krater by the Niobid Painter: Apollo and Artemis killing Niobe's children. Height 21¼ ins (54 cm). c. 460 BC. Musée du Louvre, Paris

7.35 Reverse of 7.34: Athena, Herakles, and heroes

and on various wavy ground lines. A spectral tree is shown towards the top of the scene. The old single groundline has been discarded, to be replaced by many, obviously intended, with the tree, to suggest landscape and space. Yet there is no reduction in the size of figures thought of as being in the distance. All remain on the unbroken surface of the vase. The reverse of the krater shows Herakles and Athena and other heroes (fig. **7.35**), similarly arranged over the surface, up and down. It is rather like the pediments at Olympia, which deliberately contrast a quiet scene full of foreboding at the front of the temple with hot action at the back. Herakles and his companions at ease contrast with the active violence of Artemis and Apollo (fig. **7.34**). Artemis draws an arrow from her quiver, Apollo draws his bow; one Niobid takes an arrow in the back; others dead or dying litter the field. As to the drawing, three-quarter and intermediate views are shown successfully. A profile eye at last appears in a profile head; the drapery has lost its stiff Archaic patterns and falls more freely. There is much accurately drawn foreshortening.

The arrangement of figures on various groundlines up and down the surface of the vase tallies with the detailed descriptions we have from Pausanias of the scheme used by wall painters and panel painters to suggest depth and space. Among the most illustrious of these practitioners was Polygnotos of Thasos, some of whose panels hung in the Stoa Poikile in Athens, and others in the Lesche (clubhouse) of the Knidians at Delphi. Though Pliny says that no one gained fame by painting on walls, it is possible that Polygnotos painted on walls as well as panels. It seems that most of his work appeared in the period 480–460 BC. He was regarded as a master painter by Hellenistic and Roman commentators who saw his work. He was renowned for the ''ethos'' or character with which his figures were endowed. He is said to have used posture and gesture to create these effects. The figures of the Olympia pediments and the Riace bronzes spring to mind as possible parallels. He and his circle used a four-color palette: red, yellow, black, and white. The topics favored were mostly mythological, though a historical event, the Battle of

Marathon, painted in the Stoa Poikile, was possibly the most famous. Some innovations – intermediate views of the body, unusual postures of movement and repose – were shared with vase painters. But it is the exploration of space, by putting figures on different levels to suggest depth, without, however, reducing their size (as in perspective), that seems to mark him out as an innovator. On vases like the Niobid Painter's krater, the painter may be drawing on ideas of perspective and space developed by Polygnotos and his circle.

When later writers discuss monumental painting it is often unclear whether they speak of wall painting directly on walls (murals) or of painting on wooden panels attached to walls. Yet they held large-scale Greek painting in high regard, and have recorded the names of many painters. So it is ironical that almost nothing of original Greek mural and panel painting has survived. The earliest of any substance were the terracotta metopes from Thermon (fig. **5.14**, p. 131). The rectangular shape of these seventh-century metopes encouraged single figures or small groups painted in outline technique using the colors of the vase painter: red/purple, black, white, and yellow. In spite of the absence of incision, which would have been invisible at this position on the building anyway, the metopes are compared to Corinthian vase painting for style and date. From the second half of the sixth century BC, around 530 BC, come four small wooden painted plaques found in the vicinity of Corinth. The illustration (fig. **7.39**) shows a procession of peplophoroi, musicians, and youngsters approaching an altar. Blue, red, black, and brown coloring stands out against the white ground. Whether this small plaque barely 6 inches (15 cm) high is a reflection of larger mural painting remains open to question. It is tempting to turn to the plethora of painted scenes with which the Etruscans decorated their tombs, and which have survived. Parallels to representations on Greek vases of drapery, posture, and anatomy are identifiable, but this does not help isolate traits of Greek mural painting, when we have no

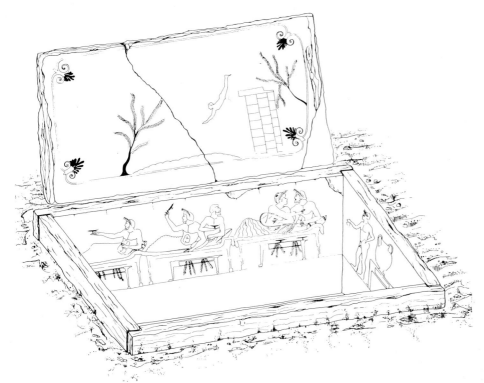

7.36 Tomb of the Diver, Poseidonia. c. 480 BC

Greek paintings with which to compare them.

From Poseidonia in south Italy, close to the Etruscans, comes the only substantial complete example of Greek wall painting of the fifth century BC that has survived. The Tomb of the Diver (fig. **7.36**) shows scenes of a typical symposium on the four sides of the tomb, with a diver on the underside of the coffin lid. The background is white stucco on the travertine slabs. Earth tones of brown, black, and yellow are the main colors used. Blue is used sparingly for couch covers and a garment. Music, drinking, and love (fig. **7.40**) are the themes of the symposium, the plunge from this life to the next (fig. **7.37**) that of the diver. There are evident similarities of pose and profile with figures painted on vases in Athens at the end of the Archaic period. This might suggest that wall painters and vase painters shared the same stylistic vocabulary, or that the symposium here is enlarged from a scene on a vase. It seems anyhow to be as dependent on vase painting as on wall painting, as far as we can judge. The theme of the Diver finds its analogies in Etruria, not Greece, so that this painter was open to local influences, and like architects and sculptors in

7.37 Painted ceiling block of the Tomb of the Diver, Poseidonia: the Diver. Height c. 3ft 4ins (1.02 m). c. 480 BC. Paestum Museum

the West was ready to select imaginatively from various sources in his work.

The information we have about monumental painting is tantalizing. There are descriptions of major paintings which survived until the third century AD. Ancient critics thought as highly of paintings as they did of sculpture. The names of leading painters are recorded, unlike the names of vase painters which we only know through their signatures. From the descriptions we learn of anatomical views, foreshortening, and arrangement of space in depth similar to features we see on contemporary vases. And details of theme, postures, and facial features on the painting in the Tomb of the Diver find parallels in red-figure Athenian vase painting. Vase painters and wall or panel painters will have been aware of one another's work. Yet wall painting differed from vase painting in scale, intention, and technique. Any precise sense of what Greek monumental painting of this period looked like and why it astonished critics remains elusive.

7.38 Attic red-figure sphinx vase (a rhyton: note the spout between the legs) by the Sotades Painter: Kekrops and daughters below the lip. Height 12¾ ins (32 cm). c. 470–460 BC. British Museum, London

7.39 *Below* Painted wooden plaque, from near Corinth: procession approaching an altar. Height c. 6 ins (15 cm). c. 530 BC. National Museum, Athens

7.40 *Bottom* Painted wall block of the Tomb of the Diver, Poseidonia: a symposium scene. Height c. 2ft 7 ins (78 cm). c. 480 BC. Paestum Museum

8
The High Classical Period
c. 450–400 BC

The period of Transition, with its mature
Doric architecture and its Severe Style
sculpture, is sometimes called the Early
Classical, preceding as it does the High
Classical of the second half of the
century. The High Classical period is
known above all for its new buildings on
the Acropolis at Athens, with their
sophisticated architecture and rich
sculptural decoration. Athens, of course,
is not the whole of Greece, but Athens
was the most creative center of cultural
activity. Athens had suffered more than
most from the Persians, and Athens had
the money to pay for the work.

The trend in sculpture toward
expressing emotional states and
complicated body movement, different
ages and different characters, as we have
seen for example in the Olympia
sculptures, was now checked. Differences
of age and anatomy are still shown in
some of the figures from the Parthenon,

Opposite Detail of the north frieze, Parthenon, Athens:
water carriers, fig. **8.21**. Marble. 447–438 BC. Acropolis
Museum, Athens

the richest repertoire of High Classical sculpture to have survived, but this interest is minor. The enthusiasms of the Severe Style were replaced by often uniform representations of young men and young women, many of whom share similar traits. Many have the same head type, with small mouth, big eyes, unbroken profile-line of nose and brow, inattentive expression, and uncombed hair. Musculature of youths is uncomplicated. Drapery undergoes radical change. It is carved more deeply, resulting in a much greater sense of light and shade. It sweeps vigorously against the body, allowing the observer to sense the limbs beneath. In these figures, sculptors sought to express an ideal of youth and beauty acceptable to and shared by the gods. The gods, after all, are shown in human form. And, by their past exploits and recent defiance of the Persians, the Athenians and their heroes seemed to share in the divine. Human anatomy is accurately shown, and movement is naturalistic, but expressions are distant and the mood is otherworldly. It is this urge to fuse the real and the ideal which exemplifies the High Classical period.

Phidias was the sculptor entrusted with supervising the sculptural decoration of the Parthenon, and he is the one most likely to have contributed most heavily to the new style and its intentions. But a workshop of sculptors was active in Argos too, and Pliny says that an Argive, Ageladas, was a teacher of Phidias. He probably also taught Polykleitos, the other great Greek sculptor of this period, known to have tried to combine ideal and real in single images.

THE PELOPONNESIAN WAR

The great war between Athens and Sparta, which broke out in 431 BC and continued until 404 BC, dominated the period. Sparta and her Peloponnesian and Boeotian allies had watched the growth of the Athenian empire with alarm, and had attempted to check Athens in a number of military campaigns in the 450s and 440s BC. Athens' leader in these years and until his death in 429 BC was Perikles. This remarkable man governed the city and the empire by the force of his personality and his powers of persuasion, in a constitutional and legal manner. The annual elections by the assembly to the board of generals saw him victorious almost every year. Externally, the states of the empire were obliged to continue their contributions, by force if necessary, and the Spartans were kept at bay. Internally, the law courts were made more democratic. Jurors were allowed to receive pay, and they were chosen by lot. This meant that the poorer citizens could participate. The power of the assembly was also increased. Yet Athens could not have functioned without slaves, women who had no vote, and resident aliens who were only partially enfranchised. Thus increasing democracy at home, however imperfect, was balanced by a policy of increased force abroad.

The military campaigns of the 440s BC were a sign of the tension between the two camps: Sparta and her allies on one side; Athens and her empire on the other. Though a truce of sorts was hammered out in the 440s BC, the resolution of the question of who was to be the leader of Greece could not be deferred indefinitely. The Peloponnesian War, as it is called, broke out in 431 BC. Within two years Perikles was dead, killed by the plague which struck Athens. The war went on year by year, Athens relying on her fleet, and Sparta on her army. Each side enjoyed successes, but little was settled. After a decade, a truce was signed in 421 BC. But the ambition of Athens was incorrigible and war was resumed in 415 BC, the Athenians stimulated by dreams of wealth and glory in Sicily. The Athenians' lamentable display of generalship at Syracuse and their defeat at the hands of the Syracusans in 413 BC were the beginning of the end. But the war dragged on until the Athenian fleet was caught by surprise and destroyed at Aegospotami on the Hellespont in 405 BC. Athens submitted in 404 BC. The long walls connecting the city to the harbors at Piraeus were dismantled, and Spartan troops entered the city.

In the West, the Syracusans had not wanted war with Athens. The tyrants had glorified the city, and made it rich in the first half of the century. On the death of Thrasybulus, however, a democracy was installed, lasting until 405 BC. The democracy enjoyed commercial success, but war was a constant threat: war against indi-

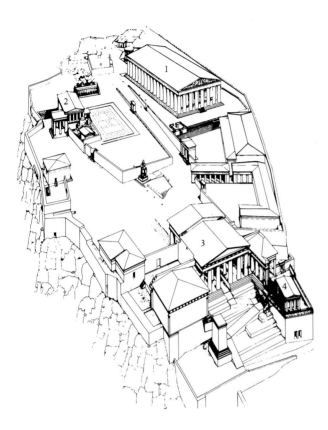

8.1 Drawing of a restoration of the Acropolis, Athens.
Late 5th century BC
   1 Parthenon
   2 Erechtheion (dotted plan to the right is of an
      Archaic temple)
   3 Propylaia
   4 Temple of Athena Nike

genous tribes, war against Etruscans infringing on trade routes, and war against Greek neighbors, notably Akragas. In all these encounters, Syracuse was successful. So she was ready when Athens sent her expedition in 415 BC, ostensibly to help Segesta, but with an eye on the wealth of Syracuse and the whole island. There was always tension between Greek colonies founded from the Peloponnese and those founded from elsewhere, Dorian and Ionian in opposition. Athens had sought to exploit these tensions by treaties with several states – Segesta, Leontinoi, Rhegium, and Gela – by which she hoped to supplant Syracuse's hegemony on Sicily. But her expedition was a disaster; the fleet was destroyed, and the army routed. Seven thousand Athenians were taken prisoner, of whom many perished in the quarries where they were imprisoned. Only a few survived.

In the decades before his death, Perikles set in motion the great program of reconstruction on the Acropolis (fig. **8.1**), using money contributed by the states of the empire. The centerpiece was the Parthenon, built between 447 and 432 BC. It was followed by the Propylaia, the monumentalized entranceway built between 437 and 432 BC, but left unfinished at the outbreak of the war. These two buildings were certainly the focal points of Perikles' scheme. The other two buildings, the Erechtheion (430s–406 BC) and the Temple of Athena Nike (420s BC), may also have been part of the original design. These four buildings mark the high point of the glorification of Athens, in a period when the city stimulated all kinds of creative genius, in architecture and sculpture, in theatre, in philosophy, and in historical writing.

The architects at work on the Acropolis were Iktinos, Kallikrates, and Mnesikles. The sculptors are less easy to identify, but the work must have been ceaseless and the decoration of the Parthenon and perhaps of the other temples, too, was under the supervision of Phidias. In fact, Plutarch says that Phidias was in charge of the whole of Perikles' scheme.

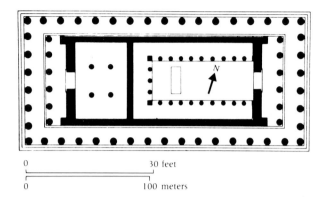

8.2 *Above* Plan of the Parthenon, Athens. c. 447–432 BC

8.3 *Below* Parthenon, Athens, view from the northwest. *Pentelic* marble. 447–432 BC

Architecture and architectural sculpture

ATHENS

The Parthenon. When the Persians arrived on the Acropolis, they found a temple being built on the site of the later Parthenon. This they burnt, leaving little that was reusable for the Temple of Athena Parthenos, the Parthenon itself (fig. **8.3**), some thirty years later. Much of the remains from the damage done by the Persians to the building under construction was used in the repair of the fortification walls on the north side of the Acropolis. Only the foundations and some

column drums were deemed of use by the Parthenon's architects, Iktinos and Kallikrates. They extended the foundations they found to accommodate a larger plan. The huge statue of Athena, which the Parthenon was to house, required an extra large cella which determined the size of the building and hence its foundations. Work began in 447 BC, the temple and statue were dedicated to Athena Parthenos, Athena the Virgin, in 438 BC, and the pedimental sculptures were finished by 432 BC.

Though the Parthenon is regarded as the epitome of Doric temple building, it incorporated unusual features. Eight columns on the façade (fig. **0.4**, p. 17) was not usual, though there were precedents: the Temple of Artemis at Corcyra 150 years earlier, and, in the West, at Metapontum (Temple A) and at Selinus (Temple G). The 17 columns of the flank peristyle show that the usual formula for the number of columns was used (fig. **8.2**). A ratio of 9:4 was to govern both plan and elevation of the temple. To allow room for a spacious cella and for a back room behind, the usual Doric porch arrangement was replaced by much shallower porches, front and back, each with six columns prostyle. Windows were installed on either side of the doorway in the back wall of the front porch. In the cella, a double-storeyed Doric colonnade surrounded the statue. A row of columns behind the statue was a new development. In the back room, where Athena's treasure was kept, Ionic columns were introduced. Another Ionic feature, a continuous sculpted frieze, encircled the exterior of the cella, the backroom, and porches, at a height which rendered it almost invisible. The elevation was normal Doric, with column shafts surmounted by capitals with their now straightsided echinus, by architrave blocks, a triglyph and metope frieze course, and by cornices (fig. **8.4**). All was marble, precisely carved and precisely fitted together.

As the Doric order developed from early Archaic to High Classical, short columns gradually changed to long, thick shafts to thin, the baggy profile of echinus to a straight-sided cone, and rectangular metopes to square ones. The sheer bulk of buildings is reduced by decreasing the height of the entablature.

8.4 Parthenon, Athens, northeast corner detail, showing Doric column and capital, architrave and frieze course (triglyph and metope), and cornices. Marble. Height (of architrave and frieze) c. 9 ft (2.75 m). 447–438 BC

As we have seen, the Parthenon is unusual in its plan. Its use of Ionic columns in the interior is also uncommon. For this it followed a precedent set in the West some 50 years before. It is unusual for its use of an Ionic continuous sculptured frieze. And it is also unusual for its mass of Doric refinements. The swelling profile of columns (entasis) is used (so that columns do not appear pinched). Angles are contracted. The columns lean inward slightly from bottom to top. The antae lean outward. The stylobate falls away slightly either side from its center in a slow curve. (Horizontal lines appear to sink in the middle if not given this upward curvature.) A similar phenomenon occurs in the entablature. Though these modifications to the horizontal and vertical are minuscule, there are nevertheless no true verticals or horizontals in the building, and hence no right angles. At the same time a sense of mobility has been given to straight lines, and a boxlike appearance has been avoided. So dignity of form was enhanced by dynamism of forms. The demands on the masons were enormous. All blocks, whether curving or not, had to fit flush; yet everywhere block fits meticulously with block, and only on one or two metopes does the carving betray signs of uncertainty and haste. The Parthenon in the last decade of the twentieth century presents a magnificent shell of a building; current work of restoration is set to change its appearance dramatically.

The building is famous for its sculptures. There were pedimental groups at front and back, and sculptured metopes on every side. There was the continuous Ionic frieze on the interior, and the great gold-and-ivory statue of Athena herself. There may have been another carved frieze over the cella door. Comparison with the Temple of Zeus at Olympia is inevitable. There were similar arrangements for pedimental sculptures, but sculptured metopes on the Parthenon take the place of the blank exterior metopes of the Temple of Zeus, and the Ionic frieze of the Parthenon replaced the Doric frieze (triglyphs and metopes) there.

The richness of decoration of the Parthenon is exceptional for a temple, and is more fitting perhaps for a treasury. In these terms, the Archaic Treasury of the Siphnians at Delphi comes to mind as a parallel and precursor. The Parthenon did not replace the old Temple of Athena on the Acropolis which had been destroyed by the Persians. Nor did it house the old revered wooden statue of the goddess, which had to await the building of the Erechtheion to be properly housed again. It was not equipped with an altar for sacrifice either. It is almost as if the Parthenon, an elaborate gift to the goddess, was as much a treasury as it was a temple. Athena's money was in fact kept in the back room. And the gold which formed much of the surface of her great statue was removable, so that the figure itself functioned at one level as a repository of wealth.

The Metopes. Of 92 metopes, those on the east, north, and west are seriously damaged. Most of those on the south are better preserved, having suffered less at the hands of Christian iconoclasts when the building was converted to a church. Eight or nine of those in the center of the south side were lost in 1687 in an explosion of gunpowder kept in the Parthenon by the Turks when the building was for some time a mosque. The themes are well known: at the east, gods and giants in combat; at the west, Greeks and Amazons (or Persians); at the north, Greeks and Trojans; and at the south, Lapiths and centaurs. The Centauromachy is reminiscent of the back pediment at Olympia, and all were vivid metaphors for the conquest of the barbaric by the civilized. All served also as reminders of the Greeks' mythical past and their recent successes.

The metope at the southwest corner of the building (fig. **8.5**) shows a Lapith and a centaur interlocked, carved almost in the round. The figures clash in an oblique charging movement, the narrative spoilt by the absence of an important metal attachment – a spit thrust into the centaur's groin – now lost.

8.5 Parthenon, Athens, southwest corner metope: Lapith and centaur in combat. Marble. Height 4 ft 5 ins (1.34 m). 447–438 BC

8.6 Parthenon, Athens, south metope 27: struggle between Lapith and centaur. Marble. Height 4 ft 5 ins (1.34 m). 447–438 BC

Another metope (fig. **8.6**) has a Lapith leaping forward and laterally from its rectangular frame. The scene is dominated by the tension of the fight and the drapery folds, originally painted, that form the backdrop to the human torso. It is a daring composition. The virtuoso execution of the heavy veined anatomy of the centaur and the flying, slightly turned Lapith body both catch the eye.

The Pediments. The east pediment was badly damaged when the construction of the apse of the Christian church destroyed the central figures. The west pediment was almost com-

pletely destroyed when Morosini tried to remove the horse groups from the center, only to have them come crashing to the ground. They had, however, been seen by Pausanias who describes them with unbelievable brevity and says nothing of the metopes and the Ionic frieze. They were also drawn in 1674 by a Flemish artist, sometimes identified as Jacques Carrey. Carrey's drawings are immensely valuable. He drew the pediments, the metopes at the south and some of the frieze. Of the original figures of the pediments, only a few survived. The figures were finished all the way round, even though positioned at a height of some 52 feet (16 m) above ground level; only parts of the figures would be seen. At Olympia, sculptors had been more economical. Hoisted aloft, the Parthenon figures were positioned in the triangular space according to a design doubtless worked out by Phidias. The composition was crowded with many figures, some of which overlapped, while others pushed limbs out through the front plane of the pediment in a manner first seen in the temple of Aphaia on Aegina.

The west pediment shows the contest between Athena and Poseidon as to who was to be the patron deity of Athens. Athena and Poseidon spring apart in a great "X" composition in the center. Their outward movement is contained by the chariot groups behind them (fig. **8.7**), while seated and reclining figures continue to the corners. One group (fig. **8.8**) is thought to be the early king of Athens, Kekrops, identified by the coiled snake beside him, and his daughter, who leans on him as she shrinks from the central

8.7 Parthenon, Athens. Drawing of a reconstruction of the west pediment (Professor Ernst Berger)

8.8 *Above* Parthenon, Athens, west pediment: Kekrops and daughter *in situ*. Marble. Height 4 ft 6 ins (1.37 m). 437–432 BC

8.9 *Below* Parthenon, Athens, west pediment: reclining male corner figure (personification of the river Ilissos). Marble. Length 5 ft 1 in (1.56 m). 437–432 BC. British Museum, London

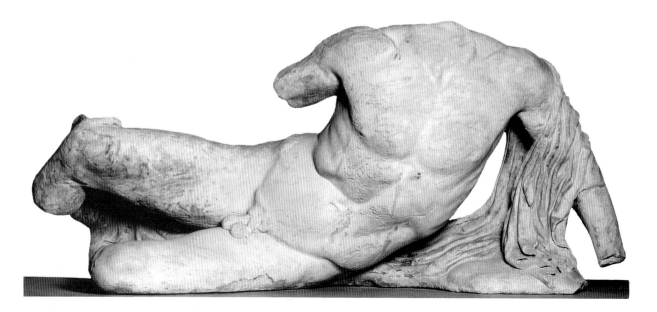

8.10 Parthenon, Athens. Drawing of a reconstruction of the east pediment (Professor Ernst Berger)

awe-inspiring incident. Another figure (fig. **8.9**) in the corner personifies one of the rivers of Attica, the Ilissos, and calls to mind the river gods of the Olympia pediment.

Another incident crucial to the myth-history of the city, the birth of Athena, appears in the front pediment (fig. **8.10**). Again, the central group is lost, though it seems Athena was shown fully armed and standing next to her father, Zeus, from whose head she has just emerged. Hephaistos and Hera must have stood nearby, while other Olympian deities crowd around. The designer specified the time of the event, dawn, by having the heads of the horses of Helios (the

Sun) rising above the floor of the pediment (the horizon) at the south end, while in the opposite corner the heads of the horses of Selene (the Moon) are all that can be seen, sinking, as night gives way to day, dark to light. Surviving figures show varying degrees of awareness of the central event. The reclining nude figure (fig. **8.11**) gazes at the rising sun, unaware of Athena's birth. He is variously identified as Ares or Dionysos, or Herakles, or even a personification of Mt

8.11 Parthenon, Athens, east pediment: reclining male figure (Dionysos? Herakles?). Marble. Height 4 ft 3 ins (1.30 m). 437–432 BC. British Museum, London

8.12 Parthenon, Athens, east pediment: two seated female figures (Demeter and Kore) and a messenger (Iris? Artemis?). Marble. Height (of messenger) 5 ft 8 ins (1.73 m). 437–432 BC. British Museum, London

Olympus to specify place, as time has been specified. Next to him (fig. **8.12**) sit Demeter and Kore, turning on their seats to hear the news, massive bodies outlined by deeply carved garments. Interest and excitement gather momentum towards the center. In the northern half, a goddess relaxing in the lap of another (fig. **8.13**) calmly awaits the passing of night, while a third, seated, turns slowly towards the center. The sculpture here is a revelation: the goddesses wear thin crinkly chitons pressed tight against upper bodies to cover but reveal the breasts beneath, while folds of the mantles over the legs are deeply carved to produce dramatic effects of light and shade, seen at a distance. Here, too, drapery pressed up against the body barely conceals knees, thighs, and lower legs.

The moment seen is the moment after the birth. It is not a moment of great activity, but of ignorance contrasting with realization, as figures demonstrate their awareness of the great event in measured physical response. Transitions in the two groups of goddesses are subtle, but all are united by superbly sculptured and understood drapery, which balances revelation of the body, covered or not, with its own texture and weight.

The Frieze. The sculptured frieze runs all the way around the central block of the building above an architrave course at front and back, and uniformly about 39 feet (12 m) above the ground (fig. **8.14**). It is just over 1 yard (1 m) high and 175 yards (160 m) long. Its position made it almost impossible to see. To improve the visibility, the upper parts of the frieze are carved in higher relief. The sculpture was brightly painted and many metal attachments were used for weapons of men and harnesses of horses. The greatest depth of carving of the frieze is nowhere more than $2\frac{2}{5}$ inch (6 cm). In antiquity it was best seen from outside the colonnade, different incidents in filmstriplike sequence. Much of the frieze is now in the British Museum in London, while large parts of it are in the Acropolis Museum, and a handsome fragment is in Paris.

At the west (fig. **8.15**) the frieze depicts 13 horsemen preparing themselves and their horses for a cavalcade which takes up much of the space of the north and south friezes. The riders of the north and south friezes are preceded by chariots, each with charioteer and warrior, and they in turn by elders standing about, musicians, and attendants walking forward, and by sheep and heifers, the sacrificial animals. At the east, the frieze shows women, who appear here for the first time, moving slowly forward from either end towards the center. They meet a group of men,

8.13 *Above* Parthenon, Athens, east pediment: three female figures (Hestia? Dione? and Aphrodite). Marble. Height (of Hestia figure) 4 ft 5 ins (1.34 m). 437–432 BC. British Museum, London

8.14 *Left* Parthenon, Athens, west frieze *in situ*, from below: cavalcade preparing. Marble. Height (of frieze) 3 ft 6 ins (1.06 m). 447–438 BC

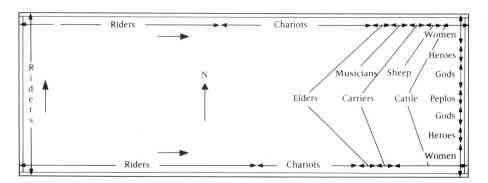

8.15 Diagram of the Parthenon frieze

8.16 Parthenon, Athens, east frieze: peplos incident. Marble. Height 3 ft 6 ins (1.06 m). 447–438 BC. British Museum, London

officials, who are apparently awaiting the arrival of the procession. Next are 12 seated Olympian gods, six on either side of the incident at the very center of the frieze. Here are five figures: two young women carrying stools are on one side of a woman generally identified as the priestess of Athena; on the other, a man, probably the Royal Archon, receives a peplos from a girl (fig. **8.16**). This is the peplos woven every four years for Athena and presented to her on the Acropolis on the occasion of the Panathenaic Festival. The procession which had begun at the southwest corner of the building finds its culmination in this encounter with the seated gods and the peplos incident which they frame. The size and complexity of this frieze imply a single designer, perhaps Phidias, as surely as its execution implies the need for many sculptors.

At the west, horsemen prepare to mount, adjust their equipment, and begin the ride

(fig. **8.17**). Pose, gesture, dress, hairstyle, and even hats are all varied. Horses, small enough when compared for size with their riders to be ponies, prance and rear, sometimes with all four hooves off the ground, while their riders' cloaks flying out behind impart a sense of forward motion. Drill holes show where metal reins and bridles were attached. The cavalcade (fig. **8.18**) shows overlapping horsemen, sometimes as many as seven in very shallow relief.

In spite of the number of riders and horses, there is no confusion or monotony. Variety is attained by contrast of human limb with horse's flank or of drapery with flesh, or by different

8.17 *Opposite top* Parthenon, Athens, west frieze: riders. Height 3 ft 6 ins (1.06 m). 447–438 BC. British Museum, London

8.18 *Opposite bottom* Parthenon, Athens, north frieze: cavalcade. Marble. Height 3 ft 6 ins (1.06 m). 447–438 BC. British Museum, London

8.19 Parthenon, Athens, south frieze: chariot and four horses. Marble. Height 3 ft 6 ins (1.06 m). 447–438 BC. British Museum, London

8.20 Parthenon, Athens, east frieze: women and elders. Marble. Height 3 ft 6 ins (1.06 m). 447–438 BC. Musée du Louvre, Paris

positions of horses' legs and heads, and of human heads and of dress and headgear. Yet the head type itself is largely the same with a rounded skull, a large eye, a small mouth, a straight nose, and a distant expression. Horse groups, chariots, charioteers, and warriors exploit the same control of overlapping forms (fig. **8.19**) to suggest recession in space. More variety is introduced by standing marshals who face against the direction of the procession, interrupting the forward momentum, and by different spacing as the procession slows to a walk. Youths carrying water jars move forward slowly (fig. **8.21**), one after another, in staccato rhythm in front of the hectic cavalcade. Around the corner and on the east frieze, stately women encounter waiting elders (fig. **8.20**). Poses are unhurried, the drapery of females heavy and voluminous, that of males clinging and contrasting with exposed arms and chests. The twelve Olympian deities, seated, are to a larger scale, as was proper, than the standing Athenians who are on either side. The outermost of the gods turn to watch the procession, but those closest to the peplos incident, Zeus on one side and Athena on the other, turn their backs on the scene. Poseidon, Apollo, and Artemis (fig. **8.22**) are seated on stools (only Zeus has a throne), slightly overlapping one another, legs

8.21 Parthenon, Athens, north frieze: water carriers.
Marble. Height 3 ft 6 ins (1.06 m). 447–438 BC.
Acropolis Museum, Athens

8.22 Parthenon, Athens, east frieze: seated deities (Poseidon, Apollo, Artemis). Marble. Height 3 ft 6 ins (1.06 m). 447–438 BC. Acropolis Museum, Athens

in front of furniture to give a sense of receding space.

Though there is uncertainty over the identity of the male figure of the five in the center of the east frieze or whether the small figure there is a boy or a girl, the scenes on the frieze doubtless refer to the Panathenaic procession. Important episodes of the Panathenaic procession are depicted in the frieze: the preparations, which actually took place outside the Agora, the chariot races, which in fact occurred down the Panathenaic Way in the Agora, and the handing over of the peplos, which took place on the acropolis. Discussion continues as to whether this is a representation of a specific Panathenaia or whether it stands as an ideal representation of all such processions. What is new is the representation of mortals in temple sculpture, when

mythological subjects would have been expected. Phidias and his colleagues had the audacity to decorate the new temple with figures of Athenians, and in the company of the gods. This bold claim that the Olympians lived among the Athenians, though discreetly placed high up under the ceiling of the peristyle, doubtless stirred the criticism of many Greeks.

There was criticism at home, too. Plutarch, writing in the first century AD, but citing a contemporary source, tells us: "Greece is clearly the victim of a monstrous Tyranny: she sees us using what she is forced to contribute for the war to gild and bedizen our city like a wanton woman hung around with costly stones and statues and thousand talent temples." In reply to this, Perikles invoked the advantages of full employment:

> The materials to be used are marble, bronze, ivory, gold, ebony, and cypress woods; the crafts required to work such materials are those of the carpenter, molder, bronzeworker, mason and sculptor, dyer, worker in gold and ivory, painter, embroiderer, metal-inlayer, and the providers and transporters of these – merchants, sailors, and pilots by sea; and by land, waggonmakers, cattlebreeders, and drovers. There are also ropemakers, weavers, leatherworkers, roadbuilders, and miners. And since each craft has its own body of unskilled workers attached to it, practically every able bodied man is employed and is receiving pay for his work.

The exceptional character of the democracy was at the bottom of Perikles' belief in Athens, according to Thucydides, who has Perikles speak in the following terms: "We are a democracy in which a citizen is advanced as reward of merit; a spirit of reverence pervades our public acts; we love the beautiful; we cultivate the mind; Athens is the school of Hellas." For Perikles, the Parthenon may have stood as an emblem of the democracy and as an instrument for the education of Greece.

The Statue of Athena. Phidias' gold and ivory statue of Athena was dedicated in 438 BC. All trace of the original has vanished, but we know about the statue from literary descriptions, from reduced copies and adaptations, and from later copies of parts of it (the shield, for example). Pliny and Pausanias give descriptions of the statue from which we gather essentials: Athena stood 26 cubits tall (nearly 38 feet or 11.5 meters high), wearing an aegis and an elaborate helmet, holding a Nike and a spear, with a shield and snake nearby. A second-century AD marble statuette (fig. **8.23**) gives a sense of what the statue actually looked like, though here the image is vastly reduced, and there is no sense of the glittering gold and the contrast with ivory flesh. The impact of this huge figure, rendered in the most costly materials, is hard to imagine. The combined effect of both statue and building must

8.23 Varvakeion statuette, a Roman version of the statue of Athena Parthenos. Marble. Height 3 ft 5½ ins (1.05 m) (with base). 2nd-century AD copy of the gold and ivory statue by Phidias of 438 BC. National Museum, Athens

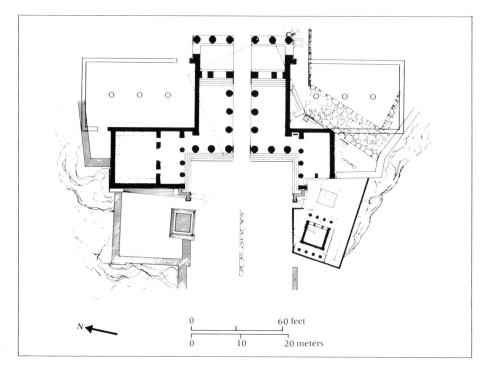

8.24 Plan of the Propylaia, Athens. c. 437–432 BC. Broken lines indicate the pre-Persian structure

have been awesome. Compelling messages were being sent concerning the religious power of Athena and the political power of Athens. That the highest level of artistic skills were at work in the service of Athena and her city was a point that no one would have missed.

The Propylaia (fig. **0.2**, p. 14).   The architect entrusted with monumentalizing the entrance to the Acropolis was Mnesikles. The Archaic entrance had been small, more in keeping with the old Mycenaean notion of the Acropolis as a fortress. Now, with the emphasis on the Acropolis as a sanctuary, the gateway was to be both more imposing and more welcoming. The plan was opened and wings extended towards the visitor. Work began in 437 BC but was abandoned on the outbreak of the Peloponnesian War, in 432 BC. The plan specified a split-level gateway (fig. **8.24**) with six columns front and back, and six (two rows of three) on the inside, with a five-doored entranceway, four of which were stepped and one unstepped for animals, with pairs of flanking units to the north and south.

The flanking units to the northeast and the southeast, perhaps intended to have been dining halls, were never completed. What was finished was the split-level gateway, with Doric columns on the exterior and Ionic either side of the main passage on the interior. The flanking unit to the northwest, the "Pinakotheke" (Picture Gallery) in which paintings on wooden panels were displayed, was also completed, having 3 columns *in antis* on the façade. Mnesikles may have intended a similar unit to the south; if so, his plans were frustrated, perhaps by the proximity of a surviving stretch of the Mycenaean fortification wall and of the sanctuary of Athena Nike. He had to content himself with a screen of three columns and a freestanding pier in front of a small space with a backing wall. This screen faced the entrance to the Pinakotheke. To the visitor climbing up the earth ramp to the entrance it would give the impression of a balancing unit to the south. The six-columned back of the gateway or inner façade shows the metopes here were blank (fig. **8.25**), nor was there any other sculpture. The material is marble throughout, finely jointed and finished, even for ceiling blocks and coffers of massive weight. The marble ceiling col-

lapsed under the strain of the bombardment of
the Acropolis by the Venetians in 1687, but
much of the southwest wing was built into a
Frankish tower which stood until the late
nineteenth century.

8.25 Propylaia to the Acropolis, Athens, from the east,
view of the inner façade. Marble. 437–432 BC

The Temple of Athena Nike (fig. **8.26**).   Built high on a bastion overlooking the approach to the Propylaia, this temple uses the Ionic order to contrast neatly with the Doric of the gateway itself. The building has four columns prostyle both at front and back, and a cella, which was an almost square room. This was entered through a doorway flanked by monolithic pillars, which were linked to antae by bronze struts. The elevation (fig. **8.27**) has Ionic bases and volute capitals for the columns with a continuous Ionic frieze above the architrave. A congregation of divinities, some seated, some standing, and some in motion make up the east frieze. The south depicts Greeks fighting Persians, and the west Greeks fighting Greeks, itself a hint that the building was constructed after the outbreak of the Peloponnesian War. Much billowing drapery, elongated figures and awkward poses anticipate developments in the next century. A decree of 449 BC authorized the construction, but the temple was not built until the middle to later years of the

8.26 *Opposite* Temple of Athena Nike, Athens, from the west. Marble. 420s BC

8.27 *Above* Temple of Athena Nike, Athens, view from the east showing *tetrastyle* columns of the façade and monolithic columns. Marble. 420s BC

8.28 Relief figure of a Nike (personification of Victory) tying her sandal, from the balustrade around the precinct of Athena Nike. Marble. Height 3 ft 6 ins (1.06 m). c. 410–405 BC. Acropolis Museum, Athens

420s BC. A little later, perhaps around 410 BC, a sculptured balustrade was added, about 3 feet (1 m) high, around the edge of the bastion on the north, south, and west. The theme was a parade of Nike figures, putting up trophies for victories or cajoling sacrificial animals along, with seated Athenas on each of the three sides. The hands of six sculptors have been detected in this work. The Nike adjusting her sandal (fig. **8.28**) demonstrates clinging drapery at its most transparent. The garment slips from the right shoulder, but the other shoulder is equally visible. The new precarious posture allowed drapery folds swinging across the figure to reveal the legs, while the clothing pressed against the torso makes the breasts visible, though covered.

The Erechtheion (fig. **0.3**, p. 16). The other Ionic building on the Acropolis was the Erechtheion, built opposite the Parthenon to the north, an unobtrusive Ionic counterweight to the Doric Temple of Athena Parthenos. This split-level building is unorthodox in plan (fig. **8.29**). Perhaps it reflects the number of earlier cults and shrines on the site, now incorporated in this single building. As well as Athena, whose old cult statue was kept here, Poseidon and Erechtheus commanded space in the building, and there were other cults in the vicinity. The building was begun in the 430s BC. Work continued intermittently, but much of the construction took place between 409 and 406 BC. In spite of the disaster of the Sicilian expedition, Athenian confidence persevered, and some building programs were continued.

A conventional Ionic six-columned façade stood at the east in front of the cella of Athena Polias. At a lower level on the north side, an Ionic porch of six more Ionic columns (four prostyle with two on the return) signaled the entrance to the lower western part of the building. This was unusual enough, but most unorthodox of all was the porch on the south side. It had six female

8.29 Plan of the Erechtheion, Athens. c. 430s–406 BC
  1 Athena Polias   2, 3, and 4 Erechtheus, Poseidon, possibly Boutes.

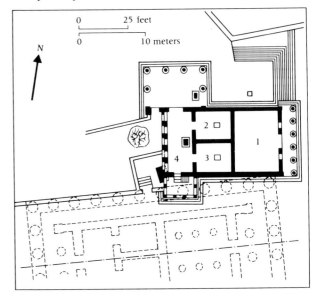

statues (Caryatids) standing on a wall to support the porch's flat roof. Access was from the east.

The Ionic order of the north porch is worth attention (fig. **8.30**). The column shaft with 24 flutes and flat fillets – compared with Doric which used 20 flutes and sharp arrises – stands on a base, and is surmounted by a volute capital. Below the capital and surrounding the neck of the column is an anthemion collar (floral carving). This ornamental motif runs all the way along the top of the north and south walls of the temple, as well as on the columns of the east façade. The channels of the volutes are concave, whereas in the Archaic period they were normally convex. In the Archaic period there had been an egg-and-dart molding between the volutes and little more; now the egg-and-dart is flanked by other decorative designs. The richness and complexity of ornament is staggering. The tall, slender proportions of the columns preserve lightness of appearance. Above the columns a frieze of white marble figures was pinned against blocks of black Eleusinian limestone. Of this frieze only fragments, which defy interpretation, survive.

The Caryatids of the south porch (fig. **8.37**, p. 263) stand with the weight leg lost beneath the vertical folds of drapery, and with the free leg pushing forward. The outer legs carry the weight of the superstructure, while the inner legs are relaxed. These are weighty figures, big and beautiful, wearing peploi with deepcut, vigorous folds over the weightbearing limbs and with transparent cloth elsewhere shaping or revealing knee, thigh and breast. As Caryatids, they are reminiscent of their counterparts in the treasury of the Siphnians at Delphi, over a hundred years earlier. Stylistically they echo the stately maidens of the east frieze of the Parthenon. The Erechtheion was the most elegant of the fifth-century buildings. Care and detail were lavished on it, and the surviving accounts of expenditures reveal how costly it was.

There was plenty of building elsewhere, too. New temples arose all over Attica, many on the sites of earlier structures, such as the Temple of Poseidon at Sunion, and many were completed before Perikles' death. Several were the work of

8.30 Erechtheion, Athens, north porch from the east. Marble with black Eleusinian limestone for frieze blocks to which marble figures were attached. Height (of columns) c. 25 ft (7.60 m). c. 430s–406 BC

the same architect, known as the Hephaisteion architect for the temple he built at the west of, and overlooking, the Agora in Athens.

The Hephaisteion (fig **0.5**, p. 18). The Temple of Hephaistos, god of metalworking, surveyed from the west the business center of the city, the Agora. It is located on the hill called the Kolonos Agoraios, where bronzeworking pits and foundry refuse prove that, in the fifth century BC, artisans

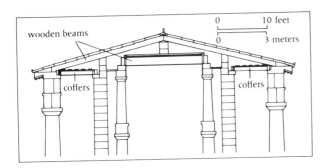

8.31 Hephaisteion, Athens. c. 450–415 BC. Restored section through the roof

metopes are decorated. Here the exploits of Theseus appear, and led to the building being called the Theseum, a name still sometimes used. The architect saw the need to introduce elements of the Ionic order, as did Iktinos and Kallikrates in the Parthenon, and the most conspicuous of these is the continuous Ionic frieze placed over the porches. At the east, the frieze extended over north and south ambulatories and showed a combat witnessed by the gods. At the back it was

had their place of work. Thus practitioners and their patron deity shared this ground. The Hephaisteion is the best preserved example of a fifth-century temple that we have. It is smaller than the Temple of Zeus at Olympia and smaller than the Parthenon. With the exception of the lowest step of limestone, wooden ceiling beams, and terracotta roof tiles, it was made entirely of marble.

The elevation is conventional Doric. It is notable, however, for unusually slender columns and a relatively high entablature. In height the columns measure 5.61 times the lower diameter compared to 4.64 or 4.72 in the Temple of Zeus at Olympia. The ceiling and roof arrangements are of special interest. Terracotta rooftiles sat on raking wooden beams (fig. **8.31**). Horizontal timbers spanned the widths of the cella from wall to colonnade, and from colonnade to colonnade. The ceiling of the peristyle was, however, made of marble, the slabs cut with *coffers* (recessed panels in the flat ceiling) to minimize the load on the wooden beams. Coffer lids were made separately and were removable, each coffer having its own lid which would not fit any other coffer. This was an expensive scheme, the reasons for which remain obscure.

That the temple was to be approached from the Agora and most often observed from that direction is shown by the arrangement of the sculptural ornament. Carved metopes at the east, now badly worn away, illustrate the labors of Herakles and run all the way across the front. On the flanks, however, only the four easternmost

8.32 Hephaisteion, Athens, frieze over back porch: centaurs pounding Kaineus into the earth, seen through exterior colonnade. Marble. Height (of frieze) 2 ft 8¾ ins (83 cm). c. 430s BC

situated only over the opisthodomos and showed the battle of Lapiths and centaurs. An episode from this popular topic shows two centaurs pounding the Lapith Kaineus (fig. **8.32**), who was otherwise invulnerable, into the earth. Only scraps of pedimental groups survive.

Bronze statues of Hephaistos and Athena, made by Alkamenes, pupil of Phidias, stood in the interior. An inscription tells us they were made between 421 and 415 BC when they were dedicated. This gives a date when the building was finished. The dates of progress of construction are based on pottery fragments from the construction fill, the style of the sculpture and architecture, and the shape of letters used in masons' marks on ceiling blocks. It seems that the friezes were perhaps carved in the 430s BC and the metopes, still somewhat Severe in style, in the 440s BC. Construction began about 450 BC and the work evidently took a long time to finish. Obviously, the Parthenon took priority.

The Agora. In spite of the toll taken by the war with Sparta, building continued in the Agora itself, too. During the decade 430–420 BC two new stoas sprang up (fig. **7.18**, p. 214). On the west side, amid the administrative buildings of the democracy and immediately adjacent to the Royal Stoa, the impressive Stoa of Zeus appeared. This unusual stoa, of the Doric order and with two wings projecting forward, was dedicated to Zeus Eleutherios (of Freedom), and so was a religious building which framed a great statue of Zeus. Its façade was partly of marble, itself unusual in the Agora, and it was decorated with paintings. Its function is unclear, though Plato says that Socrates met his friends there. Was it only a meeting place? The function of the other stoa, built on the south side of the Agora, South Stoa I is more obvious. This is a long structure, consisting of a double colonnade of the Doric order in front of 16 rooms. Materials are simple, with walls of roughly squared limestone blocks and much mudbrick. A large number of coins found here has suggested that this was a place for commerce, perhaps banking, while the shape of some of the rooms is suitable for dining couches. Since numerous members of official committees

were fed at public expense, as in the tholos, this may be the place where officials concerned with commercial activities and their regulation, such as inspectors of weights and measures, had their offices and took their meals.

Somewhere between 415–406 BC a new Council Chamber was built for the benefit of the boule. This New Bouleuterion (fig. **7.18**, p. 214) was put up directly west of its predecessor, which remained standing. The new building was rectangular, but the interior arrangement and provision for seating are uncertain. By the end of the century, a large square building identified as the Mint, where Athens struck her coinage, was built at the southeast corner of the Agora, while at the northeast one or more of the lawcourts was constructed. For the most part, these structures made use of unambitious materials, with walls of limestone and mudbrick, and floors of tamped earth.

During the sixth century BC the open space of the Agora had been used for theatrical events, whether dancing, drama, or singing, and part of it was termed the *orchestra*, the dancing place. The theatrical contests in honor of Dionysos were watched here by spectators seated on planks. These were supported by a wooden scaffolding called the "ikria," a temporary structure which could be put up or taken down at will. After a collapse of the ikria, however, and injuries to many people sometime in the fifth century BC, these events were moved to the new theatre of Dionysos on the other side of the Acropolis. In moving their dramatic performances to a theatre, which made use of a hillside, the Athenians were following Greek practice elsewhere. In the first place, suitable hollows in hillsides had been used, subsequently fitted out with wooden seating. It was not until the fifth century BC that permanent planned stone theatres were thought necessary. The plan is simple: the circle of the orchestra, where the performance took place, surrounded by an auditorium of seats rather more than semicircular in plan. On the side of the orchestra, where there were no seats, was a low stage building, unconnected to the seats, which served as dressing rooms and as backing for scenery. Orchestra and seating were unroofed.

8.33 Temple of Concord, Akragas, east façade and south flank from the east. Limestone. c. 430 BC

SICILY AND SOUTH ITALY

Theatrical events were popular in Syracuse, too. Aeschylus is said to have directed a performance of the *Persae* here around 470 BC and to have brought a production of the *Oresteia* to Syracuse in the 450s BC. The theatre where these were performed was probably on the spot where the enlarged theatre of the third century BC may now be seen. Its architect was Damocopos. It makes obvious use of a convenient hillside.

The Doric order continued to dominate temple architecture, and examples may best be seen at Akragas, where a magnificent series of structures was built along the southern ridge of the city. The Temple of Hera, built on a manmade spur of the cliff around 450 BC, is a Doric peripteral building with canonical proportions and number of columns (six by 13). Balancing porches, staircases for the inspection of the roof, and no columns in the cella complete the arrangements. Nearby, the Temple of Concord (a modern name) (fig. **8.33**) is another conventional, if remarkably preserved, Doric temple of around 430 BC. It has six by 13 columns with twenty flutes and entasis; porches front and back, staircases for access to the roof, metopes and pediment without sculpture. Yet another example with conventional plan and elevation, of the same date, is the temple of Hephaistos. This is a period of great prosperity for Akragas. Yet more and more these architects come to

8.34 Unfinished Doric temple, Segesta: interior, showing unfluted columns and missing stylobate blocks Limestone. c. 430–420 BC

espouse the conforming principles which arrived from Greece, and less and less to follow the imaginative ideas of their predecessors in the West. It is ironical that the architectural heirs of those who had had the imagination to juxtapose Doric and Ionic in the same building (as at Poseidonia two generations earlier) declined to pursue that solution. And it is paradoxical that it was mainland architects, those responsible for the Hephaisteion and the Parthenon, who ultimately adopted it.

At Segesta (fig. **8.34**), in the west of Sicily, a Doric temple outside the city was abandoned incomplete. The peristyle (six by 14) stands to this day with entablature and pediments; columns were left unfluted. Walls had been partially completed, but were subsequently robbed out, as were blocks of the stylobate. Doric refinements were included: stylobate and architrave curve slightly upward towards the middle, and columns tilt inward. The proportions of the building and the profile of the capitals place the temple somewhere around 430–420 BC. The unfinished state provides valuable evidence about the stages of construction, and it is clear in this instance – and in the Hephaisteion, too – that the outer

colonnade and its entablature were put up before the cella. The Doric refinements, so similar to those used in the Parthenon, suggest an architect from Athens. On the other hand, Western characteristics which are present argue for a local architect, who may have visited, or been told about, Athenian temples. In view of Athens' alliance with Segesta in the run-up to the Sicilian expedition, neither possibility need surprise.

At Locri in south Italy, marble *akroteria* (sculpted figures for the roof) were added to the temple, tentatively identified as a temple of Aphrodite. These take the form of the Dioskouroi leaping down from their horses, the hooves of which are supported by flying tritons, arms outstretched (fig. **8.35**). Horses and heads are reminiscent of the style of the Parthenon, though the Dioskouroi have lost the ease of movement of the Parthenon figures, and the complicated grouping with tritons below is perhaps a measure of a baroque local taste. These figures were added to the temple around 420 BC.

Terracotta remains a popular medium. Widely used in the decoration of public buildings, it was used at Locri too for representations of the Dioskouroi, as an akroterion of around 400 BC for the Temple of Zeus shows. Here the Dioskouros (fig. **8.36**) rides calmly along, his mount supported in this instance by a sphinx.

8.35 *Above* Akroteria of a temple, possibly that of Aphrodite, Locri: the Dioskouroi dismounting. Marble. c. 420 BC. National Museum, Reggio Calabria

8.36 *Below* Akroterion of the Temple of Zeus, Locri: Dioskouros mounted. Terracotta. c. 400 BC. National Museum, Reggio Calabria

Sculpture

The most reliable index to sculpture of the High Classical period is the sculpture from the Parthenon. There are the pedimental figures with the new deeply carved and revealing drapery and graduated response, physical and psychological, to the events at the center. There are the metopes with sometimes flamboyant compositions and sometimes still Severe Style theatrical expressions. And there is the frieze with its varied rhythms, mastery of figures, displaying great variety of pose, gesture, dress, and hairdo, as well as typically expressionless heads. For the standing female type, the Caryatids (fig. **8.37**) of the Erechtheion, too, are exemplary. Yet the many bases for free-standing statues, now lost, reveal how limited our perception is. The favored material was bronze, and while Roman copies give an idea of some aspects (such as the posture and the gesture and expression) of these originals, only the bronzes from Riace (figs **0.14**, **0.15**, p. 25) suggest the power and brilliance of the many bronze free-standing figures of the High Classical time. In the absence of the original bronzes, we turn to Roman copyists and adapters and to Roman commentators.

The most illustrious sculptor of the period, alongside Phidias, was Polykleitos. As well as practicing sculpture, Polykleitos wrote a book called the *Kanon*, which investigated the ideal proportions of the standing male figure. These proportions were thought to depend on the "symmetria" (commensurability) of the various parts of the body, but this term's exact meaning remains hazy: did symmetria mean volume, shape, length, breadth, or height of body parts or some equation involving these dimensions? Polykleitos is said to have made a statue, a bronze, to exemplify his "Kanon." Several copies of this statue (fig. **8.38**), the Doryphoros (Spear Carrier), have survived and are easily recognizable. The original was made about 440 BC. The figure explores the reaction of the body to the weight leg/free leg pose most vigorously. The free leg is placed both laterally and behind, the heel raised off the ground. This has been called the "walking stance," and motion forward is

8.37 Caryatid from the south porch of the Erechtheion, Acropolis of Athens. Marble. Height 7 ft 7 ins (2.30 m). c. 420–410 BC. Acropolis Museum, Athens

evidently implied in a balanced figure. Does he stand or does he walk? The horizontal axis through the hips tilts as the free leg is withdrawn, and contracted muscles set the torso in motion. The head turns to the same side as the firmly planted weight leg, and holds the figure still. The expression is the distanced, tranquil, High Classical look, seen in many figures of the Parthenon frieze. The tree trunk and the supportive strut are the contributions of the Roman marble copyist. These would not have been necessary when the statue was a bronze.

Throughout the body, tensed forms balance relaxed. Reading the statue vertically, relaxed right arm with weight leg balances tensed left arm (originally holding the spear) with free leg; reading horizontally, weight leg and free leg balance free arm and tensed arm. The term *contrapposto* is often used for this pose. Realism of bone and muscle, sinew and vein, and hair and flesh of this athletic figure is integrated into a concept of the ideal, which is dependent somehow on a system of mathematical proportions. Thus, a figure which represents the ideal is also the most visually accurate, the most real. The ambiguity of whether the Doryphoros walks or stands is matched by the ambiguity of whether he is more real or ideal.

Another work by Polykleitos was the Diadoumenos (the youth binding a fillet round his hair), again recognizable in Roman marble copies (fig. **8.39**) of the original bronze. Posture,

8.38 *Above* Doryphoros by Polykleitos, from Pompeii. Roman marble copy of a bronze Greek original. Height 6 ft 11 ins (2.12 m). c. 440 BC (original). National Museum, Naples

8.39 *Right* Diadoumenos by Polykleitos, from Delos. Roman marble copy of bronze Greek original. Height 6 ft 5 ins (1.95 m). c. 430 BC (original). National Museum, Athens

detail of the anatomy, and shape of the head are close to the Doryphoros. The more aggressive turn of the head and richer, more plastic treatment of the hair may suggest that the original was a later work, perhaps of about 430 BC.

Two of the pupils of Phidias deserve mention. Agorakritos made the cult statue for the temple of Nemesis at Rhamnus on the east coast of Attica. Alkamenes made numerous statues, according to the ancient sources. His most influential may have been a Hermes Propylaios (in front of the gates). This statue was a "herm" (an oblong block surmounted by a head and with a phallos in front). It was stylistically both retrospective, with an Archaic hairdo, and contemporary, as witnessed by the beard and face. There are many copies, and it may have been Alkamenes' original which Pausanias says he saw at the Propylaia to the Acropolis.

This Alkamenes cannot be the same Alkamenes who, Pausanias says, made the figures of the back pediment of the temple of Zeus at Olympia. The chronology does not fit. Nor does it for Paionios of Mende who, Pausanias says, made the figures of the east pediment. This illustrates the difficulties presented by literary sources. But perhaps there were two sculptors of the same name, Alkamenes, a generation or two apart. As for Paionios, an inscription on the base of a statue of a Nike in the sanctuary at Olympia says that he, Paionios, made the Nike, and that he was commissioned to make akroteria for the temple. This inscription could have been misread, or misunderstood so that Pausanias, or his source, simply made a mistake. Paionios (and Alkamenes) may have made the akroteria for the temple long after the building came into use, perhaps sometime in the 420s BC, and this information may have become garbled enough by the time Pausanias visited Olympia, or wrote up his notes to allow him to record that they had made the pediments. Information supplied by the ancient writers must be treated with caution.

Personifications of Victory (Nike), as if alighting, often functioned as akroteria on the roofs of buildings. On relief panels they decorate the balustrade around the temple of Athena Nike on the Acropolis at Athens. They also appeared as

8.40 Nike by Paionios, from Olympia. Marble. Height 6 ft 5 ins (1.95 m). C. 420 BC. Olympia Museum

independent dedications, an Archaic example of which is the Nike dedicated in the sanctuary on Delos (fig. **6.54**, p. 179). The Nike made by Paionios and dedicated at Olympia, though badly damaged, survives. The winged female figure stood out against the sky, about 33 feet (10 m) up, atop a triangular pillar. She was shown (fig. **8.40**) at the moment when she touches down, still in flight and with wings (now lost) unfolded. Her bared limb and breast contrast with the covered parts of her body. Drapery, forced against her body by the rush of her flight, accentuates her anatomy, and billowing out behind, increases the sense of forward motion about to come to a halt. Missing are her face, the rest of the drapery swirling around behind, and the outspread wings. This is, nevertheless, a masterpiece, stylistically midway between the sculptures of the Parthenon and the "wet" extravagance of the Nike balustrade (fig. **8.28**, p. 256). Paionios' Nike was dedicated around 420 BC to celebrate, as the inscription says, a victory of the Messenians and Naupaktians.

The production of grave reliefs was resumed in Attica around 430 BC, and may have been stimulated both by the outbreak of the Peloponnesian War and by the decoration of the public state graves prepared for the casualties of war. The tall, single-figured stelai of the Archaic period had been replaced in the Early Classical phase by smaller but broader reliefs, decorated with two or more figures, sometimes including seated figures. These were to be found in the Islands and in Asia Minor but not in Attica. Architectural elements were also introduced. These developments were followed in Attica when private grave monuments began to be made again.

The purpose seems to have been to represent the dead as he or she was when alive. Some figures are characterized by attributes: a soldier in armor, an old man with his stick, a girl with a doll. Other figures may be depicted with companions during life, seen saying farewell, or shaking hands. Inscriptions sometimes say who the dead person was, without identifying which of the figures in the relief is alive and which dead. It seems that many gravestones were generic, only individualized by an added epigram or other inscription.

An early example, from around 430 BC, is the so-called Cat stele, on which the dead youth is accompanied by a mourning boy attendant and an animal, perhaps a cat, seated on top of a stele (fig. **8.41**). Above the cat is a birdcage, to which the youth extends his right arm while the left hand holds a bird. Deep carved and pressed flat drapery evokes the style of the drapery of the Parthenon figures, as does the youth's head with rounded skull, small mouth, large eye, unruly hair, and faraway expression. The grave stele of Hegeso (fig. **8.42**), about 400 BC, provides a good example of the architectural format – with *antae* and the pediment of a doorway – in front of

8.41 So-called "Cat stele," from Aegina. Marble. Height c. 3 ft 5 ins (1.04 m). c. 430 BC. National Museum, Athens

which figures sit or stand. Hegeso, well dressed, has hair carefully arranged, and elegantly seated (with a footstool, even) is engaged in a familiar pastime: with the help of a servant she chooses jewelry from an opened box. Receding planes, three-quarter and intermediate views are handled with confidence. Garments exemplify the transparency of the late fifth century BC; faces are without expression of emotion. The mood is of that serenity and otherworldliness which is associated with the High Classical style of the Parthenon, and which is obviously at home here.

Votive reliefs resume at about the same time as grave reliefs in Attica. They were placed on top of pillars, like their painted wooden counterparts, and were rectangular and low in shape. Themes involve the deities concerned, sometimes approached by worshipers shown at a smaller scale, and even by the dedicator and members of

his family. Mythological scenes appear also, some inspired by lesser known local Athenian myths. The hero Echelos makes off with the nymph Basile (fig. **8.43**), encouraged by Hermes, in a fourhorse chariot. Horses neigh and rear, their heads cocked at different angles. Only two hooves of all four horses touch the ground in a group which is a clear echo of the Parthenon frieze, and which was made about 410 BC.

Evidence for sculptural production in the West is scant. This perhaps reflects difficulties in transporting marble, both in terms of communications and costs in the perilous times around the Peloponnesian War, or the accidents of survival, or preference for bronze.

Pottery and wall painting

Wall paintings such as the Tomb of the Diver at Poseidonia were painted against a white background. The white background in vase painting had been tried at the time of the experiments which led to the introduction of the red-figure technique, around 530 BC, but had not become popular. In the first half of the fifth century BC, the white-ground technique was tried again, now using outline drawing rather than the black-figure technique. A jug by the Brygos Painter (fig. **8.45**) offers a good example of this. Against the white ground the woman is drawn in outline, with contours in black relief lines. A domestic scene shows her spinning wool, using distaff and spindle, head bent in concentration. Other painters also try out the technique, and introduce new ideas. Black relief lines give way to brown dilute glaze lines, and a whiter, thicker white is used for female flesh to distinguish it from background white. It is not, however, until the High Classical era that white ground really comes into its own.

8.42 *Top* Grave stele of Hegeso, from Athens. Marble. Height c. 5 ft 2 ins (1.58 m). c. 400 BC. National Museum, Athens

8.43 *Left* One side of a two-sided votive relief: the hero Echelos and the nymph Basile ride off. Height 2 ft 6 ins (75 cm) c. 410 BC. National Museum, Athens.

The technique is used on several shapes, including the krater (fig. **8.46**), but the white ground itself is fragile and friable, and this was an obvious disadvantage, at least for pots which were to be handled much. It came to be used specially on *lekythoi*, tall flasks for holding oils and unguents and regularly deposited in burials. This meant they did not come in for a lot of use, and could be decorated with white-ground with impunity. Painters were also tempted to try more colors, which more often than not have unfortunately faded.

By the end of the century, red, black, and brown were in use for contours, and washes of green, purple, and blue were applied for broader passages of drapery. This polychrome style may best reflect the style of monumental murals and panels. Experiment went beyond color, broken contour lines attempting to suggest volume. A lekythos (fig. **8.47**) of about 410–400BC with a mournful seated woman in front of a tomb uses broken contours (of her arms, for example) to suggest mass. This may be a trick learnt from wall painting since it seems to agree with descriptions of the murals of Parrhasios, who was thought to have depicted volume by line, not by shading. Parrhasios lived in Athens during the Peloponnesian War. Shading, as a device for rendering volume in painting, is attributed by literary sources to two other late-fifth-century wall painters, Zeuxis and Apollodoros, but shading only rarely appears on vases to suggest volume in humans, and then not until the very end of the century.

These white-ground lekythoi generally show scenes appropriate to the funerary context such as departures, tombs, and visitors. Some are almost 20 inches (50 cm) high, and challenge the carved stone reliefs for prominence. Some carved reliefs even take the shape of lekythoi.

Painting vases in the red-figure technique continued, but demand slowly declined. There are fewer and fewer signatures of painters in the second half of the century and, by the early part of the fourth century BC, signatures of potters, too, had disappeared. The name-vase of the Achilles Painter, who also painted in white ground, is an amphora (fig. **8.44**), now in the

8.44 Attic red-figure amphora by the Achilles Painter: Achilles, in *contrapposto* Polykleitan stance. Height 23¾ ins (60 cm). c. 440 BC. Vatican Museums, Rome

Vatican Museum. The hero stands in solitary splendor, highlighted on a maeander groundline, shouldering his spear, his right hand on his hip. Accurate representation of the anatomy is thoroughly understood, whether it be the intermediate views of the left leg or the profile eye. The deep carving of folds of drapery of the Parthenon figures is matched in painting now by close-packed, irregular, wavy lines of garments (over the left arm), giving a subtle sense of weight and texture, and by broken lines, curls, and hooks (over the upper thighs). The mood is close to the ideal calm of the Parthenon figures, while the stance is close to that of Polykleitos' Doryphoros. The date is around 440 BC. Heroic and mythological scenes become less popular, however, and their place is taken by scenes of

8.45 *Above left* Attic white-ground oinochoe attributed to the Brygos Painter: woman spinning. Height 8⅔ ins (22 cm). c. 490–480 BC. British Museum, London

8.46 *Left* Attic white-ground krater, from Vulci: Dionysos and Nike. Height 13¾ ins (35 cm). c. 440–430 BC. Vatican Museums, Rome

8.47 *Above* Attic white-ground lekythos: seated woman in front of a tomb. Height 20 ins (51 cm). c. 410–400 BC. British Museum, London

daily life. Young women at their toilette become a favorite topic, sometimes with the women wholly nude and accompanied by numerous Eros figures.

The taste in sculpture for light, flimsy, and transparent drapery, such as that seen on the figures decorating the balustrade around the temple of Athena Nike on the Acropolis, is followed in vase painting. A practitioner who typifies the taste of the end of the century is the Meidias Painter. A hydria potted by Meidias, and now in the British Museum (fig. **8.48**), shows him at his most exuberant. The lower register shows Herakles in the gardens of the Hesperides (the daughters of the evening), and the tree whose golden apples they and the dragon protected. In the main register, the Dioskouroi and their chariots arrive to carry off the daughters of Leucippos. Pollux, successful, drives off in his chariot, hooves flying, while Castor's team awaits their master's flirtatious return. The setting is a sanctuary of Aphrodite, identified by various elements: the cult statue above and between the horse groups, the landscape suggested by trees and bushes, and the seated goddess herself below

by an altar. Figures are disposed over the surface at various levels and in various postures, as with the Niobid Painter earlier, their arms outstretched. Drapery makes no attempt to conceal the female bodies. Their limbs are plump and soft, their gestures and poses varied. The drawing is luxurious with gilding used for necklaces and bracelets and for the cult statue. The mood is warmer and more sensuous than menacing. The hydria was painted around 410 BC. The almost voluptuous sense of ease of the painted scenes is at odds both with the implied tension of the activities shown and with the rigors of the Peloponnesian War which then engulfed Athens.

As well as painted pottery, Athenian potters made large quantities of simpler wares. In the High Classical period vases decorated on a plain, shiny, tough black gloss (often inaccurately referred to as "glaze," see p. 182) became popular. These vases came in all shapes and sizes and were used for storage, pouring, and drinking of wine, water, and olive oil. The gloss was also used on other items of tableware – plates and lamps, for example. A selection of such pottery, all found in a well in the Agora in Athens (fig. **8.49**)

8.48 *Opposite* Attic red-figure hydria attributed to the Meidias Painter: bottom, Herakles in the garden of the Hesperides; top, rape of the daughters of Leucippos. Height 20½ ins (52 cm). c. 410–400 BC. British Museum, London

8.49 Shapes of plain black gloss table wares, from Athens, 5th century BC. Agora Museum, Athens

includes cups, jugs, storage pots, a cooler, plates, and lamps. Cooking pots, too, were necessary items of daily life. They were strictly utilitarian, less elegant than the table wares and handmade of coarser clay (fig. **8.51**). Such coarse wares had obviously existed before and were produced at Athens throughout antiquity.

Also made of coarse clay and undecorated were the amphoras (storage vessels) in which olive oil and wine were transported around the Mediterranean. Though all have two handles at the top and the knoblike toe at the bottom (fig. **8.50**), the profiles vary, and often signal the provenance of an amphora and its contents. The globular amphoras of the middle row in the illustration, for example, come from Mende, a state well known for its wine. Since amphoras are valuable indices of economic life, and provide evidence of trade connections, the development of their shapes and their patterns of distribution have been closely studied. Moreover, they are often stamped on the handle, especially in the Hellenistic period, with the symbol of the state where the oil or wine came from, and with the name of the governing magistrate in whose annual period of office the amphora, and perhaps its contents, were produced. Thus, these amphoras are significant chronological markers. On average, they contained about 7 gallons

8.50 Transport amphoras of various origins: top row, from Lesbos; middle row, from Mende; bottom row, from Thasos. Agora Museum, Athens

8.51 Coarse ware cooking pots and portable stoves, from Athens. 5th century BC. Agora Museum, Athens

(about 26.5 liters) and weighed about 77 pounds (35 kg) when full. They were placed on their sides for transport, as the discovery of sunk merchant ships and their cargoes on the floor of the Mediterranean has revealed, their holds containing hundreds of amphoras stacked sideways. The knoblike toe acted as another handle to help with moving the amphora, but it was no help when the owner stood the amphora up to reach the contents. In this position the amphora had either to stand in a tripod or in a hole in the ground.

In the West, Greeks had relied on imported painted pottery in the first half of the century for their prestige wares, but now they began to produce their own. The appearance of this south Italian red-figure pottery may be related to the foundation of Thurii from Athens in 443 BC. Perhaps potters and painters were involved in this late colonial venture. Their presence is certainly attested at Metapontum, a little further

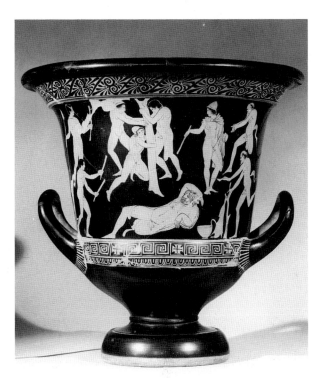

northeast along the coast from Thurii, where some of their kilns have been found.

Their work at first is undemanding, simple objects and rather stodgy figures, but, by the last quarter of the century, some are attempting more daring and innovative schemes. The calyx krater (fig. **8.52**), attributed to the Cyclops Painter, shows the drunken Polyphemos at the bottom of the scene and Odysseus and his companions at the top maneuvering the great stake with which they will blind Polyphemos. The theme goes back to the Eleusis amphora (fig. **5.7**, p. 127) painted in Athens in the seventh century BC. The arrangement of figures ''up and down'' the surface goes back to painters like the Niobid Painter (figs **7.34**, **7.35**, p. 230), and the probable appearance of such a scheme in monumental paintings of the first part of the fifth century BC. So dependence on Athens is clear. New to the scene are the figures of satyrs darting in from the right. Some have suggested that the scene may have been evoked by a satyr play, light-hearted romps performed after tragic trilogies. This calyx krater was made around 420–410 BC in Lucania.

There is evidence of another workshop which was perhaps located at Taras, and which began work around 430–420 BC. A leading painter here is the Sisyphus Painter who worked both in the conventional, relatively simple south Italian style, and also in a more elaborate, ornamental manner. From this artist developed the two main strands of south Italian painting in Apulia (the heel of Italy): the Ornate Style and the Plain Style. This Apulian pottery was to come to the fore in the next century, when vase painters in Italy began to block the Athenian vase painters from the markets in the West.

8.52 South Italian red-figure krater by the Cyclops Painter: below, Cyclops (Polyphemos) stupefied; above, Odysseus and companions. Height 18½ ins (47 cm). c. 420–410 BC. British Museum, London

9
The Fourth Century
c. 400–300 BC

The defeat at the end of the
Peloponnesian War might have been
expected to end Athens' political
aspirations. But it did not. Within a
decade, an Athenian fleet was doing
battle with Spartans, and winning, near
Knidos. By 390 BC, skirmishes had taken
place near Corinth, and the walls of
Athens and of Piraeus were rebuilt.
Though the Persians intervened in the
early 380s BC to arbitrate a treaty which
supported the claims of Sparta, the
Athenians and their allies went to war
again in the 370s BC. Finally, in 371 BC, a
peace confirmed Sparta's hegemony on
land and Athens' on sea, but the old
rivalry was still alive. The system of
independent city-states grouped in
alliances around the two protagonists
struggling for the control of Greece was
challenged first by Thebes. Employing
new military tactics, Thebes overwhelmed
Sparta in a land battle fought at Leuctra

Opposite Detail of a limestone relief, from Taras: Orestes
and Electra at the tomb of Agamemnon, fig. **9.35**.
c. 300 BC

in 371 BC, and for a brief period of ten years or so, assumed a leadership role. But the death of the great Theban general, Epaminondas, at the battle of Mantinea in 362 BC put an end to the Theban hegemony. The second more serious challenge to Athens and Sparta and the autonomous Greek states came from Macedon.

Philip II became king of Macedon in 359 BC. His early years were taken up in consolidating his authority and his kingdom's boundaries. But, in 348 BC, he moved east against the city of Olynthos, an ally of Athens, which he destroyed. Shortly thereafter, he moved south, and in 338 BC defeated the Greeks, who had at last put their rivalries behind them to face the invasion from the north, at the battle of Chaeronea. The independence of the Greek city-states was ended. Though Philip treated them leniently, they were now effectively the subjects of the king.

However much Demosthenes, the learned orator, and his friends at Athens may have railed against Macedon, and however frequently the enemies of the democracy may have been threatened by Athenian rhetoric, and even by legislative decree, the fact was that Greece was a subject, if now at long last unified, nation. Two years later (336 BC), Philip was assassinated. He was in Macedon at the time, and the finger of suspicion points at his own people. He was succeeded by his 21-year-old son, Alexander, soon to become Alexander the Great. In spite of a rebellion in Greece, which was quickly suppressed, Alexander was well disposed towards the Greeks; but he was more interested in Persia.

Alexander entered Asia Minor in 334 BC and, within a short time, had defeated the Persian king, conquered the Persian Empire, and mastered the known world from Macedonia in the north to Egypt in the south, and from the Aegean to Afghanistan (fig. **9.1**). Within a decade, Greek life and political development were irreversibly changed. Alexander's death in Babylon in 323 BC provoked disorder. Fighting broke out between his generals, who ultimately divided the empire of Alexander into kingdoms for themselves. Of these, four were to be significant – Macedon still, Egypt, Pergamon, and Syria. The history of these kingdoms is largely the

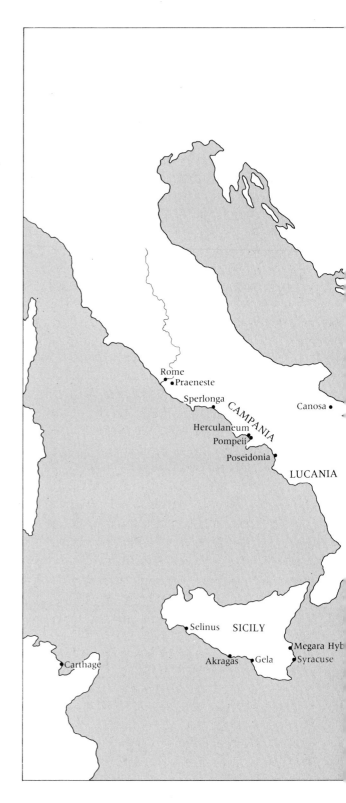

9.1 The Greek world from c. 400–30 BC

history of the Hellenistic period, but three of the four (Pergamon the exception) were independent entities by the end of the fourth century BC. The world of the Greek city-states had come to an end. Greece herself retreated to the sidelines, while great nation-states emerged, ruled by military monarchs.

Far from these great happenings in the East, Greeks in the West were under pressure, too. In Italy, Poseidonia fell into the hands of indigenous peoples, who swarmed down from the hills to capture other prosperous cities as well. But further south, Metapontum and Taras continued to prosper. In Sicily, the Carthaginians had bided their time. But in the aftermath of the disastrous Athenian expedition to Syracuse, they returned to the offensive, and Greek city after Greek city fell into their grasp. In this way, Selinus (in 409 BC) and Akragas (in 406 BC), for example, were overthrown. Syracuse survived thanks to the arrival of a new tyrant, Dionysios, who fortified the city and then carried the war to the Carthaginians in the west of the island. By turns victorious and vanquished, Dionysios battled against Carthage through the first decade of the century. Though besieged, Syracuse never fell. A hiatus of some 20 years in warfare against Carthage followed, in the course of which the philosopher Plato made the first of his visits to Syracuse from Athens. War resumed in 368 BC; Dionysios died the following year. Civil war in Syracuse engaged the attention of his son and successor, Dionysios II, and this strife was not resolved until the arrival of Timoleon from Corinth, summoned by some of Dionysios' enemies.

Timoleon left Corinth in 344 BC, and within a year was master of Syracuse. Dionysios II went into exile (at Corinth), and a moderate oligarchy, somewhat modeled after Plato's ideas, was installed. Carthage was defeated again, and under the leadership of Timoleon the damaged or destroyed Greek cities of Sicily, and their countrysides behind them, were inhabited again by new Greek colonists or returning refugees.

On the death of Timoleon, civil discord returned to Syracuse. This was resolved by Agathokles, a protagonist of the democratic party, who dissolved the council of oligarchs two

years later and assumed complete power himself. War against Carthage preoccupied him, too, but he was bold enough to take the war to Africa, and, after a successful assault on Carthage herself, peace was concluded in 306 BC.

In 307 BC, Agathokles had taken the title of King, by which he aligned himself with those other new kings of the Greek world, the successors of Alexander, in the East. His program included the unification of Sicily and south Italy into one kingdom. By 304 BC, the whole of Sicily anyway was under his control.

Conditions of dislocation, both in Greece and in the West, prevailed. Almost continuous warfare between states and between Greeks and foreigners, with its concomitant devastation, and internal struggles within cities between democrats, oligarchs and monarchs (as at Syracuse) did little to help the work of planners and architects, sculptors, and painters. But new buildings went up, and new cities were planned. The great sculptors of the fourth century BC – Praxiteles, Skopas, and Lysippos – explored further the boundaries of idealism and realism, and energetic workshops of vase painters in south Italy competed with Athens in the development of the red-figure style.

Architecture and architectural sculpture

BASSAE
High in the mountains of the Peloponnese at Bassae (fig. **9.2**) the people of Phigaleia built a Temple of Apollo. This building has many peculiarities, and its date is intriguing. Pausanias says that the architect was Iktinos, one of the architects of the Parthenon. To judge from that, and the elongated old-fashioned peristyle, it was certainly begun, and the exterior built, in the fifth century BC, perhaps in the decade 430–420 BC. But details of the architecture and the sculptured frieze suggest it may not have been finished until around 400 BC or even very early in the fourth century BC. The interior of the temple is so full of innovation and anticipates so many

9.2 Temple of Apollo, Bassae, attributed to Iktinos, one of the architects of the Parthenon. Limestone and marble. c. 430–390 BC

fourth-century developments – interior columns being non-Doric and functionally ornamental, for example – that it is included in this chapter. This building is evidently transitional between the fifth and fourth centuries BC.

The orientation is unusual, north–south. This and the Archaizing, elongated proportions were dictated by a preceding temple on the site. The temple is built almost entirely of limestone quarried nearby. The plan called for six columns by 15; porches front and back have two columns *in antis*, though the front porch is deeper than the back. The arrangement behind the porch is highly original: a cella and a kind of adyton with a side door. The transition from cella to adyton is marked by a single column with a capital of com-

pletely novel appearance. The exterior order is Doric, but columns of the cella are attached to the wall by masonry spurs, stand on broad bases, and have Ionic volute capitals of unique design. The single column screening adyton from cella introduces the Corinthian capital (fig. **9.3**).

The Corinthian capital has a bell-shaped echinus, surrounded by acanthus leaves, spirals and palmettes, and has small pairs of volutes at all four corners. Accordingly, it provides the same view from all sides, and is therefore more useful than the Ionic, whose volutes present problems at the corners of buildings. The use of the Corinthian capital is one of the hallmarks of the fourth century. Its popularity slowly increases until in the Roman period its supremacy is assured.

Although a Doric structure, this temple, like the Parthenon, was decorated with a sculptured Ionic frieze. Whereas on the Parthenon the frieze

9.3 *Above* Restored drawing of the interior of the Temple of Apollo, Bassae. c. 430–390 BC

9.4 *Below* Temple of Apollo, Bassae, frieze block: Greeks fighting Amazons. Marble. Height 2 ft (63 cm). c. 400–390 BC. British Museum, London

had run round the outside of the cella, here it decorated the interior. The subjects are commonplace: fights between Greeks and Amazons and between Greeks and centaurs. The quality of workmanship varies between convincing scenes of combat (fig. **9.4**) and others showing impossible anatomies in contorted postures. The musculature of the Greeks is emphatic , while the limbs and breasts of the Amazons are soft and fleshy, fully visible through the transparent drapery. The "wet" drapery with its billowing active folds, the ends curled into hooks and loops, is typical of Athenian work of the last decade of the fifth century BC. But the highly exaggerated postures and gestures of some figures and their theatrical expressions, with deep set eyes, are more at home in the fourth.

TEGEA

Another important temple of the Doric order in the Peloponnese was built in the middle years of the century at Tegea. The architect of this Temple of Athena Alea was Skopas of Paros. He introduced novelties of plan and elevation of which engaged Corinthian columns on the interior with Ionic above (fig. **9.5**) and a lateral entrance to the cella are conspicuous features. The elevation was

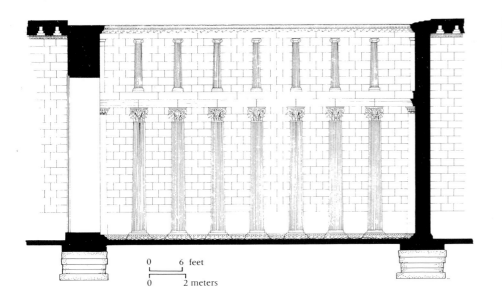

9.5 Reconstruction of the south wall of the cella of the Temple of Athena Alea, Tegea. c. 340 BC

notable for its tall proportions, which gave the temple a light and airy appearance.

EPIDAUROS

Temple building in the fourth century often involved reconstructing temples destroyed by fire or other catastrophe. The gigantic sixth-century Temple of Artemis at Ephesos, for example, was burnt down, but replaced by an equally large building almost at once. Replacement temples or the repair of damaged temples left little scope for innovation. Yet elsewhere in new complexes, architects experimented with scale, shape, and proportions, and with the new Corinthian order.

The cult of Asklepios, god of healing, medicine, and doctors, grew rapidly after its appearance, doubtless stimulated by the plague in Athens in the later fifth century BC. At Epidauros, in the Peloponnese (fig. **9.6**), an international sanctuary of enormous renown grew up in

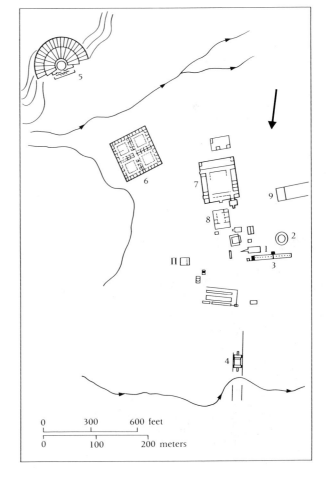

9.6 Plan of the Sanctuary of Asklepios, Epidauros. 4th century BC and later
1 Temple of Asklepios
2 Tholos (thymela)
3 Abaton (stoa)
4 Propylon
5 Theatre
6 Hotel
7 "Gymnasium"
8 *Palaestra*
9 Stadium

the fourth century BC. It paralleled Asklepios'
other great sanctuary at Kos in the eastern
Aegean.

The architect of the temple, Theodotos, chose
the Doric order, but abandoned the usual ratio of
façade columns to flank and had only 11 columns
by six to give a more square, compact plan. The
opisthodomos (back porch) also was abandoned.
The pediments were decorated with marble
figures depicting battles between Greeks and
Amazons and between Greeks and Trojans. The
seated statue of Asklepios inside was of gold and
ivory. Little of the building remains, but an
inscribed record of expenditures incurred
survives, and this yields important evidence

9.7 *Below* Tholos, Epidauros, abbreviated interior
Corinthian order. Marble. c. 360–340 BC. Epidauros
Museum

about costs for labor, transport, and materials.
The temple was built around 380 BC.

The altar was not in front of the temple but
adjacent to it, and in front of the most imposing
structure in the sanctuary. This was a circular
building known to Pausanias as a tholos, but
referred to in inscriptions as a "thymela," a
covered hearth. This building, approached by a
ramp leading straight to the door, has a diameter
of more than 24 yards (22 m), only a yard (1 m)
less than the length of the temple. The plan consisted of three concentric circles: an outer circle
of 26 Doric columns, a wall, and an inner circle of
14 Corinthian columns. The Corinthian capitals
(fig. **9.7**) display a double row of acanthus leaves,
encircling the bellshaped echinus, sharply carved
and rich in decorative value, as are the architectural moldings and the ceiling soffits. The architect was Polykleitos the Younger, whose design
dates to around 360–340 BC. The purpose of this
mysterious building is unclear. It may be a formal
precursor to the Philippeion at Olympia, the
circular building erected as a votive gift after the
battle of Chaeronea, and containing statues of
Philip and Alexander. But the tholos is placed
more emphatically in the sanctuary. Was it the
tomb of Asklepios? Was it the home of the sacred
snakes which cured many illnesses, and whose
serpentine shape was reflected in the building's
plan?

The sanctuary was well equipped with stoas,
in one of which, at any rate, the so-called
Abaton, patients seeking relief from illness were
supposed to spend the night and enjoy restora-
tive dreams. The efficacy of these is attested by
inscriptions from the site, though Aristophanes,
the famous Athenian writer of comedies, referring to an Abaton elsewhere, makes ample fun of
the whole process.

The sanctuary itself with its temple, tholos,
stoas, propylon, and boundary markers was supported by other buildings clustered on the south
side, the most important of which was the
theatre just over half a mile (1 km) away. These
structures, some built later than the fourth century BC, were all for the benefit of pilgrims. A
large two-storeyed hotel boasted 160 rooms,
arranged around four peristyle courts, and an

equally large "gymnasium" (more probably a building for ritual activity), a palaestra, and a stadium were provided for exercise and athletics. A palaestra, an enclosed exercise ground, was normally, as at Epidauros, rectangular in plan. An open court had colonnades on all sides and rooms behind the colonnade for changing, storage, meetings, and lectures.

Asklepios, his daughter Hygeia (Health), and his sacred companions the snakes (who knew how to find potent herbs and by sloughing off skins symbolized renewal) were to become influential among the Romans. But their power slowly waned, and the gradual secularization from healing sanctuary to health resort is shown in the character of subsidiary buildings at Epidauros.

Though the theatre was not built until the early third century BC, it is appropriate to con-sider it here. It was built into a hillside to make use of the slope and to reduce costs, now that theatres were to be built of stone. The illustration (fig. **9.8**) shows the circular orchestra where the dramas were enacted, with the "skene" (dressing rooms for actors and storage for props and scenery) behind. The huge auditorium, about 142 yards (130 m) in diameter, rises up the hill-side (the theatre is still in use today) in symmetri-cally arranged wedges of stone seats. Stairs separate wedge from wedge, and an upper sec-tion of seats is separated from a lower by a horizontal gangway giving access from the hill-side. The 55 rows of seats could accommodate up to twelve thousand spectators. Theatre, and theatres, were closely associated with the cult of Dionysos, so special seats at ground level were reserved for priests of Dionysos, and at Epidauros there was an altar of Dionysos in the orchestra.

9.8 Theatre, Epidauros. Early third century BC

ATHENS

The circular shape and the Corinthian column appear in Athens, too, in a monument (fig. **9.9**) commemorating a victory in a theatrical contest of a chorus sponsored by a man called Lysikrates. This was in 334 BC. The circular monument stood on a rectangular base and is the first example of the use of the Corinthian order on the exterior of a structure: six Corinthian columns are engaged in the masonry drum beneath an architrave and sculptured frieze. The apex of the roof consists of elaborately carved stone foliage, and originally supported the prize itself, a bronze tripod.

9.9 Monument of Lysikrates, Athens, showing exterior use of the Corinthian order. Marble and limestone. c. 334 BC

Elsewhere in Athens, new revenues from the silver mines at Laurion, first exploited in the 480s BC and now the site of renewed activity, allowed a new stadium to be built as well as a new theatre on the south side of the Acropolis. In the Agora (fig. **9.10**), a fountainhouse, L-shaped in plan, was built at the southwest corner between 350–325 BC, and a monumental water-clock was erected nearby, by which the opening and closing of the market and the beginning and end of trials could be timed. The small Temple of Apollo Patroos, replacing an archaic precursor, was built around 330 BC on the west side and in about 300 BC construction began on the large Square Peristyle in the northeast corner. This courtyard, with columns on all four sides, measured 38 yards (35 m) square, and was rather sloppily constructed with much reused material. It was on the site of structures taken to have been lawcourts, and may have served the same purpose.

The enclosed courtyard is a feature of domestic architecture, too. A good many houses of the fifth and fourth centuries BC (fig. **9.11**) have been excavated at Athens, particularly in the zone south and southwest of the Agora, and on the slopes of the Areopagos to the west of the Acropolis. Their sizes and plans are irregular, especially when compared with the more systematic plans for housing in other cities. Generally they are small with a single entrance from the street into a courtyard surrounded by several rooms. Occasionally, the court has a colonnade around it. The courtyard provided light and air, since windows on the exterior were few and far between for reasons of security. It was the scene of much of the household's activity. It also provided a supply of water reached by wells dug to a depth of some 39 feet (12 m), though by the fourth century BC these wells were drying up and were being replaced by cisterns which gathered rainwater from the roof. Other sources of water were the fountainhouses (e.g., at the southeast and southwest corners of the Agora) to which good, clean water for public consumption was piped from springs.

Normally, one chief room opened off the court, and this was used for entertaining. It was called the *andron* and it was here that men dined

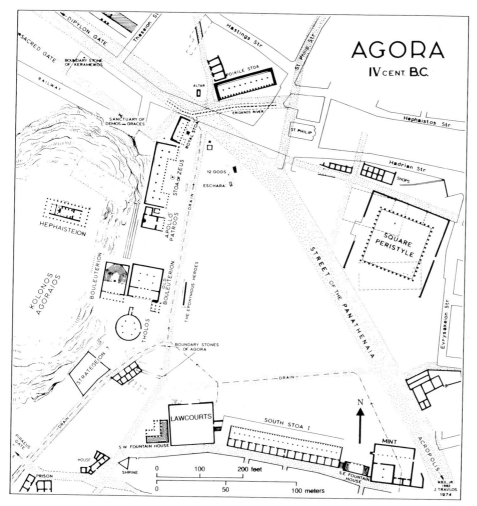

AGORA
IV CENT. B.C.

SACRED GATE
DIPYLON GATE
Thesion Str
Hastings Str
St Philip Str
BOUNDARY STONE OF KERAMEIKOS
RAILWAY
POIKILE STOA
ALTAR
SANCTUARY OF DEMOS = GRACES
ERIDANOS RIVER
Hephaistos Str
St Philip
ROYAL STOA
Hadrian Str
STOA OF ZEUS
APOLLO PATROOS
12 GODS
ESCHARA
SHOPS
HEPHAISTEION
DRAIN
SQUARE PERISTYLE
KOLONOS AGORAIOS
BOULEUTERION
OLD BOULEUTERION
THE EPONYMOUS HEROES
Evrysakeion Str
STREET OF THE PANATHENAIA
THOLOS
BOUNDARY STONES OF AGORA
STRATEGEION
DRAIN
DRAIN
N
DRAIN
PIRAEUS GATE
LAWCOURTS
S W FOUNTAIN HOUSE
SOUTH STOA I
MINT
HOUSE
SHRINE
ACROPOLIS
PRISON
S.E. FOUNTAIN HOUSE

0   100   200 feet
0   50   100 meters

W.B.D. JR. 1982
J. TRAVLOS 1974

9.10 Plan of the Agora, Athens. c. 300 BC

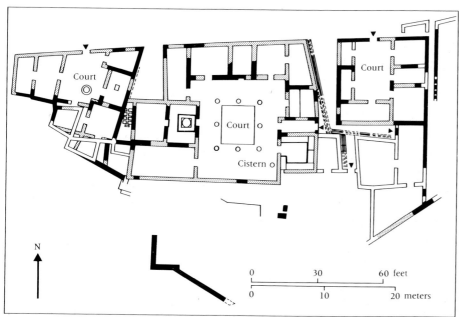

Court
Court
Court
Cistern
N

0   30   60 feet
0   10   20 meters

9.11 Domestic architecture, Athens. 5th–4th centuries BC

reclining on couches. This room was sometimes brightened by a pebble mosaic floor (pebbles set in mortar), though floors elsewhere were simply tamped earth. A kitchen, identifiable by quantities of crockery and cooking utensils, was nearby. There was also a bathroom/latrine, a small room with a drain which emptied into a drain outside the house. Other rooms around the court were storerooms, living rooms (those frequented by women often identified from quantities of loom-weights), or bedrooms, though these were often on the second floor.

Building materials were unimpressive. A foundation of rubble supported a low rubble socle for walls built almost entirely of unbaked mudbricks, and then covered with stucco to protect them from rain. Projecting eaves of the roof also provided some protection. Wood was used for roofbeams supporting the terracotta rooftiles and for frames for doors and windows. Furnishings also were modest, little more than couches, wooden chairs and stools, and small chests and tables. The overall impression of these urban private houses is of cramped conditions, of blocks of rather mean houses, sharing party walls, amid streets which resembled tortuous alleys more than thoroughfares. In the suburbs and the countryside of Attica, more spacious dwellings existed, equipped with porches, courtyards, verandahs on one or more sides of the court, and even occasionally with a tower.

OLYNTHOS

There is little evidence for town planning to be found in Athens with her rambling, irregularly shaped houses and a history more of haphazard than planned growth. Other sites, where excavation has been more feasible and widespread and where new cities were planted or new zones planned, offer better information.

Older cities, like Athens, grew up around an easily defensible point, often a hill, an Acropolis, which was protected by a wall.

Houses at the foot of the hill were also protected by a wall which tended to follow the lie of the land and dictated where future building could be. Within these walls (or wall), space was required for sanctuaries for the gods, though these could

be outside the walls, too, and for the Agora, as well as for housing. By the sixth century BC provision was also being made for administrative offices of the state which normally clustered around the Agora, and deities were propitiated in sanctuaries in high places (like the Acropolis at Athens) or in otherwise significant locations (by harbors or springs, for example). By the fourth century BC space was required also for gymnasia, theatres, and palaestras, which were often located outside the walls.

Aristotle (*Politics* 2.8.1–3), discussing questions of urban design, put forward the view that Hippodamos of Miletus, who lived in the fifth century BC, was the first man to plan towns rationally, with separate quarters for religious, public, and private use. He planned the new town of Piraeus with zones defined by function and with a grid plan. It is for the use of the grid plan that Hippodamos is most famous. He is said to have used it at Miletus for the new city, laid out in the fifth century BC after the destruction of Archaic Miletus by the Persians, and at Thurii in south Italy for the new colony planted there from Athens in 443 BC. But the grid layout had been used many years earlier, at Megara Hyblaia and Selinus in Sicily, for example, and at Smyrna in Asia Minor, so Hippodamos did not invent it. His reputation may be based on his frequent use of the plan and his enthusiasm for a rational approach to planning, whether in terms of a street plan of roads intersecting at right angles, or of zoning.

Olynthos provides a good example both of orthogonal (right-angled) grid planning (fig. **9.12**) and of domestic architecture within a grid. Urban development northwards from the old town began in the later fifth century BC and the city was destroyed by Philip in 348 BC. Reoccupation of a small part of the site then followed, before the final abandonment in 316 BC, so the street plan is of fifth-century origin, while the houses in their latest phases are fourth. North–south avenues intersect with east–west streets; each house block, measuring around 109 × 44 yards (100 × 40 m), has ten houses of equal size. Houses are arranged back to back in two rows of five, separated by a narrow alley. Within each

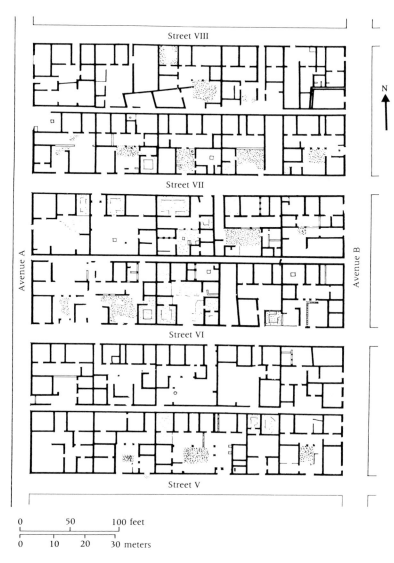

9.12 Townplanning and housing, Olynthos. 5th–4th centuries BC

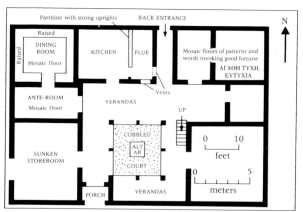

9.13 Plan of the Villa of Good Fortune, Olynthos. 4th century BC

house individual rooms vary in size. Typically, a narrow doorway opened onto a passage leading to a courtyard, the largest unit of the house. The courtyard may have columns (wooden posts) along one or more sides forming a verandah or verandahs; in which case the house may be termed a "pastas" house. The largest room, the andron (dining room), was reached from the court, with which other rooms were also linked. A second storey reached by a wooden staircase provided bedrooms. Occasionally a house reveals a more cosmopolitan flavor (fig. **9.13**). The Villa of Good Fortune, so called from an inscribed floor

9.14 *Left* Villa of Good Fortune, Olynthos, pebble mosaic floor: (central panel) Dionysos and chariot; (the surround) members of his retinue. c. 13 ft × 8 ft 2 ins (4 × 2.5 m). 4th century BC

9.15 *Below* Priene, model of the hillside town showing grid plan and zoning for agora (center), theatre, sanctuaries, council chamber, and other public uses. 4th century BC and later. Staatliche Museen, Berlin

mosaic, had rooms of unusually large dimensions, walls which were stuccoed and painted, and floors decorated with pebble mosaics (fig. **9.14**).

PRIENE

The orthogonal grid plan could be laid out not only on flat level terrain, as at Miletus or Olynthos, but also on sloping ground. Such is the case at Priene (fig. **9.15**) in Asia Minor (western Turkey), where a new city was planned on a hillside. This afforded spectacular views southward over the river Maeander and the plain towards Miletus.

The grid was laid out within the wall, broad, paved east–west roads intersecting with narrow north–south streets, often little more than stairways up and down the hill. Provision was made for all the requisite elements in a small Greek town, including housing, sanctuaries of the gods, agora with stoas, a councilhouse, a theatre, gymnasia, and a stadium. The regularity of the spacing of blocks was broken wherever necessary to accommodate large units. Thus, six blocks in the heart of the town were reserved for the agora

9.16 Drawing of a reconstruction of a "megaron" house, Priene. 4th century BC

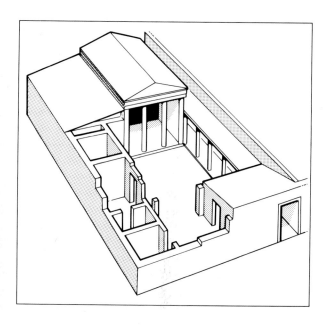

and adjacent public buildings, and the theatre absorbed almost two blocks. The grid arrangement petered out where fortification walls and grid plan met, but irregular terrain and outsize structures were neatly matched to the south, where stadium and large gymnasium were installed in the later Hellenistic phase.

The inhabitants of Priene numbered about 4000. The houses they inhabited display various plans. Some are of fourth-century date, others are later. All have courtyards, some with columns, some without. One plan (fig. **9.16**) has the main room of the house preceded by a porch with two columns *in antis* which opens on the court. This arrangement is reminiscent of Bronze Age predecessors and of temple plans, and is therefore sometimes termed a megaron plan. Similar houses have been found in seventh-century Smyrna – so this type may be a particularly East Greek manifestation. It is sometimes termed a "prostas" type, but it is the pastas type exemplified in Olynthos which gained in popularity in the Hellenistic period.

Much of the construction in Priene is of Hellenistic date, for example, the Sanctuary of Olympian Zeus, the colonnade to the south of the Temple of Athena, the Sacred Stoa and the stadium, but the agora, doubtless, and the temple of Athena certainly belong to the fourth century BC. The agora consisted of stoas on three sides – east, west, and south – with the north marked by altars, statues, other dedications, and fountains. The stoas sheltered the offices and shops, while that on the south side provided access by means of staircases to the agora for citizens arriving from the terraces below. The north side was flanked by the main east–west artery through the town, leading west to a city gate beneath the terrace on which the temple of Athena stood, and east to an arched gateway and a residential quarter beyond.

The Temple of Athena Polias (fig. **9.17**) was built higher up the hill than the agora and to the northwest. Entrance to the sanctuary was through a monumental propylon. The temple marks the revival of the Ionic order in Asia Minor after a period dominated by the Persian conquest, and the subjugation of the Greek com-

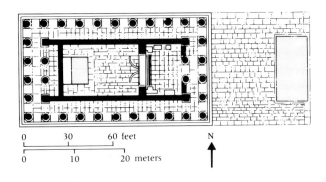

9.17 Plan of the Temple of Athena Polias, Priene. c. 340 BC. The altar is Hellenistic

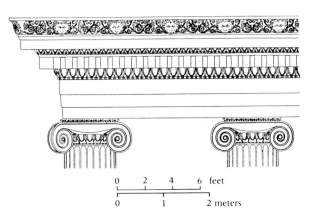

9.18 Restored superstructure of the Temple of Athena Polias, Priene. c. 340 BC

munities. It was apt that the temple, begun soon after the middle of the century, should have been dedicated by Alexander the Great, the conqueror of the Persians, in 334 BC.

The Ionic temple is now modernized and standardized. The gigantism of sixth-century Ionic temple architecture at Ephesos, Samos, and Didyma is replaced by smallness of scale and by precise proportions and ornament. This small temple (only around 40 by 21 yards (37 by 19 m)) was given an updated plan: a peristyle of six by 11 columns, and porches front and back each with two columns *in antis*. Interior columns were wholly omitted, and the porch and cella were covered with a wooden coffered ceiling. The ceiling of the peristyle, however, was formed of carved marble coffers alternating with wooden crossbeams. These coffers, richly ornamented with polychrome moldings and sculpted relief groups depicting a gigantomachy, broke the unity of the ceiling plane. The architect, Pythios, relied on easy numerical ratios to arrive at dimensions in his plan. He used multiples of the Ionic foot, and intended to make the building a mathematically derived model for the new Ionic order. An unusual feature is the use of square plinths beneath column bases. Tall, thin columns are almost nine times as high as the lower diameters. An ornamented entablature crowned the volute capitals, the carving of all of which was crisp and confident. The illustration (fig. **9.18**) shows the rich detail of the arrangement.

HALIKARNASSOS

Pythios may also have worked on the Mausoleum at Halikarnassos, a unique structure, described by Vitruvius (2:8.11) as one of the Seven Wonders of the World. Halikarnassos is in Caria, south of Miletus and Priene, and was ruled by the Persian satrap (governor) Mausolos until his death in 353 BC. This non-Greek ruler commissioned Greeks to design his tomb, and Greek sculptors to decorate it. Leading sculptors of the day – Skopas, Timotheos, Leochares, and Bryaxis – were summoned from Greece for the work. Little of the building remains, though sculptured blocks and fragmentary statues in the round have survived. Descriptions of the building have led scholars to various reconstructions (fig. **9.19**). There was apparently a high podium supporting a rectangular building surrounded by an Ionic colonnade, much decorative sculpture, a pyramid shaped roof and a four-horse chariot on the very top. It was huge, some 150 feet (46 m) high, and about 41½ yards (38 m) square at the base.

The sculptures are described by Pliny (*Natural History* 36:30–31) as the work of the four artists mentioned above, each being responsible for one side of the building. Surviving blocks worked in relief show there had been a Centauromachy, a chariot race, and an Amazonomachy, but there is little agreement about which sculptor worked which blocks. Some, however, (fig. **9.20**) on the basis of the shape of the heads of figures and the

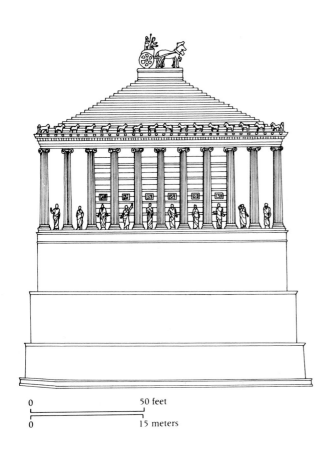

0   50 feet

0   15 meters

9.19 Conjectured reconstruction of the Mausoleum, Halikarnassos. c. 350–340 BC

9.20 Mausoleum, Halikarnassos, frieze block: Greeks fighting Amazons. Marble. Height 2 ft 11 ins (89 cm). c. 350 BC. British Museum, London

9.21 Colossal freestanding male statue from the Mausoleum at Halikarnassos. Marble. Height c. 9 ft 10 ins (3 m). c. 350 BC. British Museum, London

treatment of the eyes have been attributed to Skopas. It may be that the leading sculptors worked the freestanding figures on the podium. It now seems there were as many as three hundred figures at three different scales and on six different levels of this extraordinary structure. Some marble statues (fig. **9.21**) are over-lifesize, about 9 feet 9 inches (3 m) tall. The stance and drapery of this male figure are Greek, but his face and hairstyle are not. The long hair swept back from the forehead over the ears and to the neck is more Persian than Greek, while the broad face, challenging eyes, short beard, and fleshy mouth verge on portraiture.

SICILY AND SOUTH ITALY

The almost continuous warfare in Sicily invited architects and military engineers to concentrate on fortifications and their defense. At Syracuse the tyrant Dionysios contrived the initial ring of defenses around the Epipolae, the heights to the north commanding the city. Here masonry walls and towers, with emplacements for artillery, enfilades, and ditches, ran for some 20 miles (32 km). The pace of construction was hectic with 60,000 workers employed at the task, with competitions for the most successful architects, master masons and workers. The fortification was complete by 385 BC. This is a major monument of military architecture, and though improved in strength and equipment in the next century by Hieron II and Archimedes, it was essentially the work of Dionysios. Similar defensive works sprang up all over the Greek world, to protect cities and frontier forts.

In Sicily such fortifications, with the exception of Syracuse, had to await the refoundations of the cities organized by Timoleon. At Gela, for example, the city had been left largely abandoned after the Carthaginian sack of 405 BC, and it was not until after 339 BC that Greeks returned in numbers. On Capo Soprano a grid plan was laid out for new houses, richly provided with columns and mosaic floors. They were protected by a massive new fortification of masonry and mudbrick. The wall is about 10 feet (3 m) thick, with masonry to a height of about $11\frac{1}{2}$ feet (3.5 m) and mudbrick above. It is preserved to a height of about 42 feet (13 m) today.

Conditions in south Italy were more settled, and development can be traced, especially at Metapontum. The city, some $18\frac{1}{2}$ miles (30 km) west of Taras, controlled good farmland which stretched behind the coastline between two rivers. It had been laid out to a grid plan in the

9.22 Silver coin of Metapontum: the ear of barley, symbolizing the richness of her land, appeared on Metapontum's coinage from the 6th century to the 3rd century BC. National Museum, Collezione Gagliardi, Syracuse

mid-sixth century BC, and the construction of Doric temples both within the city walls (the sanctuary of Apollo) and outside, and of an "ekklesiasterion" (meeting place for the assembly) testify to the city's prosperity in the sixth century BC. Moreover, a treasury was dedicated at Olympia, and golden ears of corn were sent to Delphi. An impressive silver coinage struck by Metapontum (fig. **9.22**) in these years, which carries the emblem of the ear of barley, bears obvious reference to farming as the source of the city's wealth.

Aerial photography and surface survey of the land behind the city have identified some five hundred sites in an area of about 15 square miles (40 sq. km), by no means all of the land available for agriculture. These sites include sanctuaries, cemeteries, and farmhouses which range chronologically from the sixth century BC to the third. The countryside was evidently widely inhabited, people living in isolated farmhouses of modest shape and dimensions: square buildings with small rooms. Not until the fourth century BC does the large farmhouse with a central courtyard, known in Greece, put in an appearance. The first half of the fourth century BC saw a period of difficulty which had begun in the fifth, perhaps occasioned by a rising water table and flooding in the valleys. But the second half was again a period of success with density of settlement on higher ground and widespread use of the countryside.

Some details of the working of the land, such as the size of farms, are not always revealed by survey and excavation, and in this context epigraphic documents prove invaluable. The bronze tablets from Heraklea (Metapontum's neighboring city to the west) record in amazing detail the results of the work of a committee charged with investigating property lines and incomes of two sanctuaries. They disclose facts about farm size, units of measurement, lines of land division, percentages of woodland and cropland, and similar information. These inscriptions date to the end of the fourth century BC and amplify the picture of Metapontum's agricultural economic base. The land was what mattered here.

Sculpture

With the end of the High Classical period, sculpture took on more realism and began to look more naturalistic. There was a growing enthusiasm for expressing an individual's emotion, character, age, or mood, just as there had been in the Early Classical period. At the same time, those sculptors (e.g., Phidias and Polykleitos) who had attempted to represent the ideal in realistic figures, but with somewhat characterless and emotionless results, remained influential. So there is both continuity and change. The standing nude male figure remained a dominant type. Interest in movement affecting balance, and in the space surrounding figures, is strong. Control of accurate representation of the anatomy is secure. Once again a few bronze originals have survived, but mostly we rely on later copyists and commentators. The period down to the death of Alexander the Great in 323 BC is often known as the Late Classical, a term also used for the style of sculpture.

The Antikythera Bronze (fig. **9.23**), so called because it was found in the sea close to the island of Antikythera, is an example of a fourth-century BC original. The standing nude youth shows the

9.23 So-called "Antikythera Bronze". Height 6 ft 4½ ins (1.94 m). Mid-4th century BC. National Museum, Athens

influence of Polykleitan athletic figures clearly enough, in the position of legs and feet, the chiastic (X-shape) balance of muscular tension, and the emphatic structure of the anatomy. New are the smallness of the head in proportion to the rest of the body, the outstretching of the arm involving the figure in surrounding space, and the leftward swaying pose, checked by an outstretched right arm and the tilt of the head. This figure has been interpreted as a ball player,

9.24 *Above* Bronze Marathon Boy, recovered from the Bay of Marathon in 1925. Height 4 ft 3 ins (1.30 m). c. 340 BC. National Museum, Athens

9.25 *Above right* Bronze Athena, from a warehouse in Piraeus destroyed in the 1st century BC, possibly by Sulla. Height 8 ft (2.44 m). Mid 4th century BC. National Museum, Athens

and the languid mood even for an activity such as this is at home in the fourth century BC, but the gesture remains enigmatic. This figure was cast sometime around 350 BC, while High Classical influences were still strong.

Another original bronze, the Marathon Boy (fig. **9.24**), again so called because it was retrieved from the sea near Marathon, adopts a more precarious pose. Under lifesize, he seems to stand with his weight on the left leg, but the S-curve through the body is so pronounced that the volume of the torso, carried over to the right, unbalances the figure. It seems that balance can only be momentary. The smooth modeling of the surface and the soft shapes of the limbs suggest the youth of the figure, while his outstretched arms involve surrounding space on either side. He wears a fillet of a type worn by athletes in the palaestra to secure his hair. But no satisfactory explanation has yet been proposed of the gesture, or of what the object might have been on his left hand. More adventurous than the Antikythera youth, and often associated with the great Athenian sculptor, Praxiteles, the Marathon Boy was probably cast sometime around 340 BC.

Another bronze original, a statue of Athena (fig. **9.25**), was found along with other statues, which included a late-Archaic bronze Apollo (fig. **6.58**, p. 181) in excavations in the Piraeus. The whole group was doubtless waiting to be shipped from Greece to Rome when the warehouse in which it was stored burnt down. The over-lifesize Athena wears the new dense drapery of the century, an aegis and helmet, and originally held a spear in her left hand. She remains a massive, imposing figure, but, with the head tilted to the right and her gentle expression, she is rendered more approachable than her fifth-century counterpart (fig. **8.23**, p. 251). She is to be dated to approximately 360 BC.

Around 370 BC, the Athenian state commissioned the sculptor Kephisodotos, perhaps the father of Praxiteles, to make a bronze group of a mother and child, Eirene (Peace) and Ploutos (Wealth), to celebrate the inauguration of a cult of Peace in Athens. The original is lost, but marble copies (fig. **9.26**) are easily recognized, thanks to literary descriptions and the appearance of the group on the coinage of Athens. The mother, Peace, holds the child, Wealth, in the crook of her left arm, while her right hand originally held a scepter. Peace's stance and massive form echo precursors of the High Classical style. The drapery, however, is now different. She wears the heavy peplos favored as long ago as the Early

9.26 Eirene (Peace) holding the child Ploutos (Wealth), by Kephisodotos. Roman marble copy of a bronze Greek original. Height 6 ft 6½ ins (1.99 m). c. 370 BC (original). Staatliche Antikensammlungen, Munich

Classical (Transitional) period (480–450 BC) and a cloak. The clinging wet drapery of the end of the fifth century BC, which left the limbs beneath looking almost naked, is no longer so popular. The density of the drapery describes the weight and texture of the cloth itself, and conceals the body. The only anatomical forms (the right knee and both breasts) perceived beneath the drapery are those which the logical fall of the drapery would reveal. Folds are more complicated, as in nature. They stop and start, have creases and are crumpled. It is an actual, not contrived, relationship between body and cloth which is depicted. Also new, and characteristically fourth-century BC, is the expression of gentle intimacy between the two figures. This is achieved by the inclination of the mother's head towards the infant and by the infant's eager gesture and upward glance. The personification of abstract ideas was not new, but the allegorical nature of the group breaks new ground.

Kephisodotos was evidently a leading sculptor of this century, but the three whose names are most familiar are Praxiteles, Skopas, and Lysippos. A marble group of Hermes and Dionysos (fig. **9.27**), found in excavations of the Temple of Hera at Olympia, seems heavily influenced, in terms of composition, by the Peace and Wealth of Kephisodotos. Hermes holds the child Dionysos in his left arm, and inclines his head toward the infant. Dionysos looks up at and reaches for the bunch of grapes which Hermes is thought to have held in his lost right hand. This group was seen by Pausanias and described by him as the work of Praxiteles. Scholars still debate whether this is an original of the fourth century BC by the master himself, who specialized in the carving of marble, or whether it is a copy of Hellenistic or Roman date. The strut used between the tree trunk and Hermes' hip, the high polish of the surface, the recutting or miscutting of the back, and the type of sandal worn by Hermes all point to a later date. But whether it is an original or a copy, it tells us much about changes introduced by Praxiteles.

The stance is High Classical, taken from Polykleitos, and the torso, spare and heavy, is also reminiscent of the fifth century BC. The

9.27 Hermes and Dionysos by Praxiteles. Marble. Height 7 ft 1 in (2.15 m). c. 340 BC (?). Olympia Museum

slender proportions of the long legs and small head, however, are new, as is the S-curve of the awkwardly placed torso and pushed-out right hip, which introduces a note of imbalance. The contours of the body naturally echo this swinging curve, which is a characteristic of Praxiteles' work. Soft modeling of the surface blurs the smooth transitions from plane to plane – what the Italians call "sfumato" – and leaves them indistinct. This confident skill in carving and finishing marble, together with the slimmer proportions, gives the figure a certain delicacy. The drapery slung over the tree trunk contrasts with the broad expanses of the body, and shows naturalism in the variations of fold and creases, even in a single plane. As to the head, the face is typically Praxitelean, having a tapering shape, narrow eyes, a smiling mouth, detailed modulation of the forehead, and a dreamy expression. Relaxed and idle, languorous and sensuous, Hermes exemplifies a far different aspect of divine life than those depicted by sculptors in the preceding century. If original, this group was made around 340 BC.

Praxiteles' most famous statue was the Aphrodite of Knidos (fig. **9.28**). This statue for the first time presented a fullscale female nude. Literary sources are lavish in their praise of the figure's beauty, and Pliny thought it the best statue in the world. He even thought that Aphrodite herself must have helped in its creation, but others thought the statue represented Phryne, Praxiteles' mistress. It was copied again and again in Roman times, and many variations of the type developed. The statue also appeared on the coinage of Knidos. Why did it exercise the power it did? Was it just its surprising, and perhaps shocking, nudity? Aphrodite stands naked in a momentary pose, her left hand resting on the drapery thrown over the adjacent water jar, her right brought across in front in the gesture of the Venus Pudica. Like Hermes, she has long legs and a small head. Her right hip pushes out, and the S-curve rises slowly through her body. She has soft, wavy hair, and her face has a triangular forehead, shadowy eyes, a straight nose, and a small mouth. The marble original was made around 350 BC, and stood in

9.28 Aphrodite of Knidos by Praxiteles. Roman marble copy of a marble Greek original. Height 6 ft 8 ins (2.04 m). c. 350 BC (original). Vatican Museums, Rome

an open shrine visible from every side. Thus, the divine had become accessible, almost personal, seen in an intimate moment.

We learn of Skopas from literary sources and are told that he was the architect of the Temple of Athena Alea at Tegea in the Peloponnese. This building is important in its own right as an example of a Doric temple of the middle years of the fourth century BC with innovations (fig. **9.6**, p. 282.) A number of fragments of its sculptural decoration in the pediments survive. These somewhat damaged heads of pedimental figures, known as the Tegea heads (fig. **9.29**), reveal a new stylistic current in the fourth century BC. This was a depiction of stressed emotional states, by treating facial features in a pronounced way: the inner corner of the eye is deep set, there is a bulge of the eyebrow over the outer corner of the eye, the forehead is in two planes of which the lower projects markedly, the cheeks are flat, and the hair is tousled. The power and tension in these heads are undisguised. Skopas, sources say, made the freestanding marble figures which stood beside the cult statue, so we do not know for sure that he made these. But perhaps he was both architect and sculptor here.

This style is new and vigorous, and it is distinguishable at other sites where Skopas worked, such as at the Mausoleum at Halikarnassos. Some heads there display (fig. **9.20**, p. 291) similar traits to those of the Tegea heads. Skopas also worked on the new Temple of Artemis at Ephesos. This gigantic building was surrounded by over one hundred columns, more than 30 of which were decorated with sculptured bases. A surviving sculptured column drum shows Hermes, Alkestis, and Persephone. Persephone stands in a pose derived from Kephisodotos, while Hermes has the square skull and deep set eyes of the Tegea heads. So, a new and different style is widespread and popular and may logically be ascribed to Skopas.

The characteristic traits of the style – the squarish skull, the squarish forehead in two degrees, the deep set eyes, bulging brows, open mouth, and an expression of intensity and strain – are found in the statue of the celebrated hunter, Meleager (fig. **9.30**), of which some 20 copies

9.29 Head from a pedimental group. Temple of Athena Alea, Tegea (of which Skopas was the architect). Marble. Height 11¾ ins (30 cm). c. 340 BC. National Museum, Athens

are known. The type is identified by the presence of a boar's head next to the figure: Meleager was one of the leaders in the hunt for the Kalydonian boar. No literary source mentions a Meleager by Skopas, but the number of copies argues a famous Greek original, and the style of the head is consistent with that of the Tegea heads. The torso of Meleager shows strong modeling, with soft transitions from plane to plane, and more abrupt, clearcut musculature, the line of hip and groin clearly demarcated. A slow torsion pulls the left shoulder forward to balance the rightward thrust of the hip and to emphasize the importance of the intermediate view. The "full-frontal" view of Classical sculpture, still shown in the broad expanse of torso, is now on the wane. The intermediate, three-quarter view, shown by the

9.30 Meleager, probably by Skopas. Roman marble copy of a Greek original. Height 4 ft 1 in (1.23 m). c. 340 BC (original). Fogg Art Museum, Harvard University, Cambridge (Mass)

traits. Meleager is still an image of a generic powerful hero, not an individualized portrait. Skopas' original statue was probably made around 340 BC. It may have been inspired by the theme of the front pediment at Tegea, which depicted the hunt for the Kalydonian boar, and which included Meleager.

The third great sculptor of the fourth century BC was Lysippos. Since several sources connect him with Alexander the Great and state that he made portraits for the king, we can say with certainty that he was active in the period 336–323 BC. Less certainly, it seems that his career may have lasted from about 350 to 310 BC. He preferred to work in bronze, and advocated a new canon of proportions, already more modestly adopted by Praxiteles. Slenderer bodies and smaller heads were to give an appearance of greater height. A comparison of a copy of the

9.31 Head of Meleager (fig. **9.30**)

direction of the head's gaze, is now the most telling. It coordinates movement, and brings out the full power of the head.

There is an ambiguity of expression in the face which, to some, seems to carry a self-absorbed, faraway look, while, to others, it appears more determined and humanly involved (fig. **9.31**). The Meleager was made close to the end of the Classical era, when the standing nude athletic type was still able to display increasingly varied movements, as well as individualizing

Apoxyomenos (fig. **9.32**), perhaps Lysippos' most renowned work, with a copy of the Doryphoros of Polykleitos (fig. **8.38**, p. 264) makes the point. The Apoxyomenos seems taller, but both are in fact almost the same height.

The Apoxyomenos shows Lysippos directly challenging the conventional Classical four-sided approach. The athlete is using a strigil to scrape the oil off his body. One arm is stretched out directly in front of the figure with the other (holding the strigil) at right angles to it. Thus, the broad front of the torso has been broken, the visual space of the figure vastly extended, and the viewer invited, almost compelled, to contemplate views other than frontal and profile. Moreover, the torsion introduced into the lower part of the figure by the outturned foot, bent knee, and shifting horizontal axis is continued in the upper part by the position of the arms. Structured Classical frontality is here giving way to three-dimensional movement.

Portraits of Alexander were numerous, and the sources tell of characteristics – unruly hair and a certain set of the head – by which he might be recognized. Inscribed busts and coins help. Yet there is nothing to identify the work of Lysippos. The different heads of Alexander have the wild, uncontrolled hair, and the turn of the head, but still appear idealized as a superhuman regent type. Individualized, physical traits do not predominate.

Relief sculpture, other than architectural, is most commonly seen in grave reliefs, which were produced in great quantity in Athens throughout the century, until sumptuary laws forbade their production in around 310 BC. Quality varies greatly, from the work of hacks turning out stock pieces to be personalized by the addition of inscriptions and epigrams, to others which engaged the skills of master sculptors. Many of these stelai have an architectural framework of antae and pediment, within which figures are described. The figures are worked in relief which gets higher and higher through the century, until some figures are almost entirely in the round. Figures on the stele of Dexileos (fig. **9.33**) are already in high relief. An inscription identifies this gravestone as that of a young man killed in

9.32 *Above* Apoxyomenos (man scraping himself). Roman marble copy of a bronze Greek original by Lysippos. Height 6 ft 8½ ins (2.05 m). c. 350–325 BC (original). Vatican Museums, Rome

9.33 *Opposite* Grave stele of Dexileos: battle scene. Marble. Height 4 ft 7 ins (1.40 m). c. 390 BC. Kerameikos Museum, Athens

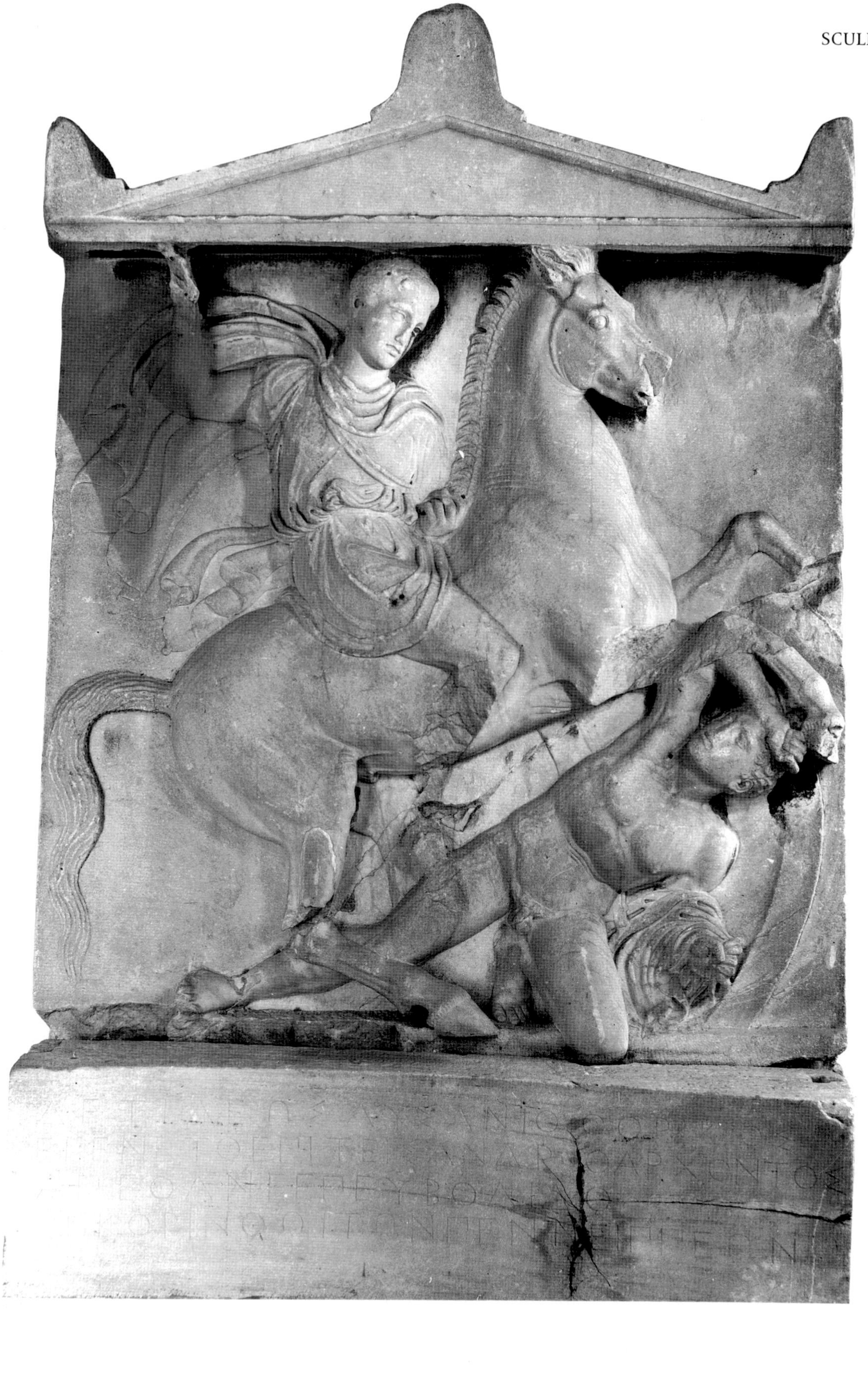

9.34 Grave stele, found near the river Ilissos, hence the "Ilissos stele": father, son, boy, and dog. Marble. Height 5 ft 6 ins (1.68 m). c. 330 BC. Kerameikos Museum, Athens

9.35 Electra and Orestes at the tomb of Agamemnon. Limestone relief, from Taras, south Italy. c. 300 BC. Metropolitan Museum of Art, New York

action against the Corinthians in 394 BC. Here he lunges from horseback at a fallen enemy; spear and reins were added in bronze. The horse and horseman are reminiscent of the Parthenon frieze, and the billowing drapery echoes that of the Nike balustrade, but Classical restraint both physical and mental is now replaced by all-out violence and collapse.

Later in the century, figures are more fully in the round, as in the Ilissos relief (fig. **9.34**). Notable for the number and variety of figures, including a grieving old man, a dead youth, a sleeping boy, and a dog, and for spatial effects, the relief is split vertically in two down the middle. The dead youth, isolated from his companions in life, gazes evenly at the visitor. The style of the youth is close to that of Skopas: he has a squarish head with deep set eyes and bulging brows. Varied views of the torso, legs, and feet introduce torsion into the body. The pathos of the scene is blatant. Sorrow and loss are openly stated by powerfully modeled and expressive figures. The relief was made around 330 BC.

The influence of the Athenian grave reliefs may be detected in the West. From Taras come a series of softstone reliefs, the style and mood of which are close to developments in Greece. These reliefs decorated miniature temples erected above the chamber tombs of the fourth-century aristocracy. One relief shows Electra and Orestes at the tomb of Agamemnon (fig. **9.35**). The posture of Orestes bears comparison with the sculptured column drum from the new Artemision at Ephesos, and hence with the style of Skopas. The inclination of heads and sorrowful expressions, speaking of profound sadness and brevity of life, derive from Athenian grave reliefs. Another relief depicts Herakles battling with Amazons. The reference is to tragic myth, obviously, and to

9.36 So-called "Alexander Sarcophagus" (more likely the sarcophagus of Abdalonymos), from Sidon: battle scene. Marble. Height (of frieze) 10⅗ ins (27 cm). c. 320 BC. Archaeological Museum, Istanbul

Classical prototypes, whether exemplified by the Parthenon or Bassae or the Mausoleum at Halikarnassos, all of which exploit the same myth. It is apparent that these Tarentine sculptors were wholly familiar with the major sculptors and workshops of Greece. At the same time, dramatic gestures and intense expressions anticipate Hellenistic sculpture. These reliefs were made around 300 BC.

Panels with sculptured figures in relief appear on a group of marble *sarcophagi* (coffins) found at the other side of the Greek world, in the tombs of the kings of Sidon, the famous city on the Phoenician coast. One of these, the so-called Alexander Sarcophagus, carries the only original contemporary representation of Alexander him-self. The coffin (fig. **9.36**) is shaped like a temple, rich with architectural moldings framing the frieze panels on all four sides of the rectangular chest, and resplendent with akroteria, water-spouts, and watchful lions at the corners of the roof. The lid (roof) of the coffin, which was worked separately, had sculptured figures of Greeks fighting Persians in the pedimental, gabled ends. The short sides of the chest show a hunting scene, and a battle scene in energetic mêlée. One long side shows Greeks and Orientals hunting together, while the other depicts Greeks and Persians fighting. Some Greeks are nude; Orientals wear traditional costume. Figures were carved with great detail and precision and were painted. The colors are well preserved and include purple, blue, yellow, and various shades of red for garments. Flesh is painted in a light yellow wash for Greeks and a darker yellow for Orientals, while hair is often accentuated with color, as is

9.37 Detail of the "Alexander Sarcophagus." Alexander with lionskin helmet

sometimes the iris of the eyes.

The composition is dense with crowded figures in closely interlocking groups. In the hunting scene, rearing horses, brandished weapons, and fluttering drapery all emphasize the action of the overlapping figures. In the battle scene, Alexander is on horseback and wearing the lionskin helmet of Herakles (fig. **9.37**), which he wears on contemporary coins. With spear poised, he attacks a Persian whose horse collapses beneath him. Alexander's face is young and smooth, his eyes painted with highlights. The intensity of his charge is matched only by that of his expression. Alexander, alone of the figures, can be identified with certainty. The prominently placed figure in the middle of the hunting scene was probably the person buried in the sarcophagus. He has been identified as Abdalonymos who was made king of Sidon by Alexander, after the battle of Issos in 333 BC. The sarcophagus was probably made around 320 BC.

Wall painting and mosaics

Alexander's court sculptor was Lysippos, who came from Sikyon in the northern Peloponnese. His court painter was Apelles, an Ionian who had studied at Sikyon, where Pamphilos began a school for painters in the middle of the fourth century BC. Once again, literary sources are the principal source of evidence about painting and painters, and the archaeological record is very thin. Pamphilos was instrumental in introducing painting into the educational curriculum for Greek youths, and insisted on the study of geometry and arithmetic as integral to painting. Apelles was famous for his portraits and for his paintings of Aphrodite.

Suitable topics for wall paintings were often mythological, showing scenes such as Hades carrying off Persephone, or Perseus freeing Andromeda. Landscape elements were entirely secondary, used only to suggest setting, though the painted stage sets in the theatre, which certainly depicted architecture, may also have shown landscape. As in the fifth century BC, wall paintings in the fourth century used a four-color palette: black, white, red, and yellow. But what the paintings were really like is still, and is likely to remain, problematical.

Like statues, however, important Classical paintings were copied by the Romans, and though probably differing from their originals in several ways, wall paintings and mosaics from Pompeii and Herculaneum may help us understand what Greek painting was like. A brilliant floor mosaic from the House of the Faun at Pompeii, of Hellenistic date, is taken by many scholars to be derived from a monumental wall painting by Philoxenos of Eretria of about 310 BC, of which we are told by Pliny. This is the so-called Alexander Mosaic (fig. **9.38**). The Pompeii mosaic, and the wall painting on which it draws, seem to depict the turning point in the battle of Issos. The mighty battle is seen by Philoxenos as a personal duel between Alexander and Darius. Alexander charges forward toward Darius, transfixing with his lance a Persian who stood in his way. Wild haired, helmetless, with shining armor and eyes alight, his attack is irresistible.

9.38 The Alexander mosaic: the culminating moment in the Battle of Issos between Greeks and Persians, the confrontation between Alexander and Darius. Floor mosaic from Pompeii, an adaptation of a Greek wall painting by Philoxenos of Eretria: (mosaic) 8 ft 10 ins × 17 ft (2.7 × 5.2 m) 1st century BC; (wall painting) c. 310 BC. National Museum, Naples

Darius in his chariot stretches out an arm towards the conqueror, while his dark horses speed away. The background is void, articulated only by lances held aloft and a blighted tree, which balances Darius in composition; except for the debris of battle, the foreground is equally void. Attention concentrates on the figures, modeled with foreshortening and bold use of light and shade. Persian garments are rendered accurately in fourth-century terms, a strong suggestion that the mosaic is a reliable facsimile of Philoxenos' painting.

In the Alexander mosaic, the small cubes (*tesserae*) of which the mosaic is made are of colored glass and stone. In earlier centuries, mosaics were made of pebble, as seen in the houses at Olynthos. But the art of decorating floors with mosaic

had begun much earlier. As early as the late eighth century BC, floors at Gordion in Phrygia had been made of pebbles arranged in simple patterns of black, white, and, very occasionally, of red stones. Phrygia was a kingdom of central Anatolia, modern Turkey, so that these are not Greek mosaics. But we know of connections between Greeks and Phrygians, and these mosaics may be thought of as precursors to Greek mosaics. The earliest examples so far recovered of Greek pebble mosaics date to the end of the fifth century BC. They are basically black and white, carefully planned, and make use of easy abstract designs, such as squares and maeanders, alongside floral patterns, and, infrequently, human and animal figures.

At Olynthos simple black and white pebble mosaics predominate, but some are more advanced, and show figures of animals and humans, and mythological scenes. In one example, borders of wave patterns and palmettes on all four sides (fig. **9.14**, p. 288) form a decorative surround. The central panel, rectangular in shape, shows Dionysos and his chariot drawn by leopards and is itself surrounded by dancing and

9.39 Pebble mosaic showing Bellerophon and the Chimaera (central medallion) with floral, maeander, and wave surrounds. From Olynthos. 9 ft 10 ins × 9 ft 10 ins (3 × 3 m). Early 4th century BC

hunting members of his retinue. Another example (fig. **9.39**) has a circular central medallion with a mythological scene, Bellerophon and the Chimaera, surrounded by florals, a maeander pattern, and a wave pattern. The design is careful, but the drawing is disappointing, the contours of bodies and the folds of drapery being fairly clumsy.

The later part of the fourth century BC shows great advances with the series of pebble floor mosaics from Pella, the capital of Alexander's successors in Macedonia. A particularly good example shows a stag hunt (fig. **9.40**) and was signed by the artist, Gnosis. The outer border, as at Olynthos, is a wave pattern, while the inner is a riotous curling floral design which frames the central scene. The comparatively small figured

9.40 Pebble mosaic showing a stag hunt, signed by Gnosis, from Pella (Macedonia). Height 10 ft 2 ins (3.10 m). c. 300 BC

panel in the middle, surrounded by its dense patterned foliage, is termed an "emblema." Pebbles are now much more closely packed and uniform in size. The central panel, as at Olynthos, has light figures against a dark background, but now the figures have musculature modeled by shading, varied views of the body confidently displayed, and contours strengthened by strips of terracotta or lead. Pebbles of colors other than black and white are used: yellows, browns, and reds appear liberally to highlight important details and contribute to the shading. All mosaics of the fourth century BC are pebble mosaics; the mosaic made of tesserae did not appear until about 250 BC.

The sources of the designs, techniques, and themes of these mosaics is a topic of eager debate. The great painter, Apelles, had visited and worked in Pella, so that his paintings may have provided one source for the Pella mosaics. Already in the fifth century, Zeuxis and his contemporaries had introduced the use of shading in monumental painting to express volume, so that knowledge of this technique, for example, must have been widespread among artists. Mythological themes were in common use for wall paintings, a case in point being the scene of Perseus freeing Andromeda which appears more than once on walls at Pompeii and may well go back to a fourth-century original by a painter called Nikias. So it may well be that wall or panel painting was copied. The question of tapestries, carpets, and rugs, however, also comes into play. About these homespun perishable objects, and the arts they represent, we are ill informed, but know that textiles of all kinds existed and were valued, and it may be that the more striking of the woven textiles were influential, and provided stimulus to the creation of mosaics also, particularly border designs.

Direct archaeological evidence about wall painting comes from the royal Macedonian tombs, and some is datable to the fourth century. A painted frieze from a tomb at Vergina, 3 feet 4 inches (1 m) high, shows a mythological scene with Hades carrying off Persephone (fig. **9.41**). Attempts at perspective for spatial effect (e.g., the wheel of the chariot) and shading to lend volume

9.41 Wall painting showing Hades carrying off Persephone, from a royal tomb at Vergina. Height (of frieze) c. 3 ft 4 ins (1 m). c. 340 BC

(the drapery, the face of Hades) are evident. Another Vergina tomb (thought to be that of Philip II, father of Alexander the Great) has a façade (fig. **9.42**) decorated with a painted frieze above the Doric entablature. The scene is remarkable in depicting a hunting episode amid many landscape elements, such as hills and trees.

9.42 Façade of a tomb with wall painting showing hunt scene and landscape, from Vergina. c. 340 BC

Pottery

In spite of disruptions following the end of the Peloponnesian War, potters continued at work in the Kerameikos in Athens, and painters continued decoration in the red-figure technique. A leading exponent of the early years of the century was the Meleager Painter, a good example of whose work is provided by the interior of the cup (fig. **9.44**) with figures of Dionysos, a woman with a tambourine, perhaps Ariadne, and Eros. This was painted around 390–380 BC. His Dionysos is a beardless, helpless stripling, whose divine authority is gone. Except Eros in flight, the painter keeps his figures on a single ground line, and ignores many of the luxuriant characteristics of the Meidias Painter (p. 271).

The florid style of the Meidias Painter is followed in a style known as the Kerch Style, so called from the site in southern Russia where numerous Athenian vases of the fourth century have come to light. The style used added color to great advantage, especially yellow, white, and gold, but also blue and green, and drew figures in a less detailed, less fussy way than had the Meidias Painter.

This last flowering of Athenian red-figure took place in the years either side the middle of the century; a *pelike* (storage jar) by the Marsyas Painter provides a good example. The scene (fig. **9.45**) shows Peleus about to capture Thetis. Eros is crowning Peleus, who is surrounded by *Nereids* and being attacked by a snake. The pos-

9.43 South Italian (Apulian) red-figure krater attributed to the Ilioupersis Painter: tomb with visitors. Height 2 ft 3 ins (69 cm). c. 380–370 BC. British Museum, London

9.44 Attic red-figure cup by the Meleager Painter (interior): Dionysos, Eros, and female. Width 9½ ins (24 cm). c. 390–380 BC. British Museum, London

tures are striking in their originality. The crouching figure of Thetis wheels towards her captor, revealing her body in several views, her head upturned. Meanwhile a naked Nereid, fleeing away, twists her body to show a full view of her back, legs almost in profile, and back view of her head. Here is a master at work. Everywhere there is added color. White is used for Thetis and for Eros, gold for Peleus' hat, for the fillet which binds Thetis' hair, and for part of Eros' wings. Other parts of the wings are blue while green appears on the drapery over Thetis' knees. Drapery is no longer transparent, but has the same renewed solidity and texture as the drapery of sculptured figures of this time. This pelike was made around 360–350 BC.

In spite of the virtuosity of painters like the Marsyas Painter, by the third quarter of the century production in Athens was weakening, and around 320 BC it stopped. Exports to the West had been checked by the success of the south Italian workshops, and soon after 325 BC other markets, for example North Africa, began to take south Italian, not Athenian products.

From the middle of the sixth century BC, the Athenians had awarded amphoras of olive oil as prizes in the Panathenaic games. These are

known, predictably, as Panathenaic amphoras and were decorated in black-figure, with Athena on one side and a scene from the games on the other. Even after the introduction of red-figure, black-figure was used for these specialized vessels, and continued in use in the fourth century BC. By about 375 BC, painters were inscribing the name of the "archon," chief magistrate, of the year on these pots, so that many can be dated precisely. The example shown (fig. **9.46**) has the name of "Niketes," who was archon in 332/1 BC, inscribed on it, a handsome striding armed

9.45 Attic red-figure pelike by the Marsyas Painter: Peleus, Thetis, Eros, and nymphs. Height 16½ ins (42 cm). c. 360–350 BC. British Museum, London

Athena on one side and on the other a scene from the "pankration" (all-in wrestling and boxing, no holds barred, except for biting and eye gouging).

As for undecorated table ware, black gloss wares remained popular, while coarse wares for cooking vessels and transport amphoras continued in widespread use.

In the West, the production of red-figure vases increased. Vases continued to be imported from Athens, but in much reduced numbers.

9.46 Attic Panathenaic amphora: striding Athena. Height 2 ft 6 ins (77 cm). 332–1 BC. British Museum, London

There were four major workshops, of which two, the Apulian and the Lucanian, had been active in the fifth century. Around 380 BC another workshop was set up in Campania, and, around 350 BC, a fourth at or near Poseidonia (Paestum). Of these four, the Apulian and the Paestan (fourth-century red-figure pottery produced in Poseidonia is always referred to as "Paestan" although the city was still called Poseidonia) are perhaps the most significant.

The Apulian painters practiced two styles: the Plain and the Ornate. The Ornate tended to be used on large vases, such as the volute krater, which was often associated with burials. About 375 BC an imaginative painter, often thought to be the Ilioupersis Painter (so called from a Sack of Troy painted on one of his vases), introduced the notion of decorating these funerary vases with funerary scenes. A volute krater in the British Museum in London (fig. **9.43**) provides an example. The principal scene shows a miniature temple building of the same shape as contemporary tombs in Taras, in front of which the dead youth leans on a *perirrhanterion*, a ritual water basin. Seated and standing figures round about have brought offerings to the tomb. There is much added white: for the building, the youth, the perirrhanterion, for gifts and for dotted ground lines. Figures in low relief cavort on the handles. Most notably there are varied viewpoints: the seated youth and the stool on which he sits, and the gable of the building including the coffered ceiling are seen from below, while the perirrhanterion and the lower step of the building are seen from above. Such attempts at spatial depth and perspective remind us that perspective as well as shading had been considered in fifth-century Athens. The pioneer in perspective, the literary sources say, had been Agatharchos of Samos.

Apulian Ornate reaches its most elaborate form in the final third of the century. A volute krater by the Baltimore Painter (fig. **9.47**) shows the funerary iconography which had become conventional in Apulian pottery, and a relentless ornamentation of the surface. The funerary tomb itself is the major feature. Spatial depth is attempted by a view of the ceiling from below, by the cuirass hung on the wall, and by obvious overlapping. Visitors gather around bringing offerings. Added whites, yellows, and browns are all in evidence. The neck of the krater is decorated with a central female (?) head framed by balancing displays of complicated, curling vegetation which entirely cover the surface. With this explosion of baroque decoration, Apulian comes to an end.

The workshops at Poseidonia were active around the middle of the century. Around 400 BC, the city had been taken over by peoples from the surrounding hills, the Lucanians, but Greeks continued to live and prosper here, as is evident not least from the red-figure pottery produced in mid-century. Two of the principal artists are known to us from their signatures, and they alone of all south Italian potters and painters signed their work. Their names are Greek, Assteas and Python. They signed in Greek on their vessels, and they used episodes of Greek myth and theatre as the subjects of the scenes they painted. Vase shapes, too, are Greek: the hydria, krater, *lekane* (a lidded dish or plate), lekythos, and amphora.

A lekythos by Assteas (fig. **9.48**) shows a scene from Classical tragedy. Orestes at Delphi contemplates the bloody dagger, flanked by Apollo and Artemis, while the Furies hover above. The mood is somber; inscriptions identify the characters; there is much added white. Rows of white dots to pick out hems of garments, belts, bootstraps, and baldrics are a Paestan innovation.

9.47 South Italian (Apulian) red-figure krater attributed to the Baltimore Painter: visitors at the tomb. Height 2 ft 11 ins (89 cm). c. 325 BC. British Museum, London

9.48 South Italian (Paestan) red-figure lekythos by Assteas: Orestes at Delphi. Height 18½ ins (47 cm). c. 350 BC. Paestum Museum

9.49 A phlyax vase. A south Italian (Paestan) red-figure krater by Assteas: scene from a phlyax (burlesque) play. Height 14½ ins (37 cm). c. 350 BC. Staatliche Museen, Berlin

An amphora by Python (fig. **9.50**) strikes a different note. The topic is the birth of Helen who emerges from a large white egg, placed on an altar, while bystanders look on with expressions and gestures of astonishment and surprise. Divinities above smile in amusement and seem to forget Helen's destiny and the fate of Troy. A master of irony, Python signed prominently on the plinth below the altar.

Other scenes derive from contemporary colonial comic theatre which typically highlighted tubby, grotesque, oddly clad male actors on a wooden stage. These *phlyax* plays often parodied the heroic tales which had been the staple diet of the Athenian tragedians. The phlyax vase illustrated (fig. **9.49**) is a calyx krater painted and signed by Assteas. On a stage supported by columns, burglars attempt to separate a miser from his strongbox. The actors all wear masks, padded tunics, and leggings, and are equipped for comic effect with exaggerated genitalia. These phlyax vases perhaps give a glimpse of what the comedies of Aristophanes in fifth-century Athens may have looked like.

Another style of pottery, perhaps produced at first in Apulia, but also in Campania and at Poseidonia, flourished in the second half of the century. This is Gnathian ware. It had the shapes of simple black gloss ware, and was decorated in white, yellow, and red. Animal and specially vegetal motifs were popular. Gnathian is the only south Italian ware to have found much favor abroad, and has turned up, for example, in Egypt, and even as far afield as sites on the Black Sea coast. Production continued into the third century BC (fig. **10.43**, p. 349).

9.50 South Italian (Paestan) red-figure amphora by Python: birth of Helen from the egg. Height 2 ft $\frac{4}{5}$ in (63 cm). c. 350 BC. Paestum Museum

10
The Hellenistic Period
c. 323–31 BC

Conventionally the Hellenistic period begins at the death of Alexander in 323 BC and concludes in 31 BC with the Battle of Actium. This watershed event saw the Romans of the West led by Octavianus, shortly to become Augustus, the first Roman emperor, defeat the Romans of the East and their Egyptian allies led by Antony and Cleopatra. It is called Hellenistic because it witnessed the dissemination of Greek and Macedonian ideas throughout what had been Alexander's empire. These ideas were taken in with varying degrees of enthusiasm. In Syria, for example, Greek customs, institutions, and language were received well in the older towns and were introduced in the new settlements, but they were spread thin, while in Egypt, Hellenism centered on the new city of Alexandria, but was challenged by the traditions of the pharaohs.

Opposite Altar of Zeus, Pergamon, north wing, fig. **10.20**. Marble. c. 175–150 BC. Staatliche Museen, Berlin

Alexander's generals divided the empire among themselves, but the new kingdoms were hostile to one another. There were upstarts and mountebanks everywhere, and bickering and warfare continued. Syria was the biggest of the new kingdoms with its capital at Antioch where the Seleucid dynasty established itself. Its control extended over most of the Asian provinces, though the easternmost fell away almost at once. Alexandria was the capital of Egypt under the Ptolemies. Many Greeks came to live here and naturally looked northward across the Aegean, which Egypt frequently controlled, along with Cyprus. Another kingdom grew up in the third century at Pergamon in western Asia Minor. This kingdom included the area of the old Ionian cities, and was therefore as open to Greek ideas as any other center. The Attalid dynasty at Pergamon was philhellene (Greek-loving), and the architecture and sculpture of Pergamon are fine examples of Hellenistic developments directly related to Hellenic precursors. Macedon remained its own kingdom.

Greeks in Greece continued to fight one another, and though, on the death of Alexander, they revolted against Macedon, their revolt was crushed, and last hopes of autonomy were snuffed out. In Athens in the first part of the third century BC, civil war between pro- and anti-Macedonian parties was almost continuous. Though the city had fallen into political insignificance in the new, larger world, it continued to enjoy cultural and academic prestige, which it turned to advantage in the second century BC. The philosophers and logicians, who could claim descent from Socrates, Plato and Aristotle, attracted many foreigners to the city for their education. These included members of royal houses. Antiochos IV, shortly before he became king, was in Athens in 176 BC and was followed by others in the second century BC. Before long, these princely students became benefactors who funded architectural projects, and there is evidence of gifts to Athens from the royal houses of Pergamon, Egypt, Syria, and Cappadocia. With the expansion of the Greek world, however, Greece itself had ceased to be the focus.

In the West, Syracuse enjoyed prosperity in the third century under the leadership of its longest living autocrat, Hieron II. He ruled during 275–216 BC, proclaiming himself king in 269 BC. Projects of urban development in the district known as Neapolis were begun, and the theatre was enlarged. With the assistance of Archimedes, wide-ranging improvements, which included wheeled catapults on rails, were made to the fortifications, and an enormous altar was constructed for Zeus. Hieron's interest in the enormous extended even to shipping. He built a super-freighter, described by Athenaeus as a floating city. Among literary figures who visited his court was Theokritos. At Taras, too, in south Italy, there is evidence of a prosperous early period, with cemeteries in the region yielding many precious metal (silver and gold) items, jewelry, and other costly objects of ivory, worked bone, amber, and bronze. But always there loomed the power of Rome. By the middle of the third century BC Taras had succumbed, and the whole of south Italy was under Rome's control. By the end of the century, Sicily too was absorbed, and the Carthaginians were at long last overcome – by Romans. A Roman praetor (a senior magistrate) was installed in Syracuse in 201 BC.

ROME AND GREECE

In the course of the second century BC, Rome was drawn into Greece across the Adriatic, at first in struggles with the Macedonians under their king, Philip V. Though he was defeated in 197 BC, enmity continued off and on until Macedon was finally broken at the battle of Pydna in 168 BC. Later, the Romans had to contend with the Achaean League, which their general, Mummius, defeated. He then sacked the league's leading city, Corinth, and from this moment (146 BC) Rome ruled Greece. (This is the very same year in which Rome razed Carthage to the ground.) Then began the large-scale removal of statuary and paintings, presumably as booty, from Greece to Rome. About a decade later, in 133 BC, the last of the kings of Pergamon, Attalos III, bequeathed his kingdom to Rome. By the end of the next century, the other kingdoms of the Macedonian inheritance, Syria and Egypt, were in Roman hands. The battle of Actium in 31 BC signaled the end of this period of absorption of the Hellenistic kingdoms into the unfolding Roman empire, and with that the end of the Hellenistic age.

The Hellenistic period is wholly different from preceding periods in many ways. Huge kingdoms have replaced the city-states of Greece, which retreat into semi-obscurity. Mighty kings required new types of architecture for which there was literally no space in cities like Athens. So centers of architectural innovation are outside traditional Greek lands, as are the vital centers of sculptural production. Yet the legacy of Greece is evident everywhere. The world changed rapidly, with new interests and new outlooks. Realism in sculpture, to the point of caricature, came to the fore, as did individualism and interest in psychological portraits. There are new expressions of movement, of drama, and violence. Renewed interest in science and scholarship led to the foundation of the great libraries of Alexandria and Pergamon. There are new religions, great increases in population, and intensified commercial contacts. This whole great world, with all its diversities of peoples, traditions and attitudes, was unified by the language of its all too plentiful bureaucracies, Greek.

Architecture

PERGAMON
In the early years of the third century BC a certain Philetairos took over the citadel of Pergamon in western Asia Minor and established the Attalid dynasty. He and his successors, whose names were either Eumenes or Attalos, all the way down to the bequest of the kingdom to Rome in 133 BC, radically altered this citadel and established it as the capital of a Hellenistic kingdom of great power and wealth. They defeated the invading Gauls. They were philhellenes to the core. And they built a city distinguished enough to challenge Athens and Alexandria for architecture, sculpture, books, and learning. This city, or its upper part on the crown of the hill, was built, not according to the rules of Hippodamos of Miletus, but with new precepts in mind. Lower down the hill was a huge gymnasium and a sanctuary of Demeter, and much domestic architecture, but it is the architectural treatment of the top of the hill, 1000 feet (300 m) high, which is of most interest.

Here, the Attalid planners used the dramatically steep landscape to frame and show off important buildings. In the plan (fig. **10.1**) the

10.1 Plan of the upper city, Pergamon. 3rd–2nd centuries BC

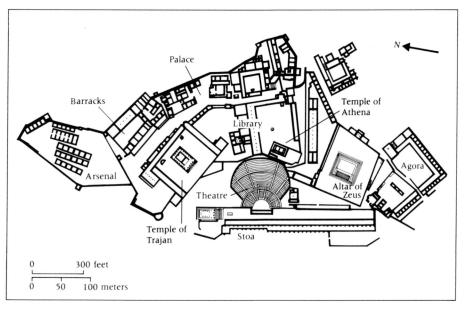

theatre is prominent. This aptly underscores the theatricality of setting, which governed the position and appearance of major buildings. Visibility of structures was important (fig. **10.3**). Equally important were the views from buildings over the impressive landscape. Panoramas of mountains spread in one direction, of rolling plains in another. The theatre with its vertiginous seats faced west. Behind it rose the buildings of the upper city, on terraces from south to north.

On the lowest terrace was a colonnaded agora, with stoas on three sides, surrounding an open space, and providing sheltered walkways in front of shops and offices on two storeys. It was an Attalos of Pergamon who saw the value of a stoa at the east end of the Agora in Athens and paid for it. On the next terrace up was the monumental altar of Zeus built in an open court. This altar was an enlargement of a type already well known in the Greek East, consisting of a wide flight of stairs between projecting wings leading to a level platform. The altar was lavishly decorated with relief sculpture, and though several sculptors worked on it, its style is uniform. This is a critical monument in the history of Hellenistic sculpture, which will be examined in the next section. The third terrace supported the Temple of Athena, one of the earliest buildings of this citadel complex, and a colonnaded court. The temple stood at the west side, at an oblique angle to the court but in line with the (later) altar of Zeus one terrace below.

10.2 *Opposite* Temple of Apollo, Didyma, from the east: note front steps of podium, deep pronaos and carved column bases. c. 330 BC and later

10.3 *Below* Pergamon, view southwestward from the top of the theatre overlooking the lower town and surrounding terrain

From this court, access was possible to the great library which housed many books and a collection of classical Greek paintings and sculpture. It challenged that of Alexandria for preeminence. A statue of Athena presided over this library. In this context she was evidently not a cult statue, but rather a patron saint of scholars and students. On the fourth terrace, at the very top, were located the palace itself of modest dimensions, the barracks for the garrison, the arsenal, and, much later, a temple built by the Roman emperor, Trajan.

A great fortification wall protected the citadel. The urban plan within, which arranged buildings on different lines on a terraced hilltop, was entirely new. It is the planning of the terraces, the coordination of the natural setting with man-made spaces, and the placement of buildings which made the upper city of Pergamon so dynamic and novel. Terraces and colonnades appeared to lead upward to the skies; the more down-to-earth realized that they led to the palace of the king and the barracks of his soldiers.

The Temple of Athena was built in the second quarter of the third century. It is a small Doric building measuring only about 24 × 13 yards (22 × 12 m), but there are new features. Columns of the peristyle are set further apart than before and are slimmer. Column heights are now 6.98 times lower diameters. Thus the bulk of the building is diminished and the airiness and lightness of the elevation are stressed. The columns were left unfluted, except directly beneath the capitals. The Doric order is rare in Hellenistic temple architecture, and Ionic is more popular. Corinthian would gradually become the order favored by Roman architects.

MAGNESIA AND DIDYMA

For temple architecture of the Ionic order, we turn to other sites in Asia Minor, Magnesia and Didyma. Creative architects working in the Ionic order tended to write about their systems of proportions and methods of planning in learned commentaries, passages of which have come down to us in the writings of the Roman critic, Vitruvius. One of these scholarly architects was Pythios who built the Temple of Athena at Priene

in the fourth century BC. Another was Hermogenes, famous for his temples at Teos, another site in Asia Minor, and at Magnesia.

Hermogenes' Temple of Artemis at Magnesia (fig. **10.4**) was raised above ground level by a podium of seven steps, and yet more light and air were admitted to the peristyle by wide spaces between the columns and by their slender form. Hermogenes was keen to relate the plan of the cella building to the peristyle columns, and these are aligned on the axis of the cella walls, and not on their outer faces. Such precision could only have derived from a drawing on a drafting board. Vitruvius was probably not the only one to insist that an architect must be able to draw. The plan (fig. **10.5**) was eight columns on the façade by 15 on the flank, and left room for another row of columns between colonnade and walls. This allowed for more air and light. The pairs of central columns at front and back are more widely spaced than other columns, emphasizing the entrances. Most radical is the treatment of the central block. The deep porch is the same size as the cella and has interior columns. The opisthodomos has the normal two columns *in antis*.

The elevation has a continuous Ionic frieze as well as *dentils*, but there was no sculpture in the pediments. Instead, the back wall of the pediment was provided with three rectangular windowlike openings, perhaps intended to reduce the weight of the superstructure. It is thought that the temple was built in the early second century BC.

10.4 Elevation of the Temple of Artemis, Magnesia. c. 175 BC

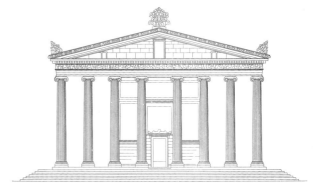

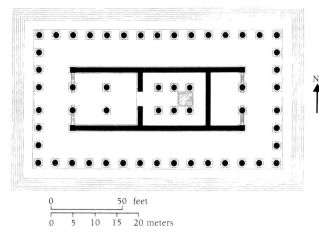

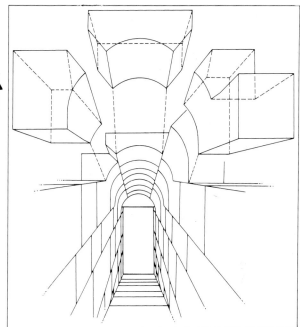

10.5 Plan of the Temple of Artemis, Magnesia. c. 175 BC

More complex was the new Temple of Apollo at Didyma (fig. **6.13c**, p. 153), begun around 330 BC and left unfinished. Work on the building was intermittent (the lintel, for example, went up in 182/1 BC), but the plan was Early Hellenistic. This huge and surprising temple replaced the gigantic Archaic temple burnt down by the Persians in 494 BC. The building was raised high on a podium of steps (fig. **10.2**, p. 318) and measured about 120 × 56 yards (110 × 51 m). The Ionic columns of the peristyle stood almost 66 feet tall, with ten on the façade and 21 on the flank in a double colonnade. A dozen more columns, with variously carved bases, stood in the porch. These columns screened a central doorway not at the level of the floor of the porch, but about 6 feet (2 m) higher, at the level of the floor of the chamber behind. The threshold is therefore more of a rostrum than an entrance, and may be the place where oracular responses were pronounced. There is no access here to the interior – a doorway exists, but it is a false entrance.

The forest of columns hides an open court with a small shrine, a temple within a temple. This interior court, with its smaller Ionic temple, evidently emulates Apollo's sacred grove and is another example of the arrangement of space to present dramatic surprises. There are more. Entrance to the interior was through a pair of sloping barrel-vaulted (fig. **10.6**) corridors leading downward from the columned porch into the

10.6 Perspective view, partially exploded, of barrel vaulted passage in the Temple of Apollo, Didyma. c. 330 BC and later

interior court, where the small shrine for the cult statue of Apollo stood. To the east, a broad flight of steps led up to a triple entrance, the central door flanked by engaged Corinthian columns (fig. **10.7**). The Apolline mysteries may have been kept in the chamber at the head of the steps, and revealed at the top of the steps on festival occasions.

Dramatic effects, whether in urban planning or spatial organization in individual buildings, are a hallmark of Hellenistic architecture. Another is the detailed interest in the proportions of architectural members and their relationships to one another, and the recording in scholarly commentaries of preferred solutions. This seems to be the case, at any rate, with the Ionic order. Doric seems to have been out of favor for big new temples, though popular among architects for large utilitarian buildings like stoas, where its simple forms could be repeated rapidly and easily. The potential convenience and brilliance of Corinthian was only slowly being realized.

ATHENS

The Corinthian order was used for the first time on the exterior of a fullscale building on the Temple of Olympian Zeus at Athens. This temple had been begun by the Peisistratid tyranny in the sixth century BC, but it got no further than the stylobate before their demise. In the second quarter of the second century BC, King Antiochus IV commissioned a Roman architect, Cossutius, to build it using the Corinthian order. The enormous building (fig. **10.8**), measuring around 118 × 45 yards (108 × 41 m), was planned to have triple rows of eight columns at front and back, with two rows of 20 columns on either flank. Examples of the Corinthian capitals were carried off to Rome after the Roman general, Sulla, sacked Athens in 86 BC (after the Athenians'

10.7 Temple of Apollo, Didyma, interior hypaethral (roofless) court, from the west: note monumental staircase to *oracular* hall, flanked by entrances to barrel-vaulted passages. c. 330 BC and later

reckless support of the revolt of King Mithridates of Pontus), and may have influenced the development of Roman Corinthian. Work was not finished on this huge temple project until the emperor Hadrian's rule in the second century AD.

Antiochos' generosity was matched by that of others, and during the second century BC Athens enjoyed a period of prosperity. Architectural growth was particularly apparent in the Agora (fig. **10.9**). The Square Peristyle of late-fourth-century date at the northeast corner, and South

10.8 Temple of Olympian Zeus, Athens, surviving columns from the southwest with the Acropolis in the background. 2nd century BC to 2nd century AD

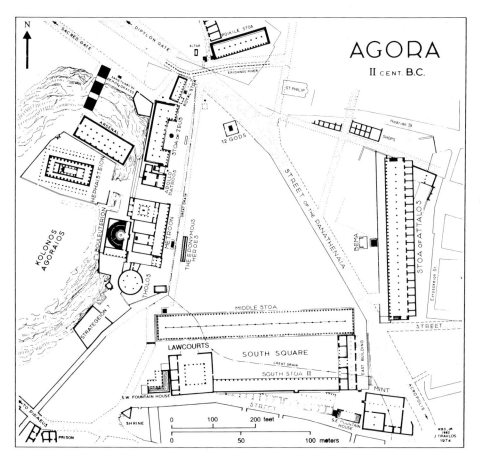

10.9 Plan of the Agora, Athens. c. 150 BC

Stoa I, built during the Peloponnesian War, were both pulled down to make way for new structures. At the south, materials from the Square Peristyle were recycled in the new South Stoa II, differently aligned from its predecessor. It is an unimpressive building consisting of a single Doric colonnade in front of a back wall, but it has to be thought of in conjunction with the new Middle Stoa. Together these two form the two long sides of a new square, a mini-agora in itself. The Middle Stoa was a big building, about 164 × 20 yards (150 × 18 m) in dimension. It faced both north and south. It is built almost entirely of limestone. The so-called East Building closed the square at the east. The function of this square has been much discussed, but many now agree that it probably had a commercial use, similar to that

enjoyed by its precursor, South Stoa I. It has also been proposed that, with the Mint nearby, the East Building may have been a convenient spot where coins could have been put into circulation.

The east side of the Agora saw the construction of the Stoa of Attalos (fig. **0.6**, p. 18), king of Pergamon from 159 to 138 BC, a gift from him and his wife to the Athenians (fig. **10.10**). It is a large (about 126 × 22 yards: 115 × 20 m) two-storeyed structure, purpose-built for shopping. There were 21 shops behind the double colonnade on each floor, 42 in all. Marble, for the

10.10 Agora, Athens, reconstructed Stoa of Attalos: ground floor interior from the south showing use of Doric order on the exterior, Ionic on the interior. c. 150 BC; reconstructed AD 1956

whole of the west side of the Agora was given a colonnaded façade (admittedly interrupted between buildings), and, together with the new stoas running the length of the south and east sides, defined in a more precise manner the commercial and administrative heart of the Hellenistic city.

MILETUS

In the zone set aside for commercial and public buildings in the rebuilt city of Miletus, a large agora with colonnaded stoas on all four sides was matched to the north by a more complex market arrangement. Here (fig. **10.12**) an L-shaped col-

10.11 Agora, Athens, Stoa of Attalos: Pergamene capital from the interior order of the upper floor. c. 150 BC

façade and the columns, and limestone were the materials used. There was wide spacing of the columns for ease of access and congregation, and variety in the use of the orders. Doric was used for the exterior on the ground level, Ionic for the interior. On the second level, Ionic columns on the exterior were linked by a balustrade, while the interior colonnade introduced a new capital type called Pergamene (fig. **10.11**), which was derived from the Egyptian palm capital. Columns of the interior colonnades were left unfluted, as was the lower part of the Doric colonnade since commercial traffic was likely to damage the column flutes. Enough of the stoa was preserved in later structures for it to be restorable with accuracy. The stoa now serves as a museum.

The other new building in the Agora was on the west side. Here a new Metroon (Temple of the Mother of the Gods) was constructed. It consisted of four rooms side by side, linked by a continuous colonnade across the front. Thus, the

10.12 Plan of the commercial and public buildings in the city center of Miletus. 2nd century BC

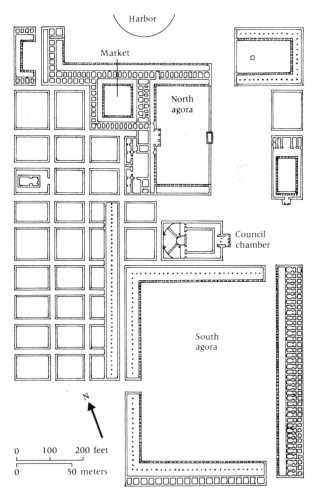

onnade, with shops and offices behind, faced the harbor. Behind the short side of this stoa stood another stoa with two projecting wings, while behind the long side were two rectangular courts. One was a peristyle market, the other an open court with colonnades on three sides (the north agora). This whole complex is a fine example of the one-time planning of a major urban market area, and of the adaptability of the stoa form in the organization of space. Differing locations, shapes, and sizes of commercial zones are all regularized by the use of the flexible colonnaded stoa. These buildings were erected in the middle years of the second century BC.

Miletus also provides a good example of the Hellenistic Bouleuterion (Council Chamber). Built around 170 BC and located between the North Market area and the huge agora, the complex consisted of a monumentalized gateway, an open peristyle court and the Chamber itself. The gateway and forecourt are innovations and were absent from the Bouleuteria of fifth-century Athens. Thus, as the real power of local government diminished with the disappearance of autonomy, its architectural manifestation became paradoxically more striking. The Chamber itself (fig. **10.13**) was arranged rather like a theatre, with rows of seats arranged in concentric semicircles around the floor, from which principal speakers could address the council. Theatres in Greek cities, incidentally, were also used for

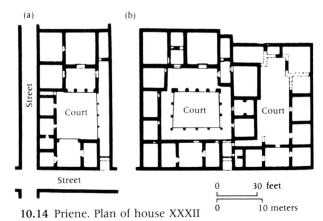

10.14 Priene. Plan of house XXXII
(a) In the 4th century BC
(b) Amalgamated with contiguous building in the 2nd century BC

political meetings. The building of the Council Chamber was roofed, and was decorated only with pilasters on the inside upper walls (above the seats). Outside, the walls are decorated with engaged Doric half-columns, a notable feature of which is the carving of the echinus with an Ionic ornament, the egg-and-dart molding. Thus, order-mixing, typical of Hellenistic architecture, was practiced even in a single architectural member. Ionic columns helped support the roof, but the interior remained bleak, and architects seem always to have been more engaged with exterior space than with interiors.

As to domestic architecture, housing of this period continued the introspective emphasis of preceding years. The interior courtyard is found everywhere, often with columns on all four sides. Occasionally, as at Priene (fig. **10.14**), houses of the fourth century BC were amalgamated in the second. At Priene, the amalgamation provides larger courts and plentiful rooms, though each house still has only a single entrance. Elsewhere, where a Hippodamian plan like that at Olynthos or Priene was not possible, private houses elbow one another in close quarters. On the island of Delos, which became an important trading center in this period, Hellenistic houses are crowded together in unsystematic blocks separated by winding streets. Congested residential areas in major cities like Alexandria may have had tall apartment blocks such as stood in later Roman towns like Ostia.

10.13 Isometric drawing, cut away, of the Bouleuterion, Miletus. c. 170 BC

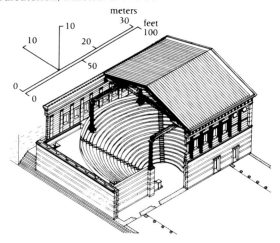

SYRACUSE

In the Greek West, Syracuse flourished during the third century BC. Writing in the first century BC, Cicero, the famous Roman orator, politician, and literary figure, described the city as "the largest Greek city, and the most beautiful of all cities." He spoke of a city which by his time was under Roman control but which had existed as an autonomous Greek city-state till the end of the third century BC. Her last tyrant, Hieron II (275–216 BC), initiated several architectural projects.

To the north, in the district known as Neapolis, a new residential zone took shape, planned with streets arranged in Hippodamian grid fashion. The nearby theatre, first constructed in the fifth century BC, was extended. New tiers of seats were added at the top with different sections named after the gods (and members of Hieron's family!), so that the diameter of the building increased to over 153 yards (140 m) and the theatre could accommodate around fifteen thousand spectators. One of the largest theatres in the Greek world, this structure had a distinctive design. The semi-circular *cavea* (auditorium) was partially framed at the top by a stoa. This also incorporated an artificial cave, into which water was brought from the uplands behind the city by a system of aqueducts. This grotto was flanked by niches for statuary and, as well as providing water for the theatre's hydraulic system, may have been the seat of the actors' guild.

With the advice of Archimedes, Hieron improved and extended the fortifications of the city. He also built a vast altar for Zeus. This rectangular structure measured about 208 × 25 yards (190 × 23 m), and was decorated with statuary. At the festival of the Eleutheria, no less than 450 bulls were sacrificed, a number which might explain the size of this mammoth altar, a structure which dwarfed its counterparts in Greece.

Sculpture

Diversification of form, and of psyche, presented in a realistic manner, are hallmarks of Hellenistic sculpture. The great variety of types, new and old, of poses and gestures and groups, taken in some instances to the point of caricature, has been explained by the influence of the new worlds opened to Greek artists by the conquests of Alexander. Yet much of what is new in Hellenistic sculpture was already implicit in the work of the great fourth-century sculptors – Praxiteles, Skopas, and Lysippos – who had consistently striven towards greater realism of human experience and expression. Lysippos' recognized enthusiasm for expanding the views of figures, his interest in mental states, his enthusiasm for surprise, for dramatic postures, for portraiture, and personification were especially influential.

The period may conveniently be divided into three chronological phases, though there is much difficulty in dating some pieces and agreement between scholars is often hard to find. The first chronological phase down to about 250 BC may be seen as a period of transition, in which revolutionary approaches appear alongside those that are conventionally Classical. The High Hellenistic phase, spanning a century from around 250 to 150 BC, follows and is typified by the style of sculptures from Pergamon. This style is often described as "Hellenistic baroque." The whole period from around 300–150 BC was seen by ancient critics, notably Pliny (*Natural History* 34.52), as a dreadful mistake in terms of art. Thus, the phases of Hellenistic sculpture perhaps most admired today were least admired by critics in the first century BC, who evidently preferred Classical restraint, moderation, and ideal types. The Late Hellenistic phase, from around 150 BC onwards, saw a resurgence of Classicism, which corresponded with the Roman conquest of Greece and the shipment of countless Greek statues from Greece to Italy. Copies, adaptations, and variants of Greek originals then proliferate in answer to the demands of Roman patrons. At the same time, the baroque trend was not bred out, but continued with some vigor and, doubtless, the disapproval of Pliny and his friends.

As to the subject matter, the standing male figure remained in use for images of gods and for commemorative statuary, and the draped female figure continued to be popular. But these were no longer the dominant types. Variety and diversity were called for, and the sculptors' vocabulary expanded accordingly. Interest in realism produced true-to-life portraits and images as individual as the aged fisherman and the drunken old woman. It also provided statues representing natural states of mind, the striving athlete or the sleepy satyr. Interest in eroticism produced sensuous statues of the nude Aphrodite, images of coupling satyrs and nymphs, and even hermaphrodites. Interest in humor produced caricatures of dwarves, slaves, and hunchbacks considered in this brutal age to be amusing, or statues of smiling, almost laughing, children evidently enjoying a natural and real, desirable, state of mind. Interest in personification and allegory multiplied. Interest in the theatrical produced statues in their settings: Eros asleep on a rock, or Nike alighting on the prow of a victorious ship on a hill high above the sea. Interest in emotion produced intense images of suffering, anguish, pain, brutality, anxiety, or pleasure. Thus, the range of subject matter was enormously wide.

The period of transition in the first half of the third century BC saw several innovations which derived from Praxiteles' startling creation of the nude Aphrodite of Knidos. She was often copied throughout the Hellenistic period, but new variations were also introduced. The Capitoline Venus (fig. **10.15**), a Roman copy of an original of the early third century BC, changes the goddess from a distant, confident figure into a more immediate, self-conscious, and seductive type. The gestures of arms and hands, rather than cloaking the female parts of the anatomy, actually draw attention to them. The Crouching Aphrodite (fig. **10.16**), similarly a Roman copy of a third-century original, presents an altogether new pose. The nude goddess at her bath offers

10.15 Capitoline Venus. Roman marble copy of a Hellenistic variant of the Aphrodite of Knidos. Height 6 ft 4 ins (1.93 m). c. 300–250 BC (original). Capitoline Museum, Rome

10.16 Crouching Aphrodite. Roman marble copy of a Hellenistic original. Height 2 ft 8¼ ins (82 cm). c. 250 BC (original). Terme Museum, Rome

various views of various limbs and roundly emphasizes the appeal of the flesh. Such creations, though new, point to continuity with the preceding century.

More revolutionary is a work of a pupil of Lysippos, Eutychides, who created an image of the Tyche (Fortune) of Antioch shortly after the foundation of that city, around 300 BC. The original was bronze, of which small-scale copies in marble and other materials (fig. **10.17**) survive. The Tyche appears as a draped female seated on a rock. She wears a crown, which represents the fortifications of the city, and in her right hand carries a wheatsheaf, symbolizing the fertility of the land. At her feet swims a youth, who

10.17 Tyche of Antioch by Eutychides. Roman marble copy of a colossal bronze original. Height 3 ft 2 ins (96 cm). c. 300 BC (original). Vatican Museums, Rome

10.18 Demosthenes by Polyeuktos. Roman marble copy of a bronze portrait statue erected in Athens. Height 6 ft 7½ ins (2.02 m). c. 280 BC (original). Ny Carlsberg Glyptothek, Copenhagen

represents the river Orontes. The personification of the city and the allegorical nature of the content are new, as is the design, which offered three principal views in a pyramidal arrangement.

Also entirely new is the posthumous portrait of the Athenian orator Demosthenes by Polyeuktos, erected in the Athenian Agora around 280 BC. The original was bronze, but again it is marble copies which have survived. Demosthenes (fig. **10.18**) faces forward with his arms lowered and his hands joined in front of him. His expression is thoughtful. The psychological portraiture is new, whereby the personality of an individual is revealed in the posture, set, and condition of the body, as well as in the facial expression. The desire to represent a generic type (e.g., the philosopher, the king, or the orator) is replaced by an interest in representing individual philosophers, kings, or orators. The psychological portrait of Demosthenes stands at the head of a long series of these portraits of personalities. At the same time, in this early Hellenistic phase, heroic portraiture, as exemplified by the portraits of Alexander, continued.

The baroque style of the High Hellenistic phase is characterized by dramatic effects, achieved by complex postures, gestures, and groupings, and by the intensity and variety of emotional representation. The tendency is first shown in softstone funerary reliefs of about 300 BC at Taras in south Italy, with their intensified expressions of sorrow and pathos.

The group of the Gaul and his Wife (fig. **10.19**) is a Roman marble copy of a bronze dedi-

10.19 Gaul killing himself. Roman marble copy of original Hellenistic group. Height 6 ft 11 ins (2.11 m). c. 220 BC (original). Terme Museum, Rome

cation associated traditionally with the dedications made by King Attalus I (241–197 BC) at Pergamon to celebrate victories over the Gauls. The defeated Gaul prefers suicide to surrender. He has already killed his wife in order to prevent her becoming a slave. The barbarian is portrayed as the noble hero. The group is completely carved in the round, affords many viewpoints, and effectively contrasts the vigorous and still vital male body with the female collapsing in death. Baroque is the twisting posture, the exaggerated musculature of the torso, and the high drama of the moment. The original of the group may date to around 220 BC.

The high point of this style is reached in the decoration of the great altar of Zeus at Pergamon, traditionally assigned to the reign of Eumenes II (197–159 BC). This altar was much smaller than Hieron's altar for Zeus at Syracuse, and took a different form. At Syracuse, Zeus was honored by size and utility, here by theme, quality, and style of ornament. The altar stood on a platform, with wings projecting forward at north and south on either side of a broad staircase (fig. **10.20**). The

10.20 Altar of Zeus, Pergamon, north wing. Marble. Height (of frieze) c. 7 ft 7 ins (2.30 m). c. 175–150 BC. Staatliche Museen, Berlin

platform supported an Ionic colonnade, while the podium below was decorated with a sculptured frieze 7 feet 7 inches (2.30 m) high. Here a colossal battle of gods and giants was depicted in local marble. The frieze consisted of some two hundred figures in such high relief and so sharply undercut that they appear almost in the round. Figures writhe and struggle, even up the steps towards the altar. Stressed moments are emphasized by tense bodies, violent postures, exaggerated muscles of torsos, legs, and arms, breathing open mouths, and deepset eyes, furrowed brows, and shocks of unruly hair. Swirling drapery enhances the dramatic effect. Zeus and Athena (fig. **10.21**) overthrow giants, whose faces are grim with horror and anguish.

The Pergamene kings had defeated the Gauls, just as the Greeks of Greece had warded off the Persians centuries before. In choosing to depict the great battle between Gods and Giants, a theme common to and known by all Greeks, the designer of the frieze of the altar evoked both those great Greek victories over barbarians and deliberately linked philhellene Pergamon with Greece and especially with Athens. There were other links to Athens. Motifs were borrowed from the Parthenon itself: the X-composition arrangement of Athena overpowering a giant on the altar is adapted from the Athena and Poseidon of the west pediment, while the Athena herself is thought to be an adaptation from the Athena of the east pediment, and Zeus an adaptation from the Poseidon of the west. These learned references point to the rise of Classicism, so that in this altar, with its confident interweaving of massive dramatic figures and horrified expressions of pain and passion, both baroque and classicizing tendencies appear side by side.

Another frieze decorated the interior of the altar showing the life of Telephos, legendary ancestor of the kings of Pergamon. Different episodes of his adventures, separated sometimes by landscape elements – a new design idea, and figures appear one above another as we are told they did in wall paintings as early as the fifth century BC. Auge and her son, Telephos (fig. **10.22**), are soon to be abandoned to the sea in the small boat visible in the foreground. The mood is calm and resigned, quite unlike the frenzy and blatant emotionalism of the outside frieze.

10.21 Altar of Zeus, Pergamon, east frieze detail: Athena fighting giants. Height (of frieze) 7 ft 7 ins (2.30 m). c. 175–150 BC. Staatliche Museen, Berlin

10.22 Altar of Zeus, Pergamon, Telephos frieze: incident in the biography of the founder of the Pergamene dynasty. Marble. Height 5 ft 2¼ ins (1.58 m). c. 175–150 BC. Staatliche Museen, Berlin

The twisting pose, swirling drapery, and dramatic setting of the famous Nike of Samothrace (fig. **10.23**) find parallels in the Pergamon altar. This personification of Victory, a marble original of around 8 feet (2.45 m) in height, harks back to iconographic precursors, such as the Nike of Paionios, and hence enjoys both Classical resonance and baroque vitality. She is shown landing from flight, wings still outspread. Originally she stood on the prow of a ship, itself set in a reflecting pool of water (unless this is a later addition) at the top of a cliff. The body lands heavily, the torso twisted slightly to the right and upward, while there is a new torsion in the drapery. A spiral rises in the thick folds between the legs towards and over the right leg, checked and balanced at the hips by another spiral system moving in the opposite direction around the left hip. Treatment of passages of drapery is paralleled in the garments of figures, such as Athena from the Pergamon frieze. The swirling folds of drapery express the rapidity of movement, while twisting of body and drapery and the theatrical setting render the Nike a masterpiece of Hellenistic baroque.

Contemporary with this baroque style are studies in the bizarre (caricatures and grotesques, for example), the erotic (hermaphrodites, groups

10.23 Nike of Samothrace, perhaps by Pythokritos of Rhodes. Marble. Height 8 ft 1 in (2.45 m). c. 180 BC. Musée du Louvre, Paris

10.24 Boy Jockey from the sea near Cape Artemision. Bronze. Height 2 ft 9 ins (84 cm). c. 220–200 BC. National Museum, Athens

10.25 Sleeping Satyr, found in Rome, possibly a Hellenistic original. Marble. Height 7 ft (2.15 m). c. 200 BC. Staatliche Antikensammlungen, Munich

of maenads and satyrs, and Aphrodite, Pan, and Eros, for example), and studies in realism. The athlete is now shown, not like the Charioteer from Delphi of the fifth century BC (fig. **7.24**, p. 220) in the moment of glory after the race, but in the throes of the competition. The bronze Boy Jockey (fig. **10.24**), recovered from a shipwreck off Cape Artemision and doubtless intended for the art market or a patron in Rome, is shown in midcontest. Astride his horse, he leans forward, one hand holding the reins and the other perhaps a whip as he urges his mount forward. There is no exaggeration of anatomy or of expression; the lightframed, wiry, boyish body and the concentration of mind are equally successfully rendered. The name of the artist is unknown; the jockey and his horse were made perhaps around 220–200 BC.

Just as a sculptor could realistically represent the emotional condition of an energetic young jockey, so keen observation of the world and its variety enabled sculptors to show other real mental states, and the relationship between mental and physical state. Thus, the Sleeping Satyr (fig. **10.25**) is a portrait of a mind at rest and a body

relaxed. But there is no mistaking the vitality of this mythological follower of Dionysos, or the detailed realism of veins, muscle, and sinew. Sometimes known as the Barberini Faun, the satyr was probably made around 200 BC and was found in Rome in 1625; it was restored by Bernini, who may have been tempted to give the figure a more baroque flavor than it originally enjoyed.

Realistic psychological portraiture flourished, even in the remotest parts of the Greek world. Greek kings of Bactria in Central Asia continued to speak Greek and enjoy things Greek. A portrait of Euthydemos I (230–190 BC) tells the tale. A Roman copy (fig. **10.26**) of an original of around 200 BC, Euthydemos appears wearing an impressive hat and no-nonsense expression. Wrinkly details around the eyes and brows, large nose (though heavily restored), and deep furrows on either side of the nose allow no compromise. This

10.26 Portrait of Euthydemos of Bactria. Roman marble copy of an original of the later 3rd century BC. Height 13 ins (33 cm). Villa Albani, Rome

10.27 Statues of Cleopatra and Dioskourides, from the peristyle of their house on Delos. Marble. Height 5 ft 6 ins (1.67 m). c. 140 BC. Delos

is a representation of the man as he was, of his external individual appearance and of his straightforward, confident character, true to life.

The Late Hellenistic phase witnessed a renewed interest in Classical sculpture. With the Roman conquest of Greece came Roman enthusiasm for Greek culture, and not least for statuary of the fifth and fourth centuries BC. Greek statues were shipped off to Italy; Roman patrons commissioned agents to find statues suitable for their gardens or their libraries or gymnasia. Wealthy Romans came to Greece to see the sights and to be educated. Less wealthy Romans and Italians came to Greece and the east to make their fortunes, and the island of Delos became a center for their activities. Trade of all kinds flourished, and Greek sculptors turned readily to the Roman market and its taste.

On Delos, the marble statues of two citizens, Cleopatra and Dioskourides (fig. **10.27**), unfortunately headless, have survived in their original position in a courtyard of the couple's house. These honorary statues, put up by Cleopatra around 140 BC, when Dioskourides dedicated tripods to Apollo, are standard types, heavily draped and conservative. The drapery has none of the devices of the deeply cut, swirling drapery of Pergamene baroque, and is markedly retrospective. Folds of cloth, seen through Cleopatra's upper garment, run counter to the upper folds, which lead the eye around the figure and thus suggest various viewpoints. To this extent, we are in the realm of the new. But the figures are reminiscent of Classical calm and control, a far cry from the exuberance and extravagance of Hellenistic baroque.

Also classicizing, and of the second half of the second century BC, is the marble Aphrodite of Melos (Venus de Milo) (fig. **10.28**), found on the island of Melos and now in the Louvre in Paris. She is over lifesize (around 6 feet 8 inches – 2.04 m tall), and stands with the left leg sharply forward, bent at the knee and turning. The Praxitelean S-curve rises through the body, while the drapery is suggestively poised. The face is Late Classical in type, and the anatomy, too. Though proportions are changed and she is higher-waisted than the Aphrodite of Knidos, the similarity is there. The new proportions, the twisting spiral of the figure between feet and hips, and the precarious drapery introduce new and distinctly Hellenistic notes, but the influence of the Classical is clear.

Increased interest in the individual meant increased interest in portraiture, and, with the greater number of Greek kingdoms following the break-up of the empire of Alexander the Great, more opportunities for regal portraiture. Rulers could be shown as identifiable individuals, like Euthydemos (fig. **10.26**), or in a more heroic manner. The bronze over-lifesize portrait of the Hellenistic ruler (fig. **10.29**) made around 150 BC offers a good example. The Classical walking stance of the nude heroic figure is modified by the Hellenistic spiral of the arms and torso, right arm twisting behind the body and the left arm around the staff on which he leans. The small head turns sharply to his right, introducing more tension, while the heavy eyebrows, thick lips, and downturned corners of the mouth suggest individualizing characteristics. The body is heavy and overmuscled, as if the muscularity of the prize-fighter were a symbol of political power. No secure identification of the figure has yet been advanced. Regal power is expressed in the firmness of the facial expression and in the sheer strength of the body, yet the characteristics which speak for individuality seem not to chime easily with those which are emblems of kingship.

10.28 *Opposite* Aphrodite of Melos: halfdraped marble statue, from the island of Melos. Height 6 ft 8¼ ins (2.04 m). c. 150–125 BC. Musée du Louvre, Paris

10.29 Hellenistic ruler, found in a Roman house on the Esquiline in 1884. Bronze. Height c. 7 ft 9 ins (2.37 m) (without lance). c. 150 BC. Terme Museum, Rome

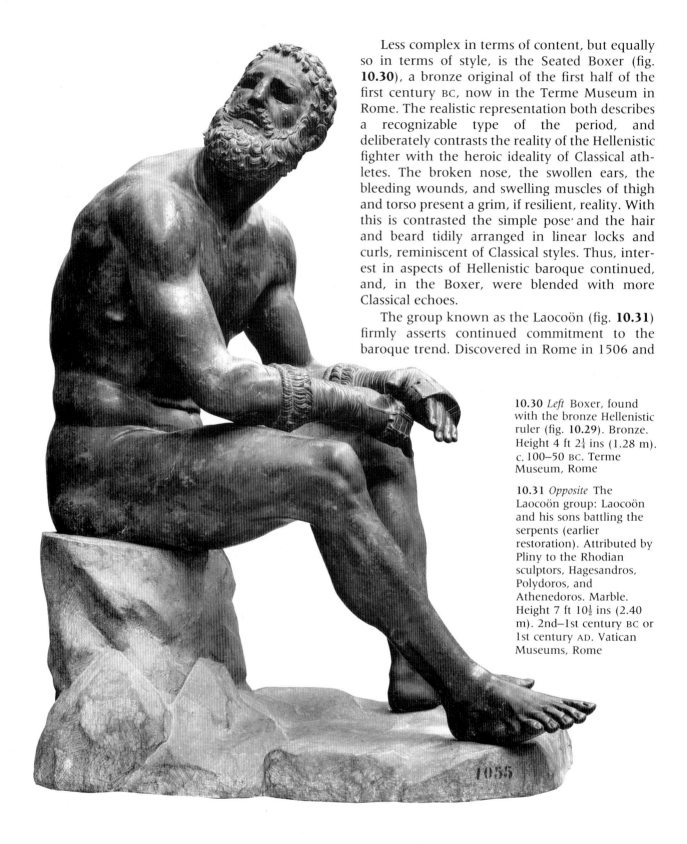

Less complex in terms of content, but equally so in terms of style, is the Seated Boxer (fig. **10.30**), a bronze original of the first half of the first century BC, now in the Terme Museum in Rome. The realistic representation both describes a recognizable type of the period, and deliberately contrasts the reality of the Hellenistic fighter with the heroic ideality of Classical athletes. The broken nose, the swollen ears, the bleeding wounds, and swelling muscles of thigh and torso present a grim, if resilient, reality. With this is contrasted the simple pose· and the hair and beard tidily arranged in linear locks and curls, reminiscent of Classical styles. Thus, interest in aspects of Hellenistic baroque continued, and, in the Boxer, were blended with more Classical echoes.

The group known as the Laocoön (fig. **10.31**) firmly asserts continued commitment to the baroque trend. Discovered in Rome in 1506 and

10.30 *Left* Boxer, found with the bronze Hellenistic ruler (fig. **10.29**). Bronze. Height 4 ft 2¼ ins (1.28 m). c. 100–50 BC. Terme Museum, Rome

10.31 *Opposite* The Laocoön group: Laocoön and his sons battling the serpents (earlier restoration). Attributed by Pliny to the Rhodian sculptors, Hagesandros, Polydoros, and Athenedoros. Marble. Height 7 ft 10½ ins (2.40 m). 2nd–1st century BC or 1st century AD. Vatican Museums, Rome

witnessed by Michelangelo, this group consisting of Laocoön and his two sons and two attacking serpents has been the subject of much scholarly debate. Pliny names the sculptors as Hagesandros, Athenedoros, and Polydoros of Rhodes. The subject matter is not in doubt: the Trojan priest, Laocoön, was about to warn the Trojans against the wooden horse when he and his sons were attacked and silenced by Poseidon by means of the sea serpents. The date of the group has, however, been controversial. The twisting contorted figures, the exaggerated anatomy of Laocoön, the anguished, fearful expressions and the high drama of the struggle have all placed the group in many scholars' minds close to the great frieze of the Pergamon altar.

10.32 Odysseus and Palladion (statue of Athena) from one of the groups found in the cave "of Tiberius" at Sperlonga, some 60 miles (96 km) south of Rome. Names of the sculptors Hagesandros, Polydoros, and Athenedoros inscribed on the ship connect these groups to the Laocoön. Marble. Cave reworked in the 1st century AD. Roman copy of Hellenistic original or Hellenistic original of the 2nd century BC. Archaeological Museum, Sperlonga

Yet the discovery in 1957 of more figures (fig. **10.32**) executed in the Hellenistic baroque style, in a cave at Sperlonga, transformed into a dining grotto belonging to an imperial villa and dated to the first century AD, has thrown the chronology into doubt. At Sperlonga, the groups depict scenes from Greek myth in big compositions. The blinding of Polyphemos, Odysseus' sailors consumed by Skylla, and the shipwreck convert the narrative from poetry to sculpture in dramatic settings and in a style similar to that of the Laocoön. Connection with the Laocoön group seems confirmed by the presence of the names of Hagesandros, Athenedoros, and Polydoros inscribed on the ship in the grotto. Were they originals of the second century BC brought to Italy from the East to adorn the emperor's underground dining room? Modern opinion inclines more to the view that both they and the Laocoön group represent concoctions of the first century AD, which drew freely on Hellenistic prototypes, emulating both the style of Hellenistic baroque, the subject matter, and the compositional arrangements. If so, one is tempted to think that the Late Hellenistic period, with respect to sculpture anyway, with its versatile adaptation of this High Hellenistic baroque style, may have continued well into the Roman empire of the first century. However that may be, the Laocoön is an excellent example of Hellenistic one-view composition, like a relief, and of Hellenistic spiraling figures. In Hellenistic fashion, the pathos of the moment is high; the hopeless struggle was doomed.

We have seen examples of architectural relief sculpture in the Gigantomacy of the Pergamene altar and the interior Telephos frieze. Other reliefs were votive. The relief known as the *Apotheosis* of Homer (fig. **10.33**), dated to around 125 BC and the work of Archelaos of Priene, combines scholarly references with allegory, a theatrical (literally) setting, landscape elements, and numerous sculptural types. Figures are arranged in registers up the relief which is only 3 feet 9 inches (1.14 m) high. At the bottom, on the stage – the backdrop for which is visible, slung along in front of columns – appears Homer crowned by personifications of Time and the World. The *Iliad*

10.33 Apotheosis of Homer: votive relief by Archelaos of Priene. Marble. Height 3 ft 9 ins (1.14 m). c. 125 BC. British Museum, London

and the *Odyssey* kneel by his side; Myth and History sacrifice; other actors represent Poetry, Tragedy, Comedy, Human Nature, and four Virtues. All salute Homer – and all are identified by inscriptions – except Human Nature, the child who prefers to contemplate the Virtues. This cluttered scene is full of learned reference, clever allusion, recognizable attributes, and personified abstractions. Above in registers on the hillside, or in the cave, are the Muses, Apollo (in the cave), Zeus (at the very summit) with his eagle at his feet and a statue of a poet to the right. Hellenistic sculptural types are used in the representation of the Muses. This complex relief speaks to the Hellenistic love of symbol, learning, sophistication, allegory, allusion, abstraction, the theatre, and poetry.

From the very earliest periods artisans had produced small figurines in terracotta, many for use as votive offerings (examples from earlier periods have been cited). South Italy continued to be a conspicuous center of production, along with Asia Minor and Athens. In Italy, the appearance of terracotta figurines of actors neatly complements their appearance on the phlyax vases (fig. **10.34**), and gives us a splendid idea of what these performers looked like in the fourth century BC and following. Towards the end of the fourth century BC a new series of terracottas, the so-called Tanagra figurines, made their appearance. They take their name from the town of Tanagra in Boeotia, where they were first

10.34 *Left* Terracotta figurine of an actor dressed as an old woman, a character in a phlyax play. c. 350 BC. Martin von Wagner Museum, Würzburg

10.35 *Above* Terracotta Tanagra figurine. Height 13 ins (33 cm). 3rd century BC. Staatliche Museen, Berlin

10.36 *Right* Pair of terracotta women conversing, from Myrina. Height 8¼ ins (21 cm). c. 200 BC. British Museum, London

found. Most come from graves, and therefore carry some specific meaning, weightier than the phlyax figures. The best known Tanagra type is the standing draped female (fig. **10.35**), which enjoyed great popularity in the Hellenistic period.

The use of several molds to make different parts of figures in different postures, and the addition of handmade sections, made production of differing types easier. Thus these artefacts readily met the Hellenistic need for variety and realism, and the draped female appeared seated (fig. **10.36**) as well as standing or playing games or dancing. The standing figure typically adopts a stylized, easy stance, is heavily draped and often

glances downward with a demure expression. A small head, slim shoulders, and broad hips are characteristic. Hundreds of these figurines have been found, and often the paint with which they were decorated is preserved. Blue paint and gilding are used on an elegant woman (fig. **10.35**) of the third century BC from Tanagra, who carries a fan and wears a sunhat. Male figures were also made, but in far fewer numbers; of these, the flying Eros figure enjoyed some favor.

The whole of this period is full of puzzles, not least in sculpture, and there are serious uncertainties of attribution, chronology, regional style, and even of identification, but the broad outlines are reasonably clear.

Wall painting and mosaics

Direct evidence for Hellenistic wall paintings is almost as scarce as it was for the fifth and fourth centuries BC, and we may reasonably suspect that what has survived is not necessarily of the first rank. At Vergina, in Macedonia, some impressive chamber tombs were discovered. Both their façades and interiors are decorated with a series of paintings. The façade of a tomb dated to about 300 BC shows Rhadamanthys (fig. **10.37**), a Judge of the Dead, cloaked and leaning on a staff. This is a figure type well known in the Greek repertoire, deriving from an earlier male type seen on fourth-century Athenian grave monuments. Other figures on the façade make up a quartet, two either side of the door. They are Hermes, who guided souls to Hades, the dead man, and another judge, Aiakos.

On the edge of the Greek world, at Kazanlak in Bulgaria, a vaulted tomb also from about 300 BC has been found, the vault painted with friezes of figures and chariots (fig. **10.38**). The standing and seated figures are drawn from the vocabulary of Greek types, while the enthroned figure to the right, placed diagonally to the foreground, is an important forerunner to the similar motif in the Roman paintings from Boscoreale. The chariot and horses careering around the dome show experiment in illusionistic perspective, and precede their counterparts in Roman paintings at Pompeii by some three hundred years. Yet the figures are flat, the use of color is unimaginative, and the draftsmanship is clumsy. This is the work of a provincial Greek artist, but is nevertheless an important survivor.

Perhaps the most important innovation of Hellenistic wall painters was a greater use of landscape. There were landscape elements on the fourth-century tomb at Vergina and schematic landscape features appear even earlier, for instance on the Tomb of the Diver wall painting (fig. **7.37**, p. 232); now literary sources tell of an important Hellenistic painter called Demetrios Topographos (the landscape painter). But because of lack of direct archaeological evidence, the topic is controversial. It is overshadowed by a magnificent series of paintings known as the

10.37 Façade of a Macedonian tomb: wall painting, Rhadamanthys, a Judge of the Dead. Height c. 4 ft 1 in (1.25 m). c. 300 BC

Odyssey Landscapes found in a house on the Esquiline in Rome. They show episodes from Odysseus' adventures set in the most dramatic landscapes. They are Late Hellenistic (first century BC) in date. But are they Greek (Hellenistic) or Roman? What precursors can be found? The elements in the painting of Macedonian tombs are evidence that landscape themes were under study, but nothing yet found prepares us for the pantheistic scale, and the brilliance of the con-

10.38 Painted dome
of circular tomb at
Kazanlak, Bulgaria: work
of a Greek artist. Diameter
of tomb c. 11 ft (3.35 m).
c. 300 BC.

10.39 Odyssey Landscape:
Odysseus and his men in
the land of the
Laestrygonians. Wall
painting, from Rome.
Height (of frieze) 5 ft
(1.52 m). c. 50 BC.
Vatican Museums, Rome

junction of narrative and illusion in the Odyssey landscapes. Odysseus (fig. **10.39**) journeys through the countryside encountering many challenges and companions. But he and his human counterparts are diminutive by comparison with the mountains, rocks, trees, the sky, and the sea. Nature herself is the real focus for the painter, so that the physical world itself becomes as important as the myth which Odysseus represents. Strong accents of light and shade emphasize the grandeur of nature, the brushwork is rapid and impressionistic. Figures are painstakingly identified, in the old Greek fashion, by inscriptions. It is difficult to believe that this phenomenon made its first appearance, fully mature, in the first century BC. Many sensitive commentators take the view that these landscapes are Roman adaptations of earlier, second-century BC Hellenistic paintings and that the three-dimensional representation of landscape as a grand setting for narrative or for its own sake began then.

Literary sources tell us that Romans copied Greek paintings, but it seems they preferred paintings of the fourth century BC, since Hellenistic paintings of the third and second century BC are seldom mentioned. Among Hellenistic painters who did attract Roman attention were Epigonos, Artemon, and Demetrios Topographos. The presence on the walls of Pompeii and Herculaneum of several versions, different in details, of a particular painting both argues the existence of a prototype and suggests the difficulty of identifying what the original looked like. It has already been suggested that the different versions of Perseus rescuing Andromeda reflect a fourth-century Greek original. Perhaps, too, Roman paintings which show either Hellenistic sculptural types or large-scale landscape elements are reflections of Hellenistic paintings.

Tessellated mosaics had replaced pebble mosaics by about 250 BC, and houses at Delos provide good examples from the second century BC. Figured panels (emblemata) (fig. **10.40**) with humans, animals, or groups could be worked separately, and inserted into a framework of abstract designs, of which the wave pattern remained popular. Most mosaics, however, for reasons of economy were made solely of abstract designs. Other examples from Pergamon show panels with figures shaped with strong accents of light and shade. One master craftsman here, Sosus by name, became famous for his illusionistic panels, notably one of birds drinking at a basin, and another of an unswept floor with the residue of a dinner party still on it.

Much larger mosaics decorated the floors of public buildings. At Praeneste (Palestrina), some 25 miles (40 km) east of Rome, is the sanctuary of Fortuna. Built in the second century BC, it echoes developments elsewhere in the Hellenistic world. Multiple terraces on a hillside and extensive use of colonnades remind one of Pergamon, and its (almost) symmetrical hillside plan, stepped terraces, and axial approach to the temple at the summit are very similar to those of the sanctuary of Asklepios on the island of Kos. A great mosaic, measuring about 6½ by 5½ yards (6 by 5 m), decorated the floor of an apsed hall.

This is the so-called Nile Mosaic (fig. **10.41**) which dates from around 100 BC and shows a Hellenistic adaptation of an old Egyptian motif. It was probably copied in Praeneste from a prototype created in Alexandria. The Nile and its

10.40 *Below* Tessellated mosaic, from Delos: figured panels (emblemata) and abstract surrounds. c. 3 ft 6½ ins × 3 ft 6¼ ins (1.08 × 1.07 m). 2nd century BC

10.41 *Right* Nile mosaic, Sanctuary of Fortuna, Praeneste. c. 19 ft 8 ins × 16 ft (6 x 4.9 m). c. 100 BC. National Museum, Palestrina

denizens, human and animal, are the subject of this polychrome mosaic. The southern regions of Egypt are shown at the top (in the apse), and the more populated estuary at the bottom. The river winding its way through the landscape is the thread which unites the whole scene. The interest in the life of the river is panoramic. The lower part depicts ships of all kinds: oared warships, sailing boats, fishing boats, and skiffs on the river populated by crocodile, hippopotamus, birds of all kinds, fish large and small, and water buffalo. Many buildings viewed from many angles stand on the banks. Soldiers gather under an awning outside an imposing columned building, a bugler sounds off, women loiter in a pergola, a peasant rides a donkey by. In the upper, more distant part, landscape elements take precedence over architecture, boats, and humans. Though there are hunting parties of tiny figures, this is the domain of wild animals, real and fantastic, most identified by Greek inscriptions. Rocks, trees, bushes, birds, and serpents are their companions. The knowledge of the river and the range of life it sustained is both encyclopaedic and fanciful. Scholarly interest in detail, the enthusiasm for landscape motifs, the great variety of boats and buildings and the varied views are all characteristically Hellenistic.

Pottery

At the end of the fourth century BC painted pottery gave way to mold-made bowls with relief decoration. These pots at first probably imitated bowls made of precious metals. They are conventionally called Megarian bowls, but were in fact manufactured all over the Hellenistic world, and enjoyed great commercial success from the third century BC down into the first. The decoration is

usually floral, but occasionally figures, and even mythological scenes, appear. The illustration (fig. **10.42**) shows part of a bowl and part of the mold from which it was made, both from Athens. This technique of making pottery was picked up by the Romans in the first century BC, and resulted in the production of the most successful of Roman tablewares, Arretine.

Painted pottery did not, however, fade out entirely. Gnathian ware continued until the end of the third century BC, as a dark ground pottery produced in the West. Its counterpart in Greece and the East was West Slope Ware, named after material found on the west slope of the Acropolis at Athens. The black surface of Gnathian was painted in whites and browns with wreaths, floral scrolls, and ribbons. Occasionally, a female head, or an Eros, or a female figure, or even a musical instrument appear as decorations. Here (fig. **10.43**) the bowl is painted with an actor's mask surrounded by decorative abstract registers and garlands. West Slope Ware typically deco-

10.42 Part of a mold-made Megarian bowl, and mold from which it was made, from the Athenian agora. 3rd–2nd centuries BC. Agora Museum, Athens

10.43 *Left* Gnathian ware bowl, made in south Italy: a comic mask and garlands. Height 7 ins (18 cm). 3rd century BC. Rijksmuseum van Oudheden, Leiden

10.44 *Below* Lagynos made near Pergamon and decorated with a lagynos and festoons. Height 6⅔ ins (16 cm). 2nd century BC. British Museum, London

10.45 *Left* Canosan askos, made in Apulia: Medusa head in relief, forepart of horses and winged Nikai attached, and elaborate painting. Height 2 ft 6 ins (76.5 cm). 3rd century BC. British Museum, London

10.46 *Above* Centuripe vase, made in Sicily: a polychrome funerary vase, painted after firing. Height 22 ins (56 cm). 3rd century BC. Catania University

rates the black surface with floral designs in white, and continued into the first century BC.

Painting on a light ground continued on Panathenaic amphoras until the end of the third century BC, and a new shape, the *lagynos* (a squat jug with a long neck), is habitually decorated with brown paint on a thick white slip. The decoration most often shows garlands of wreaths, but sometimes also different objects related to feasting (fig. **10.44**). The shape may have originated in Asia Minor, perhaps near Pergamon, and lasted till the first century BC. More ambitious were vases, essentially white-ground, with molded additions. At Canosa in south Italy in the third century BC, burials often included unusual pottery shapes to which fully three-dimensional attachments (horse heads and

necks, for example) were fixed, and atop which stood terracotta Tanagra-like Nike figures, all painted in blue, pink, and yellow on a white ground (fig. **10.45**). At Centuripe in Sicily, also in the third century BC, a similar practice was followed. The polychrome burial vase (fig. **10.46**), extravagant in shape and with molded additions (heads, architectural moldings), shows a seated woman flanked by two attendants. Pink, blue, yellow, and red are painted on the white ground. All the painting was done after the vessel was fired, so that these colors are notoriously fugitive. This technique was quite different from the Greek red-figure of the fifth and fourth centuries BC, and this style represented, in fact, the final episode in the history of Greek vase painting.

Conclusion

Though archaeology comprises much more than art, it is the major developments in Greek art from the Bronze Age to the Hellenistic era – in architecture, sculpture, pottery, and wall painting – which have been emphasized in this book. These developments continued through the Roman period and the Renaissance and can be seen as the foundation on which much of Western art came to be based.

The Greeks' interest in the representation of the human figure is evident in the Cyclades as early as the third millennium. It comes to the fore again in the two-dimensional and sticklike figures of the Geometric period and later in the increasingly realistic but stereotypical forms which prevailed until the Hellenistic period. In the fifth century BC it culminated in an understanding of natural appearances which enabled sculptors and painters of the Classical period to express accurately not only anatomy, but also human emotion, character, age, and mood. Artists had continued to struggle with the conflict between realistic and conceptual representation, and their triumph in imposing external order on the representation of nature was a major achievement of the High Classical period. From the beginning of the fourth century BC, however, balanced forms began to fragment and the exploration in art of states of mind advanced rapidly, until in Hellenistic times individualized and exaggerated postures, gestures, and expressions became common.

The Greeks' desire to represent the human figure as an object of beauty was accompanied by other expressions of creativity, most notably in architecture. Architects and planners studied measurement and scale to impose harmonious proportions on temples and more secular buildings, and to create spaces and structures suitable for sacrifice and ritual as well as for administrative, political, and commercial life. The landscape, and the relationship of architecture and landscape, was always important, whether in early sanctuaries sited on hallowed land, or in later citadels such as that at Pergamon, where geography and geometry were juxtaposed in theatrical display.

The victory of Octavianus at Actium in 31 BC can be said to mark the end of the Hellenistic era; but the influence of Greek art continued. With the absorption of the Greek cities in Italy and Sicily into the world of Rome, and with the Roman conquest of Greece, a new era had opened. Greek ideas, objects, and materials had already begun to flow into Rome. Roman generals and entrepreneurs looted Greek sites and carried off important works to decorate villas, gardens, and public places in Italy. Greek statues and paintings were copied repeatedly. Roman architects copied the Greek orders, making use of Doric and Ionic, but openly favoring Corinthian. The political Romanization of the Hellenistic world went hand in hand with the artistic Hellenization of Rome. Rome thus became the intermediary for Greek ideas to reach the Italian Renaissance and modern times.

Over a thousand years later, Renaissance artists, looking back to the ancient Greek traditions, again took up the challenge of realistically representing the structure and proportions of the human body. Renaissance architects, wishing to use ancient shapes and rules of proportion in new churches and city palaces, grappled with problems posed by the Classical orders. Renaissance painters often depicted still visible ancient monuments and sought in other ways to evoke the world of antiquity. This world, far from dying out, was thus a major influence at the dawn of the modern age and may fairly be considered the mainspring of Western civilization.

Chronology

900 BC

Greeks in Syria

800 BC

Greek settlements in south Italy and
Sicily

700 BC

Greeks in Egypt and Libya
Greeks by the Black Sea
Further settlements in south Italy and Sicily
Tyrannies in Greece
Population decline in Athens, growth
elsewhere

600 BC

Reforms of Solon at Athens
Tyranny of Peisistratos and his family at
Athens
Persians conquer Lydia and reach the Aegean
coast
Tyranny of Polykrates on Samos
Kleisthenes and democracy in Athens

500 BC

Persian invasion of Greece and war, 490–479
BC
Battle of Marathon, 490 BC
Battle of Salamis, 480 BC
Battle of Plataea, 479 BC
Western Greeks defeat Carthage at Himera,
480 BC
Western Greeks defeat Etruscans at Cumae,
474 BC
Delian League formed (becomes the Athenian
Empire) 477 BC
Tyrannies in the West: Syracuse, Akragas,
Gela
Delian League treasury transferred to Athens,
454 BC

Aeschylus, Sophokles, Euripides
Perikles
Peloponnesian War between Sparta and
Athens, 431–404 BC
Athens' expedition to Sicily, 415–413 BC
Athens' defeat at Syracuse, 413 BC
Sparta victorious, 404 BC
Aristophanes, Thucydides

400 BC

Socrates, Plato
Carthage again active in Sicily
Dionysios tyrant in Syracuse
Timoleon and oligarchy in Syracuse
Demosthenes, Aristotle
Macedonians defeat Greeks at Chaeronea, 338
BC
Alexander the Great, 336–323 BC
End of city-states in Greece
Emergence of nation states: Egypt, Syria,
Macedonia

300 BC

Hieron II rules Syracuse, 275–216 BC
Kingdom of Pergamon established
Gauls invade Asia Minor
Rome controls south Italy and Sicily by the
end of the century

200 BC

Rome defeats Macedon, 197 BC and 168 BC
Corinth sacked by Romans, 146 BC
Kingdom of Pergamon bequeathed to Rome,
133 BC

100 BC

Greece becomes a Roman province
Athens sacked by Rome, 86 BC
Battle of Actium 31 BC

Glossary

ABACUS The square-shaped flat slab forming the top of a column *capital*.

ACANTHUS A plant, the leaves of which resemble the principal decorative element of the Corinthian *capital*.

ACROPOLIS A generic term for a high place or citadel in a Greek city.

ADYTON An inner chamber at the back of a temple.

AEGIS A magic cape or shawllike garment decorated with the Gorgon's head and fringed with snakes, often worn by Athena.

AEOLIC CAPITAL An early architectural *capital*, confined geographically to Aeolis (see map, fig. **4.1**) and characterized by upward springing *volutes*.

AGORA The market place; the commercial and administrative center of a city.

AKROLITH A statue with head, hands, and feet of stone, with the rest often of wood.

AKROTERION (pl. **AKROTERIA**) The ornament at the corner of the roof of a temple or at the apex of the gable.

ALABASTRON (pl. **ALABASTRA**) A small pot with a narrow neck, and generally without foot, used for containing oil or perfume.

AMBULATORY The side and end passages around a temple.

AMPHIPROSTYLE With columns at the front and back, but not on either flank.

AMPHORA A tall, normally two-handled vessel used for storage, or, when decorated, as a container (of wine, for example) or as a prize in the games.

ANDRON A principal room of a Greek house, often the dining-room.

ANTA (pl. **ANTAE**) The broadened end of a wall often terminating a series, or pair, of columns.

ANTHEMION A *frieze* of floral decoration, frequently alternating lotus and *palmette*.

IN ANTIS Positioned between the *antae*.

APEX The highest point.

APOTHEOSIS The moment of transfer of a person or hero from human or semi-divine to divine nature.

APSE Vaulted semicircular end of a building.

APSIDAL A plan which ends in an apse.

ARCHITRAVE The course of masonry running atop the column *capitals* and supporting the superstructure.

ARRIS In the Doric order, the join of the *flutes* of a column normally forming a sharp ridge.

ARYBALLOS A small globular or ovoid flask for holding oil or perfume.

ASHLAR A masonry style of dressed and coursed rectangular blocks.

AXIAL Adjective derived from "axis." In sculpture, an imaginary line around which the human body rotates, or on either side of which the parts of the body are arranged. In architecture, a straight line which equally divides spaces and forms.

BALDRIC A belt or sash worn over one shoulder by a warrior.

BAROQUE Characterized by curved, elaborate, dynamic forms.

BLACK-FIGURE A technique for painting pottery which depended on figures in black silhouette, incised detail, and added color.

BLOOM A mass of wrought iron from a forge or furnace.

BUCRANION A frontal ox head or skull.

BURIN An incising instrument.

CAPITAL The upper, spreading element in a column, forming a transition between the vertical shaft and the horizontal elements of the *architrave*.

CARYATID A female figure supporting the *entablature* of a building.

CAVEA The seating of a Greek theatre.

CELLA The main room of a Greek temple where the cult statue was placed.

CHAMBER TOMB An irregularly shaped underground room used for burial, often approached by a corridor.

CHEVRON An inverted-V ornament.

CHIAROSCURO The use of light and shade to create effects of shape and mass in painting and sculpture.

CHITON A lightweight, single-piece garment, belted and with buttoned sleeve.

CHLAMYS A short cloak.

CHRYSELEPHANTINE Of gold and ivory.

CHTHONIC An adjective meaning "of the earth" and often referring to the gods of the underworld.

CIRE PERDUE The "lost wax" method of making bronze statues (see pp. 74, 181).

CIST A shallow rectangular grave cut in the earth or rock, sometimes stone-lined or slab-built.

COFFERS Recessed panels in a flat ceiling.

COLONNADE A range of columns supporting an *entablature*.

CONTRAPPOSTO A term applied to a pose of the

human figure in which tensed forms are balanced with relaxed forms.

CORBELING (corbel – a kind of bracket) A system for supporting courses of masonry or wood by extending successive courses beyond the face of the wall.

CORNICE The horizontal course of the *entablature* of a building immediately above the *frieze*; either raking (sloping) member of a gable.

CUIRASS Metal armor worn to protect the chest and back.

CYCLADES The southern islands of the Aegean, especially Delos, Paros, Naxos, Siphnos, and Melos.

CYCLOPEAN Of the Cyclopes, mythical primitive giants; an adjective applied to the huge, irregular masonry fortifications of the Bronze Age.

DADO The lower part of a wall, often formed of a distinctive ornamental stone.

DENDROCHRONOLOGY A means of reckoning dates and intervals of times by the examination of growth rings in trees or in dead wood.

DENTILS Small rectangular blocks used below the Ionic *cornice*, one after the other, as decoration; originally used as an alternative to, but later incorporated in, the *frieze*.

DIAZOMA A walkway dividing upper tiers of seats from the lower in a Greek theatre.

DINOS An open vessel with a rounded base needing a pedestal, used for mixing wine and water.

DROMOS A corridor leading to a chamber tomb or *tholos*.

ECHINUS The lower member of a column *capital*.

EGG AND DART A carved ornament used in architecture, so called since its continuously alternating shapes resemble eggs and darts.

ELEVATION One side or face of a building; a measured drawing of such a side, or part of a side.

EMBOSSING A technique of decoration which raises the surface into projecting knobs or studs (bosses).

ENGAGED A half or three-quarter column appearing to project from a wall.

ENTABLATURE The horizontal architectural members forming the superstructure of a building above the columns: the *architrave*, *frieze*, and *cornice*.

ENTASIS The cigarlike swelling of columns.

EPIBLEMA A cloak.

EPIGRAPHY The study of inscriptions.

EPIPHANY The appearance of a god.

EPISTYLE The *architrave*.

FAIENCE Quartz grains fused together and covered with a vitreous glaze.

FASCIA (pl. **FASCIAE**) An undecorated band on an Ionic *architrave*.

FIBULA A brooch.

FILIGREE A metalsmith's technique using thin wire for decorating.

FLUTES Shallow grooves running vertically on the shaft of a column.

FORESHORTENING An illusionistic trick to suggest depth on a flat surface by representing forms as shorter in length than they actually are.

FRESCO A wall painting made by rapid application of colors to plaster while still damp.

FRIEZE The architectural course between the *architrave* and the *cornice*.

GORGON In mythology, one of three hideous female monsters (of whom Medusa is the most famous) endowed with wings and large fangs, and having snakes for hair.

GORGONEION The head of a Gorgon.

GOURD A large fruit whose tough skin was used to hold liquid.

GRANULATION A metalsmith's technique for soldering globules of gold or silver onto jewelry.

GREAVES Armor worn to protect the shins.

GRIFFIN A mythological beast with the body of a lion, and wings and head of an eagle.

GROUND LINE In art, the line on which figures stand.

GYPSUM A sparkling limestone.

HEKATOMPEDON A temple one hundred feet long.

HEROON The shrine of a hero, a semi-divine person.

HEXASTYLE With six columns at the front, or at the front and back.

HIMATION A mantle worn over the *chiton* or *peplos*.

HIPPODAMIAN Of Hippodamos, an architect and townplanner of the fifth century BC.

HOPLITE A heavily-armed (helmet, *cuirass*, *greaves*, shield, spear) footsoldier.

HYDRIA A water jar with three handles.

ICONOGRAPHY The study of the subject matter of sculpture, painting, and the other visual arts.

INCISION The scratching of lines into a surface to form contours or patterns, especially used of the decoration of pottery, perhaps in that instance derived from the engraving of metals.

INGOT A plate of metal cast in a mold.

KANTHAROS (pl. **KANTHAROI**) A deep drinking cup with high vertical handles.

KORE (pl. **KORAI**) A standing, draped female figure.

KOTYLE A deep drinking cup with small horizontal handles.

KOUROS (pl. **KOUROI**) A standing nude male figure.

KRATER A large open vessel used for mixing wine and water.

KYLIX (pl. **KYLIKES**) A shallow drinking cup with horizontal handles.

LAGYNOS A squat jug with a long neck.

LEBES see *dinos*.

LEKANE A lidded dish or plate.

LEKYTHOS (pl. **LEKYTHOI**) A tall flask with a narrow neck and a single handle, used for containing oil or unguents.

LIGHT-WELL A small courtyard or shaft inside a building, uncovered to let in light and air.

LINTEL A horizontal block or beam bridging a door or other opening.

LUSTRAL BASIN A small rectangular space, conventionally thought sacred, accessible from above by a short flight of steps.

MAEANDER A rectilinear decorative motif, winding backwards and forwards continuously.

MAENAD A female member of Dionysos' retinue.

MAGNA GRAECIA Great Greece (Latin). The Greek settlements in south Italy, often including those of Sicily as well.

MEGALITHIC A style of construction characterized by massive, irregularly shaped blocks.

MEGARON (pl. **MEGARA**) A type of long house, characterized by a porch, a long hall, and a storage room of either *apsidal* or rectangular plan. Common at Troy, they appear in Greece by c. 2000 BC. In the Late Bronze periods, they are characterized on the mainland of Greece by a columned porch, a vestibule, and a main room with a large hearth; on Crete, by *pier*-and-door construction.

METOPE In a Doric frieze a space between two *triglyphs*, sometimes filled with a block carved with relief sculpture.

MOLDING In architecture, a continuous decorative motif.

NAOS The main room of a Greek temple (see *cella*).

NEOLITHIC The cultural period characterized by primitive farming and the use of polished stone and flint tools and weapons.

NEREID A daughter of Nereus.

NIELLO A technique for decorating metal: a black amalgam of sulphur, borax, copper, and lead inlaid in an engraved design.

NILOTIC Adjective, perhaps derived from the "Nile." Of river life.

NUMISMATICS The study of coins.

OBSIDIAN Volcanic glass.

OCTASTYLE With eight columns at the front, or at the front and back.

OINOCHOE A jug for pouring, often with a trefoil mouth.

OLPE A jug with a broad lip.

OPISTHODOMOS The back porch of a Greek temple.

ORACLE An answer given by a deity, the place where such an answer is given, or the person delivering the answer.

ORACULAR Relating to an *oracle*.

ORCHESTRA The level, horseshoe shaped space in front of the auditorium in a Greek theatre.

ORTHOSTATE An upright slab, taller than normal wall blocks and usually at the foot of a wall; a course of masonry of such blocks.

PALMETTE A floral design, consisting of leaves arranged like a palm shoot.

PANATHENAIC Of Panathenaia, the major festival of Athens. The greater Panathenaia was held every fourth year, the lesser annually.

PANHELLENIC All Greek. Most frequently used to describe either sanctuaries or games.

PEDIMENT The triangular space formed by the gable at either end of a Greek temple.

PEDIMENTAL SCULPTURES Sculpted figures, carved either freestanding or in relief, which fill the pedimental space.

PELIKE A storage jar with two handles; a container for wine or other supplies.

PENTELIC Of Mount Pentelikon.

PEPLOPHOROI Women who wore the peplos.

PEPLOS A single-piece garment, sleeveless, fixed at the shoulders with pins and belted.

PERIPTERAL Surrounded by a row of columns.

PERIRRHANTERION A ritual water basin.

PERISTYLE A *colonnade* surrounding a building (an external peristyle) or a court (an internal peristyle).

PHLYAX A comic play popular in south Italy; an actor who participated in such a play.

PIER A freestanding, rectangular mass of masonry supporting the superstructure of a building.

PILASTER A rectangular architectural member, part of which is bonded into a wall (like an engaged column) and part of which projects from it.

PITHOS (pl. **PITHOI**) A large clay storage vessel.

POLOS A tall headdress.

PORPHYRY A very hard, purple and white stone.

POSTERN A small gate or door at the back of a building or complex.

PRONAOS The front porch of a Greek temple.

PROPYLAIA A monumental entrance, having more than one doorway, to a *sanctuary*. Most frequently used of the High Classical gate building to the Acropolis at Athens.

PROPYLON (pl. **PROPYLA**) A monumental entrance to a sanctuary or other architectural complex.

PROSTYLE The arrangement whereby columns are placed in front of a building.

PROTHESIS The lying in state of a corpse.

PROTOME An independent head, or head and upper members, of an animal or human.

PSEUDO-DIPTERAL In architecture, a plan of a building showing a row of columns on all sides with unused space for a second row of columns (see p. 150).

PYXIS A lidded cosmetic or jewelry box; occasionally a knitting basket.

QUADRIGA A chariot with two wheels drawn by four horses.

RED-FIGURE TECHNIQUE A technique for painting pottery which was the direct opposite of *black-figure*: the background was painted black with figures left the color of the clay. Contours and interior details were added with *relief lines* or dilute *slip*.

REGISTER In painting, a horizontal band or *frieze* decorated with ornament or figures.

RELIEF LINE In *red-figure* vase painting, a strong line which stands up off the surface and is used for contours of figures and important interior details.

RELIEVING TRIANGLE A triangular space left in the masonry above the *lintel* of a door to relieve the lintel of some of the weight.

REPOUSSÉ Metalwork decoration in relief, achieved by beating the metal from behind.

RESISTIVITY SURVEY A survey measuring the varying resistance of subsurface areas of land to electrical current passed between electrodes stuck in the ground, and thereby revealing the presence or absence of ancient remains.

REVETMENT In architecture, a facing of stone, brick, or wood; a wall built to hold back earth.

RHYTON (pl. **RHYTA**) A ritual pouring vessel, sometimes in the shape of an animal head; a drinking horn.

ROSETTE An ornament shaped like a rose.

RUBBLE Masonry, the stones of which are broken or in a rough condition.

SANCTUARY A sacred, defined space, characterized by a boundary wall, temple(s), altars, stoa(s), treasuries, and other architectural dependencies, in which religious activities took place.

SARCOPHAGUS (pl. **SARCOPHAGI**) A coffin, of stone, terracotta, or wood.

SATRAPY A province of the Persian empire, governed by a satrap (governor).

SCARAB In Egyptian religion, a sacred beetle; seals made in this shape.

SHAFT GRAVE A grave for multiple burial, cut as a rectangular shaft in the rock.

SIREN A mythological beast combining the body of a bird with the head of a woman.

SKENE In the theatre, the dressing rooms for actors and the storage rooms for scenery and props.

SKYPHOS A two-handled drinking cup, not as deep as a *kotyle* or *kantharos*, but deeper than a *kylix*.

SLIP A coat of clay applied to cover the surface of a pot, of a different constitution from the clay of the pot itself; also used to join together parts of a pot fired separately.

SOFFIT The underside of a *lintel*, arch, or *cornice*.

SPHYRELATON A technique for making sculptured figures by hammering thin metal sheets over a wooden core.

STELE (pl. **STELAI**) A vertical slab of stone (normally) used as a grave marker, and often decorated.

STIRRUP JAR A vessel, usually globular in shape, with a small double handle like a stirrup and a thin spout, common in the Late Bronze Age.

STOA A long, rectangular, *colonnaded* building familiar in *sanctuaries* and *agoras*.

STUCCO A plaster made of lime and/or sand used to cover the surface of walls to render them smooth.

STYLOBATE The course of masonry on which columns stand.

TERRACOTTA Baked clay.

TESSERA A small square piece of stone or glass used in making a mosaic pavement.

TETRASTYLE With four columns at the front, or at the front and back.

THERMOLUMINESCENCE A method of dating clay objects by measuring radioactively accumulated energy since the clay was fired. Reheated (thermo-) clay emits energy as a form of light (luminescence).

THOLOS (pl. **THOLOI**) A circular building; a built tomb (of the Bronze Age) circular in plan.

TIEBEAM A timber tying together rafters (in a roof) or securing masonry (in a wall).

TORSION In figural art, the turning or even twisting of the body.

TRABEATED In architecture, a term for a building depending on horizontal beams and vertical posts.

TRIGLYPH In a Doric frieze, an upright grooved block with three vertical bars in relief, conventionally thought to represent the translation into stone of carved carpentry prototypes.

VOLUTE A spiral (one of two) on the face and back of an Ionic or *Aeolic capital*.

VOTIVE OFFERING An object dedicated or vowed to a deity.

XOANON (pl. **XOANA**) An early carved wooden statue of great venerability.

ZOOMORPHIC Having or suggesting the form of a living creature.

Select Bibliography

THE BRONZE AGE

GENERAL

Higgins, R. A., *Minoan and Mycenaean Art*. London and New York, 1967, 2nd ed. 1981.

Hood, S., *The Arts in Prehistoric Greece*. Harmondsworth and New York, 1978.

McDonald, W. A., *Progress into the Past*. New York, 1967.

Marinatos, S. & M. Hirmer *Crete and Mycenae*. London, 1960.

Matz, F., *The Art of Crete and Early Greece*. New York, 1962.

Nilsson, M. P., *The Minoan–Mycenaean Religion in its Survival in Greek Religion*. Lund, Sweden, 1950.

Warren, P., *The Aegean Civilisations from Ancient Crete to Mycenae*. Oxford (Equinox), 1975, 2nd ed. 1989.

CRETE

Betancourt, P. P., *The History of Minoan Pottery*. Princeton, 1985.

Boyd Hawes, H., *Gournia*. Philadelphia, 1908.

Branigan, K., *The Foundations of Palatial Crete*. London, 1970; Amsterdam, 1988.

Cadogan, C., *Palaces of Minoan Crete*. London, 1976, rev. ed. 1980.

Castleden, R., *Minoans: Life in Bronze Age Crete*. London, 1990.

Evans, A. J., *The Palace of Minos at Knossos*. 7 vols. London, 1921–35.

Graham, J. W., *The Palaces of Crete*. Princeton, 1962, 3rd ed. 1987.

Hagg, R. & N. Marinatos, eds, *The Function of the Minoan Palaces*. Stockholm, 1987.

Hood, S., *The Minoans*. London and New York, 1971.

Hutchinson, R. W., *Prehistoric Crete*. Harmondsworth and Baltimore, 1962.

Marinatos, N., *Minoan Sacrificial Ritual*. Stockholm, 1986.

Nixon, L. & O. Krzyszkowska, eds, *Minoan Society*. Bristol, 1983.

Pendlebury, J. D. S., *The Archaeology of Crete*. London, 1939, reprint New York, 1965.

Warren, P., *Minoan Religion as Ritual Action*. Göteborg, Sweden, 1988.

CYCLADES

Barber, R. L. N., *The Cyclades in the Bronze Age*. London, 1987.

Doumas, C., *Thera. Pompeii of the Ancient Aegean*. London, 1983.

Getz-Preziosi, P., ed., *Early Cycladic Art in American Collections*. Richmond, 1987.

Getz-Preziosi, P., *Sculptors of the Cyclades: Individual and Tradition in the Third Millennium BC*. Ann Arbor, 1987.

Luce, J. V., *The End of Atlantis*. London, 1969.

Morgan, L., *The Miniature Wall-Paintings of Thera: A Study in Aegean Culture and Iconography*. Cambridge, MA, 1988.

Renfrew, C., *The Emergence of Civilization. The Cyclades and the Aegean in the Third Millennium BC*. London, 1972.

Thimme, J. & P. Getz-Preziosi, eds, *Art and Culture of the Cyclades in the Third Millennium BC*. London and Chicago, 1977.

GREECE

Blegen, C. W. et al., *The Palace of Nestor at Pylos in Western Messenia*. 3 vols. Princeton, 1966–73.

Chadwick, J., *The Decipherment of Linear B*. Cambridge, 1958, 2nd ed. 1967.

Chadwick, J., *The Mycenaean World*. Cambridge, 1977.

Furumark, A., *Mycenaean Pottery. Analysis and Classification*. Stockholm, 1941.

Mylonas, G., *Mycenae and the Mycenaean Age*. Princeton, 1966.

Mylonas, G., *Mycenae Rich in Gold*. Athens, 1983.

Nordquist, G., *Asine: A Middle Helladic Village*. Uppsala, Sweden, 1987.

Taylour, Lord William, *The Mycenaeans*. London, 1964; New York, 1971.

Vermeule, E., *Greece in the Bronze Age*. Chicago, 1964.

Wace, A. J. B., *Mycenae*. Princeton, 1949.

TROY

Blegen, C. W., et al., *Troy*. 4 vols. Princeton, 1950–8.

Blegen, C. W., *Troy and the Trojans*. London, 1963.

Mellinck, M., ed., *Troy and the Trojan War*. Bryn Mawr, 1986.

AFTER THE BRONZE AGE

BACKGROUND

Andrewes, A., *Greek Society*. Harmondsworth, 1971.

Boardman, J., J. Griffin, & O. Murray, *Oxford History of the Classical World*. Oxford, 1985.

Burn, A. R., *Persia and the Greeks*. London, 1962.

Burn, A. R., *Pelican History of Greece*. London, 1966.

Bury, J. & R. Meiggs, *A History of Greece to the Death of Alexander the Great*. London, 4th ed. 1975.

Cook, R. M., *The Greeks till Alexander*. London and New York, 1962.

Desborough, V. R. D'A., *The Last Mycenaeans and their Successors*. Oxford, 1964.

Dunbabin, T. J., *The Western Greeks*. Oxford, 1948.

Finley, M. I., *The Ancient Greeks*. London, 1963.

Green, P., *From Alexander to Actium: the Hellenistic Age*. London, 1990.

Jeffrey, L. H., *Archaic Greece: the City–States ca. 700–500 BC.* London, 1976.
Jones, P. V., ed. *The World of Athens: an Introduction to Classical Athenian Culture.* Cambridge, 1984.
Murray, O., *Early Greece.* Glasgow, 1980, 1988.
Schefold, K., *Myth and Legend in Early Greek Art.* London and New York, 1966.
Snodgrass, A. M., *Archaic Greece: the Age of Experiment.* London, 1980.
Webster, T. B. L., *Everyday Life in Ancient Athens.* London and New York, 1969.

LITERARY EVIDENCE
Frazer, J. G., *Pausanias' Description of Greece.* 6 vols. New York, 1898, reprint 1965.
Herodotos, *Persian Wars.*
Homer, *Iliad.*
Homer, *Odyssey.*
Jex-Blake, K., & E. Sellers, *The Elder Pliny's Chapters on the History of Art.* London, 1896.
Pollitt, J., *The Ancient View of Greek Art.* New Haven, 1974.
Pollitt, J., *The Art of Greece: Sources and Documents.* New Jersey, 1965; Cambridge, 1990.
Strabo, *Geography.*
Thucydides, *The Peloponnesian War.*
Vitruvius, *On Architecture.*

GENERAL ART AND ARCHAEOLOGY

Biers, W., *The Archaeology of Greece.* Cornell, 1980, 2nd ed. 1987.
Boardman, J., *Greek Art.* London and New York, 1964, 3rd ed. 1987.
Boardman, J., *The Greeks Overseas.* London and New York, 1964, new and enlarged ed. 1980.
Boardman, J., J. Dorig, W. Fuchs, & M. Hirmer, *The Art and Architecture of Ancient Greece.* London and New York, 1967.
Brilliant, R., *Arts of the Ancient Greeks.* New York, 1972.
Cook, R. M., *Greek Art: Its Development, Character and Influence.* London and New York 1972, 2nd ed. 1976.
Langlotz, E. & M. Hirmer, *The Art of Magna Graecia.* London, 1965.
Richter, G. M. A., *A Handbook of Greek Art.* London, 1959, 6th ed. 1969.
Robertson, M. A., *A History of Greek Art.* Cambridge, 1975.
Robertson, M. A., *A Shorter History of Greek Art.* Cambridge, 1981.
Sparkes, B., *Greek Art.* Oxford, 1991.
Woodford, S., *An Introduction to Greek Art.* Cornell, 1986. 2nd impression 1989.

PRE-CLASSICAL
Akurgal, E., *The Birth of Greek Art: the Mediterranean and the Near East.* London, 1968.
Coldstream, N., *Geometric Greece.* London, 1977.
Homann-Wedeking, E., *Archaic Greece.* London, 1968.
Hurwit, J. M., *The Art and Culture of Early Greece 1100–480 BC.* Cornell, 1985.

Snodgrass, A. M., *The Dark Age of Greece.* Edinburgh, 1972.

CLASSICAL
Charbonneaux, J., R. Martin, & F. Villard, *Classical Greek Art.* London, 1973.
Hopper, R. J., *Trade and Industry in Classical Greece.* London, 1979.
Pollitt, J., *Art and Experience in Classical Greece.* Cambridge, 1972.
Webster, T. B. L., *Art and Literature in the Fourth Century.* London, 1956.

HELLENISTIC
Andronikos, M., *Vergina: the Royal Tombs.* Athens, 1984.
Havelock, C. M., *Hellenistic Art.* Greenwich, 1970.
Onians, J., *Art and Thought in the Hellenistic Age: the Greek World View 350–50 BC.* London, 1979.
Pollitt, J., *Art in the Hellenistic Age.* Cambridge, 1986.
Smith, R. R. R., *Hellenistic Art.* London and New York, 1991.
Webster, T. B. L., *Hellenistic Art.* London, 1967.

ARCHITECTURE
Berve, H., C. Gruben & M. Hirmer, *Greek Temples, Theatres and Shrines.* London, 1963.
Camp, J. M., *The Athenian Agora.* London, 1986.
Coulton, J. J., *Ancient Greek Architects at Work.* London, 1977.
Dinsmoor, W. B., *The Architecture of Ancient Greece.* New York, 1950, 3rd ed. 1975.
Hill, I. T., *The Ancient City of Athens.* London, 1953.
Lawrence, A. W., *Greek Architecture.* Harmondsworth, 1957, 4th ed. R. A., Tomlinson, 1983.
Plommer, W. H., *Ancient and Classical Architecture.* London, 1956.
Shoe, I. T., *Profiles of Greek Mouldings.* Harvard, 1936.
Simon, E., *The Ancient Theatre.* London, 1982.
Stuart, J. & N. Revett, *The Antiquities of Athens.* 4 vols. London, 1782–1816.
Wycherley, R. E., *How the Greeks Built Cities.* London, 1949, 2nd ed. 1962.
Wycherley, R. E., *The Stones of Athens.* Princeton, 1978.

SCULPTURE
Adam, S., *The Technique of Greek Sculpture.* London, 1966.
Ashmole, B., *Architect and Sculptor in Classical Greece.* London and New York, 1972.
Ashmole, B., *The Classical Ideal in Greek Sculpture.* Cincinnati, 1964.
Ashmole B. & H. Yalouris, *Olympia.* London, 1967.
Barron, J., *An Introduction to Greek Sculpture.* London, 1982.
Bieber, M., *Ancient Copies.* New York, 1977.
Bieber, M., *The Sculpture of the Hellenistic Age.* New York, 1954, 2nd ed. 1961.
Blumel, C., *Greek Sculptors at Work.* London, 1969.
Boardman, J., *Greek Sculpture, the Archaic Period.* London and New York, 1978.
Boardman, J., *Greek Sculpture, the Classical Period.* London and New York, 1984.
Brommer, F., *The Sculptures of the Parthenon.* London and New York, 1979.

Brown, B. R., *Anticlassicism in Greek Sculpture of the Fourth Century*. New York, 1973.

Carpenter, R., *Greek Sculpture*. Chicago, 1960.

Houser, C., *Greek Monumental Bronze Sculpture*. London, 1983.

Johansen, F., *The Attic Grave Reliefs*. Copenhagen, 1951.

Lawrence, A. W., *Later Greek Sculpture*. London, 1927.

Lullies, R. & M. Hirmer, *Greek Sculpture*. New York, 1957; London 1960, German ed. 1979.

Mattusch, C. C., *Greek Bronze Statuary from the Beginnings through the Fifth Century BC*. Cornell, 1988.

Payne, H. & G. M. Young, *Archaic Marble Sculpture from the Acropolis*. London, 1950.

Pedley, J. G., *Greek Sculpture of the Archaic Period: the Island Workshops*. Mainz, 1976.

Richter, G. M. A., *The Archaic Gravestones of Attica*. London, 1961.

Richter, G. M. A., *Korai, Archaic Greek Maidens*. London, 1968.

Richter, G. M. A., *Kouroi, Archaic Greek Youths*. London, 1942, 4th ed. 1970.

Richter, G. M. A., *Portraits of the Greeks*. Oxford, 1984.

Richter, G. M. A., *The Sculpture and Sculptors of the Greeks*. New Haven, 1929, rev. ed. 1950, 4th ed. 1970; London, 1971.

Ridgway, B. S., *The Archaic Style in Greek Sculpture*. Princeton, 1981.

Ridgway, B. S., *Fifth Century Styles in Greek Sculpture*. Princeton, 1986.

Ridgway, B. S., *Hellenistic Sculpture I: the Styles of ca. 331–200 BC*. Bristol, 1990.

Ridgway, B. S., *The Severe Style in Greek Sculpture*. Princeton, 1970.

Stewart, A., *Greek Sculpture: an Exploration*. New Haven, 1990.

PAINTED POTTERY

Amyx, D., *Corinthian Vase-Painting of the Archaic Period*. 3 vols. Berkeley, 1988.

Arias, P., M. Hirmer & B. Shefton, *A History of Greek Vase Painting*. London, 1962.

Beazley, J. D., *Attic Black-Figure Vase Painters*. Oxford, 1956.

Beazley, J. D., *Attic Red-Figure Vase Painters*. Oxford, 1963.

Beazley, J. D., *Attic White Lekythoi*. London, 1938.

Beazley, J. D., *The Development of Attic Black Figure*. Berkeley, 1951.

Beazley, J. D., *Paralipomena*. Oxford, 1971.

Beazley, J. D., *Potter and Painter in Ancient Athens*. London, 1944.

Boardman, J., *Athenian Black Figure Vases*. London and New York, 1974, reprint with corrections 1991.

Boardman, J., *Athenian Red Figure Vases: the Archaic Period*. London and New York, 1975, 2nd ed. 1988.

Boardman, J., *Athenian Red Figure Vases: the Classical Period*. London, 1989.

Coldstream, N., *Greek Geometric Pottery*. London and New York, 1968.

Cook, R. M., *Greek Painted Pottery*. London, 1960, 2nd ed. 1972.

Desborough, V. R. D'A., *Protogeometric Pottery*. Oxford, 1952.

Haspels, E., *Attic Black Figured Lekythoi*. Paris, 1936.

Kurtz, D. C., *The Berlin Painter*. Oxford, 1982.

Noble, J. V., *The Techniques of Painted Athenian Pottery*. New York, 1965.

Payne, H., *Necrocorinthia*. Oxford, 1931, reprint College Park, Maryland 1971.

Richter, G. M. A. & M. J. Milne, *Shapes and Names of Athenian Vases*. New York, 1935, reprint College Park, Maryland 1971.

Trendall, A. D., *Early South Italian Vase Painting*. Mainz, 1974.

Trendall, A. D., *Red Figure Vases of South Italy and Sicily*. London and New York, 1989.

Trendall, A. D., *South Italian Vase Painting*. London, 1966, 2nd ed. 1976.

Williams, D., *Greek Vases*. London, 1985.

MURAL AND PANEL PAINTING

Bruno, V. J., *Form and Color in Greek Painting*. New York, 1977.

Pallottino, M., *Etruscan Painting*. Geneva, 1952.

Robertson, M., *Greek Painting*. Geneva, 1959.

Swindler, M. H., *Ancient Painting*. New Haven, 1929.

OTHER

Boardman, J., *Greek Gems and Finger Rings*. London, 1970; New York 1971.

Charbonneaux, J., *Greek Bronzes*. London, 1961.

Higgins, R. A., *Greek and Roman Jewelry*. London, 1961; New York, 1962.

Higgins, R. A., *Greek Terracottas*. London, 1963; New York, 1966.

Kraay, C. M., *Archaic and Classical Greek Coins*. London, 1976.

Kraay, C. M. & M. Hirmer, *Greek Coins*. London and New York, 1966.

Richter, G. M. A., *The Engraved Gems of the Greeks and Etruscans*. London, 1968.

Snodgrass, A. M., *Arms and Armour of the Greeks*. London, 1967.

Strong, D. A., *Greek and Roman Gold and Silver Plate*. London, 1966.

Index

Bold and italic numbers
indicate illustrations